Accounting Standards

Pearson
Education

Accounting Standards

Seventh Edition

John Blake
Professor of Accounting,
University of Central Lancashire

and

Henry Lunt
Professor of Accounting,
University of Central Lancashire

An imprint of PEARSON EDUCATION
Harlow, England • London • New York • Reading, Massachusetts • San Francisco • Toronto • Don Mills, Ontario • Sydney
Tokyo • Singapore • Hong Kong • Seoul • Taipei • Cape Town • Madrid • Mexico City • Amsterdam • Munich • Paris • Milan

Pearson Education Limited
Edinburgh Gate
Harlow
Essex CM20 2JE
England

and Associated Companies around the World.

Visit us on the World Wide Web at:
www.pearsoneduc.com

First published in 1981
Sixth Edition published under the Pitman Publishing imprint 1997
Seventh Edition 2001

ISBN 0 273 64673 7

British Library Cataloguing-in-Publication Data
A catalogue record for this book can be obtained from the British Library

Library of Congress Cataloging-in-Publication Data
A catalog record for this book can be obtained from the Library of Congress

10 9 8 7 6 5 4 3 2
04 03 02 01 00

Typeset in 10/12 Adobe Sabon by 18
Printed and bound in Great Britain by T J International Ltd, Padstow, Cornwall

Contents

Preface

Accounting standards in the UK include both Financial Reporting Standards (FRSs) issue by the Accounting Standards Board (ASB) and those Statements of Standard Accounting Practice (SSAPs) issued by the old Accounting Standards Committee (ASC), insofar as these have not been withdrawn.

The new ASB is endowed with greater authority than its predecessor and is using that authority to tackle some long-standing abuses. Thus FRS 12, discussed in Chapter 13, should eliminate the abuse of provisions for restructuring and for future losses. One unavoidable consequence of this approach is that the new standards are more detailed in order to avoid ambiguity and consequent abuse.

The text has not been written to a formula and the structure of each chapter allows each standard to be discussed individually. The more common headings used in each chapter are:

(a) introduction,
(b) the basic problem addressed by the standard,
(c) the detailed requirements of the standard,
(d) practical problems of compliance with the standard,
(e) controversy over the standards,
(f) conclusion,
(g) questions (with answers at the back of the book).

A study of the controversy over each standard is important for two reasons. First, thinking accountants will wish to understand not only *what* rules they have to follow, but *why* the rules have evolved in that way. Second, users of accounts may well find that an appreciation of how accounting regulations have emerged helpful in their assessment of accounts prepared in compliance with those regulations. For instance, in discussing SSAP 15 it is observed that the standard is an example of the predominant influence of preparers rather than users of accounts on the ASC. Users who are aware of the deficiencies of SSAP 15 are thereby equipped to make their own adjustments to the accounts.

This seventh edition of the book sees some radical changes. These are:

- The Financial Reporting Standard for Smaller Entities (FRSSE) is included for the first time in Chapter 30.
- The Statement of Principles is included for the first time in Chapter 31.
- Two new Statements by the ASB are included on Interim Reports and Preliminary Announcements in Chapter 32.
- The ASB Discussion Papers are included for the first time in Chapter 34. This has the advantage that the reader has early warning of forthcoming changes to an FRS.
- The chapter on Inflation Accounting in the UK has been substantially revised.
- Each chapter now has typical exam-type questions.

- The book includes all the FRSs which have been issued since the last edition; these are FRSs 9–16. Some of these have replaced previous SSAPs and some are on new topics. For example, FRS 16 has replaced SSAP 8 but FRS 13 is on the new topic of derivatives and other financial instruments.

The book is completely up to date and covers all extant pronouncements by the ASB up to May 2000.

John Blake

Henry Lunt

Acknowledgements

We should like to express our thanks to the Institute of Chartered Accountants in England and Wales, the Chartered Institute of Management Accountants, the Association of Chartered Certified Accountants and the Institute of Company Accountants for permission to use questions from their examinations. We should also like to thank the Association of Chartered Certified Accountants for permission to reproduce material from *Accounting and Business*. Definitions from the FRSs, Figure 31.2, Examples 14.1 and 14.3 and Additional Questions in Chapter 36 are reproduced with the permission of the Financial Reporting Council.

CHAPTER 1

The Origins and Development of the Accounting Standards Programme

Background

Accounting Standards, being 'Statements of Standard Accounting Practice' (SSAPs) and 'Financial Reporting Standards' (FRSs), have become one of the major sources of authority for accountants, covering the major areas of accounting controversy. The first such statement was issued in 1971, following the issue by the Institute of Chartered Accountants in England and Wales (ICAEW) of a 'Statement of Intent' promising to issue SSAPs in December 1969.

Prior to the establishment of the accounting standards programme the ICAEW gave guidance to its members in a series of statements, 'Recommendations on Accounting Principles'. The issue of such recommendations started with the establishment of the Taxation and Financial Relations Committee (later renamed Taxation and Research Committee) in 1942, and 29 recommendations had been issued by 1969. The Taxation and Research Committee would prepare draft recommendations which would be circulated to advisory committees of each of the Institute's district societies and then forwarded to the Council of the Institute, which would decide whether to issue a recommendation, and if so the exact content of the recommendation to be issued. The following features of this procedure should be noted:

(a) There was no system for consultations with other professional bodies on topics under consideration.
(b) While the recommendations offered guidance on 'best practice', members of the institute were under no obligation to follow that guidance.
(c) There was no public announcement of topics under consideration nor was there any system for exposing proposed recommendations to public comment.
(d) While the Council of the Institute would normally accept the guidance of the Taxation and Research Committee, it retained, and on occasion exercised, the power to reject or substantially amend proposed recommendations.

'Recommendations on Accounting Principles' generally consisted of summaries of current practice rather than giving a lead in new developments, and were rarely backed up by formal research. During the 1960s a number of cases where existing accounting and auditing practice seemed to lead to an unsatisfactory result led to considerable criticism of the accounting profession.

In the USA, critics of the extent of the variety in accounting practice pointed to the example of the sale of the shares in Ethyl Corporation by its joint owners General Motors and Standard Oil; each company made a profit of some $40 million on the sale of its half share in the corporation. General Motors showed the proceeds as part of its trading income for the year, while Standard Oil did not bring in the surplus at any stage in the profit and loss account and instead took the surplus direct to the reserves. Thus, two of the largest industrial organisations in the world, audited by two of the most highly respected international firms of accountants, produced totally different treatments of earnings from identical transactions. In the UK a similar controversy arose following the takeover of AEI by GEC. While fighting the takeover, AEI had produced a forecast, in the tenth month of their financial year, that profit before tax for that year would come to £10 million. Following the takeover the accounts for AEI showed a loss of £4.5 million. A report on the difference of £14.5 million attributed £5 million to 'matters substantially of fact' and £9.5 million to 'adjustments which remain matters substantially of judgement' arising from variations in accounting policies.

A number of articles in the City pages of the national press severely criticised the failure of the accounting profession to give a lead in developing a set of consistent principles for the presentation of financial reports. The case for reform was presented with particular clarity and vigour in a number of articles by Professor Edward Stamp published in 1969, followed up by a book *Accounting Principles and the City Code: The case for reform* (Stamp and Marley) published in 1970. While leading members of the accounting profession publicly rejected many of these criticisms, clearly in private there was a realisation that at least some of the criticism was justified.

On 12 December 1969 the ICAEW issued a 'Statement of Intent on Accounting Standards in the 1970s' laying down a five-point plan to advance accounting standards by:

(a) narrowing the areas of difference and variety in accounting practice by publishing authoritative, and where possible definitive, statements of best accounting practice;
(b) recommending disclosure of accounting bases used in arriving at the amount attributed to significant items depending on judgements of value or estimates of future events;
(c) requiring disclosure of departures from definitive accounting standards in the notes to the accounts;
(d) introducing a system for wide exposure of draft proposals for accounting standards to appropriate representative bodies for discussion and comment;
(e) continuing to suggest improvements in the accounting disclosure requirements laid down by company law and regulatory bodies such as the Stock Exchange.

Professor Stamp wrote 'What is really important about this Statement of Intent is the fact that it has been made and that things will never be the same again in British accountancy. The English Institute has stood up and declared itself foursquare for progress and improvement and it deserves the greatest possible credit for having done so.' There is reason to believe that, if the ICAEW had not set up the accounting standards programme, the government would have felt it necessary to set up some form of regulatory body to deal with the problem.

Thus it can be seen that the accounting standards programme originated in response to a demand for a lead from the accounting profession in developing improved and more consistent standards in financial reporting.

The ASC and the standard setting process

As we have seen, the accounting standards programme was announced by the ICAEW in December 1969. The Institute immediately set up an Accounting Standards Steering Committee (ASSC) with 11 members, later renamed the Accounting Standards Committee (ASC); to avoid confusion the latter term will be used throughout this book. In April 1970 representatives from the Scottish (ICAS) and one from the Irish (ICAI) Institutes of Chartered Accountants joined the committee, followed by representatives of the Chartered Association of Certified Accountants (ACCA) and the Institute of Cost and Management Accountants (ICMA) in 1971 and the Chartered Institute of Public Finance and Accountancy (CIPFA) in 1976. One reason for the decision of the ICAEW to set up the ASC alone originally may well have been that at that time there were proposals to merge the major accounting bodies; following the rejection of these proposals by members of the ICAEW in June 1970, the Consultative Committee of Accounting Bodies (CCAB) was set up to enable the profession to co-ordinate activities in certain areas. From 1 February 1976 the ASC was reconstituted as a joint committee of the six governing bodies of the CCAB, committee members being nominated by the professional bodies.

The ASC's constitution defined its objectives as follows:

> Bearing in mind the intention of the governing bodies to advance accounting standards and to narrow the areas of difference and variety in accounting practice by publishing authoritative statements on best accounting practice which will wherever possible be definitive –
>
> (a) To keep under review standards of financial accounting and reporting.
> (b) To publish consultative documents with the object of maintaining and advancing accounting standards.
> (c) To propose to the Councils of the governing bodies statements of standard accounting practice.
> (d) To consult as appropriate with representatives of finance, commerce, industry and government and other persons concerned with financial reporting.

The Accounting Standards Committee, as we have seen, was composed entirely from nominees of the professional accounting bodies; in order to allow some measure of influence to the major groups the ASC set up a consultative committee of nominees from the major organisations representing those who use published accounts, including the CBI and the TUC.

In 1982 the organisational structure of the ASC was revised to reduce the number of members to 20, including five users of accounts who need not be accountants. Members were chosen with an eye to balancing various interest groups rather than purely to represent professional accounting bodies.

The procedure for developing a statement of standard accounting practice (SSAP) developed over the years. In 1990 the following stages were involved:

(a) The ASC identified a topic as requiring consideration for the possible issue of an SSAP. Identification was undertaken by a planning sub-committee which took into account suggestions from a range of sources.
(b) The planning sub-committee advised on the setting-up of working parties to prepare consultative documents.
(c) One or more research studies on a topic were commissioned, involving a review of the literature, consideration of potential problems, and tentative suggestions.

(d) On the basis of the research the ASC would decide whether to proceed towards a SSAP or other statement on a topic, and if so set up a working party.
(e) Consultative documents on a proposed statement were to be published by the ASC. These can be of three types:
    (i) A discussion paper, designed to explore the issues and stimulate debate.
    (ii) A statement of intent (SOI), summarising the way in which the ASC plans to proceed.
    (iii) An exposure draft (ED), more detailed than an SOI, and providing a draft of a proposed standard.

    Discussion papers and SOIs were optional, but an exposure draft always preceded the issue of a SSAP.
(f) The working party provided initial feedback to the ASC on its thinking at an early stage, so that an exchange of views could take place.
(g) A consultation plan would be drawn up, identifying groups with a special interest, considering any legal problems, planning full press exposure, and providing for public hearings if necessary.
(h) Technical drafting by the working party proceeded in parallel with widespread private consultations on the issues. At the same time each of the CCAB bodies would also be consulted.
(i) The ASC as a whole would be involved in finally approving issue of an exposure draft to the public. In practice over 100 000 copies of an ED would be distributed.
(j) An *exposure period* of some six months was allowed for the collection of comment, possibly accompanied by public hearings.
(k) Following exposure the working party prepared a standard, often with the benefit of further private consultations. Where fundamental changes were considered a further ED might be issued.
(l) When the ASC agreed on a standard this was finally subject to approval by each of the CCAB member bodies on whose authority the SSAP was to be issued.

If an issue was not of sufficiently widespread significance to justify a SSAP, a 'Statement of Recommended Practice' (SORP) might be issued instead. Such a SORP would have relevance and apply only to a particular industry or business sector.

The enforcement of accounting standards

Statements of Standard Accounting Practice, as we have seen, have been formulated by the Accounting Standards Committee and issued on the authority of the individual CCAB bodies. There has been no requirement in company law to comply with SSAPs; this contrasts with the situation in the USA where a government agency, the Securities Exchange Commission, effectively compels listed corporations to adopt accounting standards set by the Financial Accounting Standards Board. In certain parts of Canada there is a legal requirement that company accounts should conform to the recommendations of the Canadian Institute of Chartered Accountants. In the UK there is a strong tradition of securing improvements in standards of commercial practice by a system of voluntary self-regulation through the appropriate professional organisations rather than by legislation.

The professional bodies themselves impose compliance with SSAPs by means of their own internal disciplinary procedures. Each of the CCAB bodies has issued to its members an explanatory foreword which lays down a duty to observe accounting standards. For example, the ICAEW states that 'The Council, through its Professional Standards Committee, may inquire into apparent failures by members of the Institute to observe accounting standards or to disclose departures therefrom.' There have in fact been instances of the disciplinary committee of the ICAEW upholding complaints against members on these grounds. Members of the CCAB bodies are expected to ensure that, where they have a responsibility as directors or officers of a company for the publication of accounts, their fellow directors are fully aware of the existence and purpose of accounting standards; they should also use their best endeavours to ensure that the accounts comply with SSAPs and that the nature and effect of any departure from accounting standards is disclosed.

Where members of the CCAB bodies act as auditors or as reporting accountants they are required to ensure that any significant departures from accounting standards are disclosed, and if they concur in the disclosure to justify the departures. Since in the UK only members of the three institutes of chartered accountants and members of the association of certified accountants may become limited company auditors (apart from a diminishing number of persons who were already in practice when the relevant legislation came into force and are therefore allowed to continue) this is a highly significant requirement.

The basic rules for auditors (*see* Fig. 1.1) are:

(a) All significant departures from accounting standards should be referred to in the auditor's report 'unless the auditor agrees therewith', the extent of the detail necessary depending on whether the departure is fully explained in the note to the accounts.

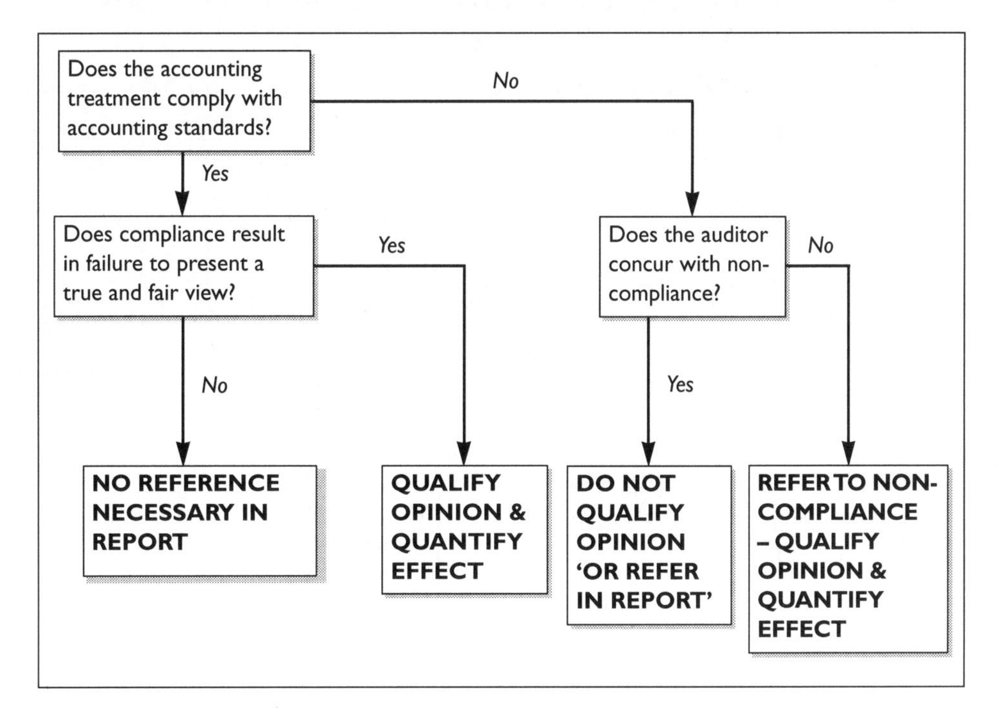

Fig. 1.1 SSAPs and the auditor

(b) Where the auditors are of the opinion that the directors have necessarily departed from an accounting standard in order to present a true and fair view then 'no reference in the audit report is necessary'.
(c) Where the auditors are of the opinion that the departure from an accounting standard is not justified they should express a qualified opinion on the accounts and quantify the financial effect of the departure if practical.
(d) In 'rare circumstances' it may happen that the auditors come to the conclusion that adherence to an accounting standard results in a failure to produce a true and fair view; in that case they should express a qualified opinion and quantify the effect on the accounts 'if practical'.

Technically *clean* audit reports in the UK are deliberately brief so as to highlight any reservation expressed by the auditor. Consequently there is a reluctance on the part of companies to incur the qualified opinion expressed when the auditor does not concur. The desire to avoid any such reference in the audit report has been one of the most significant factors leading to the acceptance of SSAPs by companies.

The Stock Exchange expects the accounts of listed companies to conform with SSAPs, and to disclose and explain any significant departures. In practice listed companies, which are subject to public comment and criticism, tend to comply with SSAPs.

The Dearing reforms

In 1987 the CCAB set up a committee under the chairmanship of Sir Ron Dearing 'to review and make recommendations on the standard setting process'. The committee reported in 1988 and in 1990 a new standard setting organisation, structured largely along the lines suggested by the Dearing Report, was established to replace the ASC.

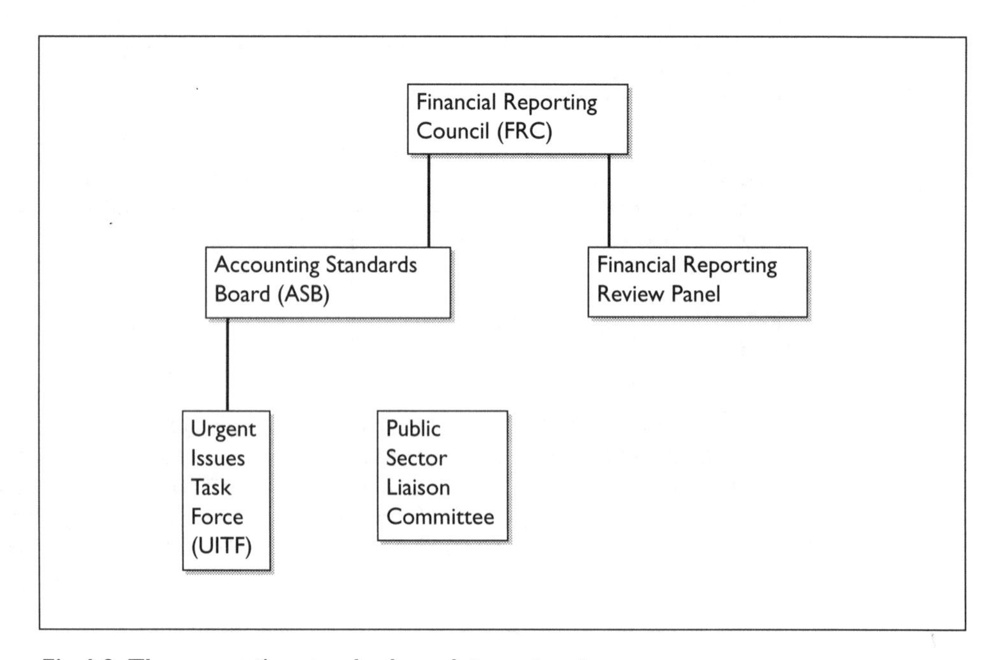

Fig. 1.2 The accounting standard regulatory structure

Figure 1.2 shows the new structure. The process of accounting standard setting is overseen by the 'Financial Reporting Council' (FRC). The chairman and three deputy chairmen of this body are appointed jointly by the Governor of the Bank of England and the Secretary of State for Trade and Industry. The other 21 members are nominated by a range of interested groups including the professional accounting bodies.

The FRC's role is:

(a) to promote good accounting and to make representations to government on how accounting legislation might be improved;
(b) to guide the Accounting Standards Board on work programmes and broad policy issues;
(c) to oversee the conduct of arrangements, arrange funding, and make appointments to the ASB and the review panel.

The Accounting Standards Board has a full-time chairman, a full-time technical director and seven part-time members, all of whom are paid. The ASB has taken over the role of the ASC in formulating accounting standards, following a similar consultative procedure but using the terms 'Financial Reporting Exposure Draft' (FRED), and 'Financial Reporting Standard' (FRS) in place of EDs and SSAPs. Initially the ASB adopted all the extant SSAPs. Unlike the ASC, the ASB has the authority to issue standards directly.

The Urgent Issues Task Force (UITF) is a sub-committee of the ASB. The UITF has some 15 members, and seeks to find consensus on how to deal with new accounting issues that emerge so as to offer an authoritative pronouncement. The Public Sector Liaison Committee is a smaller sub-committee which has the job of advising the ASB on the public sector implications of its work, with a view to minimising the differences between public and private sector practices.

The Companies Act 1989 introduced a new form of legal backing for accounting standards. Public and large private companies are required to state in their accounts whether they have been prepared in accordance with accounting standards, and to describe and explain any material departures. The Financial Reporting Review Panel examines company accounts and forms a view as to whether there is a failure to provide a true and fair view as a result of departure from an accounting standard. Where such a failure is identified the Panel seeks to agree revision of the accounts with the company. Failing such agreement, the Panel will apply to the court to seek an order compelling revision. From the point of view of the directors of the company concerned there is an unpleasant risk involved in such court proceedings; in such a case the court may order that all or part of the costs of the proceedings and the revision of the accounts should be borne by the responsible directors personally. Since no similar threat of personal liability hangs over members of the Review Panel in the event of a complaint not being upheld, this can be seen as a somewhat one-sided enforcement tool.

The new system is an expensive one. The cost of running the ASC in its last year was some £400 000, compared with a cost of some £3 300 000 in running the new system in its first year. The Dearing Report proposed a levy on the filing of company accounts to finance this structure. Instead, contributions come equally from the government, the accounting profession and private sources (mainly banks 'encouraged' to contribute by the Bank of England). Part of the costs are expected to be recovered by sale of copyright ASB publications. In the USA the Financial Accounting Standards Board (FASB) derives a substantial income from publications, giving rise to a fear of excessive detailed amendments to regulations in order to boost such income.

In 1991 the ASB announced a project to develop a 'Statement of Principles': This project was completed in December 1999 and is discussed in Chapter 31, Statement of Principles.

Comparing the ASC with the ASB a number of key areas of difference emerge:

(a) The ASB is answerable to, and appointed by, the FRC. This in turn is a body appointed by a range of interested parties. By contrast the ASC was under the control of the accounting profession. Thus accounting standard setting has moved from being an initiative of the accounting profession to being under the control of a broader-based body with government input.
(b) The ASB issues standards in its own right rather than, as the ASC did, formulating standards for final approval, and possible amendment, by the CCAB bodies.
(c) The ASB is a smaller body than the ASC with two full-time members and payment for the other seven part-time members.
(d) The UITF offers a mechanism for addressing new issues rapidly.
(e) A potentially powerful new enforcement mechanism for ensuring compliance by large and listed companies has emerged.
(f) The new system is provided with resources at a level some eight times higher than the previous system.
(g) A statement of principles is being developed to underpin accounting standards and promote consistency.

Work of the review panel

An interesting analysis of the early work of the Review Panel has been put forward by Jyoti Ghosh (*see Accountancy*, April 1993, pp. 90–91). During 1992 investigations into the accounts of ten public companies were announced.

These included some departures from accounting standards:

(a) inclusion of unrelieved ACT as part of the costs of dividends (*see* SSAP 8);
(b) reporting exceptional items net of tax, and earnings per share before exceptional items (*see* FRS 3 and SSAP 3);
(c) non-depreciation of freehold properties (*see* SSAP 12);
(d) early adoption of the proposals in the exposure draft that preceded FRS 3.

A more recent study by Sarah Perrin reports on the work of the Review Panel in 1995. Of 34 cases concluded in that year:

Public announcements of revisions to the accounts made	4
Companies persuaded Panel no correction needed	11
Companies not pursued beyond an initial examination	19
	34

(*see Accountancy*, December 1996, pp. 40–42).

Economic consequences

Observers of the work of the old ASC have noted that debate over accounting practice does not focus exclusively on technical issues. In practice, various affected parties perceive accounting standards as likely to have economic consequences, and lobby accordingly. Economic consequences can work in two ways:

(a) various user groups may respond to changes in the information in the accounts with a changed view of the business, and change their economic behaviour accordingly; or
(b) a business may be subject to some form of regulation or contract which uses the accounts as a measure of rights or obligations. As an example, the equity figure reported in the accounts is commonly used in measuring a company's borrowing powers.

It will be interesting to see how the new ASB copes with such issues.

International accounting standards

The International Accounting Standards Committee (IASC) was established in 1973, a revised constitution being agreed in 1977. As presently constituted the IASC has two classes of membership:

(a) Founder members, being the professional accounting bodies of the following nine countries:

Australia	Mexico
Canada	Netherlands
France	UK and Ireland*
Germany	USA
Japan	

**Treated as one country for this purpose.*

(b) Members, being accountancy bodies from countries other than the nine above which seek and are granted membership.

The business of the IASC is conducted by a Board comprising representatives:

(a) of each of the founder member countries;
(b) from two other member countries nominated by the nine founder members.

Each country represented on the Board shall have one vote.

The need for an International Accounting Standards Programme has been attributed to three factors:

(a) the growth in international investment. Investors in international capital markets are currently faced with making decisions based on published accounts based on accounting policies which will vary very widely according to the country of production. The harmonisation of International Accounting Standards will help investors to make more efficient decisions;

(b) the increasing prominence of multinational enterprises; such enterprises must produce accounts for the countries in which their shareholders reside and in the local country in which they operate. A harmonisation of accounting standards will help to avoid confusion and reduce the cost of producing multiple sets of accounts; and
(c) the growth in the number of accounting standard setting bodies. It is hoped that the IASC can harmonise these separate rule-making efforts.

An additional benefit of the work of the IASC has been to make available to countries, which may be poor in human or financial resources necessary to operate their own accounting standards programmes, standards which they can republish for local domestic use.

IAS procedures

The procedure for publishing an international standard involves the following stages:

(a) the IASC selects a topic for consideration;
(b) the Board sets up a steering committee;
(c) the steering committee prepares a draft standard;
(d) the Board considers the draft at various stages; the accounting research committees of the founder member bodies offer guidance, finally a proposed exposure draft is approved by a two-thirds majority of the Board;
(e) comments are received over an exposure period of some six months;
(f) the steering committee submits a revised draft standard to the IASC;
(g) the Board approves a standard by a three to four majority.

Thus, as in the UK, there is a well-established procedure for consultation in drafting each accounting standard.

The members of the ASB are committed to use their best endeavours:

(a) to ensure that accounts either comply or reveal non-compliance with international standards, and to recommend these to the appropriate authorities;
(b) to ensure that where accounts fail to comply, or disclose non-compliance, auditors refer to this fact in the accounts.

In the UK and Republic of Ireland most IASs are covered by domestic SSAPs and FRSs.

Conclusion

Accounting standards emerged in order to respond to demands from those who use company accounts for financial reports which are:

(a) comparable with those of other companies, an objective which can be met by narrowing the areas of difference and variety of accounting practice;
(b) more informative in explaining the ways in which judgement is exercised in preparing the accounts, an objective which can be met by requiring fuller disclosure; and
(c) more meaningful, an objective which is difficult to achieve because of the subjectivity of the requirement. By a system of discussion and consultation prior to

the issue of an SSAP the ASC tried to find some sort of consensus on what does constitute the most meaningful accounting practice.

In 1990 a new accounting regulatory framework was introduced. This draws on a wider base of sponsoring organisations, is more fully resourced, and has been endowed with greater authority. Some argue that this demonstrates some kind of failure of the old system. An alternative view is that the accounting standards developed by the ASC were successful in demonstrating the value of such a source of authority, leading to the more generously resourced and supported new system.

EXAMINATION PRACTICE

1.1 Compliance with accounting standards

By what means is compliance with accounting standards enforced?

FRS 1: Cash Flow Statements

Introduction

The two traditional accounting statements are the balance sheet, showing the position of the business at one point in time, and the profit and loss account, showing increases or decreases in the wealth of the business between two points in time. Accounting standard setters in the UK, as in many other countries, have seen a need for a third type of statement to focus on the flow of resources through a business between two balance sheet dates. Two types of statement have been put forward:

(a) in September 1991 the ASB issued its first standard, FRS 1: Cash Flow Statements, which analyses cash flows under five key headings; and
(b) previously, in July 1975, the ASC had issued SSAP 10: Statements of Source and Application of Funds, which focused on working capital movements. In July 1990 the ASC had issued ED 54: Cash Flow Statements, which proposed the move from the old SSAP 10 to the approach taken in FRS 1.

In October 1996 the ASB issued a revised version of FRS 1, extending the analysis of cash flows to eight key headings.

Summary of the statement

Definitions

FRS 1 defines *cash flow* as:

> An increase or decrease in an amount of cash.

Thus the focal point of the cash flow statement is identified as cash, defined as:

Cash: Cash in hand deposits repayable on demand with any qualifying financial institution, less overdrafts from any qualifying financial institution repayable on demand. Deposits are repayable on demand if they can be withdrawn at any time without notice and without penalty or if a maturity or period of notice of not more than 24 hours or one working day has been agreed. Cash includes cash in hand and deposits denominated in foreign currencies.

While cash is the focal point of the cash flow statement, another key area is:

Liquid resources: Current asset investments held as readily disposable stores of value. A readily disposable investment is one that:

(a) is disposable by the reporting entity without curtailing or disrupting its business;

and is either:

(b) (i) readily convertible into known amounts of cash at or close to its carrying amount, or
(ii) traded in an active market.

The new FRS 1 also requires a reconciliation of cash movements with movements in net debt, being:

Net debt: The borrowing of the reporting entity (comprising debt as defined in FRS 4 'Capital Instruments' (paragraph 6), together with related derivatives, and obligations under finance leases) less cash and liquid resources. Where cash and liquid resources exceed the borrowings of the entity, reference should be to 'net funds' rather than to 'net debt'.

Scope of the statement

While requiring in principle that accounts intended to give a true and fair view should include a cash flow statement, FRS 1 provides for an extensive range of exemptions:

(a) all entities falling within the size limits provided under the Companies Act 1985 for classification as a small company. This exemption applies both to companies and other entities;
(b) subsidiaries where 90 per cent or more of the voting rights are controlled within the group, provided that consolidated accounts including the subsidiary are publicly available;
(c) mutual life assurance companies;
(d) pension funds;
(e) open-ended investment funds that meet all the following conditions:
(i) substantially all of the entity's investments are highly liquid;
(ii) substantially all of the entity's investments are carried at market value; and
(iii) the entity provides a statement of changes in net assets;
(f) for two years from the effective date of the FRS, building societies, as defined by the Buildings Societies Act 1986 in the UK and by the Building Societies Act 1989 in the Republic of Ireland, that prepare, as required by law, a statement of source and application of funds in a prescribed format.

Headings in the cash flow statement

FRS 1 requires cash flows to be analysed under eight standard headings:

(a) *Operating activities.* These are the cash flows relating to operating or trading activities. They may be reported on either a *net* or a *gross* basis as discussed below. They include dividends received from associated companies if these companies' profits are included in the profit and loss account.
(b) *Returns on investments and servicing of finance.* These are receipts resulting from owning an investment and payments made for the provision of finance.

Examples of such inflows include interest received including tax recovered and dividends received net of related tax credits. Examples of such outflows include interest paid, irrespective of whether or not it is capitalised, the interest element in finance lease rentals, and finance costs under FRS 4. It also includes dividends paid on non-equity share capital.

(c) *Taxation*. This heading covers flow to and from the tax authorities relating to profits and capital gains, including ACT and purchases of certificates of tax deposit. It does not include other forms of tax such as VAT. These other forms of tax should be included along with the related activity in the cash flow statement.

(d) *Capital expenditure and financial investment*. This heading covers all acquisitions or disposals of fixed assets, other than 'acquisitions or disposals' of interests in other businesses covered in the next heading. Outflows include acquisitions of property, plant, and equipment and loans made. Inflows include sales of property, plant and equipment and receipt of loan repayments.

(e) *Acquisitions and disposals*. This heading relates to cash flows arising from acquisition or disposal of a trade or business, or an investment in a subsidiary, associate, or joint venture. Inflows or outflows relating to a subsidiary should show separately cash and overdrafts transferred or acquired as part of the sale.

(f) *Equity dividends paid*. The cash outflows relating to the equity dividend of the entity itself, or in group accounts the parent company. ACT is excluded.

(g) *Management of liquid resources*. Liquid resources are defined above. Flows will include payments into, and withdrawals from, short-term deposits, and acquisitions and disposals of other liquid investments. Cash flows within this heading may be netted off against each other if:
 1. They relate in substance to a single financing transaction, as defined in FRS 5.
 2. Are due to short maturities and high turnover.

 The accounting policy on liquid resources should be explained.

(h) *Financing*. These are receipts or payments of principal from or to external providers of finance. Inflows include receipts from share issues and borrowing other than overdrafts. Outflows include repayments of borrowing, the capital element of finance lease payments, payments to redeem shares, and payment of expenses of share issue. Financing cash flows with associated companies should be shown separately.

The first six of the above headings must be identified in the order shown. The last two may be merged, subject to each being the subject of a sub-total. Apart from the first heading, detailed breakdown of each item may be shown either on the face of the cash flow statement or by way of a note.

Operating cash flows – net or gross

There are two ways in which FRS 1 allows operating cash flows to be shown:

(a) The *net method*, otherwise called the indirect method, involves computation of the operating cash flows by adjusting the operating profits for non-cash charges and credits so that one figure of operating cash flow is shown.

(b) The *gross method*, otherwise called the direct method, involves showing individual operating cash receipts and payments such as cash receipts from customers, cash payments to suppliers, and cash payments for employees.

Whichever method is used, a note to the cash flow statement must show a reconciliation between operating profit and operating cash flow. Thus the information required by the indirect method must be given, while the information required by the direct method is optional.

This note may be shown either adjoining the cash flow statement or as a separate note.

Reconciliation to net debt

A reconciliation of the movement in cash with the movement in net debt, as defined above, must be provided. Suggested headings under which the movement in net debt might be explained are:

(a) The cash flows of the entity.
(b) Acquisition or disposal of subsidiaries.
(c) Other non-cash charges, such as the inception of finance leases.
(d) The recognition of changes in market value and finance leases.

Exceptional and extraordinary items

Cash flows relating to what are classified as exceptional and extraordinary items in the profit and loss account should be classified under the appropriate heading in the cash flow statement, with a note to the statement giving sufficient supporting detail for their effect to be understood. Exceptional cash flows that are not related to exceptional profit and loss items must also be highlighted.

Foreign currencies

The translation basis used in the cash flow statement should be the same as in the profit and loss account. For intragroup cash flows, actual transaction rates should be used if possible so that there is cancellation on consolidation. Where restrictions prevent the transfer of cash from one part of the group to another, this should be explained in a note.

Cash flows on hedging transactions should be reported together with the related hedged item.

Group accounts

The cash flow statement of a group should only deal with cash flows in and out of the group. Thus cash flows within the group should cancel out in the group accounts.

Dividends paid to the minority interest are an outflow under the heading 'returns on investments and servicing of finance', to be disclosed separately. Where equity accounting is applied, as for associated companies, only cash flows between the entity and the group should be reported.

When a subsidiary is acquired or disposed of, the amounts of cash or cash equivalents paid should be shown net of cash and cash equivalent balances within the subsidiary. A note to the cash flow statement should show the effects of acquisitions and disposals indicating:

(a) how much of the consideration comprised cash;
(b) the amounts of cash transferred within the subsidiary.

Where a subsidiary joins or leaves the group during the year, cash flows for the subsidiary should be brought into the cash flow statement for the same period as profit from the subsidiary is brought into the group profit and loss account. In the year the acquisition or disposal occurs the effect on amounts under each standard heading in the cash flow statement of the subsidiary acquired or disposed of should be shown.

Major non-cash transactions

Some material transactions do not result in cash flows. If necessary for an understanding of the underlying transactions, these should be disclosed in the notes to the cash flow statement.

Comparative figures

Comparative figures should be given for all items in the cash flow statement and such notes thereto as are required by the FRS with the exception of the note to the statement that analyses changes in the balance sheet amounts making up net debt and the note of the effects of acquisitions and disposals of subsidiary undertakings on each of the standard headings.

Preparation of the statement – exam techniques

There are two routes to the preparation of the cash flow statement:

(a) analysis of the cash books and records;
(b) adjustment of balance sheet movements by elimination of non-cash movements and their analysis under the five cash flow statement headings.

The first approach gives easy access to the data needed to show operating cash flow on a *gross* basis, but needs detailed analysis of transactions, is more complex in compilation of the reconciliation notes, and may be costly to apply. The second approach risks oversight of relevant adjustments but is easier to prepare, automatically provides a reconciliation between operating profits and operating cash flow, and is more familiar to those accustomed to preparing funds flow statements.

Given two different approaches to preparing the cash flow statement, examiners have a variety of ways in which they can present a cash flow statement. No one computational approach can embrace all of these. The well-prepared candidate will be:

(a) familiar with the format of the cash flow statement so as to be aware of the data which will need to be extracted from the question;
(b) alert to the range of differences between accrual and cash flow accounting so as to make appropriate adjustments.

Figure 2.1 shows an outline of a cash flow statement in compliance with FRS 1. This needs to be supported by the relevant notes. When preparing the cash flow statement by the indirect method, a possible sequence is:

	£000	£000
Cash flow from operating activities		
Returns on investment and servicing of finance	——	
Taxation		
Capital expenditure and financial investment	——	
Equity dividends paid		——
Cash out/inflow before use of liquid resources and financing		
Management of liquid resources	——	
Financing	——	
		——
In/decrease in cash in the year		═══

Fig. 2.1 Cash flow statement for the year ended 31 December 19X5

(a) Prepare an outline of the statement itself and the supporting notes. Preparation of the notes both provides a comprehensive answer and serves as a form of working schedule supporting the statement itself.

(b) Work through each balance sheet heading analysing each movement in the year into its cash flow components, using supporting working notes when the analysis is too complex to show on the face of the solution. Areas of complexity traditionally include:

  (i) *Fixed assets*. The net balance can change for four reasons:
   1. additions, shown as investing cash outflows;
   2. depreciation, which is an expense in the profit and loss account which has not involved any cash flow and is therefore shown as an item added back to operating profit in computing operating cash flows;
   3. disposals, where the sale proceeds are shown as an investing cash inflow and the profit and loss on disposal constitutes a final revision to the depreciation charge on the asset disposed of and accordingly is reflected in the adjustments to arrive at operating cash flows;
   4. revaluations, which do not involve any cash flow and are simply cancelled out against related changes in the revaluation reverse.

  (ii) *Working capital items* such as stock, debtors, and creditors. Normally balance sheet movements in these items are part of the adjustments to reconcile operating profit to operating cash flow. However, where opening or closing balances include non-trading items such as liabilities for outstanding plant purchases or interest obligations then these should be adjusted in arriving at the related cash flow in the statement.

  (iii) *Share capital movements* can arise because of:

1. bonus issues, involving no cash flows, where the balance sheet mov ment is cancelled out against the related transfer from reserves;
2. issues for cash, where the cash inflow should be shown in the finan section of the statement inclusive of share premium;
3. issues in exchange for non-cash assets, such as shares exchanged f shares in another company. In this case no entry in the cash flow stat ment arises, except in so far as acquisition of a subsidiary brings ca or cash equivalent balances into the group balance sheet.

(iv) *Reserve movements* arise for a variety of reasons. Changes in retain profits link back to the profit and loss accounts and relate back to ope ating profit, cash flows arising from returns on investments and servici of finance such as dividends and interest, and taxation.

Worked example

The accounts and associated notes for Lorrequer Ltd are provided below. From the we will illustrate how a cash flow statement may be drawn up.

Lorrequer Ltd – balance sheet as at 31 March 19X2

		31 March 19X2		*31 March 19X1*	
	Notes	£000	£000	£000	£000
Fixed assets	(1)		3 000		2 800
Current assets:					
Stock		2 250		1 900	
Trade debtors		1 180		860	
Other debtors	(2)	90		—	
Prepayments	(3)	30		40	
Cash at bank		—		340	
		3 550		3 140	
Current liabilities:					
Trade creditors		1 340		1 250	
Accruals	(3)	110		100	
Proposed dividends		150		200	
Taxation		410		390	
Overdraft		200		—	
		2 210		1 940	
Net current assets			1 340		1 200
			4 340		4 000
8% loan stock (repayable 31.12.X7)			1 500		1 500
			2 840		2 500
Ordinary shares of £1			1 600		1 200
Share premium			300		500
Retained profits			940		800
			2 840		2 500

Lorrequer Ltd – balance sheet as at 31 March 19X2

	£000	£000
Turnover		4 000
Cost of sales		1 800
Gross profit		2 200
Administration	445	
Distribution	820	
		1 265
Operating profit		935
Interest receivable	(5)	
Interest payable	140	
		135
Profit before tax		800
Taxation		410
Profit after tax		390
Dividends:		
Interim	100	
Final	150	
		250
Retained profit for year		140

Note 1: Fixed assets

	Freehold property £000	*Plant* £000	*Total* £000
Cost 1.4.X1	1 100	2 800	3 900
Additions at cost	320	590	910
Disposals at cost	(220)	—	(220)
Cost 31.3.X2	1 200	3 390	4 590
Depreciation 1.4.X1	100	1 000	1 100
Charge for year	20	475	495
Depreciation on disposal	(5)		(5)
Depreciation 31.3.X2	115	1 475	1 590
NBV 31.3.X2	1 085	1 915	3 000

During the year freehold property was sold for £390 000.

Note 2: Other debtors represents an amount receivable in relation to the sale of property.

Note 3: Prepayments and *accruals* relate to the following items:

	Prepayments		*Accruals*	
	19X2	*19X1*	*19X2*	*19X1*
	£000	£000	£000	£000
PAYE			20	15
Other expenses	30	40	90	85
	30	40	110	100

Note 4: On 30 June 19X1 the share premium was reduced by a 1 for 4 bonus issue. On 1 January 19X2 100 000 new shares were issued for cash £2 per share.

Note 5: Stock and cost of sales relate entirely to bought-in goods. Administration and distribution costs consist of:

	Administration	*Distribution*
	£000	£000
Depreciation	105	390
Wages and salaries	415	200
Other expenses	100	230
Profit on property sale	(175)	
	445	820

Applying this procedure to the example of Lorrequer Ltd, we would first draw up an outline of the cash flow statement above. We then work through the balance sheet as follows:

(a) The movement in fixed assets is analysed in the question:
  (i) additions at cost represent an investing cash outflow for the year, since there is no evidence of an opening or closing creditor for these;
  (ii) the depreciation charge has been recorded in the profit and loss account as an expense but does not involve any cash flow. Accordingly this is added back to operating profit in order to compute cash flow from operations;
  (iii) the sale of property may be summarised as follows:

	£000
Cost	220
Depreciation	5
	215
Profit on sale	175
Sale price	390

The *profit on sale* is the result of an investing activity, and accordingly must be deducted from the operating profit. The sale price of £390 000 has apparently not been received in full, since Note 2 tells us that £90 000 *other debtors* relates to this sale. Accordingly only cash received (£390 000 – £90 000 = £300 000) is shown under investing activities.

(b) Stock has increased by £350 000. To this extent operating profit has not resulted in cash flow, instead being tied up in increased working capital. Accordingly this amount is deducted from operating profit.

(c) The increase in trade debtors of £320 000, as with the increase in stock, must be deducted from operating profit.

(d) The increase in other debtors has already been accounted for in considering the related sale of property.

(e) Like stock and debtors, the change in prepayments (in this case a reduction) is reflected in the adjustments to operating profit.

(f) The decrease in the bank balance forms part of the change in the net cash balance, and is shown in Note 3 to the statement.

(g) The increase in trade creditors is added to operating profit to find operating cash flow.

(h) The increase in accruals is added to operating profit to find operating cash flow.

(i) To find the cash outflow on dividends a simple schedule is prepared:

	£000
Proposed dividend b/fwd	200
+ P&L appropriation for year	250
– Proposed dividend c/fwd	(150)
= Cash paid in year	300

The cash outflow is then recorded on the face of the cash flow statement as equity dividend paid.

(j) A similar schedule to that prepared above identifies the cash outflow related to tax:

	£000
Liability b/fwd	390
+ P&L change	410
– Liability c/fwd	(410)
= Cash paid	390

(k) The increase in the overdraft forms part of the cash change, and again is included in Note 3.

(l) The changes in share capital and share premium are normally best taken together. In this case the net increase of £200 000 clearly represents the proceeds of the share issue and should be shown in the financing section of the cash flow statement.

(m) The movement of retained profits is explained by the profit and loss account. Taking the items shown:
   (i) Operating profit is shown at the head of Note 1 on operating cash flows.
   (ii) In the absence of information to the contrary, interest receivable and payable is assumed to represent cash flows and accordingly is shown as *return on investment* and *servicing of finance*.

The cash flow statement as prepared above is shown in full on the next page.

Lorrequer Ltd – cash flow statement for the year ending 31 March 19X2

	£000	£000
Net cash inflow from operating activities (Note 1)		695
Returns on investments and servicing of finance:		
Interest received	5 (m)	
Interest paid	(140) (m)	
Net cash outflow from returns on investments and servicing of finance		(135)
Taxation:		
Corporation tax paid		(390)
Capital expenditure:		
Payment to acquire property	(320) (a)	
Payment to acquire plant	(590) (a)	
Receipt from sale of property	300 (a)	(610)
Equity dividends paid		(300) (i)
Cash outflow before use of liquid resources and financing		(740)
Financing:		
Issue of ordinary share capital		200 (l)
Decrease in cash ((340)(f) + (200)(k))		(540)

Notes to cash flow statement

1. Reconciliation of operating cash flows to operating profit

	£000	£000
Operating profit		935 (m)
Depreciation charge	495 (a)	
Profit on property sale	(175) (a)	
Stock increase	(350) (b)	
Debtor increase	(320) (c)	
Prepayment decrease	10 (e)	
Trade creditor increase	90 (g)	
Accrual increase	10 (h)	
		(240)
Net cash inflow from operating activities		695

2. Analysis of net debt

	At 1 April 19X1 £000	*Cash flow* £000	*At 31 March 19X2* £000
Cash at bank	340	(340)	—
Overdraft	—	(200)	(200)
		(540)	
Loan stock	(1 500)	—	(1 500)
	(1 160)		(1 700)

Controversy over the statement

Funds flow or cash flow?

As we have seen above, FRS 1 with its requirement to present a cash flow statement replaces SSAP 10 with its requirement to present a funds flow statement. In an *explanation* accompanying FRS 1, the ASB offers the following arguments in support of this change:

(a) where a funds flow statement focuses on working capital this may obscure cash movements;
(b) cash flow is a clearer concept than changes in working capital;
(c) cash flow relates directly to a business valuation model;
(d) the cash flow statement and related notes as required by FRS 1 introduces data not shown in a funds flow statement.

SSAP 10 was criticised not only for the inherent limitations of *funds flow* as opposed to *cash flow* but also because of the failure to define *funds* and to provide firm guidance on formats. As a result, companies adopted a range of approaches that meant that funds flow statements were not easily compared.

Internationally, there is a trend, particularly in the English-speaking world, to move from funds flow statements to cash flow statements. Countries making this move have included the USA (1987), New Zealand (1987) and Australia (1992).

Formats

FRS 1 offers a range of illustrative formats:

(a) a simple single company arrangement, as shown above;
(b) a group cash flow statement;
(c) a bank;
(d) an insurance company.

This comprehensive guidance responds to one of the criticisms made of SSAP 10.

The form of presentation chosen by FRS 1 contrasts with that in Australia, New Zealand and the USA, by having the five major headings rather than three. Table 2.1 (page 24) shows the differences between the four countries. During 1992 New Zealand revised its first cash flow statement, SSAP 10, to a new statement, FRS 10. It is interesting to note that, in the light of experience, New Zealand accountants moved in line with the US and Australian formats. By contrast the UK has chosen to adopt a distinctly different format, thereby making international comparison more difficult.

The new FRS 1, with eight headings, departs even further from international practice.

Gross method versus net method

By requiring a note to the funds statement to show the reconciliation between operating profit and operating cash flows, FRS 1 effectively requires that the *net method* be shown. FRS 1 also permits, but does not require, disclosure of the cash flow that constitutes the *gross* method. In the USA a similar choice is permitted, with the vast majority of companies opting for the *net* method. This is not surprising, given that

Table 2.1 Main components of cash flow statement

USA *FAS 95*	*UK* *FRS 1 (1991)*	*Australia* *AASB 1026*	*New Zealand* *SSAP 10*	*New Zealand* *FRS 10*
Operating activities (includes taxation, dividends received, interest received and paid)	Operating activities	Operating activities (illustration includes taxation, returns on investments, and interest paid)	Operating activities (includes taxation)	Operating activities (includes taxation, dividends received, interest received and paid)
	Returns on investments and servicing finance			
	Taxation			
Investing activities	Investing activities	Investing activities	Investing activities (includes returns on investments)	Investing activities
Financing (includes dividends paid)	Financing	Financing (includes dividends paid)	Financing (includes servicing of finance)	Financing (includes dividends paid)

this is simpler and less costly. However, US analysts have criticised this approach on the grounds that there is a problem of comparability. In both Australia and New Zealand the gross method is prescribed. When the requirement was reviewed in New Zealand 47 respondents supported its continuance, compared with six against.

The 'objectivity' of cash flow

One benefit argued in favour of the cash flow statement is that *cash flow* is an objective fact not subject to the manipulation that can arise with accrual accounting. While the opportunity for such manipulation is less, in practice it still exists. For example, a finance lease conceals the substance of an asset acquisition, although the note on net debt should highlight this.

Using the cash flow statement

The cash flow statement gives a useful picture of how the overall liquidity of a business has increased or diminished. For example, a glance at the example of Lorrequer Ltd above shows how:

(a) increases in stock and debtors have absorbed a major part of operating cash flow;
(b) substantial new long-term investments have not been supported by long-term finance.

A range of ratios can also be computed. Broadly speaking these are identified in two ways:

(a) the ratios used to relate the components of accruals-based accounts can be adapted to relate the equivalent components of cash flow. For example, the relationship between operating cash flows gives an insight into gearing;
(b) ratios can be computed relating cash flows to accruals-based data. For example, the ratio of cash inflows from customers to accruals-based turnover gives insight into the control of trade credit, and avoids the problem of using balance sheet debtor figures that might be distorted by the year-end date. Another example is the ratio of operating cash flow to total assets, which gives a picture of the liquidity generated from asset utilisation.

A commonly quoted ratio is that of operating cash flow to operating profit, often referred to as *quality of earnings*.

Conclusion

The cash flow statement commands widespread support as a stronger guide to a company's liquidity position than the funds flow statement. The formats used in FRS 1 are somewhat different from those used in other countries and some aspects, such as the definition of cash equivalents, are open to question.

EXAMINATION PRACTICE

2.1 Forecast cash flow statement

The balance sheet of Chiron Ltd as at 31 March 19X6, together with its projected balance sheet as at 31 March 19X7 and profit and loss account for the year ending on that date, is as follows:

Chiron Ltd – balance sheet as at:

	31 March 19X6		*31 March 19X7*	
	£000	£000	£000	£000
Ordinary share capital in £1 shares fully paid		200		250
Capital reserve:				
Share premium a/c				25
Profit and loss a/c		70		108
		270		383
Represented by:				
Fixed assets:				
Freehold premises – cost		60		90
Plant and machinery at cost less depreciation		48		125
		108		215
Current assets:				
Stock	140		170	
Debtors	100		120	
Cash	1		2	
	241		292	

Chiron Ltd – balance sheet (continued)

	31 March 19X6		*31 March 19X7*	
	£000	£000	£000	£000
Less: Current liabilities:				
Trade creditors	40		64	
Accrued expenses	1		2	
Corporation tax	16		26	
Proposed dividends	16		20	
Bank overdraft	6		12	
	79	162	124	168
		270		383

Budgeted profit and loss account for the year ended 31 March 19X7

	£000	£000
Sales		300
Cost of sales (including plant depreciation £28 000)		180
Gross profit		120
Distribution	15	
Administration	19	
		34
Operating profit		86
Bank interest		2
Profit before tax		84
Tax		26
Profit after tax		58
Proposed dividend		20
Retained profit for the year		38

You are required to prepare a predicted cash flow statement for the year to 31 March 19X7 with supporting notes as required by FRS 1.

2.2 Preparation of cash flow statement

The balance sheets of Beatem Ltd as at 31 March 19X8 (with comparative figures as at 31 March 19X7), together with other pertinent information, are given below:

Beatem Ltd – balance sheet as at:

	31 March 19X8		*31 March 19X7*	
	£000	£000	£000	£000
Share capital – ordinary shares of £1 each fully paid		1 200		1 000
Reserves:				
Share premium		550		600
Retained profits		3 725		3 500
		5 475		5 100
Debentures – 8% £1				
Convertible		2 000		—

Beatem Ltd – balance sheet (continued)

	31 March 19X8 £000	£000	*31 March 19X7* £000	£000
Current liabilities:				
Bank overdraft	1 750		1 500	
Creditors	1 450		1 550	
Taxation	820		1 150	
		4 020		4 200
		11 495		9 300
Fixed assets:				
Land and building at cost		3 500		1 800
Plant and machinery at cost	6 100		5 800	
Less: Depreciation	3 900		3 850	
		2 200		1 950
		5 700		3 750
Current assets:				
Stock and work in progress	3 435		3 150	
Debtors	2 200		1 900	
Cash and bank balance	160		500	
		5 795		5 550
		11 495		9 300

Note 1

The profit for the year 19X8, after charging all expenses including the loss on the sale of the plant, but before interest, depreciation and taxation, was £2 015 000. The corporation tax of £820 000 charged in the profit and loss account on the profits for the year was reduced by the overprovision for corporation tax on the 19X7 profit, i.e. by £150 000. The ordinary dividend paid during the year and charged against the profit after tax was £180 000. Interest of £300 000 was made up of:

	£	
Debenture interest	160 000	(£80 000 accrual included in creditors)
Overdraft interest	140 000	(all paid in year)

Note 2

During the year, plant and machinery which had cost £1 200 000 and in respect of which depreciation of £590 000 had been provided was sold for £565 000. There had been a rights issue of ordinary shares at the rate of 1 for 10 at a price of £1.50 per share payable in full on 1 April 19X7. Subsequently, a scrip (bonus) issue of 1 for 11 had been made utilising the share premium account. The convertible debentures had been issued at par on 1 April 19X7, payable in full. The conversion terms exercisable on 31 March 19Y1 are 1 ordinary share for every 4 £1 debentures. Agreed corporation tax of £1 million on the 19X7 profits had been paid on the due date.

You are required to prepare a cash flow statement for the year ended 31 March 19X8 bearing in mind the requirements of FRS 1.

2.3 Treatment of items in the cash flow statement

The directors of Vienne Ltd wish to prepare a consolidated cash flow statement in line with FRS 1: Cash Flow Statements. They are uncertain how to deal with a number of items which are listed below.

1. Consolidated creditors decreased by £70 000.
2. Vienne Ltd declared and distributed a 50% scrip issue on the share capital of £10 million, in fully paid ordinary shares of £1 each.
3. The minority interest in a cash dividend declared and paid by a consolidated subsidiary was £10 000.
4. Equipment costing £90 000 was purchased from outside the group.
5. Following the year-end date, the directors declared a final dividend of £400 000.
6. On 30 October 19X2 £48 000 had been spent on 4% loan stock with a nominal value of £50 000 maturing on 15 February 19X3.
7. Vienne Ltd's share of the profits of an associated company was £52 000 for the year. No dividend was received from the associate in the year.
8. Loan stock of £100 000 was redeemed at par during the year.
9. Plant with a net book value of £40 000 was scrapped during the year with no proceeds arising from the disposal.
10. On 30 November 19X2 damages for defective workmanship at £400 000 were awarded against the company. The court agreed that no payment need be made pending an appeal to be heard in April 19X3.

In order to identify the appropriate treatment of these items the directors have specified the following symbols:

AO Add to operating profit in determining cash flow from operating activities.
DO Deduct from operating profit in determining cash flow from operating activities.
R Include in returns on investments and servicing of finance.
T Include in taxation.
I Include in capital expenditure and financial investment.
AD Include in acquisitions and disposals.
ED Include in equity dividends.
M Include in management of liquid resources.
F Include in financing.
A Include in cash.
N No effect on the cash flow statement.

You are required to indicate how each of the items 1–10 listed above should be disclosed in the consolidated cash flow statement of Vienne Ltd, making use of the symbols specified by the directors.

You are *not* required to rewrite the question. Merely list the items in sequence and opposite each item record the symbol you think appropriate.

2.4 Preparing the statement

The balance sheets for Vienne Ltd as at 31 December 19X4 and 31 December 19X3 were:

	31 December 19X4		*31 December 19X3*	
	£000	£000	£000	£000
Fixed assets:				
Land and buildings		2 900		2 500
Plant		1 000		155
		3 900		2 655
Current assets:				
Stock	2 020		1 810	
Trade debtors	1 710		1 100	
Prepayments, etc.	71		70	
Investment	200		180	
Bank	25		120	
Cash	40		31	
	4 066		3 311	

The balance sheets for Vienne Ltd *(continued)*

	31 December 19X4		*31 December 19X3*	
	£000	£000	£000	£000
Current liabilities:				
Trade creditors	520		540	
Accruals	405		380	
Leasing obligation	370		—	
Overdraft	201		—	
Proposed dividend	180		200	
Taxation	250		230	
	1 926		1 350	
Net current assets		2 140		1 961
		6 040		4 615
10% debenture	1 500		1 000	
Lease obligation	410		—	
Deferred taxation	330		206	
		2 240		1 206
		3 800		3 410
Ordinary shares of £1		1 500		1 200
Share premium		230		530
Revaluation		750		470
Reserve				
Retained profit		1 320		1 210
		3 800		3 410

Additional information

1. The change in the revaluation reserve is due to a revaluation of land and buildings during the year. On the first day of 19X4 the entire plant was sold for £50 000 and replaced with plant held under a finance lease recorded in the accounts initially at £1 108 000.
2. The deferred tax balance consists of:

	19X4	*19X3*
	£000	£000
Revaluation surpluses	320	200
Other	10	6
	330	206

The corporation tax charge for the year was £205 000.

3. Interest payable during the year was:

	£000
10% debenture	125
Finance lease	105
	230

4. Interest receivable shown in the accounts was £52 000.

5. Prepayments and accrued income consist of:

	19X4	*19X3*
	£000	£000
Trading items	57	58
Interest receivable	14	12
	71	70

6. Accruals consist of:

	19X4	*19X3*
	£000	£000
Trading items	330	320
Interest payable	75	50
Plant purchase	—	10
	405	380

7. In both years the investments consist of short-term highly liquid investments readily convertible into known amounts of cash without notice.
8. An interim dividend of £100 000 was paid on 1 October 19X4.

You are required to prepare a cash flow statement for Vienne Ltd for the year ended 31 December 19X4.

FRS 2: Accounting for Subsidiary Undertakings

Introduction

Evolution of group accounts

The holding company originated in the USA, the first recorded instance arising in 1832. Accountants soon came to appreciate the weakness of a holding company's own accounts showing only its own income and balance sheet position. The concept of presenting group accounts to the shareholders of the holding company in order to overcome these weaknesses developed in the USA earlier than in the UK. For example, Dicksee's *Auditing* first mentions the desirability of consolidated accounts in the 1908 American edition, but the subject is only included in the English edition from 1924 onwards. The first consolidated balance sheet presented in the UK was at the AGM of Nobel Industries Ltd, in September 1922, while in 1923 Sir Gilbert Garnsey published his *Holding Companies and their Published Accounts*. In 1939 the London Stock Exchange introduced rules concerning consolidated accounts and the Companies Act 1947 (later consolidated into the Companies Act 1948) introduced a legal requirement to present group accounts. While company law defined the general nature of group accounts together with certain specific requirements relating to their production and content, experience has revealed a number of areas of controversy and variation in practice. SSAP 14, issued in September 1978, narrowed some of these areas of difference.

In the light of the Companies Act 1989 a new standard was required and FRS 2 fills this need.

Scope of the chapter

It would clearly be unreasonable to attempt to cover the whole topic of group accounts in one chapter; at the same time it is not practical to consider FRS 2 in isolation from a knowledge and understanding of consolidation procedures. Such a knowledge will therefore be assumed in this chapter, although for the sake of clarity some requirements of the accounting standard will be compared with the related requirements of the Companies Acts.

Summary of the statement

Definitions

FRS 2 identifies the legislation governing consolidated accounts as *The Act* being the *Companies Act 1985 as amended by the Companies Act 1989*. The term *undertaking* is defined as:

> A body corporate, a partnership or an unincorporated association carrying on a trade or business with or without a view to profit.

This reflects the broader responsibility to consolidate which, previously, referred only to corporate bodies.

The definition of the situation where a *parent undertaking* has a *subsidiary undertaking* identifies the following circumstances:

(a) Where

> It holds a majority of the voting rights in the undertaking.

The key term here is *voting rights in an undertaking*, defined as:

> Rights conferred on shareholders in respect of their shares or, in the case of an undertaking not having a share capital, on members; to vote at general meetings of the undertaking on all, or substantially all, matters. Schedule 10A deals with the attribution of voting rights in certain circumstances.

(b) Where

> It is a member of the undertaking and has the right to appoint or remove directors holding a majority of the voting rights at meetings of the board on all, or substantially all, matters.

(c) Where

> It has the right to exercise a dominant influence over the undertaking:
>
> (i) by virtue of provisions contained in the undertaking's memorandum or articles; or
> (ii) by virtue of a control contract. The control contract must be in writing and be of a kind authorised by the memorandum or articles of the controlled undertaking. It must also be permitted by the law under which that undertaking is established.

The key term *dominant influence* is defined as:

> Influence that can be exercised to achieve the operating and financial policies desired by the holder of the influence of any other party.
>
> (a) The right to exercise a dominant influence means that the holder has a right to give directions with respect to the operating and financial policies of another undertaking with which its directors are obliged to comply, whether or not they are for the benefit of that undertaking.
> (b) The actual exercise of dominant influence is the exercise of an influence that achieves the result that the operating and financial policies of the undertaking influenced are set in accordance with the wishes of the holder of the influence and for the holder's benefit whether or not those wishes are explicit. The actual exercise of dominant influence is identified by its effect in practice rather than by the way in which it is exercised.

And *control* is defined as:

> The ability of an undertaking to direct the financial and operating policies of another undertaking with a view to gaining economic benefits from its activities.

(d) Where```

It is a member of the undertaking and controls alone, pursuant to an agreement with other shareholders or members, a majority of the voting rights in the undertaking.

(e) Where

It has a participating interest in the undertaking and:

(i) it actually exercises a dominant influence over the undertaking; or
(ii) it and the undertaking are managed on a unified basis.

The key term *managed on a unified basis* is defined by:

Two or more undertakings are managed on a unified basis if the whole of the operations of the undertakings are integrated and they are managed as a single unit. Unified management does not arise solely because one undertaking manages another.

And the key term *participating interest* is defined as:

An interest held by an undertaking in the shares of another undertaking which it holds on a long-term basis for the purpose of securing a contribution to its activities by the exercise of control or influence arising from or related to that interest [from s 260].

(a) A holding of 20% or more of the shares of an undertaking shall be presumed to be a participating interest unless the contrary is shown.
(b) An interest in shares includes an interest which is convertible into an interest in shares, and includes an option to acquire shares or any interest which is convertible into shares.
(c) An interest held on behalf of an undertaking shall be treated as held by that undertaking.

Consolidation is defined as:

The process of adjusting and combining financial information from the individual financial statements of a parent undertaking and its subsidiary undertakings to prepare consolidated financial statements that present financial information for the group as a single economic entity.

Key terms in deciding whether or not consolidation should apply are:
(i) Interest on a long-term basis:

An interest which is held other than exclusively with a view to subsequent resale.

(ii) Interest held exclusively with a view to subsequent resale:

(a) An interest for which a purchaser has been sought, and which is reasonably expected to be disposed of within approximately one year of its date of acquisition; or
(b) An interest that was acquired as a result of the enforcement of a security, unless the interest has become part of the continuing activities of the group or the holder acts as if it intends the interest to become so.

While some subsidiaries excluded from consolidation are subject to the *equity method* defined as:

A method of accounting for an investment that brings into the consolidated profit and loss account the investor's share of the investment undertaking's results and that records the investment in the consolidated balance sheet at the investor's share of the investment undertaking's net assets including any goodwill arising to the extent that it has not previously been written off.

The equity method is discussed in detail in Chapter 10 below on FRS 9.

Scope and exemptions

The situations where a parent undertaking is excluded from an obligation to present consolidated accounts are explained in detail in company law and fall under two broad headings:

(a) a size exemption embracing most small- and medium-sized companies; and
(b) an exemption where the parent is itself a subsidiary of another EC company. The detailed conditions for this exemption to apply are specified in company law.

FRS 2 provides that a parent undertaking should disclose the grounds for exemption.

Exclusion of subsidiaries from consolidation

There are a number of circumstances where company law permits or requires the exclusion of subsidiaries from the consolidated accounts. FRS 2 defines these situations more closely, working on a broad principle that 'The FRS requires the circumstances in which subsidiary undertakings are to be excluded from consolidation to be interpreted strictly'. The company law provisions for permitting exclusion are:

(a) inclusion of the subsidiary in the consolidated accounts would not be material. Two or more subsidiaries may only be excluded where taken together they are not material;
(b) the information necessary to prepare consolidated accounts cannot be obtained without disproportionate expense or undue delay. FRS 2 effectively tightens up this provision by stating that it cannot be applied unless the subsidiaries to be excluded are not individually or collectively material to the group, i.e. the first exemption above applies in any case;
(c) severe long-term restrictions substantially hinder the exercise of the parent's rights over the assets or management of the undertaking. Where this situation arises FRS 2 *requires* exclusion, as opposed to company law which merely *permits* exclusion;
(d) the parent's interest in the undertaking is acquired and held exclusively with a view to subsequent sale. Again, whereas company law *permits*, FRS 2 *requires* exclusion in this case;
(e) company law *requires* exclusion where the activities of one or more subsidiaries are so different from those of the other undertakings included in the consolidated accounts that their inclusion would be incompatible with the obligation to give a true and fair view. FRS 2 seeks to minimise the application of this exemption by:
    (i) citing the clause in the Companies Act that exclusion on these grounds does not apply 'merely because some of the undertakings are industrial, some commercial and some provide services, or because they carry on industrial or commercial activities involving different products or provide different services';
    (ii) adding the observation that 'it is exceptional for such circumstances to arise and it is not possible to identify any particular contrast of activities

where the necessary incompatibility with the true and fair view generally occurs';

(iii) also suggesting that where the activities of different undertakings contrast then a true and fair view may be achieved by supporting the consolidated accounts with appropriate segmental information.

FRS 2 reaffirms the provision of company law that the names of any subsidiaries excluded from consolidation must be shown, with the reasons for exclusion.

Accounting for excluded subsidiaries

The way in which excluded subsidiaries should be accounted for in the consolidated accounts depends on the reasons for exclusion:

(a) Where severe long-term restrictions hinder the exercise of the rights of the parent undertaking then the treatment depends on the date at which the restrictions came into force. If the restrictions were in force at the acquisition date then the subsidiary will be carried at cost from the start. If restrictions come into force at a later date then the subsidiary will cease to be consolidated at that date and will instead be recorded as an investment at an amount based on the equity method, i.e. associated company treatment. While the restrictions are in force no further accruals should be made for the profits or losses of the subsidiary unless there is a significant degree of influence, despite the restrictions, to justify treatment as an associated company. Both the carrying value of such investments and intra-group amounts due from them should be reviewed each year and written down for any permanent diminution in value.

(b) Where an investment in a subsidiary is held exclusively with a view to subsequent resale then it should be recorded as a current asset at the lower of cost and net realisable value.

(c) Where exclusion is on the grounds of different activities then, as required by company law, the equity method (i.e. associated company treatment) should be used.

A number of special disclosure requirements for subsidiaries excluded from consolidation are provided in FRS 2:

(a) particulars of balances between the excluded subsidiaries and the rest of the group;

(b) the nature and extent of transactions of the excluded subsidiaries with the rest of the group;

(c) where the equity method is not applied to the excluded subsidiary any amounts included in the consolidated accounts for:
   (i) dividends received and receivable from the subsidiary;
   (ii) any write down of the investment in or amounts due from the subsidiary;

(d) Where a subsidiary is excluded because of different activities, separate accounts for the subsidiary. Summarised information may be provided for subsidiaries that, individually or in combination with similar operations, do not account for more than 20 per cent of any of operating profits, turnover or net assets of the whole group (including excluded subsidiaries).

Disclosure requirements for excluded subsidiaries must apply to the individual subsidiary if it accounts for more than 20 per cent of any of the operating profits, turnover or net assets of the whole group. For other subsidiaries disclosure may be made on an aggregate basis for sub-units of subsidiaries which together fall under one of the grounds for exclusion from consolidation.

Minority interests

The balance sheet should show the minority's share of capital and reserves under the heading *minority interests* while the profit and loss account should similarly show separately the aggregate of profit or loss on ordinary items attributable to *minority interest*, with the minority share in any extraordinary items shown separately. The minority share of losses in a subsidiary are attributable in principle even where this results in the interest being in a net liability rather than an asset; however, in this case the group will need to make a provision to the extent that there is a commercial or legal obligation, whether formal or implied, to finance any such deficit that cannot be recovered from the minority.

Where, on consolidation, adjustments are made to the values attributed to the assets or liabilities of a subsidiary, then the appropriate adjustment should be made to the minority interest. However, no acquisition goodwill should be allocated to the minority.

Profits or losses on transactions between group companies must be eliminated in full on consolidation, irrespective of whether the subsidiary concerned is included within the consolidation or not. The appropriate part of the consolidation adjustment must be allocated to the minority interests. In this respect FRS 2 is less flexible than company law, which permits the alternative treatment of restricting the elimination of profits or losses on intra-group transactions to the portion attributable to the controlling entity.

Consolidation accounting policies

Common accounting policies should be used in preparing the consolidated accounts with adjustments being made to the accounts of subsidiaries with different accounting policies. In exceptional cases where different accounting policies are used on consolidation then disclosure of the particulars, including details of the different accounting policies used, must be made.

In preparing the consolidated accounts the accounts of the subsidiaries should all cover the same period and run to the same date as the parent. If this is impracticable then:

(a) if possible, interim accounts should be prepared to a common accounting date;
(b) failing the above, accounts of the subsidiary for its last financial year should be used, provided that these are prepared to a date within three months of the parent undertaking's year end. In this case any material changes in the intervening period must be taken into account as consolidation adjustments. For any subsidiary where the year end or accounting period does not coincide with that of the parent the following must be disclosed:
   (i) the name of the subsidiary;

(ii) the accounting date or period of the subsidiary;
(iii) the reason for the difference.

Changes in the group

FRS 2 addresses a number of issues that arise at the time when a subsidiary becomes or ceases to be a subsidiary, or the holding in the subsidiary changes.

The date for commencing to account for a subsidiary is the day when acquisition or merger takes place. The date for ceasing to account for a subsidiary is that when the parent relinquishes control.

In the year an undertaking ceases to be a subsidiary the consolidated results will include both the appropriate share of the subsidiary's results up to the date of cessation and any gain or loss on cessation, calculated as the difference between:

(a) the amount at which the net assets of the subsidiary, including goodwill, are carried in the accounts; and
(b) any proceeds of disposal plus the amount at which any interest in the undertaking continues to be carried in the accounts.

The consolidated accounts should give the name of any material undertaking that has ceased to be a subsidiary, showing any ownership interest retained. If cessation is not attributable to a disposal then the circumstances should be explained. Similarly, where an undertaking has become or ceased to be a subsidiary other than by a purchase or share exchange then the circumstances should be explained.

Where a subsidiary is acquired in stages then the deemed date of acquisition is the date on which the part of the investment that causes the undertaking to become a subsidiary is acquired. Thus it is on that date that the fair value of all the identifiable assets and liabilities of the subsidiary must be computed, with the consequent quantification of consolidation goodwill. If a further interest in an existing subsidiary is acquired then a further valuation of identifiable assets and liabilities to compute acquisition goodwill in relation to the further interest will be required, if material.

Where there is a reduction in the interest held in an undertaking that continues to be a subsidiary then:

(a) a profit and loss on disposal will be computed as the difference between:
    (i) the disposal proceeds; and
    (ii) the reduction in the carrying amount of the subsidiary including goodwill;
(b) the portion of identifiable net assets, but not goodwill, removed from the parent share in consolidated accounts will be attributed to the minority interest.

Other disclosures

Where there are significant restrictions on dividend payments by subsidiaries, thereby limiting the parent's access to their retained profits, then the nature and extent of the restrictions should be disclosed. Where there is a possibility of tax arising on the remittance of accumulated reserves of overseas subsidiaries:

(a) the extent of any related deferred tax provision must be disclosed;
(b) the reason for not making any provision in full must be disclosed.

Conclusion

FRS 2 is unusual as an accounting standard in covering an area where company law already provides a range of highly detailed prescription. It is interesting that in that context the ASB have chosen explicitly to restrict further the limited range of choice permitted by legislation. Since these matters have recently been ruled on by Parliament in the Companies Act 1989 the ASB might be open to criticism for seeking to deny companies areas of choice that the legislation explicitly allows them.

The flow chart in Fig. 3.1 provides a summary of FRS 2s rules on exemptions from consolidation.

FRS 2 should also be considered in conjunction with a number of other standards:

(a) FRS 3 amplifies the treatment of acquired and discontinued operations;
(b) FRS 6 deals with acquisitions and mergers;
(c) FRS 9 deals with equity accounting;
(d) SSAP 20 deals with the translation of subsidiary accounts in a foreign currency;
(e) FRS 10 deals with consolidation goodwill;
(f) SSAP 25 deals with the segmental reporting rules that might help solve the *dissimilar activities* problem.

For further developments, see 'Business Combinations' in the chapter on Discussion Papers.

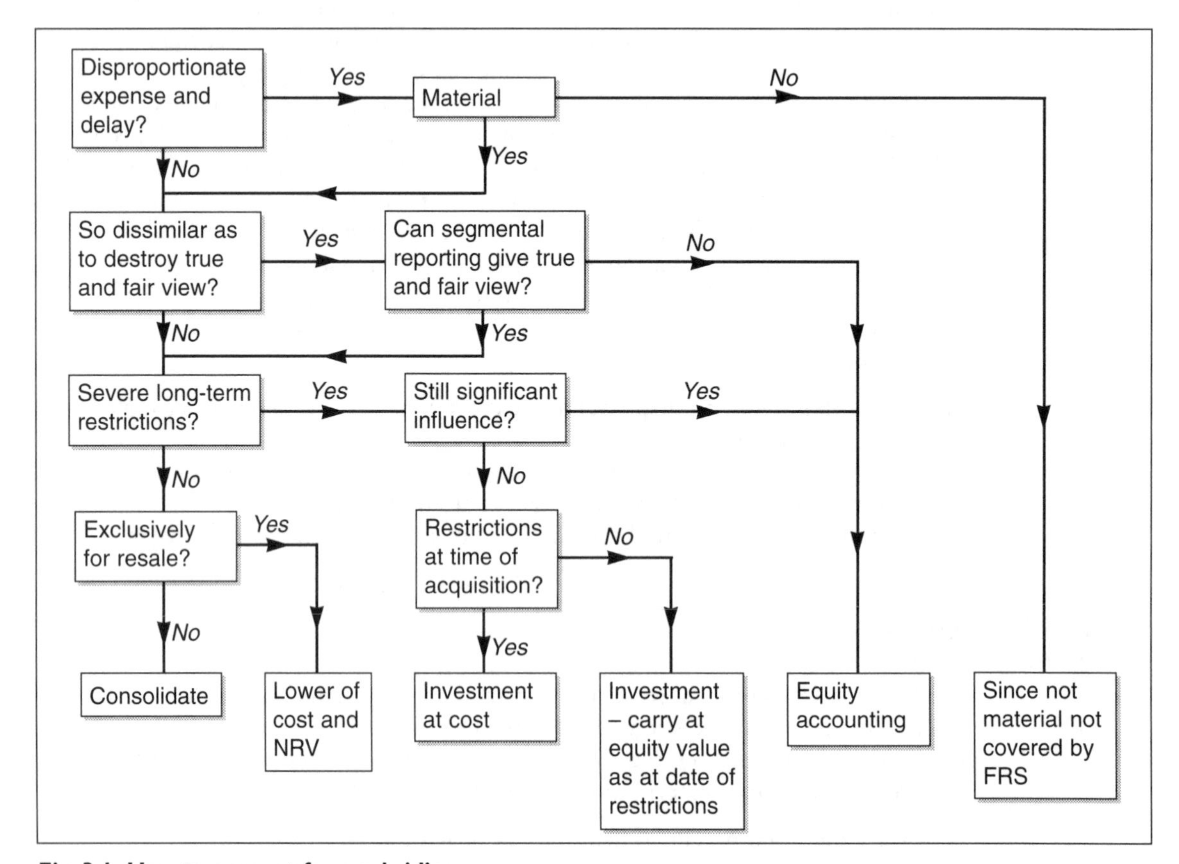

Fig. 3.1 How to account for a subsidiary

EXAMINATION PRACTICE

3.1 Exclusion from consolidation

Prepare a note on the circumstances in which UK company law and FRS 2: Accounting for Subsidiary Undertakings allow a subsidiary to be excluded from consolidation, and explain how excluded subsidiaries should be accounted for in the consolidated accounts.

FRS 3: Reporting Financial Performance

Introduction

Accountants have to decide to what extent gains or losses should be included within their definition of profit for the year, how to analyse and present that figure of profit in a meaningful way, and how to disclose other gains or losses in the accounts. In 1974 the ASC issued SSAP 6: Extraordinary Items and Prior Year Adjustments to address this issue. As we shall see below, this was a difficult standard to formulate and enforce. FRS 3, issued in October 1992, replaced SSAP 6. It is the first standard to be based on an exposure draft issued by the ASB, FRED 1, since both FRS 1 and FRS 2 were based on exposure drafts issued by the old ASC.

The basic issue

There are two broad approaches to the presentation of the profit and loss account. One, the *current operating income* approach, involves disclosing on the face of the profit and loss account only those items relating to the normal recurring activities of the company. Advocates of this approach argue that this profit figure provides a more meaningful guide to profits and gives a useful indication of management's achievement in running the business. The approach is also referred to as *reserve accounting*, on the grounds that other gains and losses are recorded as reserve movements.

The alternative is the *all-inclusive* concept of profit, that the profit and loss account should include not only the results of ordinary activities but also all other profits and losses for the year. Arguments in support of this approach are:

(a) with disclosure rules requiring separate identification of items outside the normal course of trading, the profit or loss on normal recurring items can still be identified;
(b) exclusion of certain items is necessarily subjective, and could lead to loss of comparability between companies;
(c) exclusion of certain items may also result in items being overlooked in any consideration of results over a number of years.

Both SSAP 6 and FRS 3 have been based, in principle, on the *all-inclusive* approach. The main difference between them is that SSAP 6 provided for separate identification of *extraordinary items* in such a way that these could be regarded as falling outside normal profit. This separate identification was taken up by the European

Community in the Fourth Directive and consequently enshrined in UK company law. It appears that, in formulating FRS 3, the ASB would have liked to have abolished the category *extraordinary item*. They felt unable to do this because the term is established in law, but have sought to achieve their objective by defining the term so restrictively that it is unlikely to be used in practice.

Summary of the statement

Definitions

The definitions provided in FRS 3 reflect the ASB's intention to restrict the exclusion of items from the reporting of normal activities.

Ordinary activities are defined as:

> Any activities which are undertaken by a reporting entity as part of its business and such related activities in which the reporting entity engages in furtherance of, incidental to, or arising from, these activities. Ordinary activities include the effects on the reporting entity of any event in the various environments in which it operates, including the political, regulatory, economic and geographical environments, irrespective of the frequency or unusual nature of the events.

This is a more comprehensive definition than that previously provided in SSAP 6, particularly in its reference to the inclusion within ordinary activities of all events within the various environments in which the business operates.

Acquisitions are defined in a straightforward way as:

> Operations of the reporting entity that are acquired in the period.

Discontinued operations are defined in some detail as:

> Operations of the reporting entity that are sold or terminated and that satisfy all of the following conditions:
>
> (a) The sale or termination is completed either in the period or before the earlier of three months after the commencement of the subsequent period and the date on which the financial statements are approved.
> (b) If a termination, the former activities have ceased permanently.
> (c) The sale or termination has a material effect on the nature and focus of the reporting entity's operations and represents a material reduction in its operating facilities resulting either from its withdrawal from a particular market (whether class of business or geographical) or from a material reduction in turnover in the reporting entity's continuing markets.
> (d) The assets, liabilities, results of operations are clearly distinguishable, physically, operationally and for financial reporting purposes.

Operations not satisfying all these conditions are classified as continuing.

Exceptional items, which fall within the results of ordinary activities while calling for extra disclosure, are defined as:

> Material items which derive from events or transactions that fall within the ordinary activities of the reporting entity and which individually or, if of a similar type, in aggregate need to be disclosed by virtue of their size or incidence if the financial statements are to give a true and fair view.

In contrast to the above definition, which is a broad one, the definition of an *extraordinary item* is tightly drawn:

> Material items possessing a high degree of abnormality which arise from events or transactions that fall outside the ordinary activities of the reporting entity and which are not expected to recur. They do not include exceptional items nor do they include prior period items merely because they relate to a prior period.

The term *prior period adjustments* is defined as:

> Material adjustments applicable to prior periods arising from changes in accounting policies or from the correction of fundamental errors. They do not include exceptional items nor do they include prior period items merely because they relate to a prior period.

This is the same definition as that previously used in SSAP 6 except that *period* has been used in place of *year*, presumably on the grounds that the accounting period is not necessarily of exactly one year, e.g. where there is a change of accounting date.

A new term introduced in FRS 3 is *total recognised gains and losses* defined as:

> The total of all gains and losses of the reporting entity that are recognised in a period and are attributable to shareholders.

The face of the profit and loss account

FRS 3 is supported by a number of illustrative examples. The following are shown below by way of illustration:

(a) *Example 1*, offering the minimum information to be shown on the face of the profit and loss account where the *functional format* is chosen.
(b) The necessary supporting note where the minimum disclosure has been shown on the face of the profit and loss account.
(c) An example of a *statement of total recognised gains and losses* with a *note on historical cost profits and losses.*
(d) A reconciliation of profit for the year to the movement in the shareholders' funds.

Profit and loss account example 1

	19X3	*19X3*	*19X2 as restated*
	£m	£m	£m
Turnover:			
Continuing operations	550		500
Acquisitions	50		
	600		
Discontinued operations	175		190
		775	690
Cost of sales		(620)	(555)
Gross profit		155	135
Net operating expenses		(104)	(83)
Operating profit:			
Continuing operations	50		40
Acquisitions	6		
	56		
Discontinued operations	(15)		12
Less 19X2 provision	10		
		51	52
Profit on sales of properties in continuing operations		9	6
Provision for loss on operations to be discontinued			(30)
Loss on disposal of discontinued operations	(17)		
Less 19X2 provision	20		
		3	
Profit on ordinary activities before interest		63	28
Interest payable		(18)	(15)
Profit on ordinary activities before taxation		45	13
Tax on profit on ordinary activities		(14)	(4)
Profit on ordinary activities after taxation		31	9
Minority interests		(2)	(2)
[Profit before extraordinary items]		29	7
[Extraordinary items] (included only to show positioning)		—	—
Profit for the financial year		29	7
Dividends		(8)	(1)
Retained profit for the financial year		21	6
Earnings per share		**39p**	**10p**
Adjustments [to be itemised and an adequate description to be given]		*x*p	*x*p
Adjusted earnings per share		*y*p	*y*p

[Reason for calculating the adjusted earnings per share to be given.]

Note required in respect of profit and loss account example 1

	19X3			*19X2 (as restated)*		
	Continuing £m	*Discontinuing* £m	*Total* £m	*Continuing* £m	*Discontinuing* £m	*Total* £m
Cost of sales	455	165	620	385	170	555
Net operating expenses:						
Distribution costs	56	13	69	46	5	51
Administrative expenses	41	12	53	34	3	37
Other operating income	(8)	0	(8)	(5)	0	(5)
	89	25	114	75	8	83
Less 19X2 provision	0	(10)	(10)			
	89	15	104			

The total figures for continuing operations in 1993 include the following amounts relating to acquisitions: cost of sales £40m and net operating expenses £4m (namely distribution costs £3m, administrative expenses £3m and other operating income £2m).

Statement of total recognised gains and losses

	19X3 £m	19X2 as restated £m
Profit for the financial year	29	7
Unrealised surplus on revaluation of properties	4	6
Unrealised (loss)/gain on trade investment	(3)	7
	30	20
Currency translation differences on foreign currency net investments	(2)	5
Total recognised gains and losses relating to the year	28	25
Prior year adjustment (as explained in note *x*)	(10)	
Total gains and losses recognised since last annual report	18	

Note of historical cost profits and losses

	19X3 £m	19X2 as restated £m
Reported profit on ordinary activities before taxation	45	13
Realisation of property revaluation gains of previous years	9	10
Difference between a historical cost depreciation charge and the actual charge of the year calculated on the revalued amount	5	4
Historical cost profit on ordinary activities before taxation	59	27

	19X3	*19X2 as restated*
	£m	£m
Historical cost profit for the year retained after taxation, minority interests, extraordinary items and dividends	35	20

Reconciliation of movements in shareholders' funds

	19X3	*19X2 as restated*
	£m	£m
Profit for the financial year	29	7
Dividends	(8)	(1)
	21	6
Other recognised gains and losses relating to the year (net)	(1)	18
New share capital subscribed	20	
Goodwill written off	(25)	
Net addition to shareholders' funds	15	25
Opening shareholders' funds (originally £375m before deducting prior year adjustment of £10m)	365	340
Closing shareholders' funds	380	365

A basic rule in FRS 3 is that all recognised gains and losses must appear on the face of the profit and loss account unless specifically permitted or required to be taken direct to reserves by law or by accounting standards. To reinforce this application of the *all-inclusive* concept a statement of total recognised gains and losses must also appear as a *primary statement* showing the components of total recognised gains and losses attributable to shareholders. The illustrative example of such a statement is shown above. A further requirement is that there should be a note explaining any material difference between the results as disclosed and the results on an unmodified historical cost basis; this note should reconcile the two figures both for profit on ordinary activities and for retained profit. The note should follow either the profit and loss account or, as in the example above, the statement of total recognised gains and losses. In addition, a note reconciling the opening and closing totals of shareholders' funds should be shown, as illustrated above.

As shown in the example profit and loss account above the aggregate results of each of:

(a) continuing operations;
(b) acquisitions (unless they have also been discontinued during the period);
(c) discontinued operations,

must be disclosed separately. As a minimum, this analysis must be shown for both turnover and operating profit on the face of the profit and loss account. A similar analysis for other expense items must be shown either on the face of the profit and loss account or, as in the example above, by way of note. If interest charges are allocated between continuing and discontinued operations then the basis for the allocation must be explained.

Certain types of exceptional item must be shown on the face of the profit and loss account after operating profit and before interest. These are:

(a) profits or losses on the sale or termination of an operation;
(b) costs of a fundamental reorganisation or restructuring which has a material effect on the nature and focus of the reporting entity's operations;
(c) profits or losses on the disposal of fixed assets.

The notes to the accounts should explain the impact of these items on taxation and minority interests.

Other exceptional items should be included under the statutory format headings in arriving at the results of ordinary activities, being attributed to continuing or discontinued activities as appropriate. Individual items, or categories of items, should be disclosed and explained in the notes to the accounts. Where 'necessary in order to give a true and fair view', exceptional items must be shown on the face of the profit and loss account.

The example provided in FRS 1 shows, as can be seen above, two examples of exceptional items shown immediately above the interest charge.

The taxation charge should include, with separate disclosure, the effects of any fundamental change in the basis of taxation. Any *special circumstances* affecting the tax change should be disclosed by way of note.

Extraordinary items are shown after the profit on ordinary activities after tax and after minority interests but before appropriations. They are shown net of related taxation. Related taxation is computed by:

(a) calculating the overall tax position for the period;
(b) calculating the tax position as though the extraordinary item had not arisen;
(c) taking related taxation as the difference between the two figures.

A note to the accounts should describe each extraordinary item.

Acquisition and discontinuance

When a business operation is acquired then there may be practical problems in determining the part of profits for the accounting period that are attributable to the part of that period after acquisition. In that case, an indication of the contribution of the acquisition to turnover and operating profit should be made. If this cannot be given, the fact and the reason must be explained.

Only directly related income and costs should be reported under the heading *discontinued operations*. Costs such as those of reorganising or restructuring continuing operations in response to the discontinuance should be treated as part of continuing operations.

Where a decision has been made to sell or terminate an operation then it will be necessary to make a provision to the extent that obligations arise from that decision that will not be covered by future profits of the operation or the disposal. To justify this provision the reporting entity must be able to demonstrate either:

(a) a binding sale agreement; or
(b) a detailed formal plan for termination from which withdrawal is realistically impractical.

The provision should only cover:

(a) the direct costs of the sale or termination;
(b) operating losses of the operation up to the date of termination.

In both cases, the aggregate gains expected from future operating profits or related asset disposals should be set off against the provision.

The example profit and loss account above shows how such a provision should be shown. In the year of provision, 19X2, a total provision of £30m appears in arriving at profit on ordinary activities. In 19X3, the year of discontinuance, the provision is shown on the face of the profit and loss account as an abatement of related costs, i.e.

(a) £10m set against the operating loss of the discontinued operations;
(b) £20m set against the exceptional item loss on disposal.

If an acquisition or discontinuance has a major impact on a business segment this must be disclosed.

Asset disposals

The old SSAP 6 failed to address the problem of how to account for the disposal of a revalued fixed asset. Two approaches are possible:

(a) Profit or loss is computed as the difference between disposal proceeds and the revalued amount. This is the requirement of FRS 3.
(b) Profit and loss is computed as the difference between the disposal proceeds and the historical cost, the revaluation difference being transferred from the revaluation reserve. The logic underlying this approach is that the revaluation surplus has not previously appeared in the profit and loss account and, at the time of disposal, becomes a realised profit. FRS 3 does not allow this approach but does identify the revaluation surplus as realised in the note of historical cost profits and losses, as can be seen in the example above.

Prior period adjustments

These are accounted for by:

(a) restating the comparative figures for the preceding period in the accounts;
(b) adjusting the opening balance of reserves for the cumulative effect;
(c) noting the cumulative effect of the adjustments at the foot of the current year's statement of total recognised gains and losses, as illustrated in the example above;
(d) disclosing the effect of prior period adjustments on the results for the preceding period where practical.

Comparative figures

These should be given for all items required by FRS 3. The profit and loss account comparative figures for continuing operations should include in the continuing category only those operations treated as continuing in the current period.

45
66
66
13

Investment companies

Investment companies as defined in company law should only include profits available for distribution in the profit and loss account.

Background

Extraordinary items

SSAP 6, the predecessor to FRS 3, defined extraordinary items as:

> Material items which derive from events or transactions that fall outside the ordinary activities of the company and which are therefore expected not to recur frequently or regularly. They do not include exceptional items nor do they include prior year items merely because they relate to a prior year [1986 revised version].

This was widely criticised as a broad definition that allowed company directors to exclude unwelcome items from the main profit figures. Abuse of SSAP 6 was seen as a major factor in *creative accounting*. This was particularly significant because under SSAP 3: Earnings per Share, this key ratio was computed on the basis of profit *excluding* extraordinary items. FRS 3 has amended SSAP 3 to include extraordinary items in the earnings per share computation, thereby playing down the significance of the *extraordinary item* classification. FRS 3 has also tightened up the definition of an extraordinary item, requiring *a high degree of abnormality* and that the *item is not expected to recur*. The definition of *ordinary activities* has been written so widely that it is difficult to imagine what might fall outside it. A range of activities traditionally classified as extraordinary, such as losses on discontinued activities, are

Table 4.1 Comparative treatment of *extraordinary items*

Examples of extraordinary items in SSAP 6	*Treatment in FRS 3*
1. Discontinuance of a business segment.	Exceptional item, shown after operating profit and before interest.
2. Sale of an investment not acquired with the intention of resale.	Exceptional item, treated as 1 above.
3. Provision made for permanent diminution in value of a fixed asset because of extraordinary events in period.	Since ordinary activities include '*any* event in the various environments in which it operates ... irrespective of ... frequency ... or nature' then it would appear that no such thing as an 'extraordinary event' now exists.
4. The expropriation of assets.	This is an event, as in 3 above, that now falls under ordinary activities.
5. A change in the basis of taxation, or a significant change in governmental policy.	As in 3 above, this event, of a 'political' or 'regulatory' environmental change, is within 'ordinary' activities, subject to separate disclosure.

explicitly identified as falling within ordinary activities by FRS 3. Finally, in their example, the ASB have left a space for extraordinary items but have chosen to take the view that a specific example should not be given. Overall, FRS 3 gives a clear message that, while space for extraordinary items has been entertained in line with company law, in practice such items should not arise. To illustrate this, Table 4.1 considers how the examples of extraordinary items in SSAP 6 would be considered under FRS 3.

Prior period adjustments

FRS 3 emphasises that most items relating to prior periods arise because of corrections to and adjustments of estimates inherent in preparing accounts periodically. These should be included in the accounts of the year in which they are identified. Items which justify a prior period adjustment *are rare* arising either from changes in accounting policy or from the correction of fundamental errors.

Under the consistency concept changes in accounting policy should not normally arise. Such changes arise from making a choice between two or more accounting methods. They are only justified where the new policy gives a fairer presentation of the accounts. One example of a circumstance that might justify such a rule is a change in an FRS. Where accounting methods are varied in the light of a change in the nature of transactions this does not constitute a change of policy.

A *fundamental error* is one that should have been detected at the time it was made. The term does not embrace revision of estimates made in the light of subsequent events or experience.

For further developments on FRS 3, see 'Reporting Financial Performance: Proposals for Change' in the chapter on Discussion Papers.

EXAMINATION PRACTICE

4.1 FRS 3 – allocation of items

A manufacturing company, Peel Ltd, has a turnover of £6 million and pre-tax trading profits of £1 000 000 before taking account of the following items:

(a) costs of £750 000 incurred in terminating production at one of the company's factories;
(b) provision for an abnormally large bad debt of £500 000, arising in a trading contract;
(c) profits of £150 000 on sale of plant and machinery written off in a previous year when production of the particular product ceased.

You are required to indicate whether these items should be treated as exceptional, extraordinary or normal trading transactions within the terms of FRS 3, giving your reasons.

4.2 FRS 3 – presentation

Bellamy Ltd is a company in the furniture retailing trade with 324 shops, a turnover of £79 million and pre-tax profits of £8 million in the year to 31 December 19X1, tax on profit being computed at £4 million, before taking into account the following items:

(a) As part of a programme of updating and improving shop premises 13 shop sites were disposed of during the year at a profit of £320 000 subject to capital gains tax of £104 000.
(b) During the course of audit of the accounts for the year to 31 December 19X1 it is discovered that an error was made in the previous year's accounts whereby the closing stock

of £8.7 million was brought into the accounts at £7.8 million.

(c) During the year it was discovered that certain beds imported and distributed by the company were liable, in certain circumstances, to collapse, due to a fundamental design fault. Fortunately, the company received no claims for personal injury arising from this problem, but it was necessary to recall for checking and repair all of the beds sold. The cost of this was £300 000 relating to beds sold in 19X1, £500 000 relating to beds sold in 19X0, and £180 000 relating to beds sold in previous years.

(d) During the year the directors made a decision to sell all the company's investments on the Stock Exchange and in doing so realised a profit of £2 million. These investments had been shown as fixed assets.

You are required to explain the appropriate treatment for each of the above items in the accounts of Bellamy Ltd for the year ended 31 December 19X1.

4.3 FRS 3 – conceptual basis

Discuss the merits of both the *all-inclusive* income and the *current operating* income concepts. (*Note:* The current operating income approach is sometimes referred to as reserve accounting.)

CHAPTER 5

FRS 4: Capital Instruments

Introduction

During the 1980s a variety of complex mechanisms for company financing were devised. These raised two questions:

(a) how should these be allocated between equity and liabilities? On the one hand a special class of share might carry a fixed rate of dividend and be redeemable rather like a loan. On the other hand the terms of conversion of convertible loan stock might make its value heavily dependent on the company's profitability, rather like an equity share;
(b) how should finance costs be allocated?

FRS 4 addresses these questions.

The nature of capital instruments

Capital instruments are defined as:

> All instruments that are issued by reporting entities as a means of raising finance, including shares, debentures, loans, and debt instruments, options and warrants that give the holder the right to subscribe for or obtain capital instruments. In the case of consolidated financial statements the term includes capital instruments issued by subsidiaries except those that are held by another member of the group included in the consolidation.

FRS 4 is concerned with accounting for capital instruments by entities that issue them, not for providers of capital who acquire the instruments. FRS 4 does not cover warrants under employee share schemes, leases, or equity shares in a merger.

Capital instruments appear in the balance sheet under three headings:

(a) liabilities, also referred to as 'debt';
(b) shareholders' funds;
(c) minority interests (only in consolidated accounts).

Instruments are to be regarded as liabilities if they do not constitute share capital and:

> they contain an obligation to transfer economic benefits (including a contingent obligation to transfer economic benefits).

This definition is crucial in determining whether an item falls under the heading of liabilities or shareholders' funds. In classifying a capital instrument all aspects of the agreement should be considered together unless, as in the example of *debt issued with warrants* considered below, they can be transferred independently.

Shareholders' funds are analysed between *equity* and *non-equity* interests, the latter being defined as:

> Shares possessed of any of the following characteristics:
>
> (a) any of the rights of the shares to receive payments (whether in respect of dividends, in respect of redemption or otherwise) are for a limited amount that is not calculated by reference to the company's assets or profits or the dividends on any class of equity share;
> (b) any of their rights to participate in a surplus in a winding up are limited to a specific amount that is not calculated by reference to the company's assets or profits and such limitation had a commercial effect in practice at the time the shares were issued or, if later, at the time the limitation was introduced;
> (c) the shares are redeemable either according to their terms, or because the holder, or any party other than the issuer, can require their redemption.

Similarly minority interests are divided between equity and non-equity interests.

Liabilities are divided between those which are convertible into some form of share capital and those which are not. The introduction to FRS 4 offers a useful table summarising the types of capital instrument, which is reproduced as Table 5.1.

Table 5.1 Types of capital instrument

Item	*Analysed between*	
Shareholders' funds	Equity interests	Non-equity interests
Minority interests in subsidiaries	Equity interests in subsidiaries	Non-equity interests in subsidiaries
Liabilities	Convertible liabilities	Non-convertible liabilities

Those items analysed into the left-hand column have some kind of bearing on the equity interest as compared to those analysed in the right-hand column that do not.

Allocation of debt finance costs

A finance cost is defined as:

> The difference between the net proceeds of an instrument and the total amount of the payments (or other transfer of economic benefits) that the issuer may be required to make in respect of the instrument.

Net proceeds are defined as:

> The fair value of the consideration received on the issue of a capital instrument after deduction of issue costs.

Issue costs are defined as:

> The costs that are incurred directly in connection with the issue of a capital instrument, that

is, those costs that would not have been incurred had the specific instrument in question not been issued.

On issue debt is shown at the amount of the net proceeds, while finance costs should be allocated and charged to profit and loss over the term of the debt 'at a constant rate on the carrying amount'. Thus issue costs do not have to be written off in the year incurred, but are effectively carried forward as part of the cost of finance.

The rule that finance costs be written off at a constant rate means that such costs are apportioned irrespective of the actual pattern and timing of finance costs specified in the loan agreement. The difference between the amount to be allocated each year and the actual cash flow is adjusted in the carrying amount of the liability, except that accrued finance costs may be shown as accruals rather than as part of the liability if they are to be paid in the next accounting period.

An exception to the requirement to allocate finance costs evenly over the loan term arises where the required payment is contingent on some future event, such as movement in an index. In that case the impact of the event should only be reflected in finance costs after it has occurred.

A number of practical examples of how to allocate finance costs under FRS 4 are discussed below.

Sometimes there is uncertainty as to the period over which a loan will be outstanding. The *term* of a capital instrument is defined as:

> The period from the date of issue of the capital instrument to the date at which it will expire, be redeemed, or be cancelled. If either party has the option to require the instrument to be redeemed, or cancelled and, under the terms of the instrument, it is uncertain whether such an option will be exercised, the term should be taken to end on the earliest date at which the instrument would be redeemed or cancelled on exercise of such an option.

If either party has the right to extend the period of an instrument, the term should not include the period of the extension if there is a genuine commercial possibility that the period will not be extended.

Convertible debt

In the case of the convertible debt the finance cost should be computed as though the debt will never be converted. If conversion occurs then the share issue price should be treated as the then carrying amount of the debt, including accrued finance costs, so that no gain or loss on conversion arises.

Convertible debt should be shown separately from other liabilities with the following disclosure:

(a) date of and amount repayable on redemption;
(b) number and class of shares into which debt may be converted;
(c) dates or periods for conversion;
(d) whether conversion is at the option of the issuer or the holder.

Repurchase and maturity of debt

Where there is a repurchase or early settlement of debt any gain or loss should be recognised in the profit and loss account in the period of the transaction. These gains or losses should be shown separately alongside *interest payable*.

An analysis of the maturity of debt must show amounts falling due:

(a) in one year or less;
(b) between one and two years;
(c) between three and five years;
(d) in five years or more.

The maturity date is the earliest date when the lender can demand repayment. When the agreement includes provision for refinancing then the maturity date is extended up to the point where all the following conditions are met:

(a) the debt and the facility are under a single agreement or course of dealing with the same lender or group of lenders;
(b) the finance costs for the new debt are on a basis that is not significantly higher than that of the existing debt;
(c) the obligations of the lender (or group of lenders) are firm: the lender is not able legally to refrain from providing funds except in circumstances the possibility of which can be demonstrated to be remote;
(d) the lender (or group of lenders) is expected to be able to fulfil its obligations under the facility.

Where the above situation applies, the earliest debt at which the lender could demand repayment if there were no refinancing facilities must also be disclosed.

Non-equity shares

Finance costs on non-equity shares should be allocated on the same basis as for debt, as explained above. Thus when a non-equity instrument is issued this should be shown initially as the net proceeds of the issue. Each year this will then be increased by the allocated finance cost for the year and reduced by the dividend paid. Both the dividends paid and any additional, or reduced, finance cost, should be shown as an appropriation of profit.

Warrants

A warrant is defined as:

> An instrument that requires the issuer to issue shares (whether contingently or not) and contains no obligation for the issuer to transfer economic benefits.

The net proceeds should be shown as part of the shareholders' funds, with the related type of share, i.e. *equity* or *non-equity*. If the warrant is exercised then the amount originally received is treated as part of the proceeds of the share issue. If the warrant lapses without being exercised then the amount is reported in the statement of total recognised gains and losses.

Scrip dividends

If shares are issued as an alternative to cash dividends then the proceeds at the issue are treated as the amount to be paid if the cash alternative were chosen. Where the number of shareholders who will choose to take shares is uncertain, a provision for the whole potential cash dividend must be made.

Subsidiaries

Where shares issued by subsidiaries are held outside the group then those will normally be shown as minority interests, classified into equity and non-equity headings. Finance costs of non-equity minority interests will be allocated in the same way as other non-equity interests, and a description of any rights of holders of non-equity minority shares against other group companies must be disclosed. The minority interest section of the profit and loss account should also be analysed between the equity and non-equity elements.

A special case arises where shares issued by a subsidiary carry a commitment from the group as a whole to transfer economic benefits in connection with the shares. In this case the minority interest should be shown as a liability.

Additional disclosures

Where disclosures of the existence of convertible debt, non-equity shares, and non-equity minority interests are given in the notes to the accounts then the relevant caption on the face of the balance sheet must make this clear.

Where the legal nature of an instrument included in debt includes an unusual provision, such as a conditional obligation to repay, this must be disclosed in the rules to the accounts.

Where the amount at which debt is shown in the accounts is *significantly different* from the amount payable or the claim that would arise on a winding up, a summary of all such differences must be presented.

Application notes

FRS 4 is supported by a set of application notes showing how these principles can be applied to some common forms of finance.

Index-linked loans

Sometimes the obligations under a loan are not specified in monetary terms but are made conditional on some future event. An example is that the amount repayable on a loan may be linked to an index. In that case finance costs are adjusted to reflect the future event once it has occurred, with the change in cost allocated to that reporting period. Example 5.1 gives some simple figures for such an agreement. Illustration 5.1 shows how the finance costs for each year would be computed.

Example 5.1

A loan of £1 000 is issued on 1 January Year 1, repayable after four years. Interest is at 3 percent per year based on the original amount but the sum repayable is to be uplifted to reflect the retail price index. Over the four years the retail price index moves:

Beginning Year 1	100
End Year 1	106
End Year 2	110
End Year 3	119
End Year 4	122

Illustration 5.1

Year	*Balance b/fwd*	*Balance c/fwd*	*Cost of uplift in year*	*Interest paid*	*Total finance cost for year*
1	1 000	1 060	60	30	90
2	1 060	1 100	40	30	70
3	1 100	1 190	90	30	120
4	1 190	1 220	30	30	60

Repackaged perpetual debt

A loan may be raised on the basis that it is *perpetual*, i.e. not subject to redemption, and with interest at a high rate for a number of years (the *primary period*) followed by no further interest or only a nominal amount. Since the lender cannot require that the debt be redeemed it has no value after the period of interest payments, and often arrangements are made for redemption at a token amount. Thus while the legal form of such an arrangement is to continue to owe the amount, the commercial substance is that the annual payments cover repayment of the loan by instalments as well as the finance costs.

Example 5.2 shows specimen figures for such an arrangement. Illustration 5.2 shows how annual finance costs would be computed in a similar way to the stepped interest bond calculations explained below.

Example 5.2

At the beginning of Year 1 a company borrows £1 000 which is stated to be irredeemable and to carry interest of 26.4 per cent for the first five years after which no further payments are required. Thus in effect the five payments of £2 640 will repay the sum borrowed at an annual finance charge of 10 per cent.

Illustration 5.2

Year	(1) *Balance b/fwd*	(2) *Finance cost (10%)*	(3) *Cash paid in year*	(4) *Balance c/fwd*
1	1 000	100	(264)	836
2	836	84	(264)	656
3	656	66	(264)	458
4	458	46	(264)	240
5	240	24	(264)	—

Stepped interest bonds

A stepped interest bond is one where the interest rate payable on the bond increases over the period of the loan. Example 5.3 gives a simple set of figures to illustrate such a loan. To comply with FRS 4 it is necessary to allocate the total finance costs evenly at the effective interest rate of 8 per cent, so that in the early years an accrual will gradually build up, being the difference between the low interest rate actually paid and the full finance cost provided for. This accrual will reverse in later years as the higher interest rates are paid. Illustration 5.3 shows the application of this approach to our example. In column 1 is shown the opening balance of the loan at the beginning of the year. Column 2 shows the finance cost for the year, being the constant rate of 8 per cent applied to the opening balance in column 1. Column 3 shows the cash outflow during each year, being the interest rate for that year applied to the nominal sum borrowed of £1 000; in the final year cash paid also includes the repayment of principal. Column 4 shows the final balance, being the sum of the first two columns less column 3.

Example 5.3

A company borrows £1 000, repayable after five years, at the following interest rates.

Year	*Interest rate (on nominal amount) (%)*
1	4
2	6
3	8
4	10
5	11.37

The overall effective interest rate is 8%.

Illustration 5.3

	(1)	(2)	(3)	(4)
Year	*Balance b/fwd*	*Finance cost (8%)*	*Cash paid*	*Balance c/fwd*
1	1 000	80	(40)	1 040
2	1 040	83	(60)	1 063
3	1 063	85	(80)	1 068
4	1 068	85	(100)	1 053
5	1 053	84	(1 137)	—

Deep discount bonds

Sometimes a company will raise a loan on the basis that a low nominal rate of interest is paid but the sum repayable at the conclusion of the loan exceeds the amount originally received. Thus the total finance cost is the excess amount repayable plus the interest paid. This total finance cost must be spread systematically over the period of the loan. Example 5.4 shows some figures for such a loan, while Illustration 5.4 shows how the annual finance cost will be spread, on a similar basis to that explained above when considering stepped interest bonds. Where no interest at all is paid the term *zero coupon bond* is used.

Example 5.4

A £1 000 debenture carrying a 2 per cent interest rate is issued for £696 at the beginning of Year 1. The debenture is redeemable at nominal value at the end of Year 5. The implicit annual finance cost is 10 per cent.

Illustration 5.4

Year	(1) *Balance at beginning of year*	(2) *Finance cost for year (10%)*	(3) *Cash paid in year*	(4) *Balance at end of year*
1	696	70	(20)	746
2	746	75	(20)	801
3	801	80	(20)	861
4	861	86	(20)	927
5	927	93	(1 020)	—

Debt issued with warrants

Sometimes a loan issue is made on the basis that the lender is issued with warrants carrying the rights to subscribe for shares at a specified price in the future. What distinguishes an issue of this kind from a convertible loan is that the warrants and the debt are capable of being transferred separately. Commonly such an issue is made for the par value of the debt and the debt will be redeemed at the same amount. Under FRS 4 it is necessary to compute the 'fair value' of the two separate items at the time of issue – the loan and the warrants. This can normally be done on the basis of the relative market value of the two elements immediately after the loan issue. The fair value of the warrants is then credited to the shareholders' funds and subsequently, at the option date, is treated as part of the proceeds of the share issue if the option is exercised, and transferred to the statement of gains and losses if it is not. The fair value of the loan issue is treated as the issue price, and the finance costs are computed on the same basis as a deep discounted debenture as shown above.

Limited recourse debt

This form of borrowing arises where a lender can only obtain repayment in the event of default from enforcing rights against a specific security identified in the loan agreement, so that if the proceeds of that security are insufficient to cover the loan the lender must bear the loss. In FRS 4 it is argued that unless and until the secured asset is transferred to the lender such a loan should be accounted for as a normal liability, subject to appropriate disclosure.

Subordinated debt

This arises where a loan is made subject to the rights of the lender being, in some way, less than those of other creditors. Since the lender does not forgo the ultimate right to be repaid, FRS 4 requires that such loans be included in the liabilities with appropriate disclosure.

Convertible capital bonds

As an example of this type of bond, the application notes consider the case where a special purpose subsidiary is set up outside the UK. The subsidiary issues a loan convertible into its own shares which may, in turn, be converted at the option of the bondholder – into the holding company's ordinary shares. Both the subsidiary and the holding company should show these as convertible liabilities.

Convertible debt with a premium put option

In this case the lender has the option, on a specified date, to demand repayment at an amount in excess of the issue price of the loan. In this case:

(a) the finance costs should be allocated over the period to the occurrence of the option to demand repayment. Finance costs are allocated as for a deep discount bond, as shown above.
(b) if the loan is converted into shares the assumed issue price of the shares will include not only the original loan issue price but also the accrued finance costs.

Convertible debt with enhanced interest

The loan agreement will include a clause giving the right to an increased interest rate after a certain number of years. Finance costs are allocated as for stepped interest bonds, as discussed above. If conversion occurs then the deemed proceeds of the share issue will include any accrued interest.

Auction market preferred shares (AMPS)

These are preference shares entitled to dividends based on an auction process, being transferred at a fixed price to the investor willing to accept the lowest dividend. They are redeemable at the option of the issuer, normally at issue price. These are non-equity shares. Since finance costs are not predictable, they are allocated to the period in which they accrue.

Participating preference shares

These shares carry the right to a fixed dividend plus a proportion of the dividends paid on equity shares. These are a form of non-equity share, and the separate elements of the dividend should be identified in the accounts.

Capital contributions

A holding company may provide a capital contribution to a wholly owned subsidiary in preference to a loan or a share issue. This should be shown as part of shareholders' funds.

Conclusion

FRS 4 is a complex and detailed standard responding to the increased sophistication of the financial markets.

EXAMINATION PRACTICE

5.1 Understanding the rules

Explain what exception there is to the rule that the finance costs of debt should be spread at a constant rate over the term of debt, giving two examples.

5.2 Applying the rules

On 1 January 19X5 Tegrant Ltd issues £100 000 convertible loan stock with a premium put option. Stock is convertible into one ordinary share on 31 December 19X7 for every nominal £2 of loan stock with the alternative of exercising the premium put option at £116 232. The nominal interest rate is 3% and the interest rate of financial cost is 8%.

You are required to:

(a) show the finance cost of this loan stock for each of the years to 31 December 19X5, 19X6, 19X7;

(b) draft a journal entry to be made if the option to convert into shares is exercised in full.

FRS 5: Reporting the Substance of Transactions

Introduction

FRS 5 is concerned with establishing clear principles to deal with a small number of highly complex and specialised transactions. The standard is a response to the proliferation of ingenious methods of finance which have enabled companies to increase their borrowings and risks without the substance of those transactions being reflected in the accounts. A simple example has been that of consignment stock. A company, such as a whisky distiller, that holds stock for long periods, might enter into an arrangement to sell the stock to a finance company with a binding obligation to repurchase the stock in the future at a price which equals repayment of the original amount received plus interest.

The legal form of this transaction is that there has been a sale of the goods. In commercial substance the company has retained the benefit and risks of stock holding and incurred the obligations associated with a loan. FRS 5 provides a framework within which the *substance over form* concept can be applied to such transactions.

Definitions

The requirements of FRS 5 are built around a series of key definitions that incorporate the concept of substance over form.

Assets are defined as:

> Rights or other access to future economic benefits controlled by an entity as a result of past transactions or events.

Two key terms supporting this definition are:

> Control in the context of an asset:
> The ability to obtain the future economic benefits relating to an asset and to restrict the access of others to those benefits

and

> Risk:
> Uncertainty as to the amount of benefits. The term includes both potential for gain and exposure to loss.

Liabilities are defined as:

> An entity's obligation to transfer economic benefits as a result of past transactions or events.

Having provided these terms, a key definition then explains how an item that is in substance an asset or liability should be treated:

> Recognition:
> The process of incorporating an item into the primary financial statements under the appropriate heading. It involves depiction of the item in words and by a monetary amount and inclusion of that amount in the statement totals.

The term *derecognition*, although not formally defined in FRS 5, is used to describe the situation where an item ceases to be incorporated in the accounts.

Other key terms are

> Quasi-subsidiary:
> A quasi-subsidiary of a reporting entity is a company, trust, partnership or other vehicle that, though not fulfilling the definition of a subsidiary, is directly or indirectly controlled by the reporting entity and gives rise to benefits for that entity that are in substance no different from those that would arise were the vehicle a subsidiary.

and

> Control of another entity:
> The ability to direct the financial and operating policies of that entity with a view to gaining economic benefits from its activities.

The basic principles

FRS 5 aims to ensure that the accounts of an entity should report the substance of its transactions.

To determine substance:

(a) all aspects and implications should be identified;
(b) greater weight should be given to those likely to have a commercial effect in practice;
(c) a group or series of transactions designed to achieve an overall commercial effect should be viewed as a whole.

FRS 5 does not cover the following, unless they form part of a larger group of transactions:

(a) forward contracts and futures;
(b) foreign exchange and interest rate swaps;
(c) contracts based on a movement in a price or index;
(d) expenditure commitments and orders placed;
(e) employment contracts.

Identifying assets and liabilities

In order to determine the substance of a transaction it is necessary to decide whether:

(a) new assets or liabilities have arisen;
(b) existing asset or liabilities have changed.

The rights or other access to benefits which, in line with the definition above, constitute an asset, arise if the entity is exposed, in practice, to the risks inherent in those benefits. The obligation to transfer benefits, which constitutes a liability, arises if there is some circumstance where the entity, for legal or commercial reasons, cannot avoid an outflow of benefits.

A transaction that meets this definition of creating an asset or liability should be recognised in the balance sheet if:

(a) there is sufficient evidence of the existence of the item;
(b) the monetary amount can be measured with sufficient reliability.

A transaction involving an asset already recognised in the accounts, particularly a financing transaction, where there is no significant change in either:

(a) the entity's access to benefit from that asset; or
(b) its exposure to risks inherent in those benefits,

should not result in that asset ceasing to be recognised in the account, although a linked presentation, as discussed below, may arise.

By contrast a previously recognised asset should cease to be recognised if all significant rights to benefits and exposure to risks are transferred to others.

In some special cases a transfer of an item might be restricted to only part of the item, or for only part of its life, or with some residual right to benefits or exposure to risk. In those cases there should be full provision for any probable loss, but deferral of any uncertain gain, with disclosure of any uncertainty where the effect is material.

Linked presentation

A *linked presentation* involves the gross amount of an asset being shown with related finance being deducted within a single asset caption; both the gross amount and the related deduction must be shown on the face of the balance sheet, not in the notes to the accounts. Such a presentation is only approached when the asset and related finance are *ring fenced* together so that:

(a) the finance will be repaid only from proceeds generated by the related assets; and
(b) there is no provision to keep the item on repayment of finance or reacquire it.

Linked presentation may only be used where:

(a) The finance relates only to a specific item or portfolio of items.
(b) The loan is secured on the specified item only.
(c) The entity has no obligation to repay the loan other than from the proceeds of the specified asset.
(d) The directors state in the accounts that the entity has no obligation or intention to make good any losses by the provider of finance.
(e) The provider of finance agrees in writing that repayment of finance will only be claimed from funds generated from the specified item. This agreement should be noted in the accounts where a linked presentation is used.
(f) If funds generated by the item are insufficient to repay the provider of finance this should not constitute an act of default by the entity.
(g) There must be no provision for the entity to retain or acquire the asset.

An item such as a monetary receivable, which generates cash directly, should provide the cash receipts to repay the finance. Other items should be either sold to a third party or transferred to the provider of finance at a specified time.

On entering such an arrangement, any profit should only be recognised to the extent that finance received exceeds the carrying amount of the asset. In subsequent years profits or losses should be recognised as they arise.

Offset

FRS 5 follows the Companies Act 1985 in not permitting the offset of assets and liabilities. Debit and credit balances may only be offset where they do not constitute assets and liabilities. For this purpose all the following conditions must be met:

(a) the reporting entity and another party owe each other monetary amounts in the same currencies or different but freely convertible currencies;
(b) the reporting entity must be able to insist on a net settlement; and
(c) the ability to insist on a net settlement must be secure. In particular the debit balance must mature no later than the credit balance, and the ability to insist on a net settlement must be one that would survive the insolvency of the other party.

Disclosure of substance

In whatever form a transaction is reported the supporting disclosure must enable the user of the accounts to understand the commercial effect. In particular where a transaction has resulted in items being recognised under a balance sheet heading where they differ from those normally shown, the nature of the differences must be explained.

Quasi-subsidiaries

Factors to consider in deciding whether an entity is a *quasi-subsidiary* are:

(a) whether the reporting entity is the beneficiary of the net assets of the entity, and exposed to the inherent risks;
(b) whether the reporting entity directs the financial and operating policies of the entity, and can prevent others from doing so;
(c) where the financial and operating policies of the entity are in substance predetermined then the party possessing control is the beneficiary of the net assets.

The quasi-subsidiary should be included in the group accounts as though it were a subsidiary. Such inclusion should be disclosed. A note to the accounts should summarise the accounts of each quasi-subsidiary or group of similar quasi-subsidiaries.

Applications

FRS 5 is supported by *application notes* on a number of situations that arise in practice. These are useful as illustrations of how the principles of FRS 5 should be applied.

Consignment stock

A situation, particularly common in the motor trade, may arise where a manufacturer is the legal owner of stock consigned to a dealer. The dealer only becomes liable to pay for the stock when legal title passes. Under such an arrangement it is necessary to decide when the stock, and concomitant obligation to pay for it, should be regarded as an asset and related liability of the dealer. Under FRS 5 the consignment stock becomes the dealer's asset at the point in time when the dealer has access to the benefits of the stock and exposure to the risks inherent in those benefits. This depends on an analysis of the terms on which consignments are made. Table 6.1 summarises key points.

Table 6.1

Benefit/risk	*Indicative that stock is only an asset of dealer when legal title passes*	*Indicative that stock is an asset of dealer at time of delivery*
Dealer able to retain stock to achieve sales?	Manufacturer has right to make dealer return or transfer stock, or dealer must pay penalty to stop manufacturer requiring return on stock	Manufacturer cannot require dealer to return or transfer stock Manufacturer must pay incentive for dealer to transfer stock
Dealer able to return unwanted stock?	Dealer has right, used in practice, to return unwanted stock	Dealer not allowed, or commercially unable, to return unwanted stock
Who bears obsolescence risk?	Obsolete stock returned without penalty, or manufacturer pays dealer compensation	Obsolete stock only returnable if penalty paid
When is price set?	Based on manufacturer's prices at date of transfer of legal title	Based on manufacturer's prices at date of delivery
Who bears slow movement risk?	No substantial deposit and transfer price set independently of time stock held	Dealer pays substantial interest-free deposit based on stock level *or* effectively pays interest as part of transfer price

Sale and repurchase agreements

These are arrangements where assets are sold under an agreement that includes the possibility of a repurchase. In some circumstances such an agreement effectively requires both parties to effect a repurchase by the original seller on terms which provide for repayment as the original sale price plus interest. In these cases the substance of the transaction is that the stock is retained by the seller with a secured loan from the purchaser. Circumstances that suggest that no real sale has taken place include:

(a) the sale price is different from the market price;
(b) the seller is effectively committed to repurchase the asset, either through an explicit binding option or through commercial necessity;
(c) the agreement is structured in such a way that the seller carries all fluctuations in the stock value. As an example, the stipulated repurchase price might be based on the original sale price plus interest;
(d) the seller retains the rights to determine how the asset is exploited.

Conversely, indications that a genuine sale has taken place include:

(a) the seller is not committed to repurchase the asset;
(b) the buyer carries any fluctuations in asset value. For example, the repurchase price might be based on market values;
(c) the nature of the asset is such that it will be used by the purchaser.

Even when a sale and purchase agreement does not effectively constitute a secured loan on stock, it may give rise to an effective asset or liability by virtue of the terms of any put or call option. Such an item must be accounted for on a prudent basis.

Factoring of debts

Key features of a debt factoring agreement may include:

(a) specified debts are transferred to a factor;
(b) the factor advances the seller a proportion of the debt, to be recovered out of the amounts to be paid by the debtors;
(c) the factor may offer some form of credit insurance, the effect of which is to restrict the extent to which the factor can recover unpaid debts from the seller;
(d) the factor may provide a sales ledger service.

Three accounting treatments are possible:

(a) factored debts can simply be removed from the balance sheet – this is *derecognition;*
(b) proceeds received from the factor can be shown as a deduction from related debts – this is *linked presentation;*
(c) debtors can be shown in full with amounts received from the factor shown as a separate liability – this is *separate presentation.*

Which treatment is appropriate depends on who bears the following benefits and risks:

(a) the benefit of future cash flows from payments by debtors;
(b) the risk of slow payment;
(c) the risk of default by debtors.

Table 6.2 shows some suggested considerations for deciding on an appropriate treatment.

Table 6.2

Indications that derecognition is appropriate (debts are not an asset of seller)	*Indications that a linked presentation is appropriate*	*Indications that a separate presentation is appropriate (debts are an asset of the seller)*
Transfer is for a single, non-returnable fixed sum.	Some non-returnable proceeds received, but seller has rights to further sums from the factor (or vice versa) whose amount depends on whether or when debtors pay.	Finance cost varies with speed of collection of debts, e.g. (a) by adjustment to consideration for original transfer; or (b) subsequent transfers priced to recover costs of earlier transfers.
There is no recourse to the seller for losses.	There is either no recourse for losses, or such recourse has a fixed monetary ceiling.	There is full recourse to the seller for losses.
Factor is paid all amounts received from the factored debts (and no more). Seller has no rights to further sums from the factor.	Factor is paid only out of amounts collected from the factored debts, and seller has no right or obligation to repurchase debts.	Seller is required to repay amounts received from the factor on or before a set date, regardless of timing or amounts of collections from debtors.

Securitised assets

This is a process whereby funds are lent to a company to finance a specific block of assets rather than the company as a whole. In the UK the most commonly securitised assets have been household mortgages.

Key features of such an arrangement are:

(a) the assets to be securitised are transferred by the *originator* to a specially created legal entity called the *issuer*, in return for a cash payment. Some further cash may be receivable in the future;
(b) the issuer raises cash to finance the transaction by issuing some form of loan, referred to as *loan notes*. Only a few shares are issued and, to avoid legal classification as a subsidiary, these are issued to some nominally independent third party such as a specifically created charity;
(c) loan noteholders are protected from loss on their highly geared investment by some form of credit insurance;
(d) the originator benefits from surpluses arising from any excess of repayment and interest from the mortgages over interest and repayments on the loan notes.

Three possible accounting treatments for securitised assets are:

(a) derecognition, whereby the securitised assets are removed from the balance sheet;
(b) linked presentation, whereby the securitised assets are shown as an asset with the cash received from the issuer shown as a deduction;
(c) separate presentation, showing the assets and the liability separately at their gross amounts.

Since a separate legal entity, the issuer, is involved, there is also a question as to whether this should be treated as a subsidiary in the consolidated accounts. Table 6.3 shows some factors influencing choice of appropriate treatment.

Table 6.3

	Indications supporting derecognition	*Indications supporting linked presentation*	*Indications supporting separate presentations*
	Transaction price arm's-length for outright sale	Transaction price not for outright sale	Arm's-length price
Originator's own accounts	Transfer for fixed unchangeable sum	Some future variation in transfer price possible	Proceeds received from securitised assets return to originator
	No recourse for losses	Restricted recourse for losses	Full recourse for losses
In consolidated accounts	Issuer owned by independent third party with major capital investment	Issuer is a quasi-subsidiary	Issuer is a subsidiary

Loan transfers

A loan transfer also involves the transfer of interest-bearing loans to another entity, as with securitised loans, but does not involve the use of a *special purpose vehicle*. The three possible accounting approaches are:

(a) derecognition, where the asset is simply removed from the accounts;
(b) linked presentation, where the loan continues to be shown as an asset but with deduction of the amount received for the transfer;
(c) separate presentation, where the loan is shown as an asset and the amount received as a liability.

Table 6.4 shows the indicators suggested in FRS 5 for classification.

Table 6.4

Indicator	*Supports derecognition*	*Supports linked presentation*	*Supports separate presentation*
Consideration for transfer	A single non-returnable fixed sum	Lender has some further rights following initial payment	Proceeds are returnable if loans make a loss
Recourse to original lender for losses?	None	Limited	Full
Rights/obligations of lender to transferee in relation to loan repayments	Actual repayments all go to transferee	Transferee paid only out of amounts received for loans	Original lender responsible for full repayment irrespective of timing of receipts from borrowers

Private finance initiative

The private finance initiative (PFI) is a means of supplying public services. Rather than the public sector providing a service it is contracted out to a private company. This is straightforward where it just relates to a service, for example the service of cleaning a hospital or catering for a prison. The difficulty occurs where the contract requires an asset to be built in order to supply the service. For example, the public sector may require a 'prison service' from a private sector company; it may require a 'hospital service' from a private company. In this case the private company needs to build a prison or hospital and then supply the service. The public sector makes payments to the private sector company for supplying the service. The issue is whether this payment has two parts – one for constructing the asset and another for supplying the service. If part of the payment relates to the construction of an asset, the question arises as to which entity should have the asset in its balance sheet – the private company or the public sector. Under FRS 5 the substance of the contract, and not its economic form, needs to be established. The ownership of the asset is determined by establishing who has the risks and rewards.

The PFI contract will require the public sector to make a stream of payments to the private sector company. These payments may vary, based on a formula which incorporates the amount of service provided and the standard of the service provided. This has the advantage of showing that the government (public sector) is ensuring value for money for the tax payer. The variability of the stream of the payments means that some of the risks, and rewards, for running the service are passed to the private sector company. It is the variability of the payments with regard to the property which is relevant to determining who has the risks and rewards arising from the property; the variability of the service element is not relevant.

Where it is possible to separate the payment for services from the payment for the property, the service element should be excluded from the analysis. The transaction should then be accounted for as a finance lease under the rules in SSAP 21.

Where it is not easy to separate the payment for services from the payment for the property, FRS 5 gives a list of criteria by which to judge the substance of a PFI contract in order to help identify whether the risks and rewards arising from the property belong to the government or the private company.

Where the risks and rewards belong to the government, then the asset and corresponding liability belong in the public sector 'balance sheet'; the private sector company would not therefore recognise the property in its balance sheet, but would recognise a financial asset, the debtor, for the amounts due. Conversely, where the risks and rewards belong to the private sector company, the property and related liability would be in its balance sheet, and the government would have a liability for the payments due.

The issue of accounting for PFI contracts is one of the few accounting areas which has produced concern in the public domain and provoked a debate between the ASB and the Treasury. It has been argued that the effect of accounting for the substance of a PFI contract will have economic consequences; for example, it may reduce the number of hospitals which are built, thus affecting the health of the nation.

Conclusion

FRS 5 is a standard with fairly simple objectives, combined with complex detail in its application. Applying to a small number of transactions, generally of a substantial amount, FRS 5 is a key element in the ASB's efforts to stamp out the *creative accounting* practices that have been so extensively criticised in the UK.

EXAMINATION PRACTICE

6.1 Roadroller Ltd is a caravan dealer with two suppliers, both of whom supply stock on consignment.

Dealer A supplies stock on the basis that Roadroller can be required to return that stock on request until the company agrees to buy the stock. The purchase price is based on list prices at the time of the agreed purchase.

Dealer B supplies stock on the basis that a deposit equal to 80 per cent of the purchase price must be made when stock is received. The dealer may only require return of the stock on repayment of the deposit plus a 10 per cent surcharge. On purchase the price is based on the list price of the date of the initial consignment.

You are required to explain how you would account for stock held from each of these dealers, linking in your reply to the definition of an asset in FRS 5.

6.2 Explain what provisions you would look for in a debt factoring agreement to justify removing the debtors from the accounts of the original seller.

FRS 6 Acquisitions and Mergers

Introduction

Normal practice in the preparation of consolidated accounts reflects the legal form of the amalgamation of businesses, in that the investment in a subsidiary is recorded at cost in the books of the holding company while in the group accounts only profits earned by the subsidiary after the acquisition date are treated as distributable. This treatment is acceptable when the substance of the transaction is the acquisition of one business by another, but may be regarded as less acceptable when the substance of the transaction is a merger of businesses. The problems can be illustrated by the merger of two companies, Top Ltd and Hat Ltd:

	Top Ltd	*Hat Ltd*
	£000	£000
Ordinary share capital	20	30
Retained profits	30	20
	50	50
Net assets	50	50
	50	50

Three methods of merging the two businesses are proposed:

(a) a new company, Tophat Ltd, is to be formed with an issued share capital of £100 000, half of which will be issued to the shareholders of each company;

(b) Top Ltd will issue £20 000 of ordinary shares, at a premium of £30 000, to the shareholders of Hat Ltd in exchange for their shareholding;

(c) Hat Ltd will issue £30 000 of ordinary shares at a premium of £20 000 to the shareholders of Top Ltd in exchange for their shareholding.

Each of these methods has the same commercial effect, that of merging two similarly sized businesses and sharing the expanded business equally between the former proprietors. Consolidated accounts under each scheme will appear as follows:

	(a) *Tophat Ltd* £000	(b) *Top Ltd* £000	(c) *Hat Ltd* £000
Share capital	100	40	60
Share premium	—	30	20
Retained profits	—	30	20
	100	100	100
Net assets	100	100	100
	100	100	100

Thus we can observe that, although the commercial substance of each scheme is the same, the normal method of accounting for acquisitions produces three very different amounts of distributable reserves; further, none of the figures we have produced is equal to the combined distributable reserves of the businesses that have been merged.

Merger accounting offers an alternative mechanism for consolidation that *pools* the distributable reserves of the merged companies. FRS 6 offers guidance on the situations where this practice is appropriate and the ways in which it should be applied.

Merger accounting offers a group a number of opportunities to show a more favourable accounting picture than traditional consolidation practice, termed acquisition accounting. FRS 6 is therefore written in a way that restricts the use of merger accounting.

Key definitions

A *business combination* is defined as:

> The bringing together of separate entities into one economic entity as a result of one entity uniting with, or obtaining control over the net assets and operations of, another.

A small number of business combinations can be regarded as a *merger*, being:

> A business combination that results in the creation of a new reporting entity formed from the combining parties, in which the shareholders of the combining entities come together in a partnership for the mutual sharing of the risks and the benefits of the combined entity, and in which no party to the combination in substance obtains control over any other, or is otherwise seen to be dominant, whether by virtue of the proportion of its shareholders' rights in the combined entity, the influence of its directors or otherwise.

Most will be classified as an *acquisition*, being:

> A business combination that is not a merger.

One situation where merger accounting is appropriate is a *group reconstruction:*

> Group reconstructions:
>
> Any of the following arrangements:
> (a) the transfer of a shareholding in a subsidiary undertaking from one group company to another;
> (b) the addition of a new parent company to a group;

(c) the transfer of shares in one or more subsidiary undertakings of a group to a new company that is not a group company but whose shareholders are the same as those of the group's parent;
(d) the combination into a group of two or more companies that before the combination had the same shareholders.

Shares are of two types. *Non-equity* shares and *equity shares*. *Non-equity shares* possess any of the following characteristics:

(a) any of the rights of the shares to receive payments (whether in respect of dividends, in respect of redemption or otherwise) are for a limited amount that is not calculated by reference to the company's assets or profits or the dividends on any class of equity share;
(b) any of their rights to participate in a surplus in a winding up are limited to a specific amount that is not calculated by reference to the company's assets or profits and such limitation had a commercial effect in practice at the time the shares were issued or, if later, at the time the limitation was introduced;
(c) the shares are redeemable, either according to their terms or because the holder, or any party other than the issuer, can require their redemption.

All other shares are *equity shares.*

Criteria for treatment as merger

A *business combination* should be treated as a merger where this is permitted by company law and all of the following five criteria are met:

(a) no party to the combination is portrayed as being either an acquirer or the subject of an acquisition by its own board or management or the board or management of another party to the combination;
(b) all parties to the combination must participate in setting up the new management arrangements for the combined entity, with decisions reached by consensus rather than simple majority vote;
(c) the relative size of the combining entities must not differ so greatly that one dominates the new entity by virtue of relative size;
(d) the consideration received by equity shareholders of each party to the combination for their shareholding must consist *primarily* of equity shares in the new combined entity. Only an *immaterial* proportion of the consideration may be in the form of non-equity consideration or equity shares with substantially reduced voting or distribution rights. However where a *peripheral part* of one of the parties to the combination is hived off then either the hived off part, or the proceeds of its sale, may be distributed to shareholders without being deemed to be part of the *consideration* to be taken into account in deciding whether there is a merger. A *peripheral* part of a business is one that can be disposed of without having a material effect on the nature and focus of the operations of the business; and
(e) no equity shareholders in any of the combining business should retain any material interest in the future performance of only part of the combined entity.

In relation to the above criteria any convertible shares or loan stock converted into equity as a result of the combination should be regarded as equity.

In the case of a business combination effected by using a newly formed parent company to hold the shares of each entity in the combination one of two circumstances may arise:

(a) there may be one party which can be identified as the acquirer. In that case the acquirer and the new company are consolidated by merger accounting; other parties to the acquisition are then brought in by acquisition accounting; or
(b) alternatively the whole business combination may be a merger, in which case both the new company and all the parties will be consolidated with merger accounting.

A group reconstruction may also be accounted for on a merger accounting basis if:

(a) the use of merger accounting is not prohibited by company law;
(b) the ultimate shareholders remain the same, with no change in their relative rights;
(c) no change is made in the minority interest.

Merger accounting

Key features of merger accounting are:

(a) the carrying values of assets and liabilities are *not* adjusted to fair value on acquisition. The only changes required will arise from the application of common accounting policies through the new group;
(b) the profit and cash flows of the combining entity are consolidated from the first day of the accounting year in which the combination occurs, rather than from the actual date of the acquisitions in the case of acquisition accounting. Comparative figures for previous years are also prepared for the combined entity as a whole;
(c) shares issued are recorded at nominal value, rather than with any share premium. The difference between the nominal value of shares issued, plus the fair value of any other consideration, and the nominal value of shares received, is shown as a movement in 'other reserves' in the consolidated accounts. Existing balances on share premium account or capital redemption reserve of the new subsidiary should also be brought in as a movement on other reserves;
(d) merger expenses should be charged to profit and loss at the date of the merger and accounted for as reorganisation costs in line with FRS 3.

Acquisition accounting

Any business combination not classified as a merger should be accounted for by acquisition accounting.

In this:

(a) the acquirer's consolidated balance sheet must show the identifiable assets and liabilities of subsidiaries at their fair value at the acquisition date;
(b) the results and the cash flows of acquired subsidiaries are included from the acquisition date, and are not included in the comparative figures for the previous year;
(c) the difference between the fair value of the purchase consideration and the fair value of the net identifiable assets acquired is accounted for as goodwill.

Disclosure requirements

All business combinations

There should be shown in the accounts of the entity issuing shares, in the case of a merger, or the acquiring entity, in the case of an acquisition:

(a) the names of the combining entities;
(b) whether the combination has been accounted for as an acquisition or a merger;
(c) the date of the combination.

Mergers

For each business combination accounted for as a merger, other than a reconstruction, there must be shown in the year of the merger:

(a) an analysis of the principal components of the year's profit and loss account and statement of recognised gains and losses into:
    (i) amounts for the merged entity after the merger date;
    (ii) amounts for each party to the merger before the merger date,
    and also an analysis of these principal components between the parties to the merger.
    As a minimum this analysis should show the turnover, operating profit and exceptional items, split between continuing operations, discontinued operations and acquisitions; profit before taxation; taxation and minority interests; and extraordinary items;
(b) the composition and fair value of the purchase consideration given by the issuing company and its subsidiaries;
(c) the aggregate book value of the net assets of each party to the merger at the merger date;
(d) the nature and amount of significant adjustments made to the net assets of any party to the merger:
    (i) to achieve consistent accounting policies;
    (ii) for any other reason;
(e) a statement of adjustments to consolidated reserves arising from the merger.

Acquisitions

For a material acquisition the profit after tax and minority interests of the acquired entity should be given for:

(a) the period from the beginning of the acquired entity's financial year to the date of acquisition, giving the date on which this period began; and
(b) its previous financial year.

The following disclosures should be made for each individual material acquisition and for the total of other acquisitions:

(a) the make up and fair value of the consideration given by the acquirer. Where there is any deferred or contingent element in the consideration this should be stated, with the range of possible outcomes and the principal factors affecting them;

(b) a table should show for each class of assets and liabilities of the acquired entity:
   (i) the book values immediately before the acquisition;
   (ii) fair value adjustments, analysed into revaluations, adjustments to achieve consistent accounting policies, and other adjustments with reasons;
   (iii) the fair values at the acquisition date.

   In this table provisions for reorganisation and restructuring costs of the acquired entity made up 12 months before the acquisition date should be separately identified;

(c) where at the time of reporting fair values can only be determined on a provisional basis this should be stated with reasons. Subsequent adjustments in future periods must be disclosed and explained;

(d) post-acquisition profits of the acquired entity should be included in continuing operations, as provided in FRS 3, unless they are also discontinued in the same period;

(e) any material impact on a major business segment should be disclosed and explained;

(f) sometimes there are practical problems in determining the post-acquisition results of an acquired entity to the end of the acquisition period. In such a case an indication of the contribution to turnover and operating profit should be given, and if this is not possible the circumstances should be explained;

(g) exceptional profits or losses of the acquired entity in the post-acquisition period should be identified in accordance with FRS 3 and shown as relating to the acquisition;

(h) costs of reorganising, restructuring, and integrating the acquisition should be shown separately;

(i) movements on provisions or accruals relating to the acquisition should be disclosed, analysed between those actually used and amounts released unused;

(j) the cash flow statement should show cash paid for the acquisition net of cash balances transferred as part of the acquisition, with a note summarising the effects. In the year of the acquisition the part of each cash flow heading attributable to the acquiree should be disclosed in the notes.

Substantial acquisitions

A substantial acquisition is one where:

(a) for listed companies, the combination is a Class I or Super Class I transaction under the Stock Exchange Listing Rules;

(b) for other entities, either:
   (i) the net assets or operating profits of the acquired entity exceed 15 per cent of those of the acquiring entity; or
   (ii) the fair value of the consideration given exceeds 15 per cent of the net assets of the acquiring entity,

and should also be made in other exceptional cases where an acquisition is of such significance that the disclosure is necessary in order to give a true and fair view.

In this case the consolidated accounts in the year of the acquisition must show a summarised profit and loss account and statement of total recognised gains and losses for the acquired subsidiary from the beginning of its financial year which must be shown, to the acquisition date.

The minimum content is:

(a) turnover;
(b) operating profit;
(c) exceptional items;
(d) profit before tax;
(e) tax and minority interests;
(f) extraordinary items.

The provisions of this standard which are set out in relation to *an offer* and the results thereof apply also to any scheme or arrangement having similar effect.

(a) The effective date of acquisition or merger is the earlier of:
  (i) the date on which the consideration passes; or
  (ii) the date on which an offer becomes or is declared unconditional.
  This applies even if the acquiring company has the right under the agreement to share in the profits of the acquired business from an earlier date.
(b) Equity share capital is as defined in the Companies Act 1985 s 744, namely,

> in relation to a company, its issued share capital excluding any part of that capital which, neither as respects dividends nor as respects capital, carries any right to participate beyond a specified amount in a distribution.

Summary

Merger accounting

When a business combination meets the conditions that define it as a merger, then companies are required to use merger accounting. The acquiring company will record the cost of the new investment in its books as the nominal value of the shares issued plus the fair value of any additional consideration. On consolidation, the book value of assets, liabilities and reserves will be added together and the only difference arising will be any difference between the amount of the investment recorded in the books of the holding company and the nominal value of the acquired shares. If the surplus is a credit balance this will be treated as an unrealised reserve, while a debit balance will be deducted from consolidation reserves. The consolidated profit and loss account for the year of the merger will include the profits of all the merged companies for the whole year and the corresponding amounts will be computed on the same basis.

Adjustments to the accounts must also be made if necessary to reflect common accounting policies.

Acquisition accounting

All acquisitions must be accounted for by conventional acquisition accounting, in line with FRS 2 and FRS 7.

Disclosure

For all business combinations, however they are accounted for, there must be shown:

(a) the names of the combining companies;
(b) the number and class of securities issued in respect of the combination and details of any other consideration.

Background and evolution

Merger accounting was an issue on the ASC's agenda as early as 1971, with the issue of ED 3 on the subject. However, doubts about the legality of merger accounting, confirmed by the case of Shearer v Bercain (1980), delayed any development until a change in company law. The Companies Act 1985 s 131 gives relief from the normal requirement for a share premium account to reflect the full value of the consideration for which shares are issued when at least 90 per cent of the shares in the investee are acquired.

The basic principle of SSAP 23, issued in 1985 and now withdrawn, was that a merger is regarded as occurring where 'only limited resources leave the group'. This contrasts with ED 3 which laid down more stringent conditions, including a requirement that in the amalgamated undertaking shareholders in no one of the constituent companies should have more than three times the equity in the new undertaking than shareholders from any other constituent company.

Commentators on SSAP 23 pointed out that there are techniques whereby the criteria for merger accounting could be met, although in practice the shareholders in the acquired company do not continue to hold shares in the merged undertaking. These arrangements involve acquisition by the issue of shares in the acquiring company with a related agreement for their immediate sale, either to an arranged third party in the case of a *vendor placing*, or to the existing shareholders of the acquiring company in the case of *vendor rights*. The net effect of either arrangement is that a company has been acquired for cash raised by a share issue.

The requirement that immediately prior to the acquisition the acquirer must not hold more than 20 per cent of the acquiree can be avoided by disposal of part of an existing shareholding to a financial adviser with an agreement for repurchase.

Both these measures were used in practice following the introduction of SSAP 23.

Critics of SSAP 23 questioned the choice of policy allowed for companies meeting the merger criteria. They point to the US rules which define mergers more strictly but then prescribe merger accounting.

Both these issues have been addressed in FRS 6.

For further developments, see 'Business Combinations' in the chapter on Discussion Papers.

Conclusion

FRS 6 has approached this issue with a combination of strict definition and extensive disclosure requirements.

EXAMINATION PRACTICE

7.1 Definitions

Describe what is meant by the following terms:

(a) equity method of accounting;
(b) acquisition accounting techniques;
(c) pooling of interests method of accounting.

7.2 Merger accounting

The summarised balance sheet of Sid Limited at 31 December 19X0 was as follows:

	£		£
Share capital:			
issued and fully paid 980 000			
shares of £0.25 each	245 000	Fixed assets	180 000
Reserves	300 000	Current assets	565 000
Current liabilities	200 000		
	745 000		745 000

At that date the company acquired the whole issued share capital of Toad Limited by the issue of 300 000 new ordinary shares, at the day's market price of £0.80. The balance sheet of Toad Limited immediately prior to acquisition was:

	£		£
Share capital:			
70 000 shares of £1 each	70 000	Fixed assets	90 000
Reserves	50 000	Current assets	55 000
Current liabilities	25 000		
	145 000		145 000

You are required to prepare the consolidated balance sheet of Sid Ltd;

(a) by the acquisition method;
(b) by the merger method.

FRS 7: Fair Values in Acquisition Accounting

Introduction

When consolidated accounts are prepared by acquisition accounting, i.e. when merger accounting is not used, then it is necessary to compute both the fair value of the purchase consideration and the fair value of the identifiable assets and liabilities of the acquired subsidiary or associate. FRS 7 deals with the question of what constitutes identifiable assets and liabilities and how fair value should be measured.

Definitions

Key terms in FRS 7 are:

(a) *Fair value:* the amount at which an asset or liability could be exchanged in an arm's-length transaction between informed and willing parties, other than in a forced or liquidation sale.
(b) *Identifiable assets and liabilities:* the assets and liabilities of the acquired entity that are capable of being disposed of or settled separately, without disposing of a business of the entity.
(c) *Recoverable amount:* the greater of the net realisable value of an asset and, where appropriate, the value in use.
(d) *Value in use:* the present value of the future cash flows obtainable as a result of an asset's continued use, including those resulting from the ultimate disposal of the asset.

The concept of *recoverable amount* is laid out in FRS 11. The basis for the definition is that a business may choose whether to use an asset, in which case it will enjoy the benefit of future cash flows from that use, or sell it; accordingly, assuming that an economically rational choice is made, the business will enjoy the benefit of the higher amount.

The reference to *the present value of the future cash flows* in the definition of value in use indicates that discounting is necessary. This is an interesting contrast with the position when SSAP 16 (now withdrawn) was issued in 1980 and discounting of future cash flows was *not* required. In practice the use of discounted cash flow techniques to support the figures in the financial accounts has grown substantially since 1980. See 'Discounting in Financial Reporting' in the chapter on Discussion Papers.

The principles of FRS 7

The basic principle of FRS 7 is that the identifiable assets and liabilities to be measured are those of the acquired entity that existed at the acquisition date. These are measured at fair values that reflect conditions at the acquisition date. It follows that the following should *not* affect, or be included in, the valuation of acquired assets and liabilities:

(a) changes resulting from the acquirer's intentions or future actions;
(b) changes attributable to events subsequent to acquisition;
(c) provisions or accruals for future operating losses or for reorganisation and integration costs expected to be incurred as a result of the acquisition.

Specific items

Rules identifying *fair value* for specific categories of asset are as follows.

Tangible fixed assets

Where assets similar in type and condition are bought and sold on an open market then market value should be used.

Alternatively a depreciated replacement cost should be used. The fair value should not exceed the recoverable amount.

Intangible assets

Fair value should be used on replacement cost, normally the estimated market value.

Stocks and work in progress

Normally the lower of replacement cost and net realisable value is used. Where stocks, such as commodities, are traded on a market where the acquired entity acts as both buyer and seller then current market price is used.

Quoted investments

Fair value is computed by reference to market price. Adjustment may be necessary to reflect unusual price fluctuations or the size of the holding.

Monetary assets and liabilities

Fair values of these items are based on the amounts to be received or paid and their timing, and should be determined by reference to market prices, the current price at which similar items could arise, or by discounting to present value.

Contingencies

Contingent assets or liabilities should be measured at fair values where these can be estimated, reasonable estimates of the expected outcome being used.

Pensions and other post-retirement benefits

The fair value of a deficiency or, if reasonably expected to be realised, a surplus on a funded scheme as at the acquisition date is brought into the accounts of the acquiring group. Changes in pension arrangements following acquisition are dealt with as post-acquisition items.

Deferred taxation

The fair value of the deferred tax asset or liability is determined by considering the enlarged group as a whole.

Business sold

Where part of the interest in an acquired entity may consist of a separate business which is to be sold within a year or so, that investment is treated as a single asset under FRS 7, with the fair value based on the net proceeds of the sale adjusted for any items transferred into or out of the business. If the business has not been sold by the time accounts for the year are approved then the fair value is based on the estimated net proceeds of the sale provided that:

(a) a purchaser has been identified or is being sought;
(b) the disposal is reasonably expected to occur within approximately one year of the acquisition date.

Timing problems

Timing problems arise in the application of FRS 7 for two reasons:

(a) The investigation necessary in order to establish fair values may take longer than the period between the acquisition date and the finalising of the first set of consolidated accounts. In that case the first set of published accounts will be based on provisional estimates of fair value, with any necessary adjustments to both the individual items and the related goodwill figure being made in the following year. Thereafter any further changes are treated as profits or losses in the year they are identified.
(b) The cost of acquisition may be, in part, contingent on some future event such as a multiple of earnings in a future year or years. In this case *reasonable estimate* of the likely consideration is made initially with subsequent revision until the ultimate amount is known.

Controversy over the standard

FRS 7 may appear to be a rather detailed, technical, standard dealing with a single area of interpretation in the preparation of consolidated accounts. In fact it cracks down on a major area of abuse in the preparation of accounts.

The key requirement here is that provisions or accruals for future operating losses or for reorganisation costs expected to be incurred as a result of the acquisition may *not* be included in the computation of the fair value of the identifiable assets and liabilities acquired. In the past a number of companies have made substantial provisions of this nature, which have then been credited to profit and loss in the year or years immediately following acquisition. It has been argued that this enables acquiring companies to engage in *creative accounting*, boosting the *goodwill figure* which may be written off directly to reserves, and correspondingly boosting apparent profit following the acquisition. It is characteristic of the ASB's current approach that they should have taken firm action to eliminate such abuses.

Arguments against the approach taken in FRS 7 are:

(a) the commercial reality of many acquisitions is that they take place in situations where some reorganisation to put future trading on a sound footing is necessary, so that some provision for this is justified;

(b) the requirements of FRS 7 may put UK companies at a disadvantage compared to US companies who are allowed more flexibility;

(c) acquirers may be less willing to acquire poorly managed companies in need of substantial reorganisation.

For further developments, see 'Business Combinations' in the chapter on Discussion Papers.

Conclusion

FRS 7 tackles a major area of difficulty in the area of *creative accounting*. In doing so the standard necessarily excludes some accounting provisions that might be seen as legitimate.

EXAMINATION PRACTICE

8.1 Fair value

Explain why the concept of *fair value* arises in historic cost accounting.

FRS 8: Related Party Transactions

Introduction

An important aspect of the way in which we interpret accounts is that normally transactions have been conducted on an 'arm's-length' basis. This means that a transaction has been entered into by two independent parties, each seeking to negotiate the best deal they can get. For example, if a company buys some land for £1 million then we would expect that the seller was unable to get a higher price from an alternative buyer and the company was unable to find an equally suitable piece of land at a lower price. Thus the figure for the acquisition cost at the date of purchase is likely to approximate to the market value at that date. Now let us consider the situation where the transaction was conducted between the company and a 'related party', so that one party to the transaction can control the decisions of both parties. Let us imagine that the vendor of the land is also the managing director of the company and an 80 per cent shareholder. In this case it might be that the land has a market value of £600 000 and the vendor is taking advantage of his position to make a personal profit at the company's expense, or a market value of £1 300 000, and the vendor has set a low price in an attempt to reduce a capital gains tax liability. In either case the accounts are misleading. Let us imagine that the land has a market value of £600 000. In this case the accounts need to alert users to the situation for two reasons:

1. To fulfil the stewardship role of accounting, shareholders need to be alerted to what their directors have done. In this case the over-payment for the land represents a fraud on the minority shareholders.
2. For decision-making purposes the users of accounts need to be alerted to the fact that figures may not represent market-based transactions. Thus, a bank would be unwise to regard the £1 million cost of the land in our example as a reliable figure when considering a loan secured on this asset.

To meet this need FRS 8:

(a) identifies a range of *related party* situations and transactions;
(b) prescribes disclosures to be made in these situations.

Definitions

A *related party* relationship can arise and be evidenced in a variety of ways. Therefore the definition provided in FRS 8 is necessarily extensive.

Any two or more parties are deemed to be related when at any time during the year:

(i) one party has direct or indirect control of the other; or
(ii) the parties are subject to common control from the same source; or
(iii) one party has influence over the financial and operating policies of the other to an extent that that other party might be inhibited from pursuing at all times its own separate interests; or
(iv) the parties, in entering a transaction, are subject to influence from the same source to such an extent that one of the parties to the transaction has subordinated its own separate interests.

Having defined the term *related party* in principle, FRS 8 goes on to identify situations where a related party relationship is always deemed to apply:

(i) its ultimate and intermediate parent undertakings, subsidiary undertakings, and fellow subsidiary undertakings;
(ii) its associates and joint ventures;
(iii) the investor or venturer in respect of which the reporting entity is an associate or a joint venture;
(iv) directors of the reporting entity and the directors of its ultimate and intermediate parent undertakings. For this purpose the term 'directors' includes persons in accordance with whose directions or instructions the directors are accustomed to act;
(v) pension funds for the benefit of employees of the reporting entity or of any entity that is a related party of the reporting entity.

FRS 8 then offers a list of situations where a related party relationship should be assumed unless it can be demonstrated

> that neither party has influenced the financial and operating policies of the other in such a way as to inhibit the pursuit of separate interests:
>
> (i) the key management of the reporting entity and the key management of its parent undertaking or undertakings;
> (ii) a person owning or able to exercise control over 20 per cent or more of the voting rights of the reporting entity, whether directly or through nominees;
> (iii) each person acting in concert in such a way as to be able to exercise control or influence over the reporting entity; and
> (iv) an entity managing or managed by the reporting entity under a management contract.

Two key terms are defined:

Key management: Those persons in senior positions having authority or responsibility for directing or controlling the major activities and resources of the reporting entity.

Persons acting in concert: Persons who, pursuant to an agreement or understanding (whether formal or informal), actively co-operate, whether by the ownership by any of them of shares in an undertaking or otherwise, to exercise control or influence over that undertaking.

Finally, related parties include:

(i) members of the close family of anyone falling within this related party definition;
(ii) partnerships, companies, trusts or other entities in which any individual or

member of the close family of a related party as defined above has a controlling interest.

Control is defined as 'the ability to direct the financial and operating policies of an entity with a view to gaining economic benefits from its activities'.

Required practice

At the heart of FRS 8 is a requirement that there should be disclosure of material transactions with any related party. Disclosure should consist of:

(a) the name of the related party;
(b) a description of the relationship;
(c) a description of the transaction;
(d) the amounts involved;
(e) any other elements of the transaction which need to be explained for an understanding of the accounts;
(f) amounts due to or from related parties at the balance sheet date and provisions for doubtful debts from related parties at that date;
(g) amounts written off in the period in respect of debts due to or from related parties.

These transactions may be disclosed on an aggregated basis unless disclosure of an individual transaction is required by law or is needed to understand the accounts.

Exemptions from these disclosures apply to:

(a) Consolidated accounts, where amounts have been eliminated on consolidation.
(b) The parent company's own accounts, when these are presented with the consolidated accounts.
(c) A subsidiary's accounts, as regards related transactions with other group companies, provided that:
    (i) 90 per cent or more of voting rights are controlled within the group.
    (ii) The consolidated accounts are publicly available.
(d) Pension contributions paid to the pension fund.
(e) Emoluments paid to employees.

Disclosures are also not required where the status of related party arises from the following roles:

(a) providers of finance in the course of their business;
(b) utility companies;
(c) government departments;
(d) a customer, supplier, franchiser, distributor or general agent.

Disclosure of control

When the reporting company is controlled by another party, the relationship and name of both that party and any ultimate controlling party must be shown. If the controlling or ultimate controlling party is not known, then that fact must be disclosed.

Issues in the application of FRS 8

'Control' and 'influence'

The element of judgement necessary in identifying a 'related party' is highlighted in Fig 9.1. Let us suppose that company A controls two subsidiaries, B and C. Since both B and C are subject to 'common control' then all three companies are related parties. By contrast, if company X has two associated companies, Y and Z, then each-company is related to X, since X 'has influence' over each of them. However, Y and Z, being subject to common 'influence' rather than 'control', will only be deemed to be related where the influence has been applied to the point where one of the companies has engaged in a transaction where it has subordinated its own separate interests.

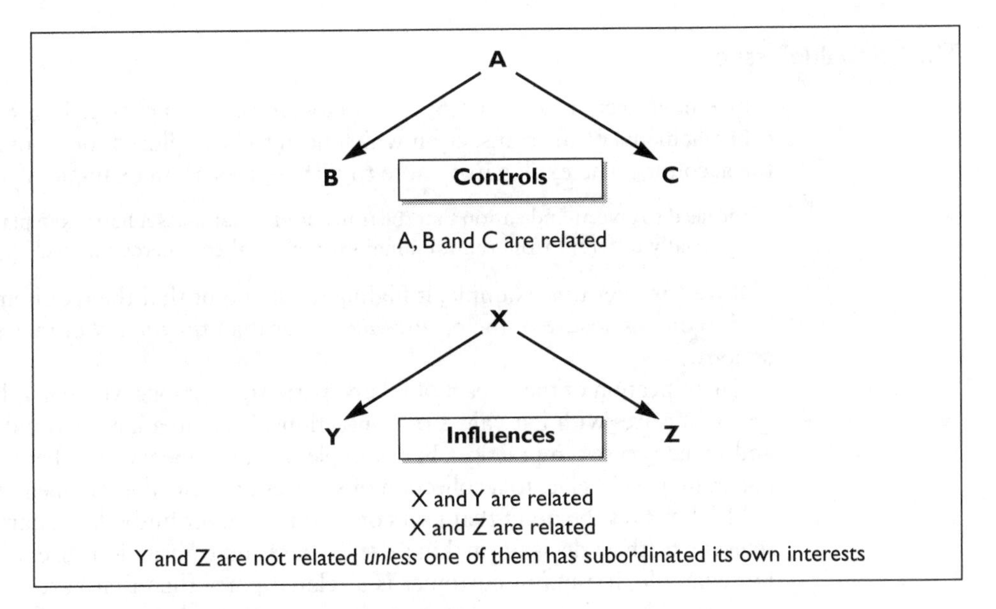

Fig. 9.1 Comparison of 'control' and 'influence'

Examples of transactions

Examples of transactions where related party disclosure will be necessary are:

1. purchases or sales of goods;
2. purchases or sales of property and other assets;
3. rendering or receiving of services;
4. agency arrangements;
5. leasing arrangements;
6. transfer of research and development;
7. licence agreements;

8. provision of finance;
9. guarantees and the provision of collateral security;
10. management contracts.

Disclosure is necessary irrespective of whether or not a price is charged.

Materiality

Where the related party is:

(a) a director, key manager or other individual in a position to influence, or accountable for stewardship of, the reporting entity; or
(b) a member of the close family of any of the above; or
(c) controlled by any of the above,

then the issue of 'materiality' is to be assessed in relation both to the reported company and in relation to the reported party. This enables the user of the accounts to make a judgement on the stewardship of the company.

The 'fair value' issue

As we have seen above, one of the disclosure requirements of FRS 8 relates to any other elements of the transaction which need to be explored for an understanding of the accounts. The explanatory note to FRS 8 gives as an example of such an issue:

> the need to give an indication that the transfer of a major asset had taken place at an amount materially different from that obtainable on normal commercial terms.

If we consider this example, it highlights the point that the requirements of FRS 8 lead to the disclosure of the *occurrence* rather than the *impact* of related party transactions.

Quantification of the impact of related party transactions would involve comparison of actual prices with fair values of transactions. Such an analysis would be both costly and, in many cases, impractical. For example, a management charge between group companies may well relate to a collection of services not traded in an open market.

FRS 8 makes the point that users of accounts might find related party transactions relevant to their decision making even where the transactions are at market value. For example, if a major customer is a related party then that part of future trading is susceptible to change arising from changes in that relationship rather than just market changes.

Conclusion

FRS 8 does not, and could not be expected to, guarantee that the accounts will identify all non-market influences on a company's transactions. It does provide a comprehensive framework to identify most of the transactions that might be influenced by related parties, but does not offer any quantification of their impact.

EXAMINATION PRACTICE

9.1 Related parties

Ghoul Ltd has two associated companies, Burnem Ltd which operates crematoria and Coffin Ltd which offers a funeral service. Mrs Slaughter is a director of Burnem Ltd. Her husband, Mr Slaughter, is a director of Wilting Ltd, a florist. Wilting Ltd has a regular arrangement to supply flowers to Coffin Ltd, which accounts for some 60 per cent of its turnover.

Is Wilting Ltd a related party of Coffin Ltd?

CHAPTER 10

FRS 9: Associates and Joint Ventures

Introduction

Until the late 1960s income from investments where the investment was less than 50 per cent of the equity of the investee was normally only included in the accounts of the investing company to the extent that dividends were receivable. Profits earned but not distributed by the investee were ignored on the grounds that the companies concerned were separate legal entities and that income should not be taken to the profit and loss account until received or receivable.

In the balance sheet the investment was valued at cost, or net realisable value if lower.

This principle can, however, lead to distortion of profit and the balance sheets of companies that conduct an important part of their business through the medium of other companies. Investors came to attach more importance to the reported profit figure, as used in price/earnings ratios and earnings per share figures, than to the dividend yield information. Furthermore, the investors' share of the net worth of the company was excluded from the balance sheet.

In the late 1960s there was considerable growth in the practice of companies conducting an important part of their business through other companies and in 1971 the ASC issued the first standard on associated companies. In the 1990s joint ventures became an increasingly popular means of gaining access to markets, technologies or scarce resources, as well as of sharing the risks, and the ASB therefore issued FRS 9 in 1997.

FRS 9 – detailed requirements

Objective

The objective of the standard is that the investor's financial position and performance should reflect its interest in investments with which it has a close involvement.

Definition of investments

FRS 9 deals with three types of investment, which are defined as follows:

1. Associated company – is a company in which the investor has a *participating*

interest and over whose operating and financial policies it exercises a *significant influence*. This means that the investment should be for the long term and that the investor should exercise some control over that investment. The investor should be actively involved with and influence the investee's financial policies with regards to, for example, products, markets, acquisitions and dividends. This will often be achieved by representation on the board of directors. Companies legislation includes a rebuttable presumption that a holding of 20 per cent or more of the shares is a participating interest and that significant influence may be exercised.

2. Joint venture – a company in which a reporting company has a long-term interest and exercises joint control together with other companies.
3. Joint Arrangement that is Not an Entity (JANET) – occurs where there is a contractual arrangement under which the participants engage in joint activities, but there is no separate legal entity which engages in its own activities. Examples might be joint marketing and distribution networks, a shared production facility and the construction of a single project.

Accounting treatments

1. Associated companies

The investor should include an associated company in its consolidated accounts using the equity method of accounting. In its individual accounts it should be treated as a fixed asset investment, i.e. valued at cost, less any amounts written off, or at valuation, and dividends received included in the profit and loss account.

In the equity method of accounting:

Consolidated balance sheet – the investor's consolidated balance sheet should include the investor's share of the net assets of its associate. Goodwill arising on acquisition, less any amount written off, should be included, but disclosed separately. (This amount in fact equals the cost of the investment plus the investor's share of retained post-acquisition profits.) Fair values should be attributed to the associates underlying assets and liabilities.

Consolidated profit and loss account – the investor's consolidated profit and loss account will show:

- the investor's share of its associate's operating results,
- any amortisation of goodwill on acquiring the associate,
- the investor's share of its associates' exceptional items, interest and tax.

Where profits and losses on the transfer of assets between investor and associate are included in the carrying value of assets, the investor's share should be eliminated.

Consolidated STRGL – the investor's consolidated STRGL should show the share of the gains and losses of the associate, separately disclosed under each heading if material.

Consolidated cash flow statement – the investor's consolidated cash flow statement should include any dividends received and any other cash flow between the associate and the investor. No other cash flows of the associate should be included, i.e. cash flows not between the investor and its associate.

Example 10.1

Example of the preparation and presentation of associated company information.

Hampden Ltd, a company with subsidiaries, acquired a 30 per cent investment in Pym Ltd on 1 January 20X1. The accounts of the Hampden group and of Pym Ltd for the year to 31 December 20X1, before consolidating the results of the associate, were as follows:

Balance sheets:	*Hampden Group*	*Pym Ltd*
	£000	*£000*
Fixed assets	500	200
Investment in associate	100	
Net current assets	200	120
	800	320
Share capital	400	200
Retained profits	400	120
	800	320

Profit and loss accounts:	*Hampden Group*	*Pym Ltd*
	£000	*£000*
Turnover	1 200	400
Profit before taxation	259	110
Taxation	144	60
Profit after taxation	115	50
Dividends	55	30
Net profit retained	60*	20
*By Hampden Ltd	25	
By subsidiaries	35	
	60	

Dividends of £9 000 receivable from Pym Ltd, an overseas company, are included as profit before tax of the Hampden Group.

The accounts of the Hampden Group will have to be adjusted to incorporate the results of the associate as follows:

(a) Turnover will not be adjusted since the turnover of the associated company is not incorporated in the group accounts.

(b) The operating profit of the group must be adjusted to exclude the dividend from the associate, while the group's share of the pre-tax profit of the associate will be brought into the accounts and shown separately.

(c) FRS 9 requires that profit for the year retained in the associated companies accounts be identified.

(d) The identifiable assets of Pym Ltd at the acquisition date were:

	£000
As at 31 December 20X1	320
Less retained profit for 20X1	20

	£000
As at 1 January 20X1	300

The group share of these assets was: 30% × 300 = 90

So that the premium on acquisition must have been:

	£000
Cost	100
Share of net assets	90
Premium	10

The group share of the associate's net assets at 31 December 20X1 is:
£320 000 × 30% = £96 000

(e) The group reserves must identify that portion of the reserves retained in the associated company.

Hampden Ltd – consolidated profit and loss account for the year ended 31 December 20X1

	£000	£000
Turnover (a)		1 200
Operating profit (259 – 9) (b)		250
Share of profit of associated company (30% × 110) (b)		33
Profit before taxation		283
Taxation: Hampden Ltd and subsidiaries	144	
Associated company (30% × 60)	18	162
Profit after taxation		121
Dividends		55
Net profit retained (c)		66*
* Analysis of retained profit		
By Hampden Ltd	25	
By subsidiaries	35	
In associated company	6	
	66	

Hampden Ltd – consolidated balance sheet at 31 December 20X1

	£000	£000
Fixed assets		500
Investment in associate (d)		
Share of net assets	96	
Premium on acquisition	10	106

	£000	£000
Net current assets		200
		806
Share capital		400
Retained profits (e)		
Hampden Ltd	220	
Subsidiary companies	180	
Associated company	6	406
		806

Where the year end of an associated company differs from that of the investor, the associate should be included on the basis of financial statements prepared to the investor's year end. Where this is not practical, then financial statements ending within three months before the investor's year end may be used.

2. Joint ventures

In consolidated accounts an investor should include joint ventures using the gross equity method.

In its individual accounts the joint venture should be treated as a fixed asset investment, i.e. valued at cost, less any amounts written off, or at valuation, and the inclusion of dividends received included in the profit and loss account .

The gross equity method is similar to the equity method, except that:

- the investor's share of the aggregate gross assets and liabilities underlying the investment are shown on the balance sheet;
- the investor's share of the investee's turnover is noted in the profit and loss account.

An illustration of the presentation of joint ventures and associates is shown below.

Profit and loss account

	£000
Turnover: group and share of joint ventures	500
Less: share of joint venture turnover	(100)
Group turnover	400

Balance sheet

	£000	£000
Fixed assets		X
Investments		X
Investments in joint ventures		
Share of gross assets	350	
Share of gross liabilities	(75)	
		275

Investment in associates

	£000	£000
Share of net assets	100	
Goodwill on acquisition less amortisation	25	125
		400

3. Joint arrangement that is not an entity (JANET)

Participants in a JANET should account for their own assets, liabilities and cash flows relating to the JANET.

Disclosure

The following disclosures should be made in addition to the information disclosed on the face of the financial statements, as discussed above. The disclosure requirements are in three parts:

- those relating to all companies,
- the 15 per cent threshold,
- the 25 per cent threshold.

The percentages refer to the investor's share in either the investee's aggregate of assets, liabilities, turnover or operating profits as a percentage of the corresponding group figures.

All associates and joint ventures

- name of assochate/joint venture,
- proportion of shares held,
- accounting year end, if different,
- nature of the business,
- material differences in accounting policy,
- restrictions on distributions,
- analysis of inter-company balances between trading and loans,
- reasons for rebutting the 20 per cent presumption, if applicable.

15 per cent threshold

Aggregate of:

- turnover of associates (this is a requirement for joint ventures in the gross equity method),
- fixed and current assets,
- liabilities: < 1 year and > 1 year.

25 per cent threshold

In addition to the requirements at the 15 per cent threshold aggregate of:

- profit before tax,
- tax,
- profit after tax.

Conclusion

The accounting for associated companies, joint ventures and JANET's has developed over a period of 30 years. FRS 9 provides users with clear information about its alliances with other companies and their effect on its financial position and performance.

EXAMINATION PRACTICE

10.1 On the 1 January 20X1 the net tangible assets of A Ltd were £300 000. The issued ordinary share capital was 100 000 £1 ordinary shares.

On 1 January 20X1 Hold Ltd bought 30 000 shares in A Ltd for £120 000.

During the year ended 31 December 20X1 A Ltd's profit, after tax, was £20 000 from which a dividend of £10 000 was paid.

Show how the associated company A Ltd would appear in Hold Ltd's :

(a) consolidated balance sheet at 31 December 20X1;
(b) consolidated profit and loss account for the year ended 31 December 20X1;
(c) consolidated cash flow statement for the year ended 31 December 20X1.

10.2 Give a definition of an associated company, a joint venture and a JANET.

FRS 10: Goodwill and Intangible Assets

Introduction

Accounting for goodwill has been one of the most contentious issues for UK standard setters. Although goodwill had long been recognised as a problem area it was not until 1982 that there was an exposure draft by the ASC, some 11 years after its first standard was issued in 1971. This was followed by SSAP 22: Accounting for Goodwill in 1984 which was revised in 1989 and withdrawn on the introduction of FRS 10 in 1997. It may well be asked why it took 26 years to issue a standard and why there have been so many changes to accounting for goodwill over the years. The answer is that there has been disagreement on the fundamental nature of goodwill and hence the appropriate accounting treatment.

The value of a business at any point in time is likely to be different from the total value of the identifiable assets, both tangible and intangible, owned by the business. This is because the value of the business as a whole will be estimated by reference to the expected future flows of income from the business. This difference is generally referred to as goodwill. In practice we would expect a successful business to build up substantial goodwill as a result of such factors as a skilled workforce and trading connections with customers and suppliers.

Goodwill is identified when a business is sold. The goodwill may appear in the acquirer's own accounts when an unincorporated business is acquired or in the group accounts when the share capital of another company is acquired.

Goodwill is only one of a number of intangible fixed assets; other examples are patents, licenses, trademarks and brands. Whilst some intangible assets are clearly separable from goodwill, such as patents, other are closely aligned to it, such as brands. This created the problem that when companies were acquired at an amount in excess of the total value of identifiable net assets, this difference was sometimes attributed to both goodwill and brands in an arbitrary manner and each element accounted for differently. The ASB therefore considered it necessary to produce a standard on goodwill and other intangible fixed assets.

The basic problem

Balance sheets are usually prepared under the historical cost convention, as modified by the revaluation of some fixed assets. Even so, the balance sheet does not, and is not designed to, reflect the value of the business. It could not, as the value will vary from one potential purchaser to another. When a business is bought, the problem arises as to how to deal with the excess paid over the total value of identifiable net assets. (The issue of where the payment is less is dealt with later in this chapter in the section on negative goodwill.) There are a number of possibilities for dealing with the goodwill, five of which are:

1. account for as a fixed asset with infinite life, subject to regular valuations, i.e. amortisation may not be necessary;
2. account for as a fixed asset with finite life i.e. amortisation is necessary;
3. write off immediately against reserves;
4. treat as a negative reserve, and deduct from shareholder's equity;
5. treat as a negative reserve, and deduct from shareholder's equity, but with annual valuations, with differences being charged to the profit and loss account .

There are arguments for and against each method. The ASC in SSAP 22 allowed methods 2 and 3 above but they clearly stated that the immediate write-off method was preferred. The ASB in FRS 10 favour number 2 with the possibility of number 1 . So in a period of eight years, between SSAP 22 (revised) being issued in 1989 and FRS 10 being issued in 1997 there has been a fundamental change.

The confusion over the treatment of goodwill is based on differing views on the nature of goodwill. One view regards goodwill as an asset that has been purchased, being the right to receive future profits in excess of what might reasonably be expected from the assets employed. This view leads to the treatment of goodwill as an asset and all that consequently follows from this treatment with regard to valuation and amortisation. The alternative view is that goodwill is an accounting anomaly which cannot be accounted for within the accounting framework as it deals with a subjective valuation at one point in time of the value of a business. It should, therefore, be eliminated with a minimum impact on the financial statements. In addition, since internally generated goodwill is not included this gives a consistency of treatment between internal and external goodwill.

Essentially the choice between these methods is whether goodwill should remain in the balance sheet unaltered and whether it is an asset or a negative reserve. Method number 3 is of particular interest because it is the most controversial. It is therefore worth listing the reasons for *not* eliminating goodwill against reserves:

1. The immediate write off of goodwill reduces the net worth to the acquirer, which may not reflect the economic reality.
2. Goodwill does not appear as an asset in the balance sheet and does not therefore appear as part of the assets on which the company should earn a return. Similarly, because it is not shown as an asset, the directors are not accountable for disclosing the cost of the asset and any subsequent fall in value.
3. Companies have internally generated goodwill and purchased goodwill. The costs of internally generated goodwill are charged to the profit and loss account and therefore, to be consistent, the cost of acquiring external goodwill should also be charged to the profit and loss account through the amortisation charge. (However, this does lead to another inconsistency, namely that purchased goodwill appears as an asset whereas internally generated goodwill does not.) Thus companies that grow by acquisition appear more profitable than those that grow organically.
4. If goodwill is eliminated against reserves, but other intangible fixed assets are

not treated in this way, then goodwill is being treated in a different `manner from other intangibles which have a similar nature to it.

The choice of method may have economic consequences. Capitalisation/amortisation has an effect on profit; immediate write off has an effect on the balance sheet structure. Thus the choice of method will impact upon performance ratios and the balance sheet ratios, including the return on capital employed and gearing.

FRS 10 has adopted a combination of methods 1 and 2 above and the detailed requirements are given below.

FRS 10 – detailed requirements

Objectives

The objectives of FRS 10 are that:

(a) capitalised goodwill and intangible assets are charged in the profit and loss account in the periods in which they are depleted; and
(b) sufficient information is disclosed in the financial statements to enable users to determine the impact of goodwill and intangible assets on the financial position and performance of the reporting entity.

Scope

FRS 10 applies whenever any company acquires a business, whether it is the acquisition of a subsidiary company by a parent company or the purchase of an unincorporated business. It also applies to an investment which is accounted for using the equity method (see FRS 9: Associates and Joint Ventures) where goodwill may arise. Certain intangible assets are excluded where these are the subject of another specific pronouncement, for example SSAP 13: Accounting for Research and Development.

Definitions

Goodwill is defined as 'the difference between the cost of an acquired entity and the aggregate of the fair values of that entity's identifiable assets and liabilities'.

Fair values are 'values arrived at in arm's-length transactions which are not forced sales'.

Identifiable assets and liabilities are 'ones that may be sold separately from selling the business as a whole'.

Intangible assets are defined as 'non-financial fixed assets that do not have physical substance but are identifiable and are controlled by the entity through custody or legal rights'.

Recognition

Positive purchased goodwill should be capitalised and included as a fixed asset in the balance sheet. Internally generated goodwill should not be capitalised.

Intangible assets which have been purchased separately from the purchase of a business as a whole should be capitalised at cost.

Intangible assets which have been acquired as part of the acquisition of a business should be distinguished from goodwill and capitalised as a separate asset, if their value can be reliably measured.

The intangible assets should be valued at *fair value*, with the proviso that, unless there is a readily ascertainable market value, this must not convert positive to negative goodwill or add to negative goodwill.

Example 11.1

	Carrying values £000	*Fair values £000*	*Recognised values £000*
Net tangible assets	100	110	110
Intangible assets	150	200	190
	250	310	300
Amount paid	300	300	300
Goodwill	50	(10)	0

If there is no readily ascertainable market value, the values of the intangible fixed assets is restricted to £190 000

Where the value of an intangible asset cannot be reliably measured then it should be included within goodwill . Examples here would be brands and publication titles.

Internally developed intangible assets may be capitalised if there is a readily ascertainable market value; this is consistent with inherent goodwill, which by definition does not have a readily ascertainable market value and is not capitalised.

Amortisation

Where goodwill and intangible assets have limited useful economic lives, they should be amortised on a systematic basis. For example, there may be legal right on a patent for a fixed number of years. There is an expectation that the life of goodwill and an intangible asset will normally be 20 years or less.

Where they have indefinite lives, then they should not be amortised. Indefinite lives or periods longer than 20 years may be used when:

(a) There are grounds for believing that the life exceeds 20 years. Relevant factors are:

- the nature of the business,
- the stability of the industry,
- the length of the product cycle,
- the barriers to entry in that industry and the level of future competition.

(b) The goodwill or intangible asset is capable of continued measurement.

Company law legislation requires fixed assets to be depreciated, so where a company argues that the life of goodwill is indefinite and does not amortise it, the company will have to disclose in a note that they have taken advantage of the law's true and fair override provisions.

In calculating the amount of the fair value to be amortised, there can be no residual value for goodwill. There may only be a residual value for other intangible assets where that residual value can be measured reliably. The amortisation method should normally be the straight line method although an alternative method, such as reducing balance, may be used if it can be justified.

The useful economic lives of goodwill and intangible assets should be reviewed at the end of each year. If a life is changed then the carrying value should be amortised over the revised remaining life. If the review increases the life to more than 20 years from the date of the acquisition of the asset, then impairment reviews are necessary.

Impairment

Impairment reviews are covered in more detail in the chapter on FRS 11: Impairment of Fixed Assets and Goodwill.

Impairment occurs when the value of goodwill or an intangible asset falls below its carrying value. A review to see whether impairment has occurred must be undertaken:

(a) for assets being amortised over a period of 20 years or less:

- at the end of the first full financial year following the year of acquisition of the asset,
- at any time that it is believed that impairment may have occurred;

(b) for assets being amortised over a period of more than 20 years or are not being amortised because they have an indefinite life:

- at the end of each financial year.

However first year impairment reviews (see (a) above) may be performed by comparing post-acquisition performance with pre-acquisition forecast performance to see whether there has been any impairment. If this initial review suggests that there has been an impairment then a full impairment review in accordance with FRS 11 must be carried out. If an impairment loss is recognised then the revised carrying value should be amortised over the remaining life. Where goodwill arising on consolidation is impaired then an impairment review should also be carried out on the fixed asset investment in the balance sheet of the parent company.

Revaluation

Where an intangible asset has an ascertainable market value then it may be revalued to its market value. It is not acceptable to 'cherry pick' and only revalue those intangible assets which have risen in value. Thus all intangible assets of the same class must be revalued. Once the decision has been made to revalue intangible assets it is not acceptable to only update when market values have risen. Thus intangible assets must be regularly revalued to ensure that their value is not materially different from the market value at the balance sheet date. (This is consistent with FRS 15: Tangible Fixed Assets).

Where the impairment of an intangible fixed asset has been recognised and subsequent events reverse this impairment so as to increase the value of the asset above its present carrying value, the gain should be recognised in the current period. Amortisation charged before the revaluation should not be written back to the profit and loss account.

However, revaluation is only allowable where the original impairment was caused by an external event which subsequent external events have reversed and which could not have been foreseen at the time of the impairment. The circumstances when this situation might occur are limited. In general, changes in values detected by an impairment review will be the result of internal factors, such as the internal generation of goodwill. In these circumstances revaluation is not permitted.

It should be noted that goodwill may not be revalued above the figure at which it was originally recognised.

Negative goodwill

Negative goodwill arises where the amount paid for a company is less than the aggregate of the fair value of an entity's identifiable assets and liabilities. Where it is believed initially that negative goodwill exists, then the fair values of the assets and the liabilities should be checked. If this confirms the existence of negative goodwill then this should be recognised and distinguished from positive goodwill.

Negative goodwill up to the fair values of the non-monetary assets acquired should be recognised in the profit and loss account for the periods in which the non-monetary assets are recovered, either by depreciation or sale. Any negative goodwill in excess of fair values of the non-monetary assets acquired should be recognised in the profit and loss account for the period expected to benefit.

Purchased goodwill on a single transaction should not be split into positive and negative components. Thus it is not acceptable to distinguish between individual assets and estimate whether the amount paid was in excess of or below fair value. The net assets are thus treated as a whole.

Example 11.2

Harvey plc acquired its investment in Jones plc in the year ended 31 December 200X. The goodwill on acquisition was calculated as follows:

	£000	*£000*
Cost of investment		500
Fair value of net assets (remaining useful life 4 years)	800	
Stock	100	
Net monetary assets	200	
		1 100
Negative goodwill		(600)

The amount of negative goodwill in the profit and loss account and balance sheet for the year ended 31 December 200X is :

Non-monetary assets recognised through the profit and loss account for the year ended 31 December 200X:

	£000
Stock (assuming all the stock is sold in the year)	100
Depreciation (£800 000/4 years)	200
	300
Total non-monetary assets at acquisition	900
Proportion recognised this year is:	1/3

The profit and loss account will be credited with 1/3 × £600 000	£200 000
The balance sheet will show negative goodwill of £600 000 – £200 000	£400 000
This will be released to the profit and loss account at 1/3 × £400 000 over the next 3 years	£133 333

Disclosure

Recognition and measurement

The following should be disclosed:

- the method of valuing intangible assets,
- a schedule which reconciles opening and closing balances on positive goodwill, negative goodwill and each class of intangible asset giving full details of all movements in the year.

Amortisation

The following should be disclosed:

- the method of amortisation and the period, with the reasons for choosing the length of the period. A full explanation is required where the period exceeds 20 years or is indefinite. In the latter case the financial statements will also have to note the departure from company law which requires goodwill to be amortised;
- where an amortisation period or method is changed, the reason and the effect.

Revaluation

Where a class of assets have been revalued, the financial statements should disclose:

- the year, the basis and the amount of the revaluation. If the valuation is during the current year, then the name and qualifications of the valuer need to be disclosed;
- the original cost / fair value and the amount of any provision for amortisation that would have been recognised if the asset had remained at original cost / fair value.

Negative goodwill

The following should be disclosed:

- the period for which the negative goodwill is being written back to the profit and loss account;
- where negative goodwill exceeds the fair values of the non-monetary assets, the amount and source of the excess goodwill and the period for which it is being written back should be explained.

Transitional arrangements

The detailed transitional arrangements are beyond the scope of this book. It is sufficient to note that companies who previously complied with SSAP 22 by writing goodwill off against reserves are not required to reinstate goodwill. Companies may, however, choose to reinstate previously written-off goodwill. In either case, additional disclosure regarding this goodwill is required.

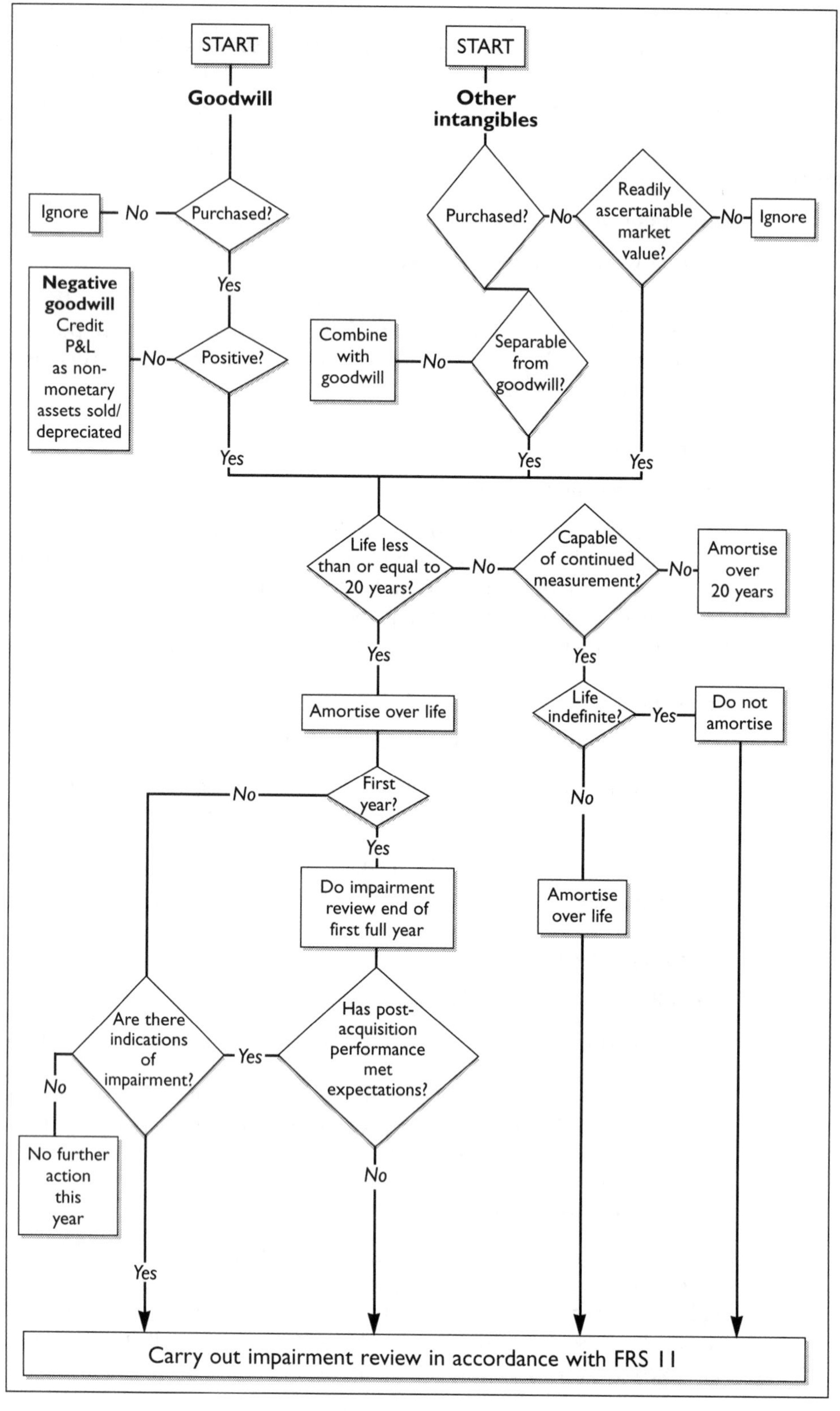

Fig. 11.1 Summary of accounting treatment for goodwill and intangible assets

Conclusion

The area of fixed assets was generally ignored by the ASC and the standards which were produced only appeared towards the end of its reign. In contrast the ASB has issued a number of standards in this area – FRSs 7, 10, 11 and 15. It has also issued the Statement of Principles, which underlies the development of these standards, with its definitions of asset and asset recognition. The ASB has also moved the UK closer to the USA position in accounting for goodwill and this is part of the harmonisation of global accounting practice.

There is thus reason to believe that the ASB has made significant progress towards a solution to the problem of accounting for goodwill and intangible assets.

EXAMINATION PRACTICE

11.1 (a) On 1 April 20X0 Cab Ltd acquired the entire share capital of Horse Ltd. The summarised balance sheets of the two companies immediately after the transaction were:

	Cab Ltd	*Horse Ltd*
	£000	*£000*
Tangible assets	800	700
Investment in Horse Ltd	1 200	
	2 000	700
Share capital	1 500	500
Retained profits	500	200
	2 000	700

The fair value of the tangible assets of Horse Ltd was £1 million.

You are required to prepare a consolidated balance sheet for the Cab group as at 1 April 20X0, prior to any amortisation of goodwill.

(b) The consolidated profit and loss account for the Cab group, before taking goodwill into account, for the two years to 31 March 20X1 and 31 March 20X2 showed:

	Cab Ltd	*Horse Ltd*
	£000	*£000*
Profit before taxation	320	350
Taxation	160	175
Profit after taxation	160	175
Dividend	130	140
Retained profit	30	35

You are required to prepare predicted balance sheets and profit and loss accounts for the two years to 31 March 20X1 and 31 March 20X2, assuming a ten-year life for goodwill.

11.2 Describe the requirements of FRS 10 regarding:

(i) the initial recognition and measurement of goodwill and intangible assets.
(ii) the amortisation of positive goodwill and intangible assets.

CHAPTER 12

FRS 11: Impairment of Fixed Assets and Goodwill

Introduction

Fixed assets may be stated in the balance sheet at historical cost less a provision for depreciation. Alternatively under FRS 15 they may be stated at current value, less an amount for depreciation (see the chapter on FRS 15: Tangible Fixed Assets). The amount stated in the balance sheet is known as the carrying value.

It is, however, accepted practice that the carrying amount should not exceed the *recoverable amount*. The recoverable amount may be defined as the higher of *net realisable value* and *value in use*. Net realisable value is the amount an asset could be sold for, less any selling costs; value in use is the net present value of the discounted future cash flows which arise from using the assets, including any proceeds on disposal.

An impairment review is the process of comparing carrying value to recoverable amount, and an impairment loss occurs if there is a reduction in the recoverable amount of a fixed asset or goodwill below its carrying amount.

Thus if the amount that a company is going to receive from an asset (recoverable amount), either through sale (net realisable value) or through use (value in use) is less than its carrying value, then it is going to incur a loss and that loss should be recognised immediately.

Prior to FRS 11 being issued there was no guidance on how to ensure that a fixed asset was not carried at more than its recoverable amount. SSAP 12: Accounting for Depreciation (now withdrawn) dealt only with the systematic writing down of the cost of an asset over a pre-determined period of time. It was therefore considered that impairments were not being recognised on a timely basis with the effect that fixed assets were being overstated in the balance sheet.

FRS 11 therefore sets out a framework on when to conduct an impairment review, when to recognise and measure an impairment loss and how to calculate recoverable amounts.

FRS 11 is also necessary as a consequence of FRS 10. This standard requires that where goodwill and intangible assets are not amortised, or are amortised over a period exceeding 20 years, then an annual impairment review must take place. This standard explains how this should be done and therefore FRS 10 and FRS 11 are closely linked. FRS 11 is also related to FRS 15: Tangible Fixed Assets.

FRS 11 – detailed requirements

Objectives

The objectives of the standard are:

- that fixed assets are recorded in the balance sheet at no more than the recoverable amount,
- that any impairment is accounted for on a consistent basis,
- that the effect of any impairment is disclosed.

The standard applies to all fixed assets, including goodwill, with the exception of financial instruments and investment properties (see the chapter on SSAP 19: Accounting for Investment Properties.)

Indications of Impairment

A review of impairment should be carried out if economic conditions suggest that the carrying amount of the fixed asset may not be recoverable. These conditions may apply directly to the assets themselves or to the related economic environment as a whole. Examples of indications of impairment are:

- past, current or forecast future operating losses or net cash outflows,
- fall in market value,
- obsolescence or physical damage to the fixed asset,
- adverse changes in the economic environment, for example greater competition or more stringent statutory requirements,
- company reorganisation,
- departure of key employees,
- significant increase in interest rates which are expected to be for the long term.

In the absence of such indicators, or of specific factors relevant to the fixed asset, then an impairment review is not required.

The inclusion of an increase in interest rates is significant. For example, if the carrying value of a fixed asset was £100 and the cash flows from the asset were expected to be £15 a year for five years i.e. £75 in total, then this would have a present value of £60 at a discount rate of 10 per cent and the impairment would be £40. If interest rates rose to 20 per cent, the present value would fall to £50, which would be an impairment of £50. Thus an asset is considered impaired if it no longer earns the current market rate of return.

Recognition and measurement of impairment

Where the recoverable amount is less than the carrying value, the fixed asset should be written down to the recoverable amount. This impairment loss should be recognised in the profit and loss account. However, where the carrying value is based on a previously revalued fixed asset, then the impairment may be charged to the statement of total recognised gains and losses (see Revalued fixed assets below).

Where it is not possible to estimate net realisable value, because, for example, there is no active market for such assets, then value in use is deemed to be the recoverable amount.

At the same time as recognising impairment, the economic life should be reviewed and the revised carrying value should be written off over any revised life.

Income generating units

Ideally, the value in use of a fixed asset would be estimated for each single asset. In practice it is rare to be able to identify cash flows arising from a single asset; examples of where this may be possible would be the hiring out of plant and equipment, such as cranes. The solution is to calculate the value in use of a 'bundle of assets' referred to as an *income-generating unit* (IGU). An IGU should be at the smallest practical level and is the net assets, including any goodwill, that is independent of any other IGU in the company. Thus the impairment review is conduced on an IGU and not on a single fixed asset.

Examples of the identification of income generating units

Example (a)

A transport company has main routes and feeder routes and the information system produces revenues for each route. However, a feeder route is *not* an IGU since it is not independent of the main route.

Example (b)

A company has ten sites, none of which operate to capacity, but there is not enough surplus capacity to close a site and reduce the number to nine sites. The company allocates production across these ten sites. Each site is not an IGU as it is dependent on the allocation process and therefore the ten sites collectively form an IGU.

Example (c)

A company has a three-stage production process – acquisition of raw materials, conversion of materials into components and assembly of components into finished products. The company also sells raw materials but there is no market for components.

The first stage, the acquisition of raw materials is independent of the second and third stages. The external price for the sale of raw materials can be used for the internal transfers. It is therefore an IGU.

The second stage is dependent on the products being sold at the third stage and these two stages should therefore be combined into a single IGU. The company thus has two IGUs.

Example (d)

A restaurant chain has 100 restaurants across the country. The income and net assets of each restaurant can be determined with some precision and each restaurant could therefore be classed as an IGU. However, an individual restaurant is unlikely to be material and therefore the restaurants may be grouped into IGUs where the same economic factors affect all the restaurants in a group. For example, the company may have four IGUs for north, south, east and west.

Income generating units and net assets

A company may be divided up into IGUs and assets and liabilities attributed to them. The IGUs are likely to reflect the different products and services of the company. The liabilities should include those relating to the operation of the business and exclude those not relating to the operation of the business, for example loans and taxation.

Head office assets and liabilities, which cannot be solely attributed to an IGU, should be apportioned to IGUs. Where this is not possible, then the impairment review needs to be conducted in two stages – at the IGU level and at the company-as-a-whole level.

Central assets

When a company has identified the IGUs and the net assets of each IGU it will then be necessary to apportion the fixed assets of the head office between them.

Table 12.1

IGU	*A* *£m*	*B* *£m*	*C* *£m*	*Total* *£m*
Direct net assets	50	75	100	225
Central net assets	5	5	5	15
	55	80	105	240

The central net assets have been apportioned on an equal basis as this reflects the use of the head office resources used by the IGUs. If there was an indication of impairment in IGU A, the recoverable amount would be compared to £55 million, not £50 million. When calculating the value in use in A, the cash flows should include an apportionment of the cash outflows for central overheads.

If it is not possible to apportion central net assets, the impairment review should be carried out in two stages – the IGU level and the company level.

Table 12.2

IGU	*A* *£m*	*B* *£m*	*C* *£m*	*Total* *£m*
Direct net assets	50	75	100	225
Central net assets				15
	50	75	100	240

In the first stage, if there was an indication of impairment in IGU A, the recoverable amount would be compared to £50 million. In the second stage, the £240 million carrying value of the company as a whole would be compared to the recoverable amount for the company as a whole.

Capitalised goodwill may be apportioned to IGUs in the same way as other central assets, as in Table 12.1 above. Alternatively, where it is not practical to allocate goodwill across the IGUs, then the two-stage procedure, as in Table 12.2, may be followed.

Table 12.3

IGU	*A* *£m*	*B* *£m*	*C* *£m*	*Goodwill* *£m*	*Total* *£m*
Carrying amount	60	80	100	50	290
Value in use	80	100	80		260

An impairment loss for IGU C is recognised of £20 million. In addition, there is an impairment loss of £30 million for the company as a whole. A further £10 million needs to be recognised and this would be written-off goodwill, reducing it to £40 million. The revised carrying values would be:

Table 12.4

IGU	*A* *£m*	*B* *£m*	*C* *£m*	*Goodwill* *£m*	*Total* *£m*
Carrying amount	60	80	80	40	260

Allocation of impairment losses

Where an IGU is impaired the carrying values of the net assets need to be reduced to their recoverable amount. If there is no obvious impairment of a specific fixed asset, the assets are to be reduced in this order:

- goodwill,
- other intangible fixed assets,
- tangible fixed assets.

However, no intangible or tangible fixed asset should be reduced below its net realisable value where this can be reliably measured.

Example 12.1

An IGU has a carrying value of £190 million. An impairment review shows that the recoverable amount is £130 million and that the intangible assets have a net realisable value of £20 million.

IGU	*Total* *£m*	*Goodwill* *£m*	*Intangible assets* *£m*	*Tangible assets* *£m*
Carrying value	190	25	45	120
Recoverable amount	130			
Impairment	60	(25)	(25)	(10)
Revised carrying value	130	0	20	110

The impairment of £60 million is allocated first to the goodwill, then to the intangible assets, but only up to their net realisable value and the remainder to the tangible fixed assets. The allocation is in a logical order as it begins with the most subjective valuation first, the goodwill, then the next most subjective, the intangible fixed asset, and finally the tangible fixed assets.

Allocation of impairment losses in merged businesses

When a business is purchased, goodwill may arise. In the acquiring company, there may be internally generated goodwill, which will not appear in its financial statements. For purposes of conducting an impairment review, however, it is necessary to value this internal goodwill. Any impairment loss will be allocated to both the purchased goodwill and the notional internal goodwill.

Example 12.2

A business is acquired and the purchased goodwill is £20 million. The value in use of the net assets in the acquiring business are £150 million and the fair values are £100 million, which implies that internally generated goodwill is £50 million.

Five years later, the carrying amount of the net tangible assets of the combined business, which is an IGU, is £105 million; the carrying value of purchased goodwill, which is being amortised over ten years, is £20 million × 5/10 = £10 million. The notional value of the internal goodwill, assuming its amortisation to be the same as the purchased goodwill, is £50 million × 5/10 = £25 million. The value in use of the IGU is £119 million.

	£m
Carrying value of tangible assets	105
Carrying amount of purchased goodwill	10
	115
Carrying amount of notional internal goodwill	25
	140
Value in use	119
Impairment	21

The impairment is first allocated to the goodwill, as explained in Example 12.1 above. The impairment has to be allocated *pro rata* between the purchased and internal goodwill at their original values, which were £20 million and £50 million respectively. Thus 2/7 of the impairment of the £21 million = £6 million is allocated to purchased goodwill, which reduces it from £10 million to £4 million. The remaining £15 million impairment loss is ignored since it relates to the internal goodwill which is itself ignored.

	£m
Carrying value of tangible assets	105
Carrying amount of purchased goodwill	4
	109

If the notional internal goodwill had been ignored, the carrying amount of the tangible assets and the purchased goodwill would be £115 million and, since the value in use is £119 million, there would be no impairment.

Thus incorporating notional internal goodwill into the computation creates an impairment, though only that fraction relating to the purchased goodwill is then written off.

The logic behind this calculation is to detect impairment in the acquired business which is being masked by the internally generated goodwill of the acquiring business. Thus under-performing assets of an acquired business are exposed and their impairment recognised.

Example 12.3

If the value in use of the combined company in Example 12.2 was £98 million, the position would be as follows:

	£m
Carrying value of tangible assets	105
Carrying amount of purchased goodwill	10
	115
Carrying amount of notional internal goodwill	25
	140
Value in use	98
Impairment	42

The impairment loss of £42 million would be allocated in the following order (as per Example 12.1):

	£m
Purchased goodwill	10
Notional internal goodwill	25
Tangible assets (the remainder)	7
	42

In this situation, had the notional goodwill been ignored, then the carrying amount of the tangible assets and the purchased goodwill would be £115 million and, since the value in use is £98 million, there would be an impairment of £17 million. This would be allocated as follows:

	£m
Purchased goodwill	10
Tangible assets (the remainder)	7
	17

Thus where value in use (£98 million) is less than the tangible assets and goodwill (£115 million) the inclusion of notional internal goodwill has no effect on which assets are written down.

Reversal of impairments

An indication that an impairment loss should be reversed would be the opposite of one of the indicators given at the beginning of this chapter that an impairment loss may have occurred.

Where an impairment loss has been recognised and subsequently the recoverable amount of the fixed asset increases, the reversal of the impairment loss should be recognised in the current period.

The reversal of the impairment losses should be recognised in the profit and loss account, unless it arises on a previously revalued fixed asset. (See below for the treatment of the reversal of impairment losses on revalued fixed assets.)

The increase in value of the previously impaired fixed asset may not exceed what the carrying amount would have been had the impairment loss not occurred. (If the fixed asset were valued at a higher amount than this carrying value, this would be a revaluation, and not the reversal of an impairment.)

The reversal of impairment losses on goodwill and intangible assets are more stringent than on tangible fixed assets. The reversal on goodwill and intangible assets should only be recognised:

- if the external event which led to the impairment loss has clearly and demonstrably been reversed;
- there has been an increase in the net realisable value of an intangible asset which has a readily ascertainable market value.

Example 12.4

An IGU consists of a production unit with the fixed assets as shown in column 1 – Carrying amount before impairment.

	Carrying amount before impairment	*Impairment*	*Reversal of impairment*
	1	*2*	*3*
	£m	*£m*	*£m*
Goodwill	40		
Patent (no market value)	20		
Tangible fixed asset	80	60	70
Total	140	60	70

If the recoverable amount of the IGU falls from £140 million to £60 million because the product it makes is obsolete there is an impairment loss of £80 million – see column 2, Impairment.

Subsequently there is a reversal of these economic circumstances because the company makes its own technological advance and the recoverable amount of the IGU is now estimated at £90 million. Supposing the carrying value of the tangible fixed assets would have been £70 million (£80 million less £10 million depreciation), if the impairment loss had not been recognised, then the value of the IGU after the reversal of the impairment loss would be as in column 3 – Reversal of impairment.

Goodwill is not restated as there has been no reversal of the original economic event which caused the impairment The old product has been replaced by a new product; a true reversal would only occur if the original product had once again become technologically acceptable.

The patent is not restated as there is no market value.

The tangible fixed assets are restated, but only up to the carrying value it would have been had the original impairment loss not been recognised.

Revalued fixed assets

Impairment losses may be categorised into two types:

1. the consumption of economic benefit – this may occur where there has been, for example, physical damage;
2. where there has been a general change in prices, for example, a slump in the property market.

Where the impairment loss on a revalued fixed assets is a result of:

1. the consumption of economic benefit, the impairment loss should be recognised in the profit and loss account;
2. a general change in prices, the impairment loss should be charged:
   - to the statement of total recognised gains and losses until the carrying amount reaches its depreciated historical cost,
   - thereafter to the profit and loss account .

Example 12.5

A fixed asset cost £4 million and has a useful life of five years with no residual value. It is depreciated on the straight line basis. At the end of year 1 and year 2 the asset had a current value of £5 million and £2 million respectively. The carrying value would be as follows:

	Historical cost	*Revaluation*
	£000	*£000*
Year 1		
Opening carrying value	4 000	4 000
Depreciation (£4m/5)	(800)	(800)
Revaluation surplus		1 800
Closing carrying value	3 200	5 000
Year 2		
Opening carrying value	3 200	5 000
Depreciation (£4m/5 : £5m/4)	(800)	(1 250)
Impairment loss	(400)	(1 750)
Closing carrying value	2 000	2 000

If the impairment loss of £1 750 million is a result of the consumption of economic benefit, the impairment loss would be charged to the profit and loss account.

In other circumstances, the impairment loss would be charged:

- £1 350 000 to the STRGL (£1 750 000 – £400 000),
- £400 000 to the profit and loss account .

A reversal of an impairment loss on a revalued fixed asset should be recognised in the profit and loss account to the extent that the original impairment loss was recognised in the profit and loss account. Any remaining balance on the reversal of the impairment loss should be recognised in the STRGL .

Income generating units and cash flows

Cash flows

Detecting an impairment loss involves comparing carrying value to recoverable amount. Recoverable amount is the higher of net realisable value and value in use, where the latter is the future cash flows discounted to a present value. Cash flows are, therefore, an essential part of ascertaining whether an impairment has occurred.

The forecast cash flows should be those of a fixed asset or an IGU. Where they are an IGU then these should include any central overheads, but exclude any cash flows relating to financing costs, for example interest on debt.

The forecast cash flows should:

- be based on underlying and supportable assumptions;
- be based on the internal budgets;
- assume a steady or declining growth rate if the cash flow extends beyond the formal budgeting period in the company. Normally, a steady or declining growth rate should be assumed after five years and the rate should not exceed the forecast long-term growth rate for the economies in which the company operates. This rate should only be exceeded where the industry is expected to grow faster than the economy as a whole and the company within that industry is expected to grow equally rapidly;
- be based on the use of the fixed asset or IGU in its current condition and future cost savings should not be anticipated. However, where the IGU consists of a new investment, such as a subsidiary, and the purchase price took into consideration future synergies with the acquiring company, then any costs and benefits expected to arise in the first year after acquisition may be included in the cash flow.

Discount rates

The discount rate used to calculate the present value of the cash flows should be commensurate with the risk attached to an equally risky investment. An appropriate discount rate could be estimated from the following three methods:

- the rate implicit in market transactions for similar assets;
- the weighted average cost of capital (wacc) of a listed company with a similar profile to the IGU;
- the wacc of the company, after allowing for the specific risk of the IGU.

The calculation of wacc is notoriously difficult. (See any book on financial management for how to find the weighted average cost of debt and equity.) Method 1 is therefore probably the easiest.

An alternative method is to adjust the cash flows for risk and then to discount at a risk-free rate such as a government bond.

The forecast cash flows should be monitored each year for the five-year period after an impairment review. If the actual cash flow is significantly less than forecast it may be necessary to replicate the calculations used in the original impairment review using the actual cash flow. If this results in an impairment loss, then this is recognised in the current period. However the assumptions underlying the cash flow forecast may be revised at the same time and if this offsets any impairment that would have been recognised had the actual and not the forecast cash flows been used, then an impairment loss should *not* be recognised.

Presentation and disclosure

Impairment losses in the profit and loss account should be included within operating profit, and disclosed as an exceptional item where appropriate. Impairment losses in the STRGL should be disclosed separately.

With regard to balance sheet disclosure:

- for assets held at historical cost, an impairment loss is added to the cumulative depreciation (i.e. it does not reduce cost);
- for assets held at current value, an impairment loss is deducted from the carrying amount;
- for assets held at depreciated replacement cost, an impairment loss:
  - charged to the profit and loss account is added to the cumulative depreciation,
  - charged to the STRGL is deducted from the carrying amount.

The following must also be disclosed:

- the discount rate used, or where a risk-free rate was used how the cash flow was adjusted for risk;
- the reason for the reversal of an impairment;
- where an impairment review of value in use is recalculated using actual rather than forecast cash flows and this would have given rise to an impairment loss had not the change in the underlying assumptions offset the loss;
- the length of the period before a steady or declining growth rate is assumed in a cash flow forecast where this exceeds five years, and the reasons for selecting this longer period;
- the long-term growth rate used where this exceeds the forecast rate for the economy in which the company operates, and the reason for this higher rate.

Conclusion

The theory behind FRS 11 is logical. It has long been recognised in the historical cost model that, where the net realisable value (nrv) of an asset is less than historical cost, then the historical cost should be departed from and nrv should be used. Whilst this concept has been applied to stock valuations it is not certain that it was as rigorously applied to other fixed assets, both tangible and intangible. In theory these fixed assets were depreciated/amortised such that their value was less than nrv but there was not a clear statement on how this should be done. FRS 11 provides a detailed policy.

Prior to FRS 11, the value of fixed assets was only required to be written down where the fall in value was considered to be permanent rather than temporary. It is not easy to judge whether a fall is temporary or permanent and many directors may have avoided writing down assets in the hope that the fall was temporary. FRS 11 considers all impairments to be permanent and this removes an element of judgement.

FRS 11 also makes a useful contribution to the long-drawn-out debate on goodwill. Those who have argued that goodwill should remain in the balance sheet indefinitely now have an opportunity to do this, provided that they carry out annual impairment tests.

As in many standards, the 'devil is in the detail' and an impairment review is complex. Whilst few would argue against the concept of recoverable amount, the calculation of nrv and particularly value in use are exceedingly difficult in practice.

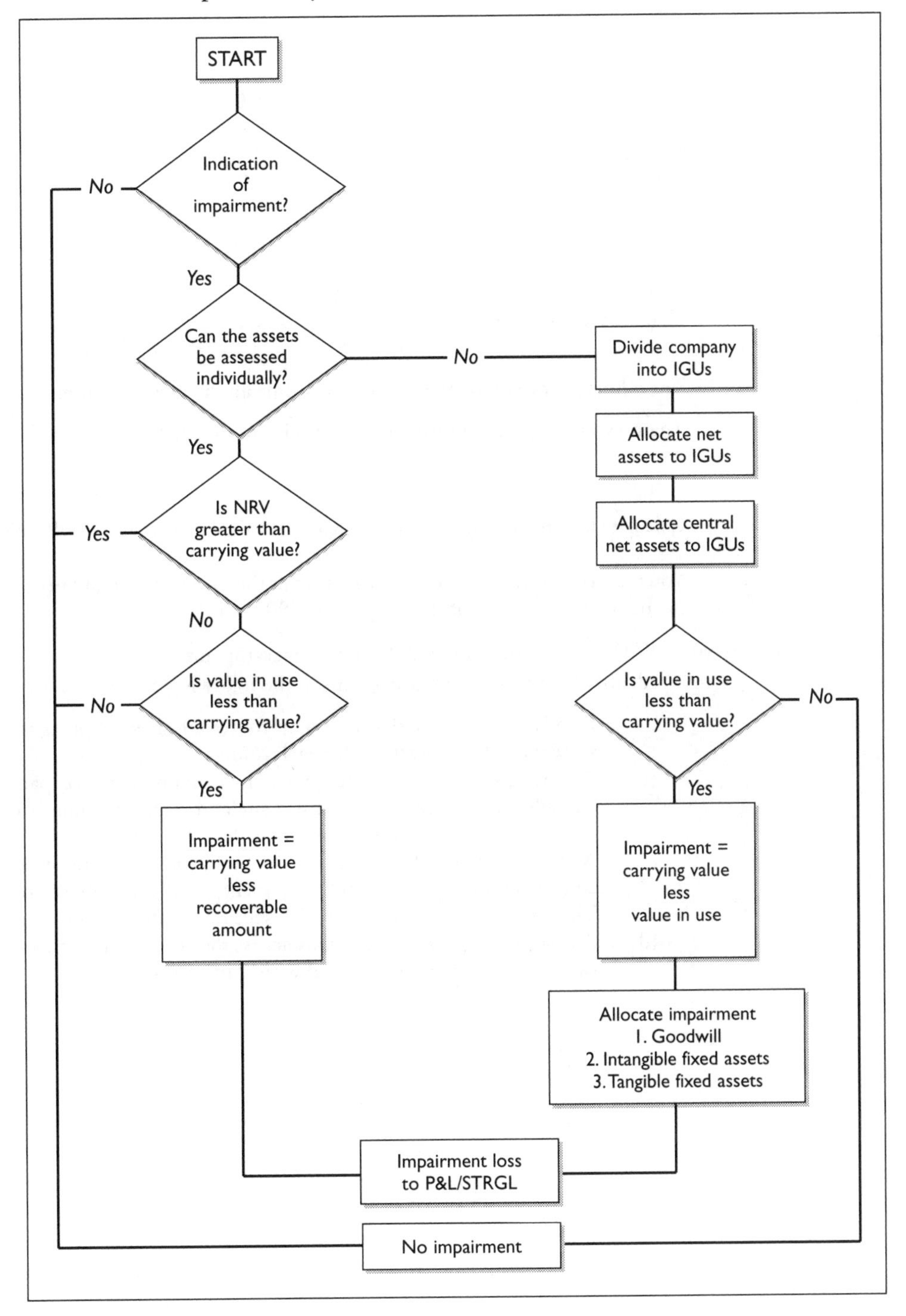

Fig. 12.1 Impairment review

Note: Goodwill and other intangible fixed assets with a life of 20 years or more require an annual impairment review. Goodwill will be part of an IGU; other intangible fixed assets may be assessed individually if recoverable amount can be calculated.

EXAMINATION PRACTICE.

12.1 Problematic plc has identified an indicator of impairment and is conducting an impairment review.

Its summarised balance sheet is:

	£000
Goodwill	600
Property	820
Plant	730
Net current assets	265
	2 415
Share capital and reserves	2 415

The whole of the company is considered to be an income generating unit.

The present value of the future cash flows is estimated at £1.2 million.

Required:

Calculate the impairment loss and prepare a revised balance sheet for Problematic plc

You may assume that net current assets are at the lower of cost and net realisable value, and the net realisable value of the property is £900 000.

12.2 (i) What is the definition of an 'income generating unit'?

(ii) Identify the income generating units in the following cases:

(a) A railway company that has main routes and feeder routes and the information system produces revenues for each route.

(b) A company that has five sites, none of which operates to capacity, but there is not enough surplus capacity to close a site and reduce the number to four sites. The company allocates production across these five sites.

(c) A company has a three-stage production process – acquisition of raw materials, conversion of materials into components, and assembly of components into finished products. The company also sells raw materials and components.

(d) A leisure group has 100 cinemas across the country. The income and net assets of each cinema can be determined with some precision.

FRS 12: Provisions, Contingent Liabilities and Contingent Assets

Introduction

The subject matter of FRS 12: Provisions, Contingent Liabilities and Contingent Assets, is one of both inherent difficulty and growing importance. The inherent difficulty is that both provisions and contingencies involve uncertainty and estimation.

To take a simple example, consider a business that inadvertently released effluent into a river. A local angling club sue the business because of depletion of fishing stocks. Both the likelihood of the company being held liable, and the amount of commercial damage involved require necessarily uncertain estimates.

The growing importance of the subject arises because:

1. Application of the 'polluter-pays' principle leads to a growing volume of environmental legislation expanding business liability.
2. Manipulation of provisions, particularly relating to restructuring costs, has been abused as a 'creative accounting' tool.

Definitions

Liabilities are 'obligations of an entity to transfer economic benefits as a result of past transactions or events'. One type of liability is a provision, being 'a liability of uncertain timing or amount'. It arises as a result of an obligating event being 'an event that creates a legal or constructive obligation that results in an entity having no realistic alternative to settling that obligation'. A legal obligation arises from a contract, legislation or other process of law. A constructive obligation arises where a pattern of practice gives rise to valid expectations that the entity accepts and will discharge some responsibility. Two circumstances where the question of a provision may need to be considered are:

1. an onerous contract, where 'the unavoidable costs of meeting the obligation under it exceed the economic benefits to be received from it';
2. restructuring, being a programme planned and controlled by management that materially changes either the scope of the business or the manner in which it is conducted.

A contingent liability is:

(a) a possible obligation that arises from past events and whose existence will be confirmed only by the occurrence of one or more uncertain future events not wholly within the entity's control; or

b) a present obligation that arises because:

   (i) it is not probable that a transfer of economic benefits will be required to settle the obligation, or
   (ii) the amount of the obligation cannot be measured with sufficient reliability.

A contingent asset is:

A possible asset that arises from past events and whose existence will be confirmed only by the occurrence of one or more uncertain future events not wholly within the entity's control.

Nature of a provision

As we have seen, the term 'provision' is defined as 'a liability of uncertain timing or amount'. This is in contrast to other liabilities:

- Trade creditors relate to goods and services received or supplied and invoiced and formally agreed with the supplier.
- Accruals relate to goods and services received but not formally invoiced. Although some degree of estimate is necessary as to the amount of accruals, the uncertainty is generally much less than for provisions.

Although a provision possesses elements of uncertainty, it is nevertheless regarded as a liability because it is 'probable' that it will materialise. This contrasts with a 'contingent liability', discussed below, where the likelihood of materialisation falls short of 'probable'.

A provision must be made when three conditions are met:

1. The entity has a present obligation as a result of a past event.
2. It is probable that a transfer of economic benefits will be required to settle the obligation.
3. A reliable estimate can be made of the amount of the obligation.

By 'probable' FRS 12 means 'it is more likely than not that a present obligation exists at the balance sheet date'.

In applying these principles a key issue is the identification of when a 'past event' has occurred. It is only when the entity has an obligation independent of the future conduct of the business that a provision arises. Examples are:

- penalty or clean-up costs for unlawful environmental damage,
- prospective decommissioning costs of an oil installation or nuclear power station.

By contrast, an intention to carry out expenditure in the future to facilitate future operations does not justify a provision. For example, if it is planned to fit smoke filters to a factory to meet new environmental requirements this is a prospective cost of future production, not a result of a 'past event'.

A change in the law may give rise to a need for a provision. For example, new environmental legislation may effectively make a business retrospectively liable for past pollution. Provision for such costs should only be made when enactment of the new law is 'virtually certain'.

Contingent liabilities

A liability will be contingent as defined above, and therefore not subject to provision, because of uncertainty.

The two elements of uncertainty, either of which can make a liability 'contingent' are:

- uncertainty as to whether the obligation will arise;
- uncertainty as to the amount of obligation. The inability to make a reliable estimate should be 'an extremely rare case'.

When reviewing a contingent liability three situations may emerge:

1. It may appear 'probable' that the obligation will be confirmed. In that case a provision should be made, and the liability ceases to be 'contingent'.
2. The possibility of any liability arising may be 'remote', in which case no disclosure is needed.
3. If the likelihood of the liability materialising falls between 'probable' and 'remote' then disclosure must be made of the nature of the contingent liability and, where practicable:
   (a) an estimate of the financial effect;
   (b) an indication of any uncertainties;
   (c) an assessment of any possibility of reimbursement.

Where an entity has joint and several liability the part expected to be met by other parties should be treated as a contingent liability.

Contingent assets

As with liabilities, an asset may be contingent and therefore not be shown in the balance sheet because of uncertainty. An example is that a company may be pursing legal action where the outcome is uncertain.

Contingent assets should be reviewed continually. Three possible conditions can arise:

1. Realisation of the asset is 'virtually certain'. In this case the asset ceases to be 'contingent'. The asset is shown in the balance sheet, and the related gain in the profit and loss account.
2. Realisation of the asset is 'probable'. In this case the item is not included in the profit and loss account or balance sheet. Instead, a note to the accounts briefly describes the nature of the contingent asset and, where practicable, gives an estimate of the financial effect. It is important not to give a misleading indication of the likelihood of any profit arising.
3. The prospects of realisation of the asset may fall short of 'probable'. In this case no disclosure is made.

Measurement

FRS 12 considers in some detail how a provision or contingent liability should be measured. In principle, the amount to be estimated is 'the amount that an entity would rationally pay to settle or transfer the obligation'. While 'caution is needed in making judgements under conditions of uncertainty' this 'does not justify the creation of excessive provisions or a deliberate understatement of liabilities'.

Estimates depend on the judgement of the entity's management, which may be supplemented by:

1. experience of similar transactions;
2. reports from independent experts;
3. post balance sheet events.

Where uncertainty involves a large population of items an 'expected value' may be found by weighting all possible outcomes by their expected probability. For example, if we have sold 100 000 items with a 5 per cent chance of guarantee work being needed at £3 per occurrence then the estimated provision would be:

$$100\ 000 \times 0.05 \times £3 = £15\ 000$$

Where a single obligation is being measured, provision is made for the best estimate of that amount.

Where provisions are likely to crystallise at some distance in time then the estimated cash outflows should be discounted to present value.

All relevant future events must be taken into account when estimating a provision. To give an example, there may be an obligation to clean up a site at the end of its life. Any reduction in clean-up costs likely to arise from developments in technology should be taken into account in making the estimate.

A situation may arise where another party is liable to reimburse the entity for the future costs being provided for. In that case the amount to be reimbursed is only taken into the accounts when receipt is 'reasonably certain', is shown as a separate asset rather than as a deduction from the related provision and is only taken into account up to the amount of the related provision.

Required disclosure of provisions

For each class of provision, disclosure is required of charges during the year, analysed into:

1. the opening and closing amount;
2. increases in, or new, provisions made in the year;
3. charges made against provisions during the year;
4. unused amounts reversed during the year;
5. charges during the year arising from the discounting process, because of the passage of time or changes in the discount rate.

Disclosure is also required of:

(i) A brief description of the nature and timing of each obligation;
(ii) An indication of the major areas of uncertainty, and the assumptions made about them;
(iii) The amount of any expected reimbursement and how it has been accounted for.

Special cases

FRS 12 reviews three special cases where consideration of a provision may arise:

1. Future operating losses do not warrant any form of provision since they do not arise from a past event. They may, however, give rise to consideration of a provision for impairment of fixed asset values.
2. Onerous contracts:

   A contract in which the unavoidable costs of meeting the obligations under it exceed the economic benefits expected to be received under it.

   The unavoidable costs will be the lower of:

(a) The excess of the cost of completing the contract over the income to be derived from it.
(b) The penalties to be incurred as a result of withdrawing from the contract.

Where such an unavoidable cost arises, consideration should be given to writing down, as an impairment loss, assets dedicated to the contract. Any remaining unavoidable cost should be recognised as a provision.

3. Restructuring is defined as:

   'A programme that is planned and controlled by management and materially changes either:

   (a) the scope of a business undertaken by an entity; or
   (b) the manner in which that business is conducted.'

A provision for restructuring costs is made only when there is an obligation to restructure. A 'constructive obligation' to restructure arises only when:

- there is a formal plan identifying issues such as the part of the business concerned, locations affected, number of employees to be affected, expenditure involved and a timetable for implementation;
- there is a valid expectation in those affected that the restructuring will take place.

Only the direct expenses of restructuring should be provided for.

Decision tree

A large part of the standard is usefully summarised as a decision tree shown in the Appendix to the Standard and reproduced here as Fig 13.1. From this we can see that:

- A provision is made where there is a present obligation, a probable consequence outflow and where a reliable estimate of the amount can be made. Inability to make such an estimate should be 'rare'.
- A contingent liability is disclosed where there is a possible obligation and the prospect of a consequent outflow is greater than remote.

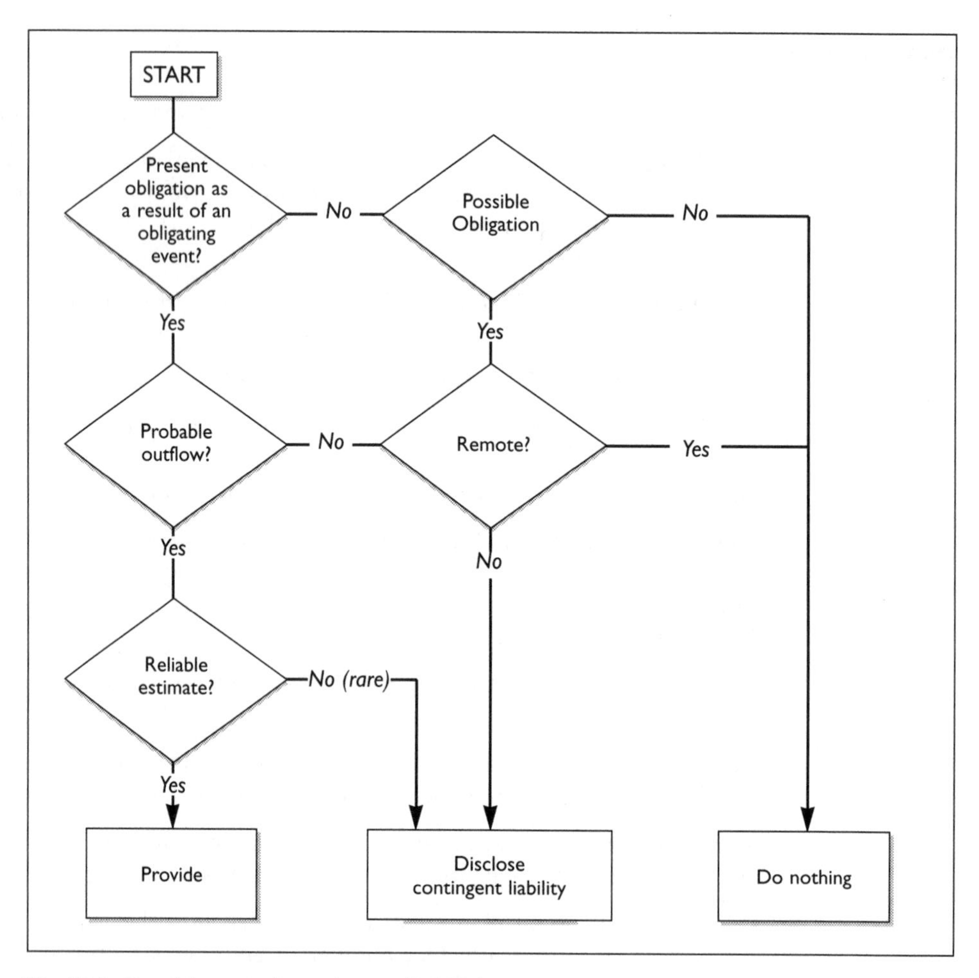

Fig. 13.1 Provisions and contingent liabilities

Conclusion

FRS 12 lays out clear guidance on the principles that should guide companies in accounting for uncertain obligations. For the analyst, scrutiny of the disclosure on movement in provisions gives a clear indication of how successfully companies have predicted uncertain outcomes in the past.

EXAMINATION PRACTICE

13.1 ABC plc has the following items to consider in the accounts for the year to 30 September 1999:

1. A claim from a customer in relation to defective goods is nearing settlement. ABC's legal advisers think it probable that a sum of some £400 000 will be paid by ABC in settlement, in addition to all legal costs.

2. ABC sells goods with a warranty. If minor defects arose in all products sold, repair costs of £2 million would arise. If major defects arose in all products sold, repair costs of £8 million would arise. ABC's experience is that 20 per cent of sales lead to claims for minor defects and 5 per cent lead to claims for major defects.
3. In July 1999 ABC relocated to a new factory. The lease on the old factory runs to 30 September 2001 at a rent of £100 000 per year. No sub-tenant can be found for the old factory.
4. A law passed in August 1999 requires the fitting of new smoke filters at a cost of £150 000 by December 1999. This work has not yet been done.
5. ABC has a provision of £150 000 brought forward at 1 October 1998 against a legal claim. In the year 1998/99 ABC won this court action so that the provision is no longer needed. However, environmental penalties of some £150 000 have been threatened by the Local Council, and it is probable that this cost will have to be paid. Accordingly it is proposed that the provision be carried forward.

You are required to explain, quantifying your answer where necessary, how you would account for each of these items in compliance with FRS 12.

13.2 Explain the points of similarity and of difference between a 'provision' and a 'contingent liability' as discussed in FRS 12, 'Provision, Contingent Liabilities and Contingent Assets'.

CHAPTER 14

FRS 13: Derivatives and Other Financial Instruments: Disclosures

Introduction

A business represents an investment to its owners. When considering an investment, there are two primary questions – what is the return and what is the risk? The risk comprises two components – the business risk and the financial risk. The business risk depends upon the goods and services supplied by the company and the market in which it operates. A pharmaceutical company, for example, engaged in cutting-edge research is inherently more risky than a retailer of food and clothes. Financial risk, at its simplest level, is measured by the gearing ratio. Thus a high-geared company has a greater financial risk than a low-geared company.

The role of the accountant/finance director has been broadened to include the management of financial risk. Financial markets have become increasingly sophisticated and as well as the traditional forms of finance, equity and debt, there have arisen highly complex forms of finance.

The ASB recognised that guidance on accounting for financial instruments and derivatives lagged behind this change in the use of financial instruments. This was a serious omission as financial instruments may have a significant impact on the financial performance, financial position and risk of a company and this was not being reflected in financial statements.

The ASB decided to tackle this topic in two stages – a standard on disclosure to be followed by a standard on recognition and measurement issues. The first issue is dealt with by FRS 13; the second issue is currently the subject of a discussion paper (see the chapter on Discussion Papers).

The key definitions are:

Financial instruments – any contract that gives rise to both a *financial asset* of one company and a *financial liability* or *equity instrument* of another company. Financial instruments include bonds, shares, debtors and creditors and *derivatives*.

> *financial asset* – cash or the right to receive cash or another financial asset,
> *financial liability* – obligation to pay cash or a financial asset to another company,
> *equity instrument* – shares or other evidence of ownership interest,
> *derivatives* – a financial instrument whose value is derived from the value of some underlying item, such as shares, bonds, foreign exchange rates and interest rates.

Capital instrument – all financial instruments which are issued by a company as a means of raising finance, for example shares and debentures. (For a full definition see the chapter on FRS 4: Capital Instruments.)

FRS 13 – detailed requirements

The objectives of FRS 13

The objectives of FRS 13 are that it should ensure that companies disclose sufficient information about their derivatives and other financial instruments to allow users to assess:

- the financial risk of a company,
- the significance of the derivatives and financial instruments to the financial performance, position and cash flows of the company.

Scope

FRS 13 applies to all companies which have a capital instrument, for example shares, quoted on a stock exchange.

Certain financial instruments are excluded from FRS 13. In general these are excluded because they are the subject of another FRS or SSAP. Thus financial instruments relating to subsidiaries, associated companies, pensions and leases are all excluded.

The standard is in three parts: Part A deals with non-financial institutions; Part B deals with banks; and Part C deals with other financial institutions, for example insurance companies. Parts B and C are considered to be beyond the scope of this book, although much of what is in Part A does apply to financial institutions.

Instruments required to be disclosed

The definition of financial instruments is drawn so widely that it includes short-term debtors and creditors. However the standard recognises that these are not normally relevant to the objectives of the FRS, and companies therefore have the option of excluding them when disclosing information about financial instruments.

The standard also has another simplification: non-equity shares, for example preference shares, are deemed to be financial liabilities. This removes the necessity for companies to categorise their non-equity shares as either equity instruments or liability instruments. However, they are disclosed separately within the financial liabilities.

The disclosure requirements of FRS 13 are in two parts:

- narrative disclosure,
- numerical disclosure.

Narrative disclosure

The standard requires the disclosure of objectives, policies and strategies with regard to the management of financial risk. The risks may be categorised into:

- credit risk – for example, non-payment by a debtor;
- liquidity risk – the inability to realise assets to meet financial liabilities when they fall due;
- cash flow risk – the fluctuation in cash flows;
- market price risk – the fluctuation in the value of financial instruments as a result of changes in interest rate, foreign exchange rates, commodity prices, shares prices, etc.

This narrative disclosure may be included in the Operating and Financial Review (see the chapter on Statements by the Accounting Standards Board). This has the advantage of placing the report on financial instruments in the wider context of the business as a whole. Thus a company which has low business risk and high financial risk will be perceived differently than one which has both high business risk and high financial risk. Alternatively, the disclosures may be in the notes to the financial statements or in the directors' report.

The narrative disclosure should include an analysis of the main reasons for holding or issuing financial instruments. Possible categories are:

- financing – as a source of finance;
- risk management or hedging – hedging occurs where the value of a financial instrument is expected to change inversely to the value of the transaction being hedged;
- trading or speculation – the purpose of trading is to make a gain from short-term changes in market prices.

Where the objectives, policies and strategies have changed from those reported previously, the reasons for the change should be given. Where there has been a change between the year end and the signing of the accounts, this should also be disclosed in accordance with SSAP 17: Accounting for Post Balance Sheet Events.

The narrative disclosure should also include commentary on the numerical disclosures (see below). The directors should explain how the numerical data are consistent with their objectives. This will not be possible if the numerical data at the year end are unrepresentative of the position during the year. If this situation occurs an explanation should be provided.

Where financial instruments are used as hedges, the details of the financial instruments and the risks being hedged should be disclosed.

Example 14.1 An example of a narrative disclosure

(The discussion set out below will usually be preceded by a general discussion of, *inter alia*, the entity's activities, structure and financing. This discussion will typically consider the financial risk profile of the entity as a whole as a prelude to the narrative disclosures required by the FRS.)

The Group's financial instruments, other than derivatives, comprise borrowings, some cash and liquid resources and various items, such as trade debtors, trade creditors, etc. that arise directly from its operations.

The Group also enters into derivatives transactions (principally interest rate swaps and forward foreign currency contracts). The purpose of such transactions is to manage the interest rate and currency risks arising from the Group's policy that no trading in financial instruments shall be undertaken.

The main risks arising from the Group's financial instruments are interest rate risk, liquidity risk and foreign currency risk. The Board reviews and agrees policies for managing each of these risks and they are summarised below. These policies have remained unchanged since the beginning of 19x0.

INTEREST RATE RISK

The Group finances its operations through a mixture of retained profits and bank borrowings. The Group borrows in the desired currencies at both fixed and floating rates of interest and then uses interest rate swaps to generate the desired interest profile and to manage the Group's exposure to interest rate fluctuations. The Group's policy is to keep between 50 per cent and 65 per cent of its borrowings at fixed rates after taking account of interest rate swaps.

LIQUIDITY RISK
As regards liquidity, the Group's policy has throughout the year been that, to ensure continuity of funding, at least 50 per cent of its borrowings should mature in more than five years. At the year end, 57 per cent of the Group's borrowings were due to mature in more than five years.

Short-term flexibility is achieved by overdraft facilities.

FOREIGN CURRENCY RISK
The Group has one significant overseas subsidiary – Foreign – which operates in the USA and whose revenues and expenses are denominated exclusively in US dollars. In order to protect the Group's sterling balance sheet from the movements in the US dollar/sterling exchange rate, the Group finances its net investment in this subsidiary by means of US dollar borrowings.

Numerical disclosures

The numerical disclosure is in eight parts:

1. interest rate risk,
2. currency risk,
3. liquidity,
4. fair value,
5. financial instruments held for trading,
6. financial instruments held for hedging,
7. commodity contracts,
8. additional discussion of the numerical disclosure (non-mandatory).

FRS 13 recommends that the numerical disclosure should be a summary rather than a detailed analysis. This will involve aggregating and offsetting the data to a greater extent than is normal in financial reporting. This may mean that it is not possible to trace the numerical data back to the financial statements, in which case FRS 13 prefers the link to be made, unless this would further complicate the information provided.

Interest rate risk

An analysis of financial liabilities and financial assets should be given, analysed by currency, showing those with fixed, variable and no interest, and the period covered. Examples are given in Tables 14.1 and 14.2.

Table 14.1 Financial liabilities (1)

Currency	*Total*	*Floating rate*	*Fixed rate*	*No interest*
	£m	*£m*	*£m*	*£m*
Sterling	415	150	250	15
US dollar	200	80	120	0
Total	615	230	370	15

Table 14.2 Financial liabilities (2)

Currency	*Floating rate*	*Fixed rate*		*No interest*
		Weighted average interest	*Weighted average period*	*Weighted average maturity period*
		%	*Years*	*Years*
Sterling	based on bank rate	10	5	2
US dollar	based on US prime rate	7	8	–
Total		–	6	2

Similar tables would be produced for financial assets.

Currency risk

An analysis of the financial instruments should be given showing the amount in each currency, analysed by reference to the functional currency of operations. This provides an analysis of the currencies which give rise to the currency gains and losses which are recognised in the profit and loss account . This will be consistent with SSAP 20: Foreign Currency Translation.

Table 14.3 Net financial assets and financial liabilities in £m

Functional currency of group	*Sterling*	*Dollar*	*Yen*	*Total*
Sterling	–	80	30	110
Dollar	40	–	50	90
Yen	50	(20)	–	30
Total	90	60	80	230

Liquidity disclosure

A profile of the financial liabilities should be given showing amounts falling due:

- less than 1 year,
- between 1 and 2 years,
- between 3 and 5 years,
- more than 5 years.

Table 14.4 Maturity of financial liabilities

	£m
Less than 1 year	100
Between 1 and 2 years	150
Between 3 and 5 years	175
More than 5 years	400
	825

An analysis of undrawn committed borrowings, i.e. finance which a lender is committed to lending but which the borrower (the company) has not requested, and the period at which the lender's obligations expire, should be given. A simple example of such an arrangement is a bank overdraft facility. The data should be analysed into:

- less than 1 year,
- between 1 and 2 years,
- more than 2 years.

Table 14.5 Borrowing facilities

	£m
Less than 1 year	50
Between 1 and 2 years	75
More than 2 years	40
	165

The analysis is only required for financial liabilities, but companies may voluntarily disclose the maturity of financial assets so that any matching of these financial instruments can be appreciated by the user.

Fair value

The company should categorise its financial assets and financial liabilities. This would normally follow the headings used in the narrative disclosure as discussed above for credit risk, liquidity risk, cash flow risk and market price risk. For each category it should disclose fair value and the balance sheet carrying value.

Fair value is defined as the amount at which an asset or liability could be exchanged under an arm's length transaction between informed and willing parties, other than in a forced or liquidation sale.

Where the carrying value is not materially different from fair value, then carrying amount may be used as fair value, and so there is no difference between the two valuations.

The method and assumptions in arriving at fair value should be disclosed.

If it is not possible to provide a fair value, then the company should disclose:

- a description of the financial instrument and its carrying amount;
- why fair value could not be measured;
- the characteristics of the financial instrument which would affect its fair value, for example cash flow.

Table 14.6 Fair values of financial assets and liabilities

	Carrying Value £ m	*Fair Value £m*
Financial instruments held to finance operations		
Short-term loan	(220)	(230)
Long-term loan	(1 000)	(1 200)
Derivative financial instruments held to manage interest/currency profile		
Interest rate swap	–	(30)
Forward foreign currency contract	–	10
Derivative financial instruments held to hedge currency exposure		
Forward foreign currency contract	–	20
Financial instruments issued for trading		
Debt securities	30	30

Financial instruments held for trading

Where a company trades in financial instruments the following should be disclosed:

- the gain or loss, analysed by type of financial instrument;
- the fair value – if this is not representative of the year as a whole, then an average position should be disclosed.

Table 14.7 Gains and losses on financial instruments held for trading

	£m
Investment in debt securities	2
FTSE futures	(1)
Forward foreign currency contract	3
	4

Financial instruments held for hedging

Financial instruments used for hedging are usually accounted for using 'hedge accounting'. In this method, gains and losses on the hedge are not recognised immediately in the profit and loss account. They are either ignored or carried forward in the balance sheet. They are recognised only when the hedged transaction occurs. Any gain or loss on the hedge is either used to adjust the carrying value of the hedged item in the balance sheet or recognised in the profit and loss account at the same time as the hedged item.

The following should be disclosed about gains and losses on financial instruments where 'hedge accounting' has been used:

- cumulative gains and losses which are unrecognised,
- cumulative gains and losses which are included in the balance sheet,
- the extent to which the gains and losses above are expected to be recognised in the profit and loss account in the next period,
- gains and losses in the profit and loss account which were either unrecognised or in the balance sheet in the prior period.

Table 14.8 Gains and loss on hedges

	Gains £m	*Losses £m*	*Total £m*
Unrecognised gains and losses at 1.1.2000	9	12	(3)
Gains and losses arising in previous years recognised in 2000	8	9	(1)
Gains and losses arising before 1.1.2000 not recognised in 2000	1	3	(2)
Gains and losses arising in 2000 not recognised in 2000	18	6	12
Unrecognised gains and losses at 31.12.2000	19	9	10
Gains and losses expected to be recognised in 2001	12	6	6
Gains and losses expected to be recognised after 2001	7	3	4
	19	9	10

Example 14.2

A company has a 30 June year end. On 1 June 1999 the directors decide to buy materials in December 1999 from a foreign supplier for $150 000. It places the order and covers the transaction with a forward purchase of $150 000 in December for £100 000. In December 1999 it receives the goods and resells them in July 2000. At 30 June 1999 '$150 000 in December' could be bought for £97 000 and in December 1999 $150 000 could be bought for £95 000.

The following disclosures would be made :

- 30 June 1999 – there is an unrecognised loss of £3 000.
- 30 June 2000 – there is a loss carried forward in the balance sheet of £5 000.
- 30 June 2001 – there is a loss in the profit and loss account of £5 000.

Commodity contracts

Commodities may be hard, such as copper, or soft, for example coffee. Where contracts for commodities are settled in cash they are treated like financial instruments.

Exemption from disclosure of commodity contracts is allowed where:

- the market in which the commodity is traded is illiquid,

- to disclose the information would be prejudicial to the company.

The non-disclosure and the reasons for the non-disclosure must be disclosed.

Market price risk

Companies are encouraged to provide a discussion which sets the numerical information in the context of the business. This is a more focused discussion than the narrative disclosure discussed above.

This discussion should include:

- the method used to manage risk, its main parameters and the underlying assumptions. If the parameters or assumptions are changed, then the reason for the change should be given and the comparative figures should be restated using the new parameters or assumptions. An example of this would be the use of sensitivity analysis;
- an explanation of the objectives of the method and its possible limitations;
- reasons for changes in reported risk compared to last year.

Example 14.3

An example of a discussion of market price risk:

MARKET PRICE RISK

The Group monitors its interest rate and currency risks and other market price risks to which it is exposed primarily through a process known as 'sensitivity analysis'.

This involves estimating the effect on profit before tax over various periods of a range of possible changes in interest rates and exchange rates.

The model used for this purpose makes various assumptions about the interrelationships between movements in interest rates and exchange rates and about the way in which such movements may impact on the economies involved. Although these assumptions are based on past experience, such experience may not be reflected in the future. Furthermore, the results of the analysis cannot be simply extrapolated to other price changes. For these reasons, the figures disclosed below need to be treated with a degree of caution.

The Group accepts a degree of interest rate risk, currency risk and other market price risk as long as the effects of various changes in rates and prices, as calculated using its sensitivity analysis model, remain within certain prescribed ranges. The figures disclosed below are well within those ranges.

On the basis of the Group's analysis, it is estimated that the maximum effect of a rise of one percentage point in one of the principal interest rates to which the Group is exposed would, after taking into account the most likely consequential impact on other interest rates and on exchange rates, be a reduction in profit before tax for 19x1 of between 1.6 per cent and 2.4 per cent and the maximum effect of a rise of three percentage points would be a reduction in profit before tax for 19x1 of between 6.5 per cent and 9.8 per cent. Similarly, it is estimated that a strengthening of sterling by 10 per cent against all the currencies in which the Group does business would generate currency losses equal to about 3 per cent of profit before tax for 19x1, whereas a 30 per cent strengthening would have generated currency losses equal to about 8.4 per cent of 19x1 profit before tax. The Group's exposure to other market price risk is not material.

Disclosure of accounting policies

In addition to the narrative and numerical disclosures required by FRS 13, SSAP 2: Disclosure of Accounting Policies requires explanations of the accounting policies used in financial statements. With respect to financial instruments this would include such matters as:

- the method used to account for derivatives and financial instruments;
- the recognition and measurement of financial instruments and associated income/expenses and gains / losses;
- the treatment of financial instruments *not* recognised, and how any provision for losses is recognised in these circumstances.

Conclusion

Accounting standards are generally about measurement, presentation and disclosure. All three issues are usually covered within a single standard.

FRS 13 is therefore unusual in that it deals only with disclosure. The issue of measurement is the subject of a Discussion Paper (see the chapter on Discussion papers). It therefore seems illogical to release a standard which only covers disclosure and not the more important and controversial issue of measurement. It may well be that, in the light of any new standard on measurement issues, FRS 13 will need to be amended.

The ASB may argue that this was an important area that needed to be tackled and could not be delayed pending the resolution of any debate on the measurement of financial instruments. FRS 13 is a recent standard to be implemented for year ends after March 1999 and time will tell whether its release, before a standard on measurement issues, was justified.

EXAMINATION PRACTICE

14.1 A company has used hedge accounting for a number of years. It made a gain of £36 000 on a hedge during the year but it did not recognise this gain as the hedged transaction had not yet occurred. However, a profit on a hedge made in a previous year of £5 000, which was not previously recognised, has been recognised, as the hedged transaction has now occurred. The company expects that 50 per cent of the unrecognised gains and losses will be recognised in the following year and 50 per cent the year after. At the beginning of the year, there were unrecognised gains of £15 000.

Required:

Prepare a suitable table for disclosure of the above information in the financial statements of the company, in accordance with FRS 13. The year end was 31 December 20X1.

14.2 (a) What are the objectives of FRS 13?

(b) What are the different types of risk identified in FRS 13?

(c) Why do you think FRS 13 requires disclosure of:

- the analysis of liabilities with fixed and floating interest rates (see Table 14.2);
- the maturity profile of financial liabilities (see Table 14.4);
- the maturity profile of undrawn borrowing facilities (see Table 14.5)?

(d) What do you consider is the importance of the narrative disclosure requirements in FRS 13?

FRS 14: Earnings per Share

Introduction

During the 1960s investors became more interested in earnings than dividend yield measures of company performance. Earnings per share (EPS) is the earnings of a company divided by the number of ordinary shares, and it has become one of the most widely used measures of performance. It is related to the price/earnings ratio, which is the market value of shares divided by the EPS. The ASB considered it necessary to have a standard on EPS so that all companies would calculate it in a consistent way. The first standard was issued in 1972 and it was revised on a number of occasions; it was finally replaced in 1998 with FRS 14.

Although the ASB issued FRS 14 it did so with a repeat of the warning it gave in FRS 3. The ASB considers that all components of a company's activities should be considered when assessing its performance. It is therefore unwise to place undue reliance on any single performance measure and thus EPS is only a starting point for the analysis of corporate performance.

FRS 14 – detailed requirements

Objective

The objective of FRS 14 is to prescribe the basis for calculating EPS and the related disclosures.

Scope

FRS 14 is mandatory for listed companies.

Basic and diluted EPS

The standard is divided into the following sections:

- *Basic EPS*
  This is the earnings divided by the ordinary shares. The number of shares may change without there being a corresponding change in the resources, for example where there is a bonus issue.

- *Diluted EPS*
  Where a company has securities which do not currently have a claim to equity earnings but may do so in the future then these additional shares will dilute the EPS. An example is convertible loan stock.

Companies are required to calculate both a basic EPS and a diluted EPS.

Basic EPS

Basic earnings per share should be calculated by dividing the net profit or loss for the period attributable to ordinary shareholders by the weighted average number of ordinary shares outstanding in the period.

The net profit or loss should be after deducting dividends and other appropriations in respect of non-equity shares, for example preference dividends (see FRS 4 for a definition of non-equity shares).

Example 15.1

EPS plc
Profit and loss account (extract)

		£000
Profit before tax		1 200
Taxation		(400)
Profit after tax		800
Minority interest		(160)
Profit for the year		640
Preference dividend	100	
Ordinary dividend	140	240
Retained profit for the year		400

Issued ordinary share capital:

1 000 000 50p ordinary shares £500 000

$$\text{EPS} = \frac{\text{Profit after minority interest and preference dividends}}{\text{Number of shares}}$$

$$= \frac{£540\ 000}{1\ 000\ 000}$$

$$= 54\text{p per share}$$

If the market value of the share is £8.10, then the price earnings (p/e) ratio is:

$$\frac{\text{market price}}{\text{EPS}} = \frac{£8.10}{54\text{p}} = 15$$

Example 15.2

Weighted average number of shares

	Issued shares	*Shares bought back*	*Balance*
1 January 20X1	12 000	–	12 000
31 March 20X1 issue of new shares for cash	4 000	–	16 000
1 July 20X1 purchase of shares for cash	–	2 000	14 000
31 December 20X1 year end balance	16 000	2 000	14 000

Weighted average

$(12\ 000 \times 3/12) + (16\ 000 \times 3/12) + (14\ 000 \times 6/12) = 14\ 000$

or

$12\ 000 + (4\ 000 \times 9/12) - (2\ 000 \times 6/12) = 14\ 000$

Changes in the number of shares without a corresponding change in resources

1. Bonus issue

In a bonus issue ordinary shares are issued to existing shareholders for no additional consideration. The number of shares therefore increases without there being an increase in resources. The EPS is calculated as if the bonus issue had occurred at the beginning of the previous corresponding period.

Example 15.3

Bonus issue

	20X1	*20X2*
Net profit 31 December	£1 600	£2 000

Ordinary shares until 30 June 20X2 500

Bonus issue 1 July 20X2: one share for every five ordinary shares held at 30 June 20X2.

Bonus $500 \times 1/5 = 100$

EPS for 20X2 $\frac{2\ 000}{(500 + 100)} = 333\text{p}$

Adjusted EPS for 20X1 $\frac{1600}{(500 + 100)} = 267\text{p}$

Since the bonus issue is without consideration, the issue is treated as if it had occurred at the earliest period reported, i.e. 1 January 20X1.

A share consolidation, which is the opposite of a bonus issue, is calculated in the same way as a bonus issue.

2. Rights issue

In a rights issue the exercise price is often less than the fair value of the shares and thus the issue includes a bonus element. The number of shares before the rights issue needs to be adjusted by the following factor:

$$\frac{\text{Fair value of current share}}{\text{Theoretical ex-rights fair value per share}}$$

The theoretical ex-rights price is found by adding the fair value of the shares prior to the rights issue to the proceeds of the rights issue and dividing by the number of shares after the rights issue. This is logical since, in theory, the value of the company cannot increase by more than the amount of cash introduced from the rights issue, and this is now divided by a greater number of shares.

Example 15.4

Rights

	20X0	*20X1*	*20X2*
Net profit as at 31 December	£40 000	£50 000	£60 000
Shares before the rights issue	200 000		

The rights issue is one share for every four held. The rights price is £2.
The rights issue takes place on 31 March 20X1.
The fair value of an ordinary share before the rights issue is £2.50.

Theoretical ex-rights value per share is:

$$\frac{\text{Fair value of current shares + Amount received from rights issue}}{\text{Number of current shares + Number of shares issued}}$$

$$\frac{(£2.50 \times 200\,000 \text{ shares}) + (£2 \times 50\,000)}{200\,000 \text{ shares} + 50\,000} = \frac{600\,000}{250\,000}$$

Theoretical ex-rights value = £2.40

Adjustment factor

$$\frac{\text{Fair value of current share}}{\text{Theoretical ex-rights value}} = \frac{£2.50}{£2.40} = 1.04$$

Earnings per share

	20X0	*20X1*	*20X2*
20X0 EPS as originally stated: £40 000 / 200 000 shares	20p		
20X0 EPS restated for rights issue: £40 000 / (200 000 shares × 1.04)	19p		

	20X0	20X1	20X2
20X1 EPS allowing for the rights issue: $\frac{£50\,000}{(200\,000 \times 1.04 \times 3/12) + (250\,000 \times 9/12)}$		21p	
20X2 EPS £60 000 / 250 000			24p

Note that the adjustment factor is used on the original number of shares. Once the rights issue has taken place, the new number of shares (in this case 250 000) is included. For 20X1 the weighted average principle is applied.

Diluted EPS

Where a company has an existing obligation to issue new shares then those who hold the option have a potential claim on the earnings of the company, with the consequence of diluting the EPS. Where the possibility of dilution arises from the existence of some form of option to subscribe for new equity shares in the future then in order to compute the diluted EPS it is necessary to calculate the effect on the number of shares in issue and, in some situations, on the earnings also.

For the purpose of calculating diluted EPS, the net profit attributable to ordinary shareholders and the weighted average number of shares outstanding should be adjusted for the effects of all dilutive potential ordinary shares. A potential ordinary share is a financial instrument or a right which entitles a holder to ordinary shares. Examples are :

1. share warrants and options which give the holder the right to purchase or subscribe for ordinary shares;
2. rights granted to employees as part of remuneration or share purchase plans;
3. rights to ordinary shares that are contingent upon certain conditions, for example the purchase of a business, or share incentive schemes;
4. debt and preference shares which are convertible to ordinary shares.

Effect on number of shares

The weighted average number of shares is calculated in the same way as for basic EPS, plus the weighted average number of ordinary shares that would be issued on the conversion of all the dilutive potential ordinary shares. Potential ordinary shares are deemed to have been converted into ordinary shares at the beginning of the period, or the date of the financial instrument giving the rights, if later.

1. Share warrants and options

A share option allows the purchase of shares at a favourable price, i.e. less than their fair value. The calculation in effect assumes that a proportion of these shares was issued for no consideration. The proportion is:

$$\text{shares under option} \times \frac{\text{exercise price}}{\text{fair value}}$$

Example 15.5

Effects of share options on diluted earnings per share

Net profit for 20X1	1 200 000
Weighted average number of ordinary shares for 20X1	8 million
Average fair value of one ordinary share	£3.00
Weighted average number of shares under option during 20X1	3 million
Exercise price for shares under option in 20X1	£2.00

	Shares	*Net profit*	*EPS*
Net profit for 20X1		1 200 000	
Weighted average shares for 20X1	8m		
Basic EPS			15p
Number of shares on option	3m		
Number of shares that would have been issued at fair value: 3m × (£2/£3)	(2m)		
Diluted EPS	9m	£1 200 000	13.3p

The net profit has not been increased because the calculation only includes shares deemed to be issued for no consideration.

2. Employee share and incentive plans

Share options are increasingly popular as incentive schemes. The schemes may take many forms, but for purposes of calculating diluted EPS there are only two basic divisions: schemes in which awards are based on performance criteria and other schemes. The former are effectively 'contingently issuable shares' and are dealt with below. The latter are considered as options. As with the share option approach, only those shares deemed to have been issued for no consideration are included. The deemed proceeds consist of the consideration from the employee, if any, and the cost of the shares calculated in accordance with UITF 17 (see the chapter on UITFs). Under UITF 17, part of the consideration consists of the future services from the employee not yet received.

Example 15.6

Share option scheme (not performance related)

A share option scheme is based on the employee's period of service with a company.

As at 31 December 20X1 the provisions of the scheme were:

Date of grant	1 January 20X1
Market price at grant date	£4.00
Exercise price of option	£1.00
Date of vesting	31 December 20X3
Number of shares under option	4 million

Under UITF 17, £1 per option (£4.00–£1.00 / 3 years) is charged to the profit and loss in each of the three years 20X1–20X3

Net profit for the year 20X1	£1 500 000
Weighted average number of ordinary shares	12 million
Average fair value of an ordinary share	£3.50

Assumed proceeds from each option		£3 (Exercise price of £1.00 plus the cost relating to future service not recognised of two years at £1 = £2. The following year would be £2 (i.e. £1 plus £1)	
	Shares	*Net profit*	*EPS*
Net profit for 20X1		£1 500 000	
Weighted average shares for 20X1	12m		
Basic EPS			12.5p
Number of shares on option	4m		
Number of shares that would have been issued at fair value: (4m × £3) / £3.50	(3.4m)		
Diluted EPS	12.6m		11.9p

3. Contingently issuable shares

These are financial instruments or rights to ordinary shares which are contingent upon the satisfaction of certain conditions. Such shares are included in the calculation of diluted EPS as of the beginning of the period, or at the time the right was granted if later. As noted above, many employee share and incentive plans operate as contingently issuable shares.

Example 15.7

Contingently issuable shares

A company has 600 000 ordinary shares in issue at 1 January 20X1.A recent business acquisition has given rise to the following contingently issuable shares.

- 20 000 ordinary shares for every new branch opened in the three years 20X1–20X3.
- 2 000 ordinary shares for every £5 000 of earnings in excess of £1 million over the three years ended 31 December 20X3.

Shares will be issued on 1 January following the period in which a condition is met.

A new branch was opened on 1 July 20X1, another on 31 March 20X2 and another on 1 October 20X3.

Reported earnings over the three years were £400 000, £500 000 and £600 000 respectively.

Basic EPS	*20X1*	*20X2*	*20X3*
	£	*£*	*£*
Earnings	400 000	500 000	600 000
Denominator			
Ordinary shares	600 000	620 000	640 000
Branch contingency (i)	10 000	15 000	5 000
Earnings contingency (ii)	–	–	–
Total shares	610 000	635 000	645 000
Basic EPS	65.6p	78.7p	93.0p

Diluted EPS	*20X1*	*20X2*	*20X3*
	£	£	£
Earnings	400 000	500 000	600 000
Denominator			
Ordinary shares in basic EPS	610 000	635 000	645 000
Additional shares:			
Branch contingency (iii)	10 000	5 000	15 000
Earnings contingency (iv)	–	–	200 000
Total shares	620 000	640 000	860 000
Diluted EPS	64.5p	78.1p	69.8p

(i) This figure is the shares due for opening a branch pro-rated over the year.

(ii) It is not certain that the earnings condition has been satisfied until after the three-year period.

(iii) The contingently issuable shares are included from the start of the period they arise so these figures are increasing the denominator to the full 20 000 shares.

(iv) This is (£1 500 000 – £1 000 000) / £5 000 × 2 000.

4. Debt and preference shares and the effect on earnings

The profit in the EPS calculation is after preference dividends and loan interest. Dilution may therefore affect earnings as well as the number of shares. This may occur:

- where preference shares are converted into ordinary shares,
- where debt is converted into ordinary shares,
- where there is any other changes in income or expenses. For example, if debt is converted into ordinary shares, profit will increase because interest is reduced, but this may increase the payments due on a profit-sharing scheme.

Example 15.8

Convertible bonds

Net profit	£200 000
Ordinary shares in issue	1 000 000
Basic EPS	20p
Convertible 10% bonds	£250 000

Each block of five bonds is convertible to ten ordinary shares. The tax rate including deferred tax is 30 per cent.

Interest expense relating to the bonds £250,000 @ 10%	=	£25 000
Tax at 30%	=	£7 500
Adjusted net profit £200 000 + £25 000 – £7 500	=	£217 500
Number of ordinary shares resulting from the bond conversion	=	500 000

Number of ordinary shares used for the diluted EPS calculation
1 000 000 + 500 000 = 1 500 000

Diluted EPS $\frac{£217\ 500}{1\ 500\ 000}$ = 14.5p

Dilutive v non-dilutive

The purpose of calculating dilutive EPS is to help users forecast EPS and warn them that the EPS may fall. However, in some circumstances the effect of potential ordinary shares may be antidilutive, i.e. EPS would rise. FRS 14 requires any antidilutive affects to be ignored. In order to distinguish between dilutive and antidilutive, it is necessary to rank each potential issue of shares from most dilutive to least dilutive. EPS is calculated after each potential issue and if the EPS increase, then that, and any subsequent potential issues, are ignored.

The profit to be used for purposes of assessing dilutive and antidilutive affects should be net profit attributable to the ordinary shareholders, less any profit attributable to discontinued operations, as defined in FRS 3. It may be necessary to allocate any interest and tax paid to the discontinued operations as FRS 3 does not require this apportionment, but it is necessary for the purposes of FRS 14. Once any antidilutive affects has been identified the EPS is calculated in the normal way.

Example 15.9

Ranking dilutive securities in the calculation of weighted average number of shares

Net profit attributable to ordinary shareholders	£15 000 000
Net profit for discontinued activities	£5 000 000
Ordinary shares outstanding	30 000 000
Average fair value of one ordinary share	£5.00

Potential ordinary shares

Options	7 million with exercise price of £4
Convertible preference shares	1 million entitled to a cumulative dividend of £6 per share. Each is convertible to 4 ordinary shares.
4% convertible bond	Nominal amount £50 million. Each £2 000 bond is convertible to 80 shares. Tax rate 30%.

The effect on earnings on conversion of potential ordinary shares

	Increase in earnings £	*Increase in ordinary shares Number*	*Earnings per share £*
Options			
Increase in earnings:	nil		
Incremental shares 7 million × (£5 – £4) / £5		1 400 000	nil
Convertible preference shares			
Increase in net profit (£6 × 1 000 000)	6 000 000		
Incremental shares (4 × 1 000 000)		4 000 000	1.50

	Increase in earnings £	*Increase in ordinary shares* Number	*Earnings per share* £
4% convertible bonds			
Increase in net profit			
£50 million × 4% × (100% – 30%)	1 400 000		
Incremental shares (£50m / £2 000 × 80)		2 000 000	70p

The potential share issues are considered from the most dilutive to the least dilutive.

	Net profit from continuing operations £	*Ordinary shares* Number	*Per share* £	
Reported	10 000 000	30 000 000	0.33	
Options	–	1 400 000		
	10 000 000	31 400 000	0.32	Dilutive
4% convertible bonds	1 400 000	2 000 000		
	11 400 000	33 400 000	0.34	Antidilutive
Convertible preference shares	6 000 000	4 000 000		
	17 400 000	37 400 000	0.46	Antidilutive

The diluted EPS is increased by both the bonds and the preference shares. These are therefore ignored in the diluted EPS calculation.

Basic EPS

Net profit	£15 000 000
Number of shares	30 000 000
Basic EPS	50p

Diluted EPS

Net profit (remains at)	£15 000 000
Number of shares	31 400 000
Diluted EPS	48p

The earnings for the purposes of ranking the dilutive shares is net profit from continuing operations only. The EPS calculation includes the amount of net profit attributable to ordinary shareholders, which includes the discontinued operations.

Restatement

Comparative figures should be restated if the number of ordinary or potential ordinary shares outstanding is changed, other than the conversion of potential ordinary shares, without a corresponding increase in resources. If this change occurs after the year end then this new number of shares should be used, and this fact disclosed.

Other share transactions after the year end which do involve resources, or the conversion of potential ordinary shares, should be disclosed; examples are the issue and purchase of shares.

Disclosure

The following should be disclosed:

- basic and diluted EPS should be presented, for each class of ordinary share with different rights, on the face of the profit and loss account. The figures should be disclosed even if the amounts are negative, i.e. a loss per share;
- the earnings figure used for both basic and diluted EPS, and a reconciliation of this figure to the profit or loss for the period;
- the weighted average number of shares used for basic and diluted EPS;
- where a company chooses to calculate an additional 'EPS' figure other than the basic and diluted EPS required by FRS 14, then it should use the same weighted average number of shares; be calculated on a consistent basis; be reconciled to the EPS figures required by FRS 14; be at least as prominent as the EPS figures required by FRS 14; and an explanation should be given as to why an additional EPS had been calculated.

It is interesting that the ASB allow disclosure of alternative 'EPS' figures; they normally wish to reduce the number of options. However, this is consistent with the ASB's view that it is unwise of users to concentrate on a single number. The ASB is therefore allowing companies to use different components of the profit and loss account to calculate alternative 'amounts per share'.

Conclusion

The previous accounting standard on EPS worked well and the ASB would probably not have made any changes to it had there not been pressure to follow international standards in this area. The changes required were fairly minor and FRS 14 has therefore proved uncontroversial. The acceptance of FRS 14 was helped by the ASB's willingness to allow companies to experiment with their own versions of 'EPS' and to present these in their financial statements.

EXAMINATION PRACTICE

15.1 A company has the following profits and share capital.

	20X0	*20X1*	*20X2*
Net profit as at 31 December	£35 000	£48 000	£62 000
Ordinary shares £1	300 000		

The following rights issue takes place:

The rights issue is one share for every six held. The rights price is £2.50.
The rights issue takes place on 31 March 20X1.
The fair value of an ordinary share before the rights issue is £3.00

You are required to calculate:
(i) the EPS and restated EPS for 20X0,
(ii) the EPS for 20X1 and 20X2.

15.2 You are required to answer the following questions in connection with FRS 14:

(a) What is the difference between basic EPS and diluted EPS, and give an example of when diluted EPS would be calculated?

(b) In what circumstances may dilution affect both the number of shares and the earnings, and give an example?

(c) What is meant by antidilutive and state the implication for calculating diluted EPS?

FRS 15: Tangible Fixed Assets

Introduction

Although tangible fixed assets are often the most contentious part of company balance sheets, there were surprisingly few standards on this topic until recently. Until the release of FRS 15 there was no standard on:

- what may be capitalised as part of the cost of a fixed asset,
- the revaluation of tangible fixed assets,
- the procedures to be followed if a company did not depreciate some of its tangible fixed assets.

FRS 15 is one of a number of standards which deal with fixed assets. Ideally there would have been one standard as this would have avoided the cross-referencing which is now necessary. The relevant standards are:

Intangible fixed assets

SSAP 13: Accounting for Research and Development,
FRS 10: Goodwill and intangible assets.

Tangible fixed assets

SSAP 19: Accounting for investment properties,
FRS 15: Tangible fixed assets.

Standards relevant to tangible fixed assets and intangible fixed assets

FRS 11: Impairment of fixed assets and goodwill,
FRS 3: Reporting financial performance. (This is relevant for the measurement and classification on the disposal of a fixed asset.)

FRS 15 – detailed requirements

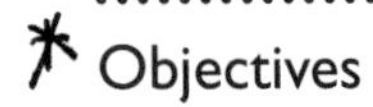

Objectives

The objectives of FRS 15 are to ensure that:

- consistent principles are applied to the initial measurement of tangible fixed assets;

- where a business has revalued tangible fixed assets, then:
  - the valuation is carried out on a consistent basis,
  - the valuation is kept up to date,
  - the gains/losses on revaluation are recognised on a consistent basis,
  - depreciation is calculated on a consistent basis,
  - there is sufficient disclosure to enable users to assess the impact of a company's accounting polices regarding tangible fixed assets on the profit and loss account and balance sheet.

Scope

The only tangible fixed assets excluded are investment properties (see the chapter on SSAP 19: Accounting for Investment Properties).

Content of FRS 15

FRS 15 is in three parts:

- initial measurement,
- valuation,
- depreciation.

Initial measurement

Cost

A tangible fixed asset should initially be measured at its cost. The cost should include all those costs which are directly attributable to bringing the asset into working condition.

The cost will be purchase price, less any trade discount. The directly attributable costs may include employee costs where appropriate, for example on the construction of a building.

Examples of directly attributable costs which may be capitalised are:

- acquisition costs, e.g. stamp duty on property and import duties;
- cost of building site preparation;
- delivery costs;
- installation costs;
- professional fees, e.g. legal, architect and engineer's fees;
- estimated costs of dismantling, removing an asset and restoring the site may be capitalised, either at the time of acquisition or subsequently if the company is obliged to do this. These costs should be recognised in accordance with FRS 12: Provisions, Contingent Liabilities and Contingent Assets.

Examples of costs which may not be capitalised:

- administration costs;
- costs in selecting a building site;
- abnormal costs, e.g. rectification of design errors and wasted materials;

- operating losses which arise because of lost revenue during the construction of a tangible fixed asset. For example, if an extension is built on a hotel and there is lost revenue because the rooms next to the extension cannot be used, the lost revenue cannot be capitalised.

Capitalisation of directly attributable costs should cease when the tangible fixed asset is ready for use, i.e. physically constructed, even if the asset has not been brought into use or met its target capacity. For example where a health club is being constructed and interest is being capitalised (see the section below on the capitalisation of finance costs) this should cease when the health club is constructed, not when it first accepts members or has hit its membership target.

Costs associated with a start-up or commissioning period should be included in the cost of a tangible fixed asset where for technical or legal reasons it is incapable of operating at normal production levels. Technical reasons might be where a machine has to be run-in and tested before it can be allowed to run at full capacity. Legal reasons might be where for health and safety reasons a tangible fixed asset may not be used to its full capacity until it has been awarded a licence, and a licence is not issued until the tangible fixed asset has been in use for some time. Such essential costs of a commissioning period should be capitalised. An example of this might be the construction of a power station or a theatre.

However, a distinction must be made between an essential commissioning period and the build-up of demand for a new venture. For example, costs relating to a start-up period where a new hotel has been fully constructed and could run at full capacity, but is operating at less than full capacity as demand builds up, cannot be capitalised.

Finance costs

FRS 15 permits the option of capitalising finance costs, such as interest. (Finance costs are defined in the chapter on FRS 4: Capital Instruments.) A company may capitalise finance costs which are directly attributable to the construction or acquisition of a tangible fixed asset and include such costs as part of the cost of that asset. If the company adopts this policy, then it must be applied consistently to all assets. For example, if a company constructs a building for itself, then the interest will be for the purchase of the materials, etc.; when a company engages a building contractor to construct a building, the interest will be for financing progress payments.

Directly attributable finance costs are those that would not have been incurred had the tangible fixed asset not been constructed / purchased. This would include:

- specific loans to finance the tangible fixed asset,
- the interest which would have been saved if the amount spent on the asset had been used to repay company debt.

The amount of interest capitalised must not exceed the interest incurred in the period.

It is more difficult to calculate the interest charge where the company has not made specific borrowings to construct an asset. In these circumstances a weighted average of interest is applied to the average of the carrying value of the asset.

Example 16.1

A company finances the construction of a tangible fixed asset from its general borrowings. The capitalised expenditure at the start of the year and at the end of each quarter is shown in row 1 of Table 16.1. The average for the year (balance brought forward and quarters 1 to 3) is £6 000.

The borrowings at the start of the year and at the end of each quarter are shown in row 2. The interest paid is shown in row 3.

The percentage of interest paid is shown in row 4 and the average for the year (balance brought forward and quarters 1 to 3) is 4 per cent. The capitalised interest for the year is therefore £240, being the average capitalised expenditure × the average percentage (£6 000 × 4%) and this is added to the capitalised expenditure at the end of the year to give a total of £13 240.

Table 16.1

	Bal b/f	*Q1*	*Q2*	*Q3*	*Average*	*Bal c/f*
Capitalised expenditure (£)	2 000	5 000	7 000	10 000	6 000	13 000
Total borrowings (£)	10 000	8 000	9 000	12 000		
Interest paid (£)	300	320	450	480		
Interest rate	3.00%	4.00%	5.00%	4.00%	4.00%	240
						13 240

The capitalisation of interest should start when:

- the finance costs are being incurred,
- expenditure on the tangible fixed asset is being incurred,
- activities to get the asset ready for use are in progress.

The activities to get the tangible fixed asset ready for use might include technical and administrative work, for example obtaining permits and the development of land. There must however be activity; where land is held, for example by a speculative builder in a land bank, there is no activity and therefore no interest should be capitalised. Where these activities are disrupted, then capitalisation of interest should be suspended until the work recommences. The reason for this is that costs incurred during a suspended period are deemed to be for merely holding partially completed assets without there being any activity.

Capitalisation of finance costs should permanently cease when the activities necessary to get the tangible fixed asset ready for use are substantially completed. Where the construction is completed in separate parts, and each separate part can be used independently of the other parts, then capitalisation should cease as each part is completed. For example, where a business park is being constructed with several buildings, each of which can be used individually, the capitalisation should cease as each building is completed. In contrast, where a factory is being built and the product passes through several processes, capitalisation does not cease as each process is completed, as the factory cannot be used until all the processes are completed.

Disclosure of capitalised finance costs

The following should be disclosed:

- the accounting policy,

- the aggregate amount of finance costs included in the cost of tangible fixed assets,
- the amount of finance costs capitalised in the period,
- the amount of finance costs recognised in the profit and loss account in the period,
- the capitalisation rate (4 per cent in Table 16.1).

Controversy over the capitalisation of interest costs

Although in general the ASB opposes choice, the capitalisation of finance costs is discretionary. Its reasons seem to be that:

- It recognises there are some difficult conceptual issues related to the capitalisation of finance costs which need to be resolved and until this is done it is unwise to make capitalisation of interest mandatory.
- In the absence of an internationally agreed approach it is unwise to insist on a method.

The arguments *for* capitalisation of interest are:

- Finance costs are just as much a cost of constructing a tangible fixed asset as other directly attributable costs.
- Capitalisation of interest ensures a consistency of treatment within a company between those assets which are self-constructed and those which are purchased. If a company had two buildings, one it purchased as a new building and the other it built itself, then since the price of the purchased building would comprise all costs to the vendor, including interest costs, it is therefore consistent to include interest costs in the self-constructed building.
- Similarly to the point above, capitalising finance costs results in consistency between different companies, as regardless of whether a tangible fixed asset was purchased or self-constructed, finance cost would be included.
- Depreciation is calculated on cost less residual value. Since residual value is based on a current value figure, which in theory includes an element for interest, then interest should also be included in the cost.
- Capitalisation of interest conforms to the concept of matching revenues and expenses.
- The financial statements are more likely to show the true success or failure of a project.

The arguments *against* capitalisation are:

- Borrowings fund an entire business rather than a specific asset and it is an unnecessary, arbitrary allocation to attempt to assign interest to a particular tangible fixed asset.
- Interest should always be regarded as a period cost; the fact that it is for a tangible fixed asset under construction should not alter this treatment. Showing interest as a period cost enables important ratios to be calculated, for example interest cover.
- Where a company has no loans, and is entirely financed by equity, the construction of a tangible fixed asset is financed by shares. Since it would be inconsistent for the same asset to have a different value depending on how it was financed, there would need to be included 'notional interest'. This presumably would either be an estimate of what interest the company would pay if it bor-

rowed, or an estimate of its cost of equity. Neither choice is attractive, and therefore it is preferable not to include any finance costs.

- It is not possible in practice to arrive at an appropriate cost of interest. The use of the actual rate on specific borrowings or a weighted average of all borrowing costs ignores the fact that as debt increases the *next* loan arranged may bear a higher interest charge, because the risk increases as the gearing increases. This will not be recognised in the capitalised interest charge.

Recoverable amount

If the amount recognised on initial measurement of a tangible fixed asset exceeds its recoverable amount, it should be written down to recoverable amount.

A tangible fixed asset needs to be reviewed for impairment on initial recognition only if there is some indication that impairment has occurred. (These factors and the impairment review are discussed in the chapter on FRS 11: Impairment of Fixed Assets and Goodwill.)

Subsequent expenditure

The issue of subsequent expenditure concerns the distinction between revenue and capital expenditure.

Subsequent expenditure which ensures that a tangible fixed asset maintains its previously assessed standard of performance, for example repairs and maintenance expenditure, is revenue expenditure and should be charged to the profit and loss account. If this expenditure was not incurred then the previously estimated life may be shortened and the residual value of the tangible fixed asset reduced. This would result in extra depreciation which would also be charged to the profit and loss account. Examples of this type of expenditure are servicing of machinery and painting of premises.

In three situations, however, subsequent expenditure should be capitalised. These are:

- Where the expenditure enhances the economic benefits beyond those previously assessed.

This may occur where a machine is upgraded by fitting improved parts; for example, if a 2000 cc vehicle engine were replaced with a 3000 cc engine.

- Where the separate components of a tangible fixed asset are being separately depreciated, and one of those parts is replaced.

This may occur, for example, where the roof, lift and central heating of a building are depreciated separately from the building itself. If one of these items was replaced, then any carrying value of the old asset would be written off and the new expenditure capitalised. Similar principles would apply to aircraft, for example, where some of its separate components would be depreciated as if they were separate assets.

Example 16.2

A machine costing £100 000 has an estimated life of ten years and no residual value. The machine includes a component which is a motor with an estimated cost of £20 000 and a life of five years. The single machine would be regarded as two assets for purposes of calculating depreciation. The machine (excluding the motor) valued at £80 000 would be depreciated over ten years, and the motor costing £20 000 would be depreciated over five years. (see UITF Abstract 23 in the chapter on UITF Abstracts.)

- Where the expenditure restores the economic benefits which have been consumed through its use and these have already been included in the depreciation charge.

This may occur where there are regular major inspections and overhauls which restore a tangible fixed asset to its former condition. An example would be a boat which periodically returns to dry-dock for inspection and refit.

Example 16.3

A boat is purchased for £100 000, with an estimated life of ten years assuming the boat is properly maintained, and no residual value. The company uses the straight line method for depreciation. The first overhaul is expected in five years time at an estimated cost of £10 000. The boat may be capitalised at £90 000 and the 'overhaul' at £10 000.

If the overhaul occurred in year 4 at a cost of £12 000, then the remaining £2 000 on the estimated sum initially capitalised (£10 000 less 4 years × £2 000) would be written off, and the £12 000 overhaul would be capitalised and written off over five years.

The boat of £90 000 would be depreciated at £9 000 p.a. over its ten year life.

Controversy over major inspections and overhauls

Before FRS 12: Provisions, Contingent Liabilities and Contingent Assets was issued, it was the practice for companies to make a provision for future overhauls and then to allocate this cost over the period to the next overhaul. This practice is not allowed under FRS 12 (see the chapter on FRS 12).

FRS 15, however, offers companies an alternative, as seen above, which is to capitalise the cost of a refit as part of the cost of the asset. This will result in a similar charge to the profit and loss account as the pre-FRS 12 position. However, the essential difference is that it is not a provision but relates to expenditure that has been incurred, although the cost of the first overhaul will have to be estimated.

The capitalisation of inspections and overhauls as a separate part of the cost of an asset is similar to the capitalisation of the separate components of an asset. There are, however, important differences. The inspection may result in a certificate that, for example, the boat is seaworthy and this has the characteristics of an intangible rather than a tangible fixed asset. It is somewhat artificial to analyse a single fixed asset into parts which are not separable and have no value.

Although FRS 15 allows the capitalisation of refits, it does state that the decision to identify future expenditure on overhauls over a shorter period than the related asset should reflect:

- that the period of between overhauls is substantially different from the life of the asset itself;
- the degree of irregularity of the amount of the expenditure, i.e. the need to smooth out any fluctuations in expenditure;
- materiality to the financial statements as a whole.

Valuation

The revaluation of tangible fixed assets is discretionary. Although many commentators believe that the ASB is intent on moving to a form of current value accounting, this is not (yet) the case.

Where a company chooses to revalue its tangible fixed assets, then:

- All tangible fixed assets of the same class should be revalued.

This requirement prevents companies from 'cherry-picking' and just revaluing those assets which have increased in value and ignoring those which have fallen in value.

- Not all classes of tangible fixed assets need to be revalued.

This allows a company, for example, to revalue all (or none) of its buildings without having to revalue its plant and machinery.

- Where the policy is to revalue a class of assets, then the carrying amount in the balance sheet should be its current value, and this will be achieved by frequent revaluations.

Frequency

Property

In the case of property, there should be a full valuation every five years and an interim valuation in year three. More frequent interim valuations should only be undertaken where it is likely a material change in value has occurred.

As an alternative to a full valuation every five years, a five-year rolling programme may be adopted. This will only be appropriate where the properties are non-specialised and of a similar nature. It will be necessary to divide the properties into five groups of similar size. Interim reviews within rolling programmes would only be necessary where it is likely a material change in value has occurred.

A full valuation must be carried out by a qualified valuer, who may be either internal or external to the company. Where the valuer is internal, the work must be reviewed by an external valuer.

An interim valuation must be carried out by a qualified valuer, but there is no requirement for a review where the valuer is internal.

Other tangible fixed assets

Where there is an active second-hand market, or reliable indices, then:

- the directors themselves may value tangible fixed assets (other than properties),
- the valuation must be done annually.

Where there is no second-hand market or reliable index, the same procedures for properties apply.

Valuation basis

Property

FRS 15 refers to two valuation bases; these are 'existing use value' (EUV) and 'open market value' (OMV). These are terms used by the Royal Institution of Chartered Surveyors (RICS) and is based on their manual for valuing properties. The essential difference is that the EUV assumes that the property can only be used for its existing use in the foreseeable future.

A distinction is also made between specialised and non-specialised properties. Specialised buildings are normally sold for a continuation of their existing use as part of the sale of the business as a whole. Examples are power stations, museums, universities and hospitals. Demand for such properties is limited.

Non-specialised properties can be used for their existing or similar use and there is generally an active market . Examples are shops and offices.

The rules for valuation are:

- specialised properties should be valued at depreciated replacement cost;
- non-specialised properties should be valued at EUV, with a note to the accounts if OMV is materially different;
- properties surplus to requirements should be valued at OMV

Other tangible fixed assets

These are valued at market value, being the amount for which the asset could be sold. Where this value is not obtainable, depreciated replacement cost is used.

Gains and losses on revaluation

Gains

These are recognised in the profit and loss account and the statement of total recognised gains and losses (STRGL) according to the circumstances.

Example 16.4

A company bought an asset at the beginning of 2002 for £120 000. The estimated useful life was ten years and estimated residual value nil. Depreciation is on a straight line basis.

At the beginning of 2005 the asset is revalued at £105 000.

The financial statements would show:

Performance statements

	2004	*2005*
	£	*£*
Profit and loss account 120 000/10	(12 000)	
Profit and loss account 105 000/7		(15 000)
STRGL	–	21 000
Balance sheet		
Fixed asset	120 000	105 000
Provision for depreciation £12 000 × 3 years	(36 000)	
Provision for depreciation £105 000 / 7 years		(15 000)
Book value/carrying value	84 000	90 000

	2004	*2005*
	£	*£*
Revaluation reserve	–	18 000
Profit and loss reserve – depreciation	(12 000)	(15 000)
Profit and loss reserve – transfer from revaluation reserve		3 000

The £21 000 is transferred from the STRGL to the revaluation reserve as an unrealised gain. However, this unrealised gain may be transferred to the profit and loss account reserve as a realised gain over the life of the asset. Thus £21 000 / 7 = £3 000 will be transferred annually.

In the first three years of the asset's life, £12 000 × 3 = £ 36 000 depreciation was charged to the profit and loss account. It might be thought that since the asset is now valued at £105 000 the asset has only lost £15 000 in value (£120 000 less £105 000) and that the difference of £21 000 (£36 000 less £15 000) could be credited back to the profit and loss account. FRS 15, however, regards this as a change in value and not an adjustment to the economic benefit consumed, and must therefore be credited to the STRGL.

However, where revaluation losses have previously been recorded in the profit and loss account, and these are reversed by revaluation gains, then these should be recognised in the profit and loss account. This gain is reduced by the additional depreciation that would have been charged had the asset not been reduced in value. This effectively restores the position to where it would have been had there been no loss and subsequent gain.

Losses

Revaluation losses caused by the consumption of economic benefits are charged to the profit and loss account.

Other losses are recognised in the STRGL until the carrying value reaches its depreciated historical cost, and then it is charged to the profit and loss account.

There is an exception to this rule, which is that where the recoverable amount is greater than the revalued amount, then the loss may be recognised in the STRGL until such time as the revalued amount is equal to the recoverable amount. When the revalued amount falls below recoverable amount, then the loss is charged to the profit and loss account.

The reasoning behind this is that, whilst recoverable amount exceeds the valuation, any changes are valuation adjustments and should properly be included in the STRGL; once recoverable amount falls below the valuation, this is an impairment and should be recorded in the profit and loss account.

Example 16.5

A company buys a property for £1 million, with an estimated life of ten years and no residual value. It uses straight line depreciation.

The following valuations are obtained:

	End year 1	*End year 2*
Valuation	£1 080 000	£700 000
Recoverable amount	£1 200 000	£760 000

The accounting treatment would be as follows:

	Year 1
	£000
Opening book amount	1 000
Depreciation 1/10	100
Depreciated book amount	900
Revaluation gains/losses	
• STRGL	180
• P&L a/c	–
	1 080

Since there has been no previous recognised losses, the whole of the gain of £180 000 is recognised in the STRGL. The property is valued at the valuation figure since this is the lower of the valuation of £1 080 000 and the recoverable amount of £1 200 000.

	Year 2
	£000
Opening book amount	1 080
Depreciation – nine years remaining 1/9	120
Depreciated book amount	960
Valuation	700
Loss	260

Initially, the difference between the carrying value and depreciated historical cost would be recognised in the STRGL i.e. £960 000 less (£1 000 000 × 8/10) = £160 000 and the remaining £100 000 in the profit and loss account. However, since the recoverable amount exceeds the valuation (£760 000 less £700 000) then a further £60 000 may be recognised in the STRGL, making a total of £160 000 + £60 000 = £220 000. The profit and loss account is charged with the remaining £40 000.

Thus

	Year 2
	£000
Opening book amount	1 080
Depreciation – 9 years remaining 1/9	120
Depreciated book amount	960
STRGL	(220)
P&L a/c	(40)
Closing book amount	700

Extracts from the financial statements would be as follows:

	Year 1	*Year 2*
Profit and loss account		
Depreciation	(100)	(120)
Impairment		(40)
Statement of recognised gains and losses		
Surplus/(deficit) on revaluation	180	(220)

	Year 1	*Year 2*
Fixed assets		
Cost or valuation at beginning of year	1 000	1 080
Surplus/(deficit) on revaluation	80	(380)
Cost or valuation at end of year	1 080	700
Depreciation at beginning of year	nil	nil
Charge for year	100	120
Depreciation written back on revaluation	(100)	(120)
Depreciation at end of year	nil	nil
Net book value	1 080	700
Revaluation reserve		
At beginning of year	nil	180
Surplus / (deficit) on revaluation	180	(220)
At end of year	180	(40)

These figures may be explained as follows. The total loss is £1 000 000 – £ 700 000 = £300 000. Of this, £260 000 is in the profit and loss account, which is the depreciation of £220 000 and the further loss of the difference between depreciated historical cost and recoverable amount (£800 000 – £760 000 = £40 000). The remaining loss of £40 000 is in the STRGL.

Gains and losses on disposal

The profit or loss on the disposal of a tangible fixed asset should be accounted for in the profit and loss account in the period in which it is sold, being the difference between the proceeds and the carrying amount. This profit or loss is shown in accordance with FRS 3 (see the chapter on FRS 3: Reporting Financial Performance).

Controversy over reporting gains and losses on disposal

The treatment of gains and losses on disposal is inconsistent with the gains and losses on revaluation. A revaluation gain is recognised in the STRGL but a subsequent gain on disposal is recognised in the profit and loss account. The previous FRED on Tangible Fixed Assets had a solution to this problem which was to revalue assets to their disposal value at the time of sale – the so-called 'death-bed' valuations. This had the effect that there was no gain or loss on disposal and all of the gain was a revaluation which was recognised in the STRGL.

FRS 15 did not adopt this practice, for the following reasons:

- FRS 3 is being reviewed and it was felt that such changes should not be made until FRS 3 was amended (see the chapter on Discussion Papers and 'Reporting Financial Performance')
- where assets are held at historical cost, profits/losses on disposal represent over/under depreciation and these are included in the profit and loss account. It

was therefore considered to be consistent if profits/losses on revalued assets should also be recorded in the profit and loss account.

There is also a conceptual problem with the capital maintenance concept which underlies FRS 15. FRS 15 defines current value as the lower of replacement cost and recoverable amount, where recoverable amount is the higher of value in use and net realisable value. This is the 'value to the business' model which is a feature of current cost accounting. However, in current cost accounting, holding gains are credited to a capital maintenance reserve to maintain the physical (operating capability) capital of the business, and are not credited to a performance statement, whether this be the profit and loss account or the STRGL.

Disclosure

Where a class of tangible fixed assets has been revalued, the following should be disclosed:

- name and qualifications of the valuers, and whether they are internal or external to the business,
- basis of valuation,
- date and amounts of valuation,
- the depreciated historical cost value,
- a statement that interim valuations have not been carried out where this is the case,
- the date of the last full valuation.

Depreciation

Depreciation is defined as :

> The measure of the cost or revalued amount of the economic benefits of the tangible fixed asset that have been consumed during the period. Consumption includes the wearing out, using up or other reduction in the useful economic life of a tangible fixed asset whether arising from use, effluxion of time or obsolescence through either changes in technology or demand for the goods and services produced by the asset.

The depreciable amount of a tangible fixed asset should be allocated on a systematic basis over its useful economic life. The depreciation method should reflect the pattern of its consumption. The depreciation charge should be included as an expense in the profit and loss account.

The fundamental objective of depreciation is to reflect in operating profit the cost of the economic benefits of the tangible fixed asset consumed in the period. This is applicable regardless of whether the asset has risen in value. Where a tangible fixed asset has been revalued the depreciation charge is calculated on the carrying value and the remaining life.

FRS 15 recognises two methods of allocating depreciation – straight line and reducing balance. Straight line assumes that there is an equal amount of consumption of the economic benefits of the tangible fixed asset each year. Reducing balance assumes that the benefits consumed in earlier years are greater than those in later years. This may occur where a machine is more liable to break down as it becomes older or the quality of its production deteriorates. However, straight line is normally adopted unless there are good reasons for choosing reducing balance. Companies may change methods only if this results in a fairer presentation of its financial statements.

FRS 15 replaced SSAP 12: Accounting for Depreciation. One of the reasons for the new standard was the non-compliance by many companies with the requirement to depreciate property. A number of companies, prior to FRS 15, argued that:

- Increases in value meant there was no consumption and therefore depreciation was unnecessary. They argued that since the residual value was increasing and was at least equal to carrying value there was no need for depreciation.

FRS 15 rejects these arguments and makes it quite clear that property has a finite life and must therefore be depreciated. (An exception is investment properties – see the chapter on SSAP 19: Accounting for Investment Properties).

- Other companies argued that the amount they spent on repairs maintained the carrying value of the asset and to record depreciation as well would be double-counting.

FRS 15 makes it quite clear that subsequent expenditure to ensure a tangible fixed asset delivers its economic benefits does not remove the necessity for depreciation. In certain circumstances this subsequent expenditure may be capitalised (see above) but it must also be depreciated.

Tangible fixed assets (with the exception of land) should be reviewed for impairment (as per FRS 11) when:

- There has been no depreciation charge, on the grounds that it was immaterial. This may occur because:
  - there is a long estimated remaining life;
  - residual value is not materially different from carrying value. It should be noted that residual value should be based on prices prevailing when the asset was acquired, or revalued, and not current values.

The materiality is judged at the aggregate as well as the individual asset level. For example, depreciation on a single property may not be material, but if a company has 100 properties, then in aggregate the depreciation charge may be material.

High residual values may occur:

  - where the amount spent on repair maintains the previously assessed standard of performance of the asset;
  - the asset is unlikely to suffer from obsolescence;
  - the company normally sells assets before the end of their lives and there is no evidence that the amounts received have been significantly less than carrying value, i.e. there have been no losses on disposal;
- The remaining life of the asset exceeds 50 years.

A consequence of FRS 15 is that many companies who did not previously depreciate buildings, and who could continue with non-depreciation, either on the grounds of immateriality or life exceeding 50 years, will probably choose to depreciate rather than have to do an annual impairment review. Impairment reviews are complex and may result in one-off large charges to the profit and loss account; a steady depreciation charge over 50 years will seem the better option.

The life of a tangible fixed asset and its residual value should be reviewed annually and if changes are made to either life or residual value, the depreciation charge should be revised.

Example 16.6

The cost of a tangible fixed asset is £120 and the estimated residual value and life was valued at £20 and ten years respectively. The depreciation would be as shown in Table 16.2 row (a).

If after three years the further life was estimated at only five years, the question arises as how to account for this:

(b) immediate write off;
(c) recalculate the depreciation charge as if it had been known in year 1 that the life would only be eight years, and take the back-log adjustment to the current profit and loss account;
(d) reallocate the net book value at the time of reassessment over the remaining life.

Each of these methods is illustrated in Table 16.2.

Table 16.2

Year	*1*	*2*	*3*	*4*	*5*	*6*	*7*	*8*	*9*	*10*	*Total*
(a) Depreciation	10	10	10	10	10	10	10	10	10	10	100
(b) Depreciation	10	10	10	30	10	10	10	10			100
(c) Depreciation	10	10	10	20	12.50	12.50	12.50	12.50			100
(d) Depreciation	10	10	10	14	14	14	14	14			100

(a) Depreciation – assumes allocation over full ten years
(b) Depreciation – anticipated depreciation charge in years 9 and 10 (£10 + £10) written off in year 4
(c) Depreciation – £100/8 = £12.5, with back-log (three years at (£12.5 – £10) in year 4
(d) Depreciation – net book value end year 3 of (£120 – £30) less residual value £20 = £70 written off over five years

Method (d) is the favoured approach as it has a smoother effect on the income statement. A similar computation, and conclusion, would be reached if the estimated residual value was estimated at less than £20 in year 3.

Renewals accounting

Prior to FRS 15, infrastructure assets of certain public utilities, for example water companies, were not depreciated. It was argued that the amount spent on maintenance removed the necessity of depreciation. This was a similar argument to that of commercial companies, for example for hotels and public houses. However, the ASB recognised this as an issue for public utilities and allowed renewals accounting as a solution to the problem.

Where an infrastructure has definable tangible fixed assets, they are accounted for in accordance with FRS 15. However, for all other assets, for example water mains, they may be accounted for using renewals accounting, providing:

- the infrastructure asset is a system that operates as a whole to a defined service level;
- the level of annual expenditure required to maintain the service level is set out in an asset management plan which is certified by a qualified and independent person;
- the system is in steady state, neither expanding or contracting.

Under renewals accounting, the level of annual expenditure required to maintain the system is deemed to be the depreciation charge. This is charged to the profit and loss account and deducted from the carrying value. The actual expenditure on maintaining the system is capitalised as part of the cost of the asset and added to the carrying value. The carrying value of that part of the infrastructure asset which is replaced or restored by the subsequent expenditure should be eliminated.

Disclosure

The following should be disclosed:

- the depreciation method used;
- useful economic lives, or depreciation rate;
- total depreciation charge for the period;
- the effect of a change in life or residual value;
- a schedule of opening and closing values for cost/revalued amount, cumulative provisions for depreciation/impairment, and carrying amount, with a reconciliation of the movement analysed between additions, disposals, revaluations, depreciation, impairment losses and impairment losses written back;
- the reason and the effect of a change in depreciation method.

It should be noted that, where a tangible fixed asset is revalued, the cumulative depreciation is normally eliminated. However, where the valuation is calculated on depreciated replacement cost, both the revalued amount and the depreciation provision are restated so that their net carrying value equals the valuation.

Transitional arrangements

Where a business elects not to adopt a policy of revaluation as set out in FRS 15, but it has revalued fixed assets in the past prior to FRS 15, it may either:

- 'Freeze' the existing valuations, and disclose that the valuations have not been updated, and give the date of the last revaluation.
- Restate the carrying amounts to historical cost, less deprecation on historical cost.

Conclusion

FRS 15 was a long overdue standard and to a large extent it has codified good practice and is therefore to be welcomed. It has tackled, for example, the issues of:

- **out-of-date revaluations,**
- **valuations on selected assets,**

- 'split-level' depreciation, whereby companies would revalue assets and charge the depreciation on the historical cost element to the profit and loss account and on the revalued element to the STRGL.

However, there are a number of issues which are still not satisfactorily resolved.

- FRS 15 allows a choice on the capitalisation of interest. It would have been better if FRS 15 had a positive view and either allowed or disallowed it.
- The treatment of subsequent expenditure and the ability to capitalise a portion of the cost of a tangible fixed asset as a future overhaul expense is theoretically weak. It looks as if the controversy surrounding FRS 12 has had an impact on the ASB and they have allowed this in order to give an alternative to those companies which can no longer make provisions for overhaul expenditure.
- FRS 15 may need to be revised when any amendments have been made to FRS 3. It was perhaps unfortunate that FRS 15 was released whilst the ASB were considering how to measure performance, and this may lead to changes soon after companies, and analysts, have learnt its requirements.
- There is no mention in FRS 15 of investment properties. Given that FRS 15 is so clear on the necessity of depreciating property, and one of the major reasons for issuing the standard was the non-compliance with SSAP 12, it is disappointing that FRS 15 does not make the case for why investment properties should be exempt.
- FRS 15 develops the reporting of tangible fixed assets, regardless of whether they are at historical cost or current value. However, there are weaknesses in the modified historical cost model and it has been argued that there should be a mandatory requirement for large / listed companies to revalue non-specialised properties where these account for more than 20 per cent of gross assets.
- The transitional arrangements allow a company which has previously revalued tangible fixed assets but no longer wishes to do so to freeze the current carrying value. Although the ASB are clearly in favour of current values, the requirements which apply when a policy of current value is adopted may seem so onerous to many companies that many will revert back to historical cost. This is ironic and it is the opposite of what the ASB had hoped would happen. Thus three categories of valuation will exist – historical cost, current market value and out-of-date valuation.

EXAMINATION PRACTICE

16.1 A company buys a property for £2 million, with an estimated life of ten years and no residual value. It uses straight line depreciation.
The following valuations are obtained:

	End year 1	*End year 2*
Valuation	£2 160 000	£1 500 000
Recoverable amount	£2 200 000	£1 550 000

You are required to show how this property should be accounted for in the financial statements, showing all your workings for years 1 and 2.

16.2 In connection with the initial measurement of tangible fixed assets:

(a) A property company acquires land, subsequently builds property and then lets out the property. When should the company start to capitalise interest and when should it stop?

(b) A public house opens in February and it does not achieve its target turnover until March. Could the costs incurred between February and March be capitalised as part of the start-up costs?

(c) A boat is constructed for pleasure cruises on a river, but it is not granted a licence to operate until it has undergone sea trials. Could the costs incurred between the boat being completed and the licence being granted be capitalised?

(d) An aircraft is purchased for £700 000, with an estimated life of seven years assuming the plane is properly maintained, and no residual value. The company uses the straight line method. The first overhaul is expected in four years time at an estimated cost of £14 000. Show two methods by which the company could account for the aircraft.

CHAPTER 17

FRS 16: Current Tax

Introduction

FRS 16: Current Tax replaced SSAP 8: The Treatment of Taxation under the Imputation System in the Accounts of Companies.

FRS 16 deals with current taxation which is the tax payable, or recoverable, in respect of an accounting period. (This is in contrast to FRED 19 which deals with deferred taxation, which relates to a number of periods – see the chapter on FREDs.)

FRS 16 was introduced because of changes in the tax system, notably restrictions on the reclaimability of tax credits and the abolition of ACT. However, it should be noted that these changes did not of themselves necessitate a new standard. FRS 16 represents a change in principle to the old SSAP 8.

The basic problem

The basic problem concerns dividends received. Dividends received from UK companies are received with a tax credit; dividends received from overseas companies are usually received net, after the deduction of a withholding tax. The distinction between a tax credit and withholding tax is fundamental to the accounting treatment in FRS 16.

A tax credit is the tax attributable to the recipient of a UK dividend, and arises because the dividend is paid out of income which has already been taxed. The rate of tax credit is set by tax legislation. On the other hand, a withholding tax is the tax deducted from dividends on behalf of the recipient and is paid over to the tax collecting authority by the company paying the dividend.

There are three possibilities:

1. 'Gross up' all dividends received, regardless of whether they have tax credits or withholding tax, so that the dividends are shown gross, with the related tax shown in the tax charge. The argument for this approach is that the tax and the income should not be offset; the income is better shown gross, and the tax included with the other tax that a company pays. (This was the treatment in SSAP 8.)
2. All dividends received should be shown at the net amount received. The argument for this approach is that given that there are different tax systems around the world, it is more consistent if all dividends received are shown net.
3. Dividends received with a tax credit are not grossed up; dividends received net of a withholding tax are grossed up. The argument for this approach is that

there is a fundamental difference between a tax credit and withholding tax, and this should be reflected in a different accounting treatment. It is argued that tax credits are notional, and should therefore be ignored, but that withholding tax is real and should be accounted for.

The ASB has opted for the latter method – number 3 above.

FRS 16 – detailed requirements

FRS 16 requires:

- Dividends received with a UK tax credit should be shown 'net'; overseas dividends which have suffered withholding tax should be shown gross, with the withholding tax included in the tax charge.
- Outgoing dividends should be accounted for in the same way as dividends received.
- Tax relating to items in the profit and loss account should be shown in the profit and loss account; tax relating to items in the statement of total recognised gains and losses should be shown in that statement.
- Other income and expenses subject to non-standard rates of tax should be included at the amount actually received or paid, without any notional tax adjustment to reflect that the rate of tax for that particular transaction is different from that of the other transactions.
- That if the rate of corporation tax is not known, then the existing rate should be used. However, if legislation setting a new rate is 'substantively enacted', then that new rate may be used.

Disclosure

The following should be disclosed separately in the profit and loss account and STRGL:

- UK tax – showing estimated tax, adjustments for prior periods and double taxation relief.
- foreign tax – showing estimated tax and adjustments for prior periods.

An example is given in Table 17.1 below.

Table 17.1

	£000	£000
UK corporation tax		
Current tax on income for period	50	
Adjustments in respect of prior periods	75	
	125	
Double taxation relief	(30)	
		95
Foreign Tax		
Current tax on income for period	40	
Adjustments in respect of prior periods	60	

	£000	£000
		100
Tax on profit on ordinary activities		195

Conclusion

In the main, FRS 16 codifies best practice and the standard has therefore proved uncontroversial. The only exception perhaps is the distinction FRS makes between a tax credit and a withholding tax and whether such income should be 'grossed up'.

EXAMINATION PRACTICE

17.1 You are required to answer the following questions in connection with FRS 16.

(a) A company receives two dividends as follows:
dividend received from a UK company of £1 000; tax credit £111
dividend received from an overseas company of £1 000 ; withholding tax £111
What is the total income from dividends in the profit and loss account?

(b) A company has a tax charge relating to profit of £500 000; it also has a tax charge relating to an item in the STRGL of £100 000. In which financial statement should these tax charges be presented?

(c) A company wishes to raise finance. Bank A offers a loan; Bank B offered to subscribe for preference shares in the company (so-called 'preference share lending'). Bank A would receive interest and Bank B preference dividends and these are taxed in a different way. Should an adjustment be made in the profit and loss account of Bank B to reflect any notional tax ?

(d) At the year end of T Ltd the rate of corporation tax is 30 per cent. However a bill has passed through the House of Commons and is currently with the House of Lords proposing to change the corporation tax rate to 28 per cent. What rate of corporation tax should be used when preparing the year-end accounts?

CHAPTER 18

SSAP 2: Disclosure of Accounting Policies

Introduction

One of the methods by which the 'Statement of Intent' on accounting standards in the 1970s proposed to advance accounting standards was by recommending disclosure of accounting bases used in arriving at the amount attributed to significant items depending on judgements of value or estimates of future events. SSAP 2 issued in November 1971 can be seen as an attempt to ensure such disclosure.

The terminology of SSAP 2 is frequently used in other accounting standards.

Summary of the statement

Definitions

A number of terms, such as accounting *principles, practices, rules, conventions, methods* and *procedures* have in the past been treated as interchangeable. For the purposes of SSAP 2 a distinction has been made between three terms:

(a) *Fundamental accounting concepts* are 'the broad basic assumptions which underlie the periodic financial accounts of business enterprises'.

(b) *Accounting bases* are 'the methods developed for applying fundamental accounting concepts to financial transactions and items, for the purpose of financial accounts. Such methods are necessary:
   (i) to decide in which periods revenue and expenditure should be brought into the profit and loss account;
   (ii) to decide the amounts at which material items should be shown in the balance sheet'.

(c) *Accounting policies* are 'the specific accounting bases selected and consistently followed by a business enterprise'. Management should select those accounting policies which are believed to be appropriate to the circumstances of the business and best suited to present fairly the results and financial position.

The statement specifically identifies four fundamental accounting concepts as having *general acceptability*. These are defined as follows:

(a) *The going concern concept*, that 'the enterprise will continue in operational existence for the foreseeable future. This means in particular that the profit and loss account and balance sheet assume no intention or necessity to liquidate or curtail significantly the scale of operation'.

(b) *The accruals concept*, that 'revenue and costs are accrued (that is, recognised as they are earned or incurred, not as money is received or paid), matched with one another so far as their relationship can be established or justifiably assumed, and dealt with in the profit and loss account of the period to which they relate; the accruals concept implies revenue and profit dealt with in the profit and loss account will be matched with related costs and expenses where these are material and identifiable'.

(c) *The consistency concept*, that 'there is consistency of accounting treatment of like items within each accounting period and from one period to the next'.

(d) *The prudence concept*, that 'revenue and profits are not anticipated, but are recognised by inclusion in the profit and loss account only when realised in the form either of cash or of other assets the ultimate cash realisation of which can be assessed with reasonable certainty; provision is made for all known liabilities (expenses and losses) whether the amount of these is known with certainty or is a best estimate in the light of the information available'.

While the statement says that the relative importance of these four concepts will 'vary according to the circumstances of the particular case', it is made clear that where the accruals concept is inconsistent with the prudence concept the latter should prevail.

Required practice and disclosure

The basic requirement laid down in SSAP 2 is that there should be disclosure in the accounts of the accounting policies followed for dealing with items 'judged material or critical in determining profit or loss for the year and in stating the financial position'. The explanations given should be 'clear, fair, and as brief as possible'. There is also a requirement that where the accounts are based on assumptions which depart from the four fundamental concepts the facts should be explained. It follows that, unless there is a clear statement to the contrary, there is a presumption that the four fundamental concepts have been observed.

The fundamental concepts

SSAP 2 does not claim to lay down a conceptual foundation on which to erect the accounting standards programme. The statement lays down that:

> It is not the purpose of this statement to develop a basic theory of accounting. An exhaustive theoretical approach would take an entirely different form and would include, for instance, many more propositions than the four fundamental concepts referred to here. It is, however, expedient to recognise them as working assumptions having general acceptance at the present time.

Altogether academic writers on accountancy have contrived to list more than 150 accounting concepts. The list given in SSAP 2 is only a selection of particularly important concepts which it can be assumed will always apply. However, the treatment decided on in SSAPs is often explained and justified by reference to SSAP 2; for example, the first paragraph of SSAP 13: Accounting for Research and Development discusses the application of the *accruals* and *prudence* concepts to the subject matter of the statement.

Accounting policies

SSAP 2 requires that explanations of accounting policies should be 'clear, fair, and as brief as possible'. There is no specific requirement in the statement that information on accounting policies should be disclosed as one note to the accounts rather than in individual notes under the relevant headings, but in practice most companies show an *accounting policies* statement attached, or as a note, to the accounts. SSAP 2 lists a number of topics for which different accounting bases are recognised as follows:

(a) depreciation;
(b) treatment of intangibles such as research and development, patents and trade marks;
(c) stocks and work in progress;
(d) long-term contracts;
(e) deferred taxation;
(f) hire purchase, leasing, and rental transactions;
(g) conversion of foreign currencies;
(h) repairs and renewals;
(i) consolidation policies;
(j) property development transactions;
(k) warranties for products or services.

Most of these are now covered by individual FRSs or SSAPs or exposure drafts. Clearly the list is not exhaustive.

There are a number of disclosure requirements laid down by the Companies Acts which are now normally complied with by inclusion in the statement of accounting policies, such as the method of calculating turnover and the basis of the computation of tax liability.

For further developments, see FRED 21: Accounting Policies in the chapter on FREDs.

EXAMINATION PRACTICE

18.1 Defining the terms

Define the terms:

(a) fundamental accounting concepts;
(b) accounting bases;
(c) accounting policies.

18.2 Understanding the concepts

List and define the four fundamental accounting concepts, and explain in what order of priority they rank.

18.3 Accounting bases

List four significant matters for which different accounting bases are recognised, and give two examples of a different accounting base for each.

18.4 Accounting policies

Draft an 'accounting policies' note for a limited company covering five different items.

CHAPTER 19

SSAP 4: The Accounting Treatment of Government Grants

Introduction

Successive governments have produced a variety of different grant schemes to encourage specific aspects of industrial activity. The appropriate accounting treatment has not always been obvious – in the late 1960s the English and Scottish Institutes contrived to publish opposing recommendations on the topic. Following the Industry Act 1972 this was an obvious area for the ASC to tackle.

SSAP 4 was issued in April 1974. A revised version was issued in July 1990 to allow for changes in types of grant and in company law.

Summary of the statement

Definitions

Government grants are 'assistance by government in the form of cash or transfers of assets to an enterprise in return for past or future compliance with certain conditions relating to the operating activities of the enterprise'. Government includes government and inter-governmental agencies and similar bodies whether local, national or international.

The original SSAP 4 divided government grants between *revenue-based* grants linked to revenue expenditure and *capital-based* grants linked to capital expenditure. The revised SSAP 4 drops this distinction, preferring a more flexible statement that 'in the absence of persuasive evidence to the contrary, government grants should be assumed to contribute towards the expenditure that is the basis for their payment'.

Required practice

The key issue to be addressed is that of when government grants should be credited to profit and loss. A grant should not be recognised until:

(a) conditions for its receipt have been complied with;
(b) there is reasonable assurance that the grant will be received.

Once these conditions are met then grants should be credited to profit and loss so as to match them with related expenditure.

Thus:

(a) grants made to reimburse costs previously incurred, or to give immediate assistance to the business, are recognised as income in the year when they become receivable;
(b) grants made to finance the general activities of the enterprise over a specific period should be credited to profit in that same period;
(c) where grants are made to contribute towards specific expenditure on fixed assets they should be credited to profit and loss over the expected useful lives of the related assets.

In principle, SSAP 4 recognises two ways of achieving the objective of crediting grants to profit over the life of the related assets as in (c) above:

(a) The objective can be met by setting off the amount of the grant against the cost of the acquisition of the asset. The effect of this method is that the depreciation charge in each year will be based on the net cost of the asset and the grant will effectively be credited to profit and loss over the period that the asset is depreciated.

    While recognising this method *in principal*, SSAP 4 points out that counsel's opinion argues that this is not acceptable under the Companies Act 1985.
(b) The objective can also be met by treating the amount of the grant as a deferred credit and transferring a portion to revenue in each period of the asset's expected useful life. In this case the amount of the deferred credit should be shown separately in the balance sheet if material and must not be shown as part of the shareholders' funds.

Potential liabilities to repay grants in specified circumstances should only be provided for if repayment is *probable*. Such potential liabilities may require disclosure in line with FRS 12: Provisions, Contingent Liabilities and Contingent Assets.

Disclosure

Disclosure should include:

(a) the accounting policy adopted for grants;
(b) the effects of government grants on the accounts;
(c) where the enterprise receives material government assistance in a form other than grants the nature of the assistance should be disclosed, with an estimate of the financial effects if possible.

Practical application

Recording in the accounts

SSAP 4 considers bookkeeping methods for crediting a capital-based grant to revenue over the life of an asset. The two methods will be illustrated with the simple example of a company buying a machine costing £5 000 on 1 April 19X3 on which a grant of 20 per cent is received. Assuming that the plant is written off evenly over a period of four years and that the company makes up its accounts to 31 March the machine will be recorded in the books as follows:

(a) If the company's accounting policy is to reduce the cost of the asset by the amount of the grant:

Plant Account

		£			£
1.4.X3	Bank (cost of machine)	5 000	1.4.X3	Bank (grant rec'd)	1 000
31.3.X4	Depreciation c/f	1 000	31.3.X4	Profit and loss (depreciation)	1 000
			31.3.X4	Cost c/f	4 000
		6 000			6 000
1.4.X4	Cost b/f	4 000	1.4.X4	Depreciation b/f	1 000
31.3.X5	Depreciation c/f	2 000	31.3.X5	Profit and loss (depreciation)	1 000
			31.3.X5	Cost c/f	4 000
		6 000			6 000
1.4.X5	Cost b/f	4 000	1.4.X5	Depreciation b/f	2 000
31.3.X6	Depreciation c/f	3 000	31.3.X6	Profit and loss (depreciation)	1 000
			31.3.X6	Cost c/f	4 000
		7 000			7 000
1.4.X6	Cost b/f	4 000	1.4.X6	Depreciation b/f	3 000
31.3.X7	Depreciation c/f	4 000	31.3.X7	Profit and loss (depreciation)	1 000
			31.3.X7	Cost c/f	4 000
		8 000			8 000

Balance sheet extracts

Fixed assets	*31.3.X4*	*31.3.X5*	*31.3.X6*	*31.3.X7*
Plant:				
Cost	4 000	4 000	4 000	4 000
Depreciation	1 000	2 000	3 000	4 000
Written down value	3 000	2 000	1 000	—

(b) If the company's accounting policy is to treat the amount of the grant as a deferred credit, a proportion being transferred to revenue annually, see next page:

Plant Account

		£			£
1.4.X3	Bank (cost of machine)	5 000	31.3.X4	Profit and loss	
31.3.X4	Depreciation c/f	1 250		(depreciation)	1 250
			31.3.X4	Cost c/f	5 000
		6 250			6 250
1.4.X4	Cost b/f	5 000	1.4.X4	Depreciation b/f	1 250
31.3.X5	Depreciation c/f	2 500	31.3.X5	Profit and loss	
				(depreciation)	1 250
			31.3.X5	Cost c/f	5 000
		7 500			7 500
1.4.X5	Cost b/f	5 000	1.4.X5	Depreciation b/f	2 250
31.3.X6	Depreciation c/f	3 750	31.3.X6	Profit and loss	
				(depreciation)	1 250
			31.3.X6	Cost c/f	5 000
		8 750			500
1.4.X6	Cost b/f	5 000	1.4.X6	Depreciation b/f	3 750
31.3.X7	Depreciation c/f	5 000	31.3.X7	Profit and loss	
				(depreciation)	1 250
			31.3.X7	Cost c/f	5 000
		10 000			10 000

Investment Grant Account

		£			£
31.3.X4	Profit and loss	250	1.4.X3	Bank (grant received)	1 000
31.3.X4	C/f	750			
		1 000			1 000
31.3.X5	Profit and loss	250	1.4.X4	B/f	750
31.3.X5	C/f	500			
		750			750
31.3.X6	Profit and loss	250	1.4.X5	B/f	500
31.3.X6	C/f	250			
		500			500
31.3.X7	Profit and loss	250	1.4.X6	B/f	250

Balance sheet extracts

Fixed assets	*31.3.X4*	*31.3.X5*	*31.3.X6*	*31.3.X7*
Plant:				
Cost	5 000	5 000	5 000	5 000
Depreciation	1 250	2 500	3 750	5 000
Written down value	3 750	2 500	1 250	—
Deferred liabilities:				
Investment grant				
deferred credit	750	500	250	—

The original exposure draft on the accounting treatment of government grants, ED 9, would have required the second of these two methods, crediting the grant to a deferred credit account, to be used. Arguments in favour of this approach include:

(a) assets acquired at different times and locations are recorded on a uniform basis, leading to greater comparability;
(b) accounting controls on the ordering, construction and maintenance of assets will be based on the gross value;
(c) where an estimate of grant receivable made in one year requires an amendment on receipt of the grant in a subsequent year the necessary adjustment can be made more easily.

The principal argument in favour of the alternative approach, of crediting the amount of the grant to the relevant asset account, is its simplicity, in that by means of the reduced depreciation charge the grant is automatically credited to revenue over the life of the asset.

The legal position

The Companies Act 1985 includes provision that:

(a) the amount to be included in the balance sheet in respect of any fixed asset shall be its purchase price or production cost (Sch 4, para 17);
(b) the purchase price of an asset shall be determined by adding to the actual price paid any expenses incidental to its acquisition (Sch 4, para 26.1).

The CCAB has received counsel's opinion that the combined effect of these provisions is to rule out the setting off of a grant against the cost of a fixed asset. However, this method does continue to be acceptable for any enterprise not covered by company law.

EXAMINATION PRACTICE

19.1 Accounting for grants

On 1 January 19X4 Labrador Ltd purchased an item of plant costing £100 000 with an estimated useful life of five years and no residual value. An investment grant of £20 000 was received relating to this asset on 31 January 19X4. Labrador Ltd makes up its accounts to 31 December.

(a) You are required to show, for the year ended 31 December 19X4, the entries in the books of account and the entries in the balance sheet relating to this item of plant under both methods considered by SSAP 4.

(b) Discuss the relative merits of the two methods and explain, with reasons, which method is not permitted under company law.

CHAPTER 20

SSAP 5: Accounting for Value Added Tax

Introduction

Background

Value added tax (VAT) was introduced in the UK on 1 April 1973. The main implications for the accountant related to adaptations to the bookkeeping system needed in order to meet the requirements of the Customs and Excise and to enable registered businesses to complete their quarterly VAT returns. Indeed because the VAT system obliged small businesses to maintain detailed and up-to-date records of their transactions one benefit was to make the life of the small practitioner specialising in incomplete records considerably easier! The appropriate accounting treatment of VAT is generally self-evident from an understanding of the principles and workings of the system. SSAP 5, therefore, is not a controversial or complex statement. The ASC issued SSAP 5 in April 1974 with application to accounting periods starting on or after 1 January 1974, and so contrived to establish standard practice at an early stage.

Nature of VAT

The decision to introduce value added tax into the UK was taken at the time of the UK's application to join the then EEC, and brought the UK into line with other member states of the EEC. A proportion of VAT receipts is set aside as part of the income of the Community, and the principles of coverage (but not the rate of tax) have been harmonised throughout the EC.

If we imagine a transaction in a standard rated product, assuming a VAT rate of 15 per cent:

	Selling price	*VAT*	*Paid to Customs and Excise*
	£	£	£
A Ltd, a producer of raw materials, sells £100 worth to B Ltd, a manufacturer	100	15.00	
A Ltd pays over output tax			15.00
B Ltd, the manufacturer, produces a widget with the raw materials and sells it to C Ltd, a wholesaler	200	30.00	

	Selling price	VAT	Paid to Customs and Excise
	£	£	£
A Ltd pays output tax – input tax (30 – 15)			15.00
C Ltd sells the widget to D Ltd, a retailer	250	37.50	
C Ltd pays output tax – input tax (37.50 – 30)			7.50
D Ltd sells the widget to John Smith, an accountancy student who has heard a lot about widgets and has always wanted to own one	300	45.00	
D Ltd pays output tax – input tax (45 – 37.50)			7.50
Total VAT paid			45.00

John Smith, the individual customer, pays £345 for his widget to D Ltd; of this £300 is the purchase consideration due to D Ltd and £45 is the value added tax collected by D Ltd and paid over to the Customs and Excise. Customs and Excise have collected their £45 in four stages, on each occasion when the product has changed hands. Each of the four companies involved has acted as a collector of the tax, paying over to the Customs and Excise tax they have collected (output tax) after deducting tax they have borne themselves.

There are currently two rates of VAT, 'zero rate' of 0 per cent and 'standard rate' of 17.5 per cent. The total amount of tax collected by the Customs and Excise will depend on the rate applicable to the transaction entered into with the final customer; a registered business will be able to recover input tax relating to its purchases even if its sales are 'zero-rated' so that an amount is repaid to the business by the Customs and Excise. A registered business cannot reclaim input tax on motor cars used in the business or expenditure on business entertainment (other than of overseas customers) so that the burden of this 'non-deductible' input tax falls on the business itself.

Certain types of supply are 'exempt', in that the business is not required to charge VAT on goods and services it supplies but is not able to recover input tax on its own purchases; thus in this case the business itself is the final consumer and VAT on purchases is part of their cost. A complication arises in relation to businesses whose trade is part taxable and part exempt; such 'partially exempt' businesses may only recover a part of their input tax.

Summary of the statement

General principles

SSAP 5 is based on the view that the accounting treatment of VAT should reflect the role of the business as a *collector* of tax, VAT being, as we have already seen, 'a tax on the supply of goods and services which is eventually borne by the final consumer but collected at each stage of the production and distribution chain'. Thus VAT will not be included in income and expenditure except where the business itself bears the tax. The provisions of SSAP 5 cover two areas:

(a) accounting for the normal situation where the business acts as a collector of VAT;

(b) accounting for the position where the business bears the cost of VAT.

The collection of VAT

SSAP 5 provides that turnover shown in the profit and loss account should exclude the related VAT. If the company wishes to show gross turnover as well, the related VAT should be shown as a deduction in arriving at turnover exclusive of VAT.

The net amount due to or from the Customs and Excise in respect of VAT should be shown as part of debtors or creditors and will not normally require separate disclosure.

SSAP 5 provided guidance on appropriate disclosure during the transitional period, when comparative figures for sales in the accounts covering the period prior to the introduction of VAT might include purchase tax. The statement suggested that to provide comparability both the net and the gross figures be shown for each period.

VAT borne by the business

Where VAT paid on goods and services acquired by the business is not recoverable, either because the business is *exempt* or because input tax on those specific goods and services is *non-deductible*, then VAT forms part of the cost of those goods and services and should be accounted for accordingly. Specifically irrecoverable VAT allocatable to fixed assets and to other items separately identified in the published accounts should be included in cost where 'practicable and material'.

A practical problem does arise in the case of the partially exempt business where, normally, the proportion of input tax disallowed will be equal to the proportion of sales which are exempt. Where the financial and VAT accounting periods do not coincide it may be necessary to make an estimate of irrecoverable VAT for the year. Having found the proportion of input tax which is irrecoverable that amount should be allocated over the cost of the related goods and services, if material.

SSAP 5 and the examiner

It is difficult to envisage a situation when a question on accounting would be totally devoted to VAT. The subject is only likely to arise as part of a *published accounts* or *tax in accounts* question, when it is important to remember the principles of SSAP 5.

EXAMINATION PRACTICE

20.1 VAT and turnover

Should the turnover figure shown in a set of published accounts include VAT?

20.2 VAT and fixed assets

Should the amount at which additions to fixed assets is stated in a limited company's published accounts include or exclude VAT?

CHAPTER 21

SSAP 9: Stocks and Long-term Contracts

Introduction

In practice no area of accounting has produced wider differences than the valuation put on stock and work in progress in the financial accounts. SSAP 9 was issued with the following objectives:

(a) to narrow the areas of difference and variation in accounting practice on stock and work in progress; and
(b) to ensure adequate disclosure in the accounts.

The problems involved in laying down a coherent set of rules which will cover the practical problems of stock valuation in all kinds of trading activity, and in all kinds of accounting systems, are very considerable. SSAP 9 is made up of a fairly brief set of principles laying down a wide-ranging set of requirements relating to accounting practice and disclosure, together with extensive guidance given in the explanatory notes and appendices relating to the practical problems of complying with the standard.

Summary of the statement

Definitions

The definition of terms in SSAP 9 is particularly important because of the technical detail they contain; many companies had to change their accounting policies in order to come into line with these definitions.

The term *stocks and work in progress* is defined in terms of its component parts, which are listed as goods purchased for resale, consumable stores, materials purchased for manufacture into products for sale, products and services in the course of completion and finished goods. The following terms are important in valuing stock:

(a) *Cost* is defined as the expenditure 'incurred in the normal course of business in bringing the product or service to its present location and condition'. The statement specifically lays down that this expenditure includes both the *cost of purchase*, defined as the purchase price including such items as import duties and handling costs and deducting such items as trade discounts and rebates, and the *cost of conversion*, defined as comprising direct costs, *production overheads*, and any other attributable overheads. *Production overheads* are defined as those incurred in respect of materials, labour and services for production, based on the normal level of activity. It is therefore necessary to classify each overhead as to function, such as production, selling or administration, so as to include in the cost of stock all overheads relating to production, including depreciation.

(b) *Net realisable value* is defined as estimated selling price less all costs to completion and all costs relating to sale of the product.

The following terms are important in valuing long-term contract work in progress:

(a) *Long-term contract:* a contract entered into for the design, manufacture or construction of a single substantial asset or the provision of a service (or of a combination of assets or services which together constitute a single project) where the time taken substantially to complete the contract is such that the contract activity falls into different accounting periods. A contract that is required to be accounted for as long-term by this accounting standard will usually extend for a period exceeding one year. However, a duration exceeding one year is not an essential feature of a long-term contract. Some contracts with a shorter duration than one year should be accounted for as long-term contracts if they are sufficiently material to the activity of the period that not to record turnover and attributable profit would lead to a distortion of the period's turnover and results such that the financial statements would not give a true and fair view, provided that the policy is applied consistently within the reporting entity and from year to year.

(b) *Attributable profit:* that part of the total profit currently estimated to arise over the duration of the contract, after allowing for estimated remedial and maintenance costs and increases in costs so far as not recoverable under the terms of the contract, that fairly reflects the profit attributable to that part of the work performed at the accounting date. (There can be no attributable profit until the profitable outcome of the contract can be assessed with reasonable certainty.)

(c) *Foreseeable losses:* losses which are currently estimated to arise over the duration of the contract (after allowing for estimated remedial and maintenance costs and increases in costs so far as not recoverable under the terms of the contract). This estimate is required irrespective of:
   (i) whether or not work has yet commenced on such contracts;
   (ii) the proportion of work carried out at the accounting date;
   (iii) the amount of profits expected to arise on other contracts.

(d) *Payments on account:* all amounts received and receivable at the accounting date in respect of contracts in progress.

Stock

SSAP 9 requires that stock and work in progress, other than long-term contract work in progress, should be valued at the total of the lower of the cost and the net realisable value of each individual item or, where this is impractical, of each group of individual items. The statement specifically rejects the idea of taking the lower of the total of cost and the total of net realisable value on the grounds that this could result in setting off foreseeable losses on items with a net realisable value lower than cost against unrealised profits on items where cost is less than net realisable value. A summary in the notes to the accounts should show the amounts of stock held in each of the main categories.

Long-term contracts

For long-term contracts an assessment must be made on a contract-by-contract basis. In the profit and loss account turnover and related costs relating to each contract should be recorded as the contract activity progresses. Where it is considered that the outcome of a long-term contract can be assessed with reasonable certainty before its conclusion, then *attributable profit* should be recognised in the profit and loss account as the difference between the reported turnover and related costs for that contract.

The following balance sheet treatment of long-term contracts is required:

(a) If recorded turnover is in excess of payments received on account then the excess is disclosed separately within debtors as *amounts recoverable on contracts*.

(b) If payments received on account exceed related turnover and related long-term contract balances the excess is disclosed separately within creditors as payments on account.

(c) The long-term contract costs less:
   (i) amounts transferred to cost of sales; and
   (ii) foreseeable losses and payments on account not matched with turnover should be shown as *stocks*.

   The balance sheet note should identify separately:
   (i) net cost less foreseeable losses; and
   (ii) applicable payments on account.

(d) If the provision or accrual for the foreseeable losses exceeds the cost incurred (after transfer to cost of sales) the excess should be included within either provisions for liabilities and charges or creditors as appropriate.

Accounting policies

The accounting policies that have been applied to stock and long-term contracts should be stated and applied consistently. In particular the methods of ascertaining turnover and attributable profit must be disclosed.

Practical problems

Types of problem

The basic principles to be applied in placing a value on stock and work in progress are laid down by the SSAP and by the accompanying definitions of terms. While these principles are in themselves quite straightforward, there can be considerable practical difficulties in their application; many of these difficulties will arise from circumstances relevant to particular types of business or will depend on the nature of the company's accounting system. The practical difficulties of application are dealt with in some detail in the appendices to SSAP 9.

Ascertaining cost

As we have seen, the definition of *cost* in SSAP 9 requires that an appropriate portion of related production overheads should be added to the direct costs of stock, in order to reflect the expense of bringing the product 'to its present location and conditions'.

Where the company needs to exercise prudence in valuing stock and work in progress this should be taken into account in arriving at the net realisable value, not by excluding from cost selected overheads.

Overheads should be allocated on the basis of function (e.g. production, marketing or selling) rather than according to whether the overhead arises from usage or on a time basis; therefore it will be necessary to exercise judgement in allocating overhead expenses to specific units of production. General management expenses are not directly related to production and therefore should not be included in the cost of stock, but in a small organisation where management responsibility may cover a number of functions including production it may be necessary to allocate management costs accordingly. Where a business has service departments it will be necessary to allocate these costs in proportion to the use made of them by the main functions of the business. For example, the accounting department might serve the production function by paying production wages and salaries and operating the purchase ledger function, the marketing function by paying sales staff salaries and controlling the sales ledger, and the general administrative function by the preparation of annual accounts and financial information for management purposes – in such a case only the costs of servicing the production function will be included in the *cost of conversion.*

There is an exception to the rule that only production overheads should be included in the *cost of conversion:* where there is a specific contract to supply goods and services then overheads relating to design and the selling expenses related to the contract may also be included, while in the case of a long-term contract interest payments on borrowings specifically related to financing the work may also be carried forward as part of the cost. These circumstances should be rare in practice, and where non-production overheads are carried forward in the stock figure the accounting policy should be disclosed and explained.

When including overheads in the cost of stock and work in progress, allocations should be made on the basis of the normal level of activity, and abnormal costs should be excluded. There are a number of reasons why a factory might, during a period, run at less than its full capacity. For example, there may be stoppages due to industrial action, or there may be reduced production during the starting up, closing down, or reorganisation of a production line. In these cases indirect production expenses will remain constant, and if allocated over the reduced quantity of production would result in increased costs being carried forward in the stock valuation. The rule is that the cost of unused capacity should be written off in the year incurred, and costs carried forward should be based on the normal level of production. For example, supposing a factory with a capacity for producing a million corkscrews a year only produces 500 000 during one year because of industrial action, there are direct costs of £1 per corkscrew and overheads of £400 000, and stock at the year end is 250 000 corkscrews. If the total costs of the year were evenly spread over actual production then stock would be valued as follows:

	£
250 000 × £1 direct costs	250 000
$\frac{250\,000}{500\,000}$ × £400 000 overheads	200 000
Cost including *conversion cost*	£450 000

Whereas based on the normal level of activity:

	£
250 000 × £1 direct costs	250 000
$\frac{250\ 000}{1\ 000\ 000}$ × £400 000 overheads	100 000
Cost including *conversion cost*	£350 000

If costs were allocated on the basis of actual production we would have carried forward in the stock valuation £100 000 of costs which in fact arose not from producing that stock but from the failure during the year to achieve normal production; clearly this is unacceptable.

The practical problems of actually allocating cost will depend on the company's own costing system. Where a standard costing system is in operation, the variance accounts should be examined and, where substantial variances are shown, it may be necessary to adjust the stock value accordingly. Where a marginal costing system is used it will be necessary to calculate the appropriate portion of production overheads to add on to the direct costs of stock for the purposes of the financial accounts.

Normally a number of identical items will have been purchased or manufactured over a period of time, and there will be a problem in relating cost to specific stock items. Methods used include FIFO, LIFO, base stock, average cost and replacement cost. The appendix to SSAP 9 rejects LIFO, base stock and replacement cost but makes no recommendation on which of the other methods should be applied. In practice LIFO is rarely used in the UK, except for companies with USA subsidiaries where, for tax reasons, LIFO is a commonly used method.

SSAP 9 refers to the method used by some companies, particularly retail stores, of estimating the cost of stock by deducting from the sales value the gross profit percentage. While acknowledging that in some circumstances this may be the only practical method of finding a cost figure, the statement advises that it is only acceptable where it can be demonstrated that this method does give a reasonable approximation to actual cost.

Net realisable value

The net realisable value of stock is the amount which will be realised from the disposal of stock less all costs to complete the product and costs of marketing, selling and distribution. The principal situations in which net realisable value may be lower than cost are:

(a) obsolescence of stock, through technical or marketing developments;
(b) physical deterioration of stock;
(c) excessive or overpriced stockholdings arising from errors in production or purchasing;
(d) a fall in the market price of stock;
(e) a deliberate management decision to sell goods at a loss for marketing purposes.

The first three items can be linked to such factors as age, movements in the past and forecast movements, and companies may have standard formulae for making provisions against stock values based on age and movement analysis of stock. While such formulae will be helpful in establishing a consistent policy, it is still necessary to review any provision in case other circumstances apply. Where stocks of spares are held for resale then it may be possible to predict obsolescence by reference to the number of units sold to which the spares are applicable. In forecasting net realisable value, events occurring between the balance sheet date and completion of the accounts need to be considered.

SSAP 9 specifically rejects reduction to estimated replacement cost when this is lower than cost and net realisable value, on the grounds that the object of a provision against cost is to achieve a breakeven position, not to create profits for the future. However, the statement acknowledges that in some circumstances replacement cost will constitute the best guide to realisable value.

Comparison of cost and net realisable value

The comparison of cost and net realisable value needs to be made in respect of each item of stock separately. Where this is impractical it may be necessary to take groups of similar items together. Thus supposing a garage has the following stocks:

	Cost	*NRV*	*Lower of cost and NRV*
	£	£	£
Used car ABC 1	500	600	500
Used car ABC 2	1 200	1 000	1 000
Used car ABC 3	1 400	1 600	1 400
Spare engines	1 000	800	800
Other spares	900	1 200	900
	£5 000	£5 200	£4 600

The correct value to put on cost is £4 600. If the lower of total cost or total net realisable value were taken then the result would be to set off foreseen losses against unrealised profits.

Long-term contracts

The basic principle of SSAP 9 is that where there is reasonable certainty that a profit will be made on a long-term contract then the attributable profit should be included in the profit and loss account. Where a loss is expected on the contract then the whole of the loss should be provided for immediately.

The standard included a simple example to illustrate this, reproduced here as Table 16.1. Letters of the alphabet to designate lines have been added to help explanation.

For each project the results of the most recent evaluation are shown. Line (a) shows the estimated value of work done and line (h) shows the related costs – the totals of both lines are shown in the profit and loss account.

Table 21.1 Example as given in SSAP 9

Line		Project number 1	2	3	4	5	Balance sheet total	Profit and loss account
(a)	Recorded as turnover – being value of work done	145	520	380	200	55		1 300
(b)	Cumulative payments on account	(100)	(600)	(400)	(150)	(80)		
(c)	*Classified as amounts recoverable on contracts*	45			50		95 DR	
(d)	Balance (excess) of payments on account		(80)	(20)		(25)		
(e)	Applied as an offset against long-term contract balances – see below		60	20		15		
(f)	*Residue classified as payments on account*		(20)	—		(10)	(30) CR	
(g)	Total costs incurred	110	510	450	250	100		
(h)	Transferred to cost of sales	(110)	(450)	(350)	(250)	(55)		(1 215)
(j)		—	60	100	—	45		
(k)	Provision/accrual for foreseeable losses charged to cost of sales		—	—	(40)	(30)		(70)
(l)			60	100		15		
(m)	*Classified as provision/accrual for losses*				(40)		(40) CR	
(n)	Balance (excess) of payments on account applies as offset against long-term contract balances		(60)	(20)		(15)		
(p)	*Classified as long-term contract balances*		—	80		—	80 DR	
	Gross profit on long-term contracts	35	70	30	(90)	(30)		15

Projects 1, 2 and 3 are running profitably. On the assumption that work is sufficiently advanced to predict the outcome with *reasonable certainty*, profits on these projects will be:

	Project 1	2	3
Sales	145	520	380
Cost of sales	110	450	350
	35	70	30

Projects 4 and 5 are not running profitably so that a provision for a foreseeable loss, as shown at line (k), is needed. The total required provision is added to cost of sales, giving a total loss of:

	Project 4	5
Sales	200	55
Cost of sales	(250)	(55)
Foreseeable loss	(40)	(30)
Total loss	90	30

We now turn to the balance sheet. Where payments received on account (line (f)) are less than the value of work done then the difference is shown as a debtor, as in the case of projects 1 and 4 (see line (c)). In the case of projects 2, 3 and 5, payments received exceed the value of work done to the extent identified on line (d). In all three of these projects there is a balance of costs incurred to date after deduction of cost of sales (see line (j)), and after deducting provisions for losses (see line (l)). In the case of projects 2 and 5 this balance can be offset in full against the balance of payments on account leaving a net balance (line (f)) to be shown as a creditor in the balance sheet. In the case of project 3 only £20 of the balance of £100 cost can be offset against the excess of payment on account. The remaining £80 is classified as a long-term contract balance as part of stock (see line (p)).

In the case of project 4 the provision for losses cannot be offset against the accumulated costs of the contract, so is shown as a provision in the balance sheet. In the cases of projects 2, 3 and 5 a note to the account should disclose separately the net cost and applicable payment on account:

		Project		
	2	3	5	*Total*
Net cost (line (l))	60	100	15	175
Applied payment on account (line (e))	60	20	15	95

Controversy over the statement

The first SSAP 9, issued in May 1975, had been preceded by ED 6 issued in May 1972. SSAP 9 adopted the substance of ED 6, reducing the extent of the disclosure requirements, and the reason for the delay in issuing SSAP 9 was to permit time for discussions with the taxation authorities. Following the issue of SSAP 9 the *Survey of Published Accounts* showed failure to comply with SSAP 9 as the single largest cause of qualification or comment in auditors' reports. A number of companies felt sufficiently strongly in disagreement with SSAP 9 to refuse to comply with the statement, while some companies felt unable to comply with the statement because of special circumstances of their trade.

The revised SSAP 9, as described in this chapter, is similar to the original except that the required detail of information has been expanded substantially to avoid conflict with company law changes in the 1980s, particularly on *set off* of balances.

Major areas of controversy have been as follows.

Prudence in defining cost and attributing profit

Both the requirement to include a proportion of overheads in stock and the requirement to include an appropriate portion of profit on incomplete long-term contracts have been rejected by a number of companies on grounds of prudence. Some companies have been reluctant to adopt the SSAP 9 principle of including a portion of estimated profit on long-term contracts because of the Revenue's insistence on taking the closing long-term work in progress of the last period of the old basis of accounting as the opening figure for the first period of the new basis of accounting.

Use of LIFO

Although LIFO, even prior to the issue of SSAP 9, was not widely used in the United Kingdom, it is a method of allocating cost to stock widely used in the USA, where it is accepted as a method of stock valuation by the tax authorities. Where a UK company has subsidiaries in the USA it may, therefore, find itself consolidating LIFO stock figures into the UK group accounts.

Crops valued at selling price

A number of plantation companies have a long-established policy of valuing crops harvested and held in stock at the year end on the basis of the realised selling price. This method, which is not mentioned in SSAP 9, goes against the traditional accounting convention of recognising income at the point of sale; however, it will probably continue to be used on the grounds that it provides the only fair way of stating the results in the position where cost is very difficult to quantify.

Dealers in investments and commodities

A case can be made against the 'lower of cost and net realisable value' rule when valuing stocks held by dealers in items such as investments and commodities where a well-organised market exists; it can be argued that carrying forward such stocks at their market value gives a fairer view. Dealers who follow the rules in SSAP 9 can manipulate their results by *bed and breakfast* operations, selling stocks at the end of one day's trading and buying back the following morning so as to incorporate the profit on sale and the new cost of stock in the accounts.

Interest on long-term contracts

The appendix to SSAP 9 advises that where borrowings can be related to the financing of specific long-term contracts then it may be appropriate to include the interest on these borrowings in the cost of work in progress. This view has been challenged on the grounds that once funds have been borrowed then, whatever the purpose for or security given on the loan, the money borrowed becomes part of and indistinguishable from the total liquid funds of the business.

Disclosure

An example of how major *categories* of stock might be reported in the notes to the accounts is:

Stocks and work in progress

Stocks and work in progress comprise:

	19X9		19X8	
	£000	£000	£000	£000
Engineering				
Raw materials	530		490	
Work in progress	1 175		995	
Finished goods	625		720	
		2 330		2 205

While the requirement to disclose the component parts of stock is normally met by disclosing the split between raw materials, work in progress and finished goods, in the case of a company carrying on different trades it may be helpful to show the split between categories of business. In some businesses, such as a chain of retail food stores, it may be that only one category of stocks will be held and that therefore no further analysis will be necessary.

EXAMINATION PRACTICE

21.1 SSAP 9

(a) Explain what is meant by the term *long-term contract.*

(b) A company has four long-term contracts as at the balance sheet date. All four are sufficiently advanced to predict the outcome with reasonable certainty. Compute the amounts to be included in the profit and loss account and balance sheet in respect of these contracts, showing any additional information to be given in the notes.

	Contract			
	1	*2*	*3*	*4*
Value of work done	500	350	700	220
Related costs	450	400	600	230
Total costs to date	600	400	720	280
Payments received on account	525	200	610	235
Foreseeable additional loss	—	60	—	10

21.2 SSAP 9 terminology

'The amount at which stocks and work in progress (other than long-term contract work in progress) is stated in periodic financial statements should be the total of the lower of cost and net realisable value of the separate items of stock and work in progress or of groups of similar items' – Statement of Standard Accounting Practice No. 9.

You are required in the context of that accounting standard:

(a) to define the phrase *net realisable value*;

(b) to say whether 'replacement cost' is acceptable as an alternative basis of valuation and if so in what circumstances;

(c) to say whether overheads should be included in cost and if so to what extent;

(d) to explain *briefly* the following methods of valuing stock and work in progress:

(i) adjusted (discounted) selling price;

(ii) first in, first out;

(iii) last in, first out;

(iv) base stock.

CHAPTER 22

SSAP 13: Accounting for Research and Development

The basic problem

For a number of companies research and development expenditure constitutes a substantial and essential part of their activity. Such expenditure, by its very nature, tends to be speculative in character, and this poses a serious problem to the accountant preparing annual financial reports. Following the accruals concept it would seem logical to carry forward research and development expenditure as an asset in the year it is incurred, and to write off the asset against future related revenue; this is known as the deferral method. On the other hand, bearing in mind the speculative nature of such expenditure, it may be held that its relationship with the revenue of a future period cannot be established with reasonable certainty, and so in accordance with the prudence concept research and development expenditure would be written off in the year that it is incurred: this is known as the write-off method.

The main arguments used to support the deferral method rather than the write-off method are:

(a) the method is more realistic in commercial terms. Companies invest large sums of money in research and development expenditure with the intention of earning future profits, not as an overhead expense necessary for current production;

(b) a write-off policy may lead to distortion of profit trends, artificially depressing profits in the years leading up to the introduction of a new product, and inflating profits in the years of commercial production. This may lead to a misleading impression being given of rising profitability; and

(c) it is generally accepted that investment in research and development is socially desirable, but the write-off method may well deter management from such investment since, in the short term, it results in a reduction of reported profits.

In support of the write-off method, it is argued that:

(a) since cash resources absorbed by research and development are only released when revenue is earned, a profit figure arrived at under a write-off policy is a better indication of funds available for dividends;

(b) the deferral method calls for the exercise of subjective judgement regarding future revenue, while the write-off method is quite straightforward; and

(c) there may be considerable practical difficulties in relating research and development expenditure to specific future income.

In 1971 public attention was drawn to the problem of accounting for research and development expenditure with the financial collapse of the Rolls Royce group; the balance sheet of the group included a large deferred asset account for development expenditure in respect of a project which could not be completed profitably. Thus the question of research and development was an early candidate for consideration by the ASC.

SSAP 13 was first issued in 1977. A revised standard was issued in 1989.

Summary of the statement

Overview

SSAP 13 draws a distinction between research expenditure aimed at gaining new scientific or technical knowledge, and development expenditure aimed at using scientific or technical knowledge for a specific commercial project. All research expenditure must be written off as it is incurred. For development expenditure companies are allowed to choose between a write-off policy and a deferral policy, but where the latter policy is chosen then deferral is only permitted to the extent that the related project can meet a number of stringent tests to assess viability.

SSAP 13 requires disclosure of accounting policies on R&D, and details of movements on any deferred development account. The revised SSAP 13 also requires large (as defined below) companies to disclose their total R&D charge for the year.

Definitions

SSAP 13 offers the following definition:

> Research and development expenditure means expenditure falling into one or more of the following broad categories (except to the extent that it relates to locating or exploiting oil, gas or mineral deposits or is reimbursable by third parties either directly or under the terms of a firm contract to develop and manufacture at an agreed price calculated to reimburse both elements of expenditure):
>
> (a) *pure (or basic) research:* experimental or theoretical work undertaken primarily to acquire new scientific or technical knowledge for its own sake rather than directed towards any specific aim or application;
> (b) *applied research:* original or critical investigation undertaken in order to gain new scientific or technical knowledge and directed towards a specific practical aim or objective;
> (c) *development:* use of scientific or technical knowledge in order to produce new or substantially improved materials, devices, products or services, to install new processes or systems prior to the commencement of commercial production or commercial applications, or to improving substantially those already produced or installed.

The distinction between pure and applied research on the one hand, and development on the other, is essential to the application of a deferral policy under SSAP 13. The introduction in the revised SSAP 13 of a requirement for certain companies to disclose total R&D expenditure has also made it necessary to consider what expenditure does, or does not, fall under the *research and development* heading. As a broad principle the revised SSAP 13 states:

> Research and development activity is distinguished from non-research based activity by the presence or absence of an appreciable element of innovation. If the activity departs from

routine and breaks new ground it should normally be included; if it follows an established pattern it should normally be excluded.

To illustrate how this principle might be applied SSAP 13 offers the following examples of R&D activity:

(a) experimental or theoretical work to discover new knowledge or advance existing knowledge;
(b) searching for applications of knowledge;
(c) formulation and design of possible application of such work;
(d) testing to search for, or evaluate, alternative products, processes or services;
(e) work on pre-production prototypes;
(f) design of products, processes or services involving new technology or substantial improvements;
(g) construction and operation of pilot plants.

By contrast examples of items which would not normally be classified as R&D include:

(a) tests and analyses for quality control or quantity control;
(b) periodic alterations to existing products, processes or services;
(c) operational research not tied to a specific R&D activity;
(d) cost of corrective action for breakdowns in commercial production;
(e) legal and administration costs for patents and related litigation;
(f) costs of constructing facilities or equipment unless related to a specific R&D project;
(g) market research.

Required practice

Expenditure on fixed assets to provide R&D facilities should be capitalised and depreciated in line with SSAP 12. All other research costs should be written off in the year of expenditure.

In the case of development expenditure companies must choose either a write-off or a deferral policy. Whichever policy is chosen must be applied consistently to all development expenditure.

Where a write-off policy is chosen all development costs should be written off in the year of expenditure.

Where a deferral policy is chosen then development expenditure is deferred to future periods if all of the following conditions can be met:

(a) There must be a clearly defined project.
(b) Related expenditure must be separately identifiable.
(c) The outcome of the project must be assessed with reasonable certainty as to:
   (i) technical feasibility;
   (ii) commercial viability, covering factors such as market conditions (including competition), public opinion, and consumer or environmental legislation.
(d) Future revenues from the project must be 'reasonably expected' to exceed the total of deferred development costs, any further development costs and related costs of production, selling and administration.

(e) Adequate resources must be available, or reasonably be expected to be available, to complete the project, bearing in mind working capital needs.

When development costs are deferred to future periods then as soon as commercial application is under way amortisation must be commenced. Amortisation should be over the expected period of commercial exploitation, on either a time or a usage basis. Each year deferred development expenditure must be reviewed on a project-by-project basis, and if future recovery is considered doubtful an appropriate write-down must be made.

SSAP 13 explicitly states that if a deferral policy is chosen then it must be applied consistently to all development projects. However, in practice, management can apply a write-off policy to any project they choose simply by professing doubts about future viability.

Fixed assets

Where fixed assets are acquired or constructed in order to provide facilities for research or development work, such assets should be capitalised and written off over their estimated useful lives. Depreciation on such fixed assets will be included in the total depreciation charge disclosed in accordance with the Companies Act, and will also form part of any total of research or development expenditure disclosed.

Work under contract

If a company carries out development work under a firm contract on behalf of third parties on such terms that all related expenditure will be reimbursed, then any such expenditure not reimbursed at the balance sheet date should be included in work in progress.

Exceptions

Costs incurred in locating and exploiting oil, gas and mineral deposits do not fall within the scope of SSAP 13. However, developments of new surveying techniques and methods during the course of such activity do fall within the SSAP 13 definition of research and development.

Required disclosure

The accounting policy on research and development must be stated and explained.

Movements on deferred development expenditure, and the amounts carried forward at the beginning and end of the period, must be disclosed. Deferred development expenditure should be shown in the balance sheet as an intangible fixed asset.

The revised SSAP 13 includes a further requirement to disclose the total R&D expenditure charged in the profit and loss account. This should be analysed between the current year's expenditure and amounts amortised from deferred development expenditure. This new disclosure requirement does not apply if:

(a) the company is not a plc, a holding company with a subsidiary plc, or a *special category* company; and
(b) the company satisfies the criteria, multiplied by 10, for definition as a medium-sized company under the Companies Act 1985.

Summary of SSAP 13

Figure 22.1 provides a summary of the main points covered by SSAP 13.

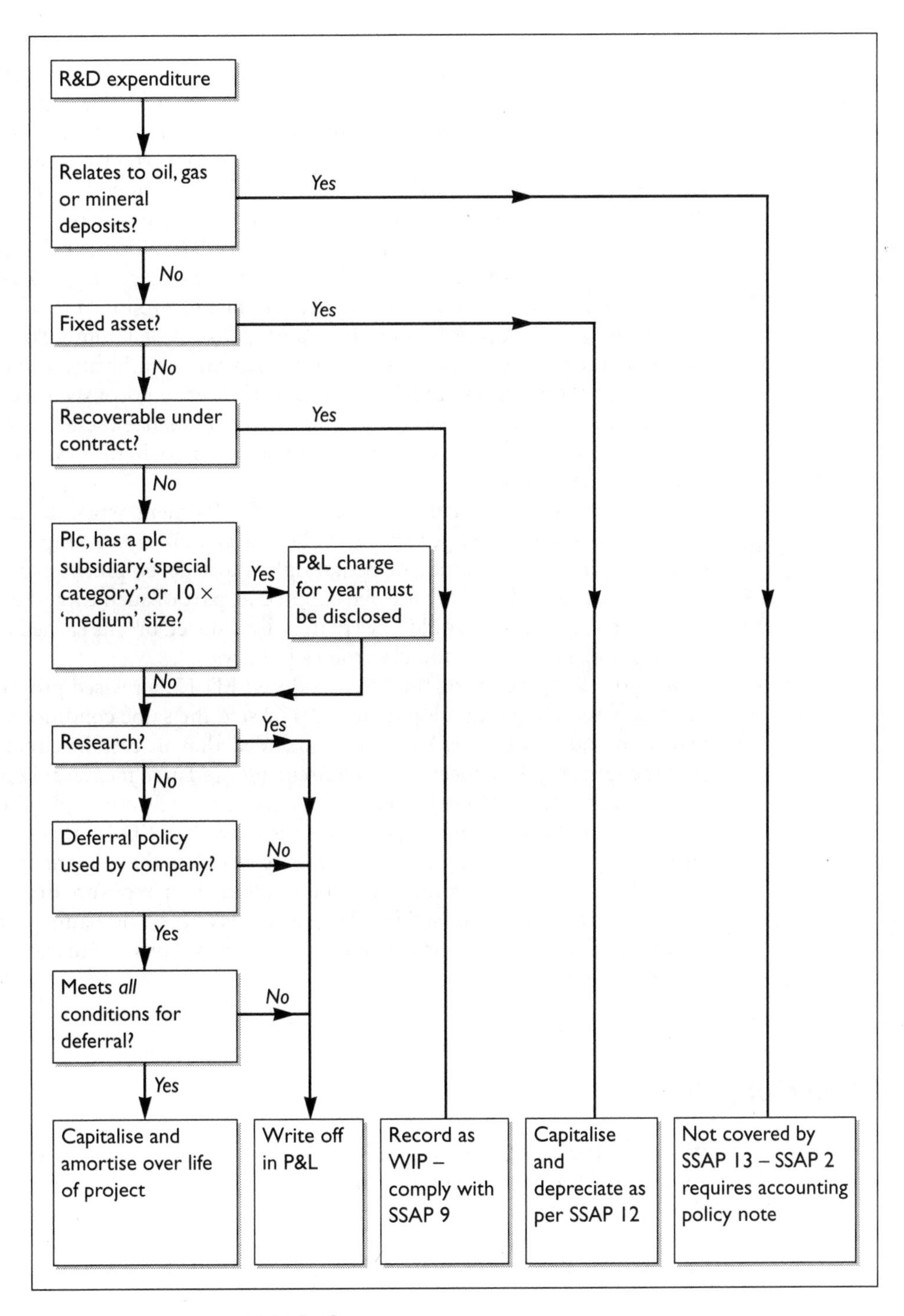

Fig. 22.1 Summary of SSAP 13

Background

The first SSAP 13 was preceded by two exposure drafts, ED 14 issued in January 1975 and ED 17 issued in April 1976. ED 14 defined pure research, applied research and development in terms similar to those finally adopted in SSAP 13, argued that pure and applied research could only be treated on a write-off basis, and, having listed the conditions required to be met in order to defer development expenditure prudently (these conditions were identical to those eventually listed in SSAP 13), concluded that for practical purposes the elements of uncertainty inherent in the conditions made the deferral method unacceptable, and required that all research and development expenditure be written off in the year incurred. ED 14 would also have required the disclosure of the total of research and development expenditure written off in the year. A leading article in *The Accountant*, describing ED 14 as a grasp at an awkward nettle, remarked that the requirement to follow a total write-off policy would have a significant effect on the reported results of a number of companies and might be regarded as an 'intrusion, without legislative authority, into the proper area of managerial discretion'. In fact, the proposals were vigorously attacked by companies in the aerospace and electronics industries, and since these areas accounted for over half of the total research and development activity in the UK, such criticism had to be taken seriously.

In the 1970s government contracts for development work on defence projects allowed an agreed profit percentage to be charged on capital employed in contracts by developers. The government would only allow development expenditure shown in the published balance sheet to be counted as part of such capital employed. Thus a write-off requirement would have materially reduced profits earned by defence contractors in the aerospace and electronics industries.

In April 1976, therefore, the ASC produced ED 17, a revised proposal for a statement on research and development. ED 17 listed the same conditions for deferral as had been laid down in ED 14, but concluded that in certain circumstances companies might be able to meet these requirements, and in that case laid down that development expenditure should be deferred against future revenue arising from the project. While ED 17 enjoyed a more favourable response than ED 14, there was some resistance to the idea of making deferral compulsory. Thus the element of choice allowed in SSAP 13 represents a compromise between the two exposure drafts.

The revised SSAP 13, issued in 1989, responds to the Companies Act 1985 and the European Community Fourth Directive with provisions for disclosure of the total R&D write-off in the year.

Choice of policy

We have already seen the arguments between a write-off approach and a deferral approach. Clearly company management will have in mind these arguments when choosing a company policy on research and development. Since SSAP 13 offers a choice between the two approaches the standard is presumably based on the assumption that conditions specific to the individual company may make one or the other approach more appropriate. Surprisingly, SSAP 13 offers no guidance on what relevant conditions might be expected to influence such a choice. Factors that might usefully be considered by management include:

(a) the amount of development expenditure relative to the total scope of the company's activities. Operation of a deferral policy involves a time-consuming, and therefore costly, annual review of projects. This is only worthwhile if the impact on the accounts is going to be material;
(b) the policies generally adopted by other companies in the same industry. Clearly it is useful to analysts if companies in the same industry adopt similar, and therefore comparable, accounting policies. From the company's point of view, failure to follow general industrial practice may cause analysts to query why the company feels reluctant to be portrayed in the same way as competitors;
(c) for a company that is not in the SSAP 13 category for which disclosure of the R&D write-off for the year is required, a write-off policy may be attractive because it involves less disclosure than a deferral policy;
(d) any contractual restrictions on the company which are based on the reported balance sheet figures. For example, a company with tight borrowing power restrictions might welcome the opportunity to boost reported equity with a deferral policy. As we have already seen, some defence contractors find a deferral policy helps boost permitted profits under government contracts;
(e) the company's competence and experience in handling budgeting and forecasting techniques. As we have seen, in order to apply a deferral approach a company needs to make a wide range of forecasts. These must be supported with convincing evidence for the auditors;
(f) the company's sensitivity to *income smoothing*. A write-off approach depresses profits in the years when a new project is developed. Conversely profits are artificially boosted in the years when commercial exploitation occurs because related development costs have already been written off. A deferral approach *smooths* reported profits, and this may be important to a listed company sensitive to shareholder reaction.

Company law

The Companies Act 1985 provides that deferred development costs may only be included in the balance sheet in *special circumstances*. Where such an amount is included then the notes to the accounts should include:

(a) details of the write-off period for the deferred costs;
(b) reasons for the capitalisation.

Where the unamortised costs are not treated as a realised loss in the computation of distributable reserves the notes to the accounts must state that fact, and explain the circumstances relied on by the directors to justify this treatment.

In practice, compliance with the stringent criteria for deferral laid down in SSAP 13 should offer sufficient justification.

Conclusion

SSAP 13 provides an interesting example of how the ASC dealt with an accounting problem on which accountants were divided, in that ED 14 prescribed a total write-off policy, ED 17 prescribed a deferral policy subject to a number of strict conditions being met, while SSAP 13 permits choice between two methods. While allowing this element of choice the statement, in laying down stringent conditions for deferral and providing detailed rules for amortisation, does in practice narrow considerably the range of possible treatment.

EXAMINATION PRACTICE

22.1 Allocation of R&D items

Current items charged to a research and development (R&D) suspense account in the books of Simple Limited, a company in the electronics industry, are analysed as follows:

		£
1.	Expenditure on applied research related to Project X (note 1)	500 000
2.	Contribution to University U for pure research related to the industry	50 000
3.	Expenditure on the development of Project Y (note 2)	100 000
4.	R&D expenditure relevant to a patent currently granted for Project Z, now being launched as Product Z (note 3)	125 000
5.	Cost of purchase of know-how of an efficient method of carrying out Process P	20 000

Note 1: Your enquiries show that the expenditure on Project X is the first annual instalment of the cost of the applied research which is likely to be repeated over the next two years. Management were cautiously optimistic about the successful development and sale of the resultant new product.

Note 2: Project Y is regarded enthusiastically by management and they believe they have sufficient evidence from pilot studies to support their view that there will be profitable returns from the new product launched in the near future.

Note 3: The £125 000 costs include £1 000 fees paid to the Patent Office and to a patent agent.
You are required to advise management on the accounting treatment of each of the five items.

22.2 Treatment of R&D

During the course of a year Venture Ltd incurred expenditure on many research and development activities. Details of three of them are given below.

Project 3: To develop a new compound in view of the anticipated shortage of a raw material currently being used in one of the company's processes. Sufficient progress has been made to suggest that the new compound can be produced at a cost comparable to that of the existing raw material.

Project 4: To improve the yield of an important manufacturing operation of the company. At present, material input with a cost of £100 000 p.a. becomes contaminated in the operation and half is wasted. Sufficient progress has been made for the scientists to predict an improvement so that only 20 per cent will be wasted.

Project 5: To carry out work, as specified by a creditworthy client, in an attempt to bring a proposed aerospace product of that client into line with safety regulations.

Costs incurred during the year were:

Project	*3*	*4*	*5*
	£	£	£
Staff salaries	5 000	10 000	20 000
Overheads	6 000	12 000	24 000
Plant at cost (life 10 years)	10 000	20 000	5 000

You are required to:

(a) Define the following:
  (i) pure research expenditure,
  (ii) applied research expenditure, and
  (iii) development expenditure.

(b) State the circumstances in which it may be appropriate to carry forward research and development expenditure to future periods.

(c) Show how the expenditure on Projects 3, 4 and 5 would be dealt with in the balance sheet and profit and loss account in accordance with SSAP 13. *(ICAEW)*

CHAPTER 23

SSAP 15: Accounting for Deferred Taxation

The need for a statement

The profit or loss of a company as calculated for the purposes of taxation is often substantially different from that reported in the financial accounts. This rises from two types of difference:

(a) certain types of income or expenditure shown in the financial accounts may be non-taxable or non-allowable, for example, dividend income or entertainment expenditure relating to UK customers; and
(b) certain items of income or expenditure may be included in the computation of taxable profit in one period and in the financial accounts in another. These are known as *timing differences* and we will be considering examples of these in some detail below.

Three approaches to accounting for the tax effects of these *timing differences* have been put forward:

(a) The *flow through* approach, whereby the tax charge is taken to be the tax assessment for the year and the question of timing differences is ignored.
(b) The *full deferral* approach which, following the accruals concept, would charge to the profit and loss account the full tax effects of all timing differences.
(c) The *partial deferral* approach whereby provision is made for the tax effect of timing differences except to the extent that it can be foreseen that the effect of these will continue indefinitely.

This became a particularly important topic during the 1970s with the introduction of 100 per cent first-year allowances on plant and of stock appreciation relief since abolished. Moreover the basing of the calculation of earnings per share on the reported figure of profit after tax increased the significance of the company's approach to deferred taxation. The abolition of first-year allowances in 1984 again changed the position, although small/medium firms are eligible for first-year allowances of 40 per cent.

Computation of deferred taxation

There are two main methods of computing a deferred tax balance, the liability method and the deferral method.

The liability method

Under this method the taxation effects of timing differences are regarded as liabilities for taxes payable in the future or as assets representing recoverable taxes. Thus the deferred taxation balances will be calculated on the basis of the current rate of tax on the grounds that the most recent rate of tax is the best available guide to the likely position when tax is actually paid or recovered. Whenever there is a change in the rate of taxation there will be a revision of the opening balance of deferred taxation; the effect of such a revision will normally be shown in the profit and loss account as part of the taxation charge.

The deferral method

This is a procedure whereby the taxation effects of timing differences are regarded as deferrals of taxation payable or recoverable to be allocated to future periods when the differences reverse. Balances on the deferred taxation account are regarded as deferred credits or deferred charges rather than as amounts payable or recoverable and are not revised on changes in the rate of taxation.

The deferral method can be applied in two ways:

(a) by accounting for each reversing timing difference in a year by the rate of tax applying in the year that difference originated. Originating timing differences will be accounted for by applying the current rate of tax; or

(b) by using the *net change* method whereby the net amount of all originating and reversing timing differences is calculated. If this produces a net *originating* difference then the current tax rate will be applied, while if there is a net *reversing* difference then either:

  (i) a *first in, first out* basis is used, whereby the rate applying to the earlier timing differences making up the deferred tax account is used;

  (ii) an *average basis* is applied, a rate being arrived at by comparing the balance on the deferred taxation account at the beginning of the period with the total of related timing differences.

Example of the two methods

Consider the very simple example of a company with only one sort of timing difference arising from accelerated capital allowances.

Simplesoul Limited commenced business on 1 January 19X1 and trading in the four years to 31 December 19X4 was as follows:

	19X1	19X2	19X3	19X4
	£	£	£	£
Profit before depreciation	1 500 000	1 600 000	1 700 000	1 800 000
Depreciation	200 000	320 000	320 000	460 000
Profit before tax	1 300 000	1 280 000	1 380 000	1 340 000
Purchase of machines:				
A	1 000 000	—	—	—
B	—	600 000	—	—
C	—	—	—	700 000
Tax rates	50%	52%	54%	53%

Depreciation is provided at 20 per cent on a straight line basis and first-year allowances of 100 per cent were available and used in each year. Taxation computations for the four years show:

	19X1	*19X2*	*19X3*	*19X4*
	£	£	£	£
Profit for the year	1 300 000	1 280 000	1 380 000	1 340 000
Add: Depreciation	200 000	320 000	320 000	460 000
Less: First year allowance	(1 000 000)	(600 000)	—	(700 000)
Taxable profit	500 000	1 000 000	1 700 000	1 100 000
Tax rate	50%	52%	54%	53%
Taxation	250 000	520 000	918 000	583 000

An extract from the company's fixed asset register reads as follows:

		Machines		
	A	B	C	*Total*
	£	£	£	£
19X1				
Cost in year	1 000 000	—	—	1 000 000
Depreciation	(200 000)	—	—	(200 000)
NBV c/fwd	800 000	—	—	800 000
19X2				
NBV b/fwd	800 000	—	—	800 000
Cost in year	—	600 000	—	600 000
Depreciation	(200 000)	(120 000)	—	(320 000)
NBV c/fwd	600 000	480 000	—	1 080 000
19X3				
NBV b/fwd	600 000	480 000	—	1 080 000
Cost in year	—	—	—	—
Depreciation	(200 000)	(120 000)	—	(320 000)
NBV c/fwd	400 000	360 000	—	760 000
19X4				
NBV b/fwd	400 000	360 000	—	760 000
Cost in year	—	—	700 000	700 000
Depreciation	(200 000)	(120 000)	(140 000)	(460 000)
NBV c/fwd	200 000	240 000	56 000	1 000 000

Deferred taxation will now be computed using the liability and deferral methods.

The liability method

In 19X1 the company enjoyed first-year allowances of £1 000 000 and charged depreciation of £200 000 giving us an originating timing difference of £800 000. At a tax of 50 per cent the deferred tax provision for the year will be £800 000 @ 50 per cent = £400 000 and this will be the amount carried forward.

In 19X2, because of the change in the tax rate, it will be necessary to revise the opening provision. During 19X2 the company has enjoyed first-year allowances of £600 000 and charged depreciation of £320 000 giving a net timing difference of £280 000. (This is made up of an originating timing difference of £480 000 on Machine B less a reversing difference of £200 000 on Machine A.) Thus the provision to be made in 19X2 can be computed:

	£
Revision of opening balance (£800 000 × 2%)	16 000
Net timing difference in year (£280 000 × 52%)	145 600
Charge for year	161 600
Balance b/forward	400 000
Balance c/forward	561 600

In 19X3 it will again be necessary to revise the opening provision in the light of the change in the tax rate while, there being no capital allowances and a total depreciation charge of £320 000, there will be a net reversing timing difference of £320 000.

	£
Revision of opening balance (£1 080 000 × 2%)	21 600
Net timing difference in year (£32 000 × 54%)	(172 800)
Deferred tax written back in year	(151 200)
Balance b/forward	561 600
Balance c/forward	410 400

In 19X4, following the reduction in the tax rate, there will be another version of the opening balance together with a provision on the net timing difference in the year of £240 000 (£700 000 – £460 000).

	£
Revision of opening balance (£760 000 × 1%)	(7 600)
Net timing difference in year (£240 000 × 53%)	127 200
Charge for year	119 600
Balance b/forward	410 400
Balance c/forward	530 000

Under the liability method it is possible to verify the balance on the deferred taxation account by comparing the balance sheet value of fixed assets with the tax value, i.e.

	19X1	*19X2*	*19X3*	*19X4*
	£	*£*	*£*	*£*
Balance sheet value of fixed assets	800 000	1 080 000	760 000	1 000 000
Tax written down value	—	—	—	—
	800 000	1 080 000	760 000	1 000 000
Tax rate	50%	52%	54%	53%
Deferred tax balance	400 000	561 600	410 400	530 000

Strict deferral method

Following the deferral method we have a deferral of a liability of £800 000 at 50 per cent in 19X1 on Machine A, a deferral of a liability of £480 000 at 52 per cent in 19X2 on Machine B, and a deferral of a liability of £560 000 at 53 per cent on Machine C in 19X4; each of these deferrals will be written back over the following four years.

		Machines			
	A	B	C	*Charge (write back) in year*	*Total c/fwd*
	£	*£*	*£*	*£*	*£*
19X1					
Originating difference (800 000 @ 50%)	400 000	—	—	400 000	400 000
19X2					
Originating difference (480 000 @ 52%)	—	249 000	—		
Reversing difference	(100 000)	—	—	149 600	549 600
19X3					
Reversing difference	(100 000)	(62 400)	—	(162 400)	387 200
19X4					
Originating difference (560 000 @ 53%)	—	—	296 800		
Reversing difference	(100 000)	(62 400)	—	134 400	521 600

Net change deferral method

Under the 'net change' deferral method the computation of deferred tax is simplified by taking net timing differences and applying the appropriate rate; in the case of a net originating timing difference the appropriate rate will be that applying to the current year, while in the case of a net reversing difference the rate used will be either:

(a) that applied on the earlier portion of the originating timing differences accounting for the opening balance of deferred taxation (first in first out method); or
(b) the weighted average rate relating to the balance accumulated on the deferred taxation account.

Thus taking the figures in our example we would arrive at the results shown in Table 23.1.

Table 23.1 Net change deferral method

Year	Net difference	Tax rate	Average charge to (write back from) P & L	Balance c/forward	FIFO charge to (write back from) P & L	Balance c/forward
	£		£	£	£	£
19X1	800 000	50%	400 000	400 000	400 000	400 000
19X2	280 000	52%	145 000	545 600	145 600	545 600
19X3	(320 000)	50.52%*	(161 664)	383 936		
		or 50%			160 000	385 600
19X4	240 000	53%	127 200	511 136	127 200	512 800

$$* \frac{\text{Deferred tax balance b/forward}}{\text{Total related timing differences}} = \frac{£546\ 600}{£1\ 080\ 000} = 50.52\%$$

In practice when the deferral method is used it would be far too time-consuming to use a *strict deferral* approach and either the *average* or FIFO approach is used. As we can see from this example, differences between the two approaches only arise in the year of net reversing timing differences.

Summary of the statement

Definitions

Key definitions are:

(a) *Deferred tax* is the tax attributable to timing differences.
(b) *Timing differences* are differences between profits or losses as computed for tax purposes and results as stated in financial statements, which arise from the inclusion of items of income and expenditure in tax computations in periods different from those in which they are included in financial statements. Timing differences originate in one period and are capable of reversal in one or more subsequent periods.
(c) The *liability method* is a method of computing deferred tax whereby it is calculated at the rate of tax that it is estimated will be applicable when the timing differences reverse. Under the liability method, deferred tax not provided is calculated at the expected long-term tax rate.

The definitions section of SSAP 15 considers three types of timing difference:

(a) tax losses available for relief against future taxable profits are regarded as a timing difference;

(b) revaluation surpluses on fixed assets are regarded as a timing difference, unless rollover relief is expected to defer tax indefinitely;
(c) retention of overseas earnings leads to a timing difference only if there is an intention to remit them *and* remittance would result in a tax liability after taking into account double taxation relief.

Basis of provision

SSAP 15 takes a *partial deferral* approach, requiring that deferred tax should be accounted for to *the extent that is is probable* that a liability or asset will *crystallise* and should not be accounted for to the extent that it *is probable* that the item will *not crystallise.*

In exercising judgements on the probability of crystallisation 'a prudent view should be taken'. Assumptions to be taken into account will include all information on events and management intentions up to the date the accounts are signed, including financial plans on projections.

The deferred tax provision should be computed by the liability method. Debit timing differences should be set off against credit timing differences.

Pension costs

In 1993 the ASB amended SSAP 15 to permit companies to use either the partial deferral or the full deferral approach for the deferred taxation effects of pension costs.

Debit balances

Net debit balances arising on deferred taxation should be written off unless they are expected to be recoverable without replacement by equivalent debit balances.

Required disclosure

In the profit and loss account, deferred taxation should be shown separately as a part of the total tax charge for the year; there should also be an indication of the extent of any unprovided deferred tax for the year. Where there is a change in the rate of taxation, any resulting adjustment to the deferred taxation account should be disclosed separately as part of the total charge for the year.

The deferred tax balance and its major components should be disclosed in the accounts or the notes thereto, while transfers to or from deferred tax should be disclosed in a note.

Transfers to or from the deferred taxation account arising from reserve movements (e.g. fixed asset revaluations) should be shown as part of those movements. Where any note in or attached to the accounts shows that an asset has a value different from the related amount in the balance sheet then the note should also state the taxation effects of realising the asset at that value.

The total amount of any unprovided deferred tax should be shown in a note to the accounts, analysed into its component parts. If an asset revaluation has been regarded as not giving rise to a timing difference, the fact should be stated and the potential tax effect should be quantified.

Groups

In the case of a company in a group any assumptions made as to the impact of group relief in its effect on deferred tax should be stated, together with details of any payment due for group relief.

Making estimates

If a partial provision is to be made for deferred taxation then it is necessary to consider the circumstances in which each major category of timing difference is likely to crystallise.

(a) *Short-term timing differences* are those which arise from the use of the receipts and payments basis for tax purposes and the accruals basis in financial accounts. Some examples of short-term timing differences are:
   (i) interest or royalties payable and receivable treated on a *cash* basis for taxation purposes and on an *accruals* basis in the financial accounts;
   (ii) general provisions for bad debts in the financial accounts only allowed for taxation purposes where they become specific;
   (iii) inter-company profits on stock deferred in the consolidated accounts until stock is sold to third parties but taxed when profit is taken in the accounts of the individual subsidiary.

   By their nature such timing differences are likely to crystallise, although they may be offset by other timing differences.

(b) *Accelerated capital allowances timing differences* arise where capital allowances in the taxation computations exceed related depreciation charges in the financial accounts. Such timing differences were particularly significant from 1972 to 1984 when the first-year allowance on plant and machinery was 100 per cent. This is a timing difference that can be of a recurring nature, in that the reversing difference may be offset or exceeded by new originating differences. Thus a company with a stable or growing investment in fixed assets may in each year enjoy capital allowances on purchases of fixed assets in that year in excess of the depreciation charge on fixed assets bought in previous years. The following example illustrates the nature of a recurring timing difference:

Example

Mercury Limited commenced business on 1 January 19X5 manufacturing gloves. The company used a standard type of glove-making machine that had a life of five years with no residual value at the end of that time. Over a period of five years the company steadily expanded its production capacity by acquiring a new machine each year and thereafter maintained that capacity level by replacing a machine each year.

Table 23.2 Mercury Limited

Year to	Machine purchased	Cost of machine	Capital allowances on machine					Depreciation on machine					Total allowance for year	Total depreciation for year
			A	B	C	D	E	A	B	C	D	E		
31.12.X5	A	100	100	—	—	—	—	20	—	—	—	—	100	20
31.12.X6	B	120	—	120	—	—	—	20	24	—	—	—	120	44
31.12.X7	C	150	—	—	150	—	—	20	24	30	—	—	150	74
31.12.X8	D	200	—	—	—	200	—	20	24	30	40	—	200	114
31.12.X9	E	250	—	—	—	—	250	20	24	30	40	50	250	164

Table 23.2 illustrates how accelerated capital allowances can lead to a recurring timing difference. If we look at each individual machine the originating timing difference in the year of purchase is reversed in the following years. However, in each year *total* capital allowances continue to exceed *total* depreciation, and as long as there is a stable and consistent programme of fixed asset replacement, and fixed asset prices do not fall, the timing difference will continue to recur.

Assuming a steady increase in the price of glove-making machines and continuing first-year allowances of 100 per cent, total capital allowances and total depreciation in each of the first five years, might appear as shown in Table 23.2.

In this example an originating timing difference of £80 arises in respect of Machine A in 19X5. In 19X6 £20 of this difference reverses but a new originating timing difference of £96 arises in respect of Machine B. We can see that in each year the new originating timing difference exceeds the reversal of previous timing differences. Even if the cost of glove-making machines ceases to rise and stays steady at £250, depreciation provided in 19X4 at 20 per cent on five machines costing £250 each will be exactly equal to first-year allowances of £250 on the machine purchased in that year. The timing difference will only cease to recur if the company ceases to replace its fixed assets or there is a reduction in the rate of first-year allowance.

Under the current UK system of capital allowances this position is unlikely to occur, and the relatively small timing differences between capital allowances and depreciation will generally call for full provision. It is, nevertheless, important to appreciate the effect of high first-year allowances because:

(i) these may still arise in the UK in the case of special regional incentives;
(ii) they may also arise in overseas subsidiaries;
(iii) in the history of the deferred tax debate it is important to be aware of the large timing differences attributable in the 1970s to accelerated capital allowances.

(c) *A timing difference arises on the revaluation surpluses on fixed assets* in that a tax liability will arise at the time when the asset is disposed of at a price in excess of original cost (or tax written down in value) but this surplus, or part thereof, will already have been brought into the financial accounts at the time of revaluation. A taxation liability will only arise where a company disposes of the fixed asset and does not benefit from rollover relief. SSAP 15 therefore lays down that provision for deferred taxation on a revaluation surplus should be made as soon as a liability is foreseen, which would normally be the time when the company decides in principle to dispose of the fixed asset.
(d) *A timing difference arises on rollover relief* in that tax on a capital gain arising on a disposal of a fixed asset may be deferred until the replacement asset is

disposed of, although the capital gain will have been shown as a surplus in the financial accounts at the time of the original disposal. Deferred tax arising from rollover relief should be treated in the same way as on a revaluation surplus, provision being made as soon as it is foreseen that a liability will arise.

As we have seen, SSAP 15 specifies that, in estimating whether a timing difference will crystallise, *reasonable assumptions* will involve use of financial plans or projections. An appendix suggests that a period of three to five years will often be adequate, but a longer period of forecasts may sometimes be needed.

Controversy over the statement

History of SSAP 15

The range of views relating to the subject of deferred taxation is reflected by the variations in official guidance published on the subject:

(a) ICAEW recommendations N19 (1958), and N27 (1968) advised that deferred taxation should be provided for by the liability method;
(b) ED 11 issued in 1973 would have required provision in full for deferred taxation by the deferral method;
(c) SSAP 11 issued in 1975 required provision in full for deferred taxation and allowed companies to use either the deferral method or the liability method;
(d) ED 19 issued in 1977 laid down conditions for partial provision for deferred taxation similar to, though somewhat less precise than, those eventually adopted in SSAP 15, and prescribed the liability method;
(e) SSAP 15 issued in 1978 required provision for deferred taxation on timing differences other than those that can be foreseen with reasonable probability. There was no guidance given in the statement on whether the liability or deferral methods should be used, but a technical release issued by the ASC advised that in most circumstances the liability method will be appropriate, but that companies may use the deferral method if they prefer;
(f) ED 33 issued in 1983 proposed a change of emphasis in the criteria for partial deferral, based on the balance of probabilities, and argued the case for the liability method;
(g) a revised SSAP 15, issued in 1985, followed ED 33 in prescribing partial deferral based on the balance of probabilities and prescribed the liability method.

Clearly there are two major areas of controversy over deferred taxation, the first relating to the appropriate method to be used in making a provision, and the second, which has overshadowed the first, being concerned with the more fundamental question of the extent to which it is appropriate to provide for deferred taxation at all.

Deferral versus liability method

The advantages of the deferral method may be summarised thus:

(a) the deferral method is more in accordance with the *accruals* concept, in that the actual benefit enjoyed from an originating timing difference is carried forward to the years of reversal;

(b) use of the deferral method avoids undue fluctuations in the deferred tax charge arising from changes in the tax rate;
(c) the deferral method is required practice in the USA, so that for companies which are, or have, US subsidiaries this can be the more convenient method.

The advantages of the liability method are:

(a) the figure for deferred taxation in the balance sheet represents the best current estimate of the future liability;
(b) since the liability method has been recommended practice in the UK for many years and has been adopted by most companies, its continuance will save companies from a change in accounting policy in this respect;
(c) calculations under the liability method are considerably more straightforward;
(d) under a system of partial deferral there are practical difficulties in making the specific identification of originating timing differences required for operating the deferral method; and
(e) conceptually the liability method, representing an estimate of the liability which will actually arise, is more in line with the principles of partial deferral.

The debate over full deferral

As we have seen, the issue of SSAP 11, requiring a full deferral policy, caused considerable controversy leading to the eventual withdrawal of the statement. The arguments against a full deferral policy can be summarised as follows:

(a) full deferral goes against the *going concern* concept since in times of inflation increased costs of replacing stock and fixed assets will mean that deferred taxation will rarely in practice become payable unless the company goes into liquidation;
(b) if companies are required to provide for deferred tax in full then the benefits enjoyed by a company from good tax planning will not be reflected in the accounts;
(c) similarly, it can be argued that to require a full deferral policy is against the public interest, in that this frustrates the policy of the government in giving relief at an earlier date;
(d) the requirement to provide for deferred taxation in full had the effect of reducing the reserves of some companies to a point where their borrowing powers would be severely restricted. It is interesting to note that the CBI joined in the opposition to SSAP 11;
(e) some commentators considered there to be a political danger in having companies show large balances of deferred taxation, since this might be seen as a form of government investment and as a result lead to some call for the government to exercise some form of voting right in proportion to the amount invested;
(f) many companies were, in practice, likely to ignore SSAP 11 with a consequent danger to the authority of the ASC; and
(g) the full deferral method ignores the advantages enjoyed by a company from postponing payment of tax for a considerable period; one suggestion made was that a prediction of the future cash flow relating to tax deferral be made and the tax liability discounted to present value.

Arguments for a full deferral policy included:

(a) that failure to provide for deferred taxation in full is against the *prudence* concept, since there is always a risk that deferred taxation will become payable;
(b) similarly, failure to provide deferred taxation goes against the *accruals* concept, since it can be argued that a liability arises at the time of the originating timing difference;
(c) any system of partial deferral involves an exercise of judgement which will result in the reported earnings of companies being heavily dependent on the attitude of the directors, with a resultant lack of comparability in earnings per share figures;
(d) not to provide for deferred taxation results in a failure to account for a major source of company finance – postponement by the government of its demands for taxation. One suggestion made has been that deferred taxation should be described in the balance sheet as 'government funds invested by deferment of tax payments';
(e) since, in practice, the main reason why deferred taxation does not become payable is because of the effects of inflation, it can be argued that it is inconsistent to acknowledge this effect in historical cost accounts and that partial deferral should only be made in inflation adjusted accounts.

The ASC was eventually convinced of the merits of a partial deferral rather than a full deferral approach; the technical release accompanying SSAP 15 pointed out that there was a majority in favour of a partial deferral approach from those who commented on ED 19. It is, however, significant that the arguments against full deferral come mainly from those who present financial reports, and the arguments against come mainly from those who use published accounts. It can be argued that SSAP 15 is an example of the predominant influence of the former in setting accounting standards.

Audit problems

The auditor's responsibility under SSAP 15 can be considered in three parts:

(a) to check the accuracy of the calculation of the total liability for deferred taxation;
(b) to form an opinion as to whether the directors have based the actual provision made for deferred taxation on the requirements laid down in SSAP 15. Where the directors state that in their opinion the tax effects of originating timing differences cannot be demonstrated with reasonable probability to continue in the future it is difficult to see how any auditor could in practice dispute this view and object to a full provision being made. Where the directors take the view that part of the potential deferred tax liability need not be provided, the auditors must examine the evidence advanced to justify this view, taking into account the success of forecasts made by the company in the past and secure written representations from the directors to support their action.

SSAP 15 does give opportunities to unscrupulous directors to manipulate the published results of a company; in particular a company might make a full provision for deferred taxation when the requirements of SSAP 15 are first complied with, and then increase the portion of the liability for which provision is not made over a period of time claiming that, with experience, increased confidence can be placed on forecasts. In such a case the auditor will have to form his or her own opinion on the motives and intentions of the directors in deciding whether SSAP 15 has been complied with in such a way as to give a true and fair view; and

(c) to ensure that the accounts give full and clear disclosure as laid down in the accounting standard. Where a material part of the deferred tax charge arises from a change in forecasts made in previous years the auditor may wish to see the effects of such changes identified separately as an 'exceptional' item.

For futher developments, see FRED 19: Deferred Tax in the chapter on FREDs.

EXAMINATION PRACTICE

23.1 The rules in SSAP 15

(a) Explain under what circumstances and to what extent SSAP 15 requires provision to be made for deferred taxation.

(b) Under what circumstances can a deferred tax charge be
  (i) shown as a prior year adjustment?
  (ii) transferred direct to the reserves?

(c) Explain the difference between 'liability' and 'deferral' methods of computing deferred taxation.

23.2 Deferred taxation

In relation to Statement of Standard Accounting Practice No 15 – Accounting for Deferred Taxation, you are required to:

(a) distinguish between:
  (i) *permanent differences*, and
  (ii) *timing differences*;

(b) outline five main categories under which timing differences may arise; and

(c) state the general criteria to be used in deciding whether a provision for deferred taxation is necessary. *(CIMA)*

CHAPTER 24

SSAP 17: Accounting for Post Balance Sheet Events

Background

In October 1978 the IASC issued IAS 10: Contingencies and Events Occurring after the Balance Sheet Date; in the UK the ASC responded by issuing SSAP 17 in rather more detail.

Summary of the statement

Definition of terms

The following definitions included in SSAP 17 are essential to an understanding of the statement.

Post balance sheet events are 'those events, both favourable and unfavourable, which occur between the balance sheet date and the date on which the financial statements are approved by the board of directors'. The statement draws a distinction between two types of post balance sheet event.

(a) *Adjusting events* are those which provide new or additional evidence of conditions existing at the balance sheet date, and therefore need to be reflected in the accounts. Specifically they include items decided on after the balance sheet date, such as the proposed dividend and reserve transfers for the period which, because of statutory requirements, are shown in the accounts; and
(b) *Non-adjusting events* are those which concern conditions which did not exist at the balance sheet date, and have arisen since. Normally these events will not affect the accounts for the year but, nevertheless, it may be necessary to refer to them in the notes to the accounts.

It is clearly necessary in defining a 'post balance sheet event' to identify clearly the date when the accounts are approved by the directors. It is recognised in SSAP 17 that companies will have various procedures for approving the accounts, depending on the company's management structure. SSAP 17 defines the date of approval as the 'date of the board meeting at which the financial statements are formally approved', and requires disclosure of this date in the accounts.

Preparation of the accounts

SSAP 17 is based on the principle that the accounts must be prepared on the basis of conditions existing at the balance sheet date. Accordingly a post balance sheet event will only affect the amounts stated in the accounts in one of two circumstances:

(a) where it is an *adjusting event*, that is, as we have seen above, where it provides or brings to light evidence of circumstances already existing at the balance sheet date; or
(b) where the event indicates that it is not appropriate to apply the going concern concept to a material part of the company.

Disclosure of non-adjusting events

Although non-adjusting events should not be taken into account in computing the amounts in the accounts (unless and in so far as they provide evidence of the validity of applying the going concern concept) disclosure will be necessary in either of two cases:

(a) where the event is so material that non-disclosure would affect the ability of those using the accounts to have a proper understanding of the financial position of the company; or
(b) where the nature of the post balance sheet event is to reverse or complete a transaction entered into before the year end, the substance of which was primarily to alter the appearance of the company's balance sheet, i.e. what is commonly known as *window dressing*.

In such circumstances disclosure will consist of:

(a) the nature of the post balance sheet event; and
(b) an estimate of the financial effect or a statement that it is not possible to quantify the effect. Such an estimate should be given before tax, the tax implications being explained where necessary for a proper understanding of the position.

Complying with the statement

Window dressing

The requirements of SSAP 17 relating to window dressing were not included in the original exposure draft on post balance sheet events, ED 22. SSAP 17 does not require that artificial transactions designed to alter the appearance of the company's balance sheet should be reversed in the accounts, instead requiring that the effect of such a transaction should be disclosed. It is interesting to reflect that a company can comply with SSAP 17 by presenting accounts showing amounts which are distorted in this way and, provided that the nature of the transaction is disclosed in the notes to the accounts, avoid any comment from the auditors on failure to comply with an SSAP. It is hoped that, in a material case of *window dressing*, the auditors would in any case draw the attention of shareholders to the consequent failure of the accounts to present a *true and fair view*. Presumably the ASC has felt unable to lay down stricter rules on *window dressing* because of the practical difficulties of defining and identifying such transactions.

Classification of post balance sheet events

An appendix to SSAP 17 gives some examples of *adjusting* and *non-adjusting* events. These examples can be summarised:

Adjusting events

(a) where fixed assets purchased or sold *during* the year have a purchase or selling price determined *after* the year-end date. SSAP 17 does not give any guidance on how to determine the date of sale. Purchases or sales after the year-end date will be *non-adjusting* events;
(b) a valuation of property which indicates a permanent diminution in value existing at the year-end date; where it can be demonstrated that the decline in value took place after the year-end date this will be a *non-adjusting* event;
(c) the receipt of the accounts of, or other information relating to, an unlisted company, providing evidence of a permanent loss of value of the investment; again, if it can be demonstrated that the loss in value took place after the year-end date this will be a *non-adjusting* event;
(d) evidence from transactions or events after the year-end date as to the net realisable value attributable to stock and work in progress, or as to the accrued profit on a long-term contract;
(e) the insolvency of a debtor, or renegotiation of an amount owed by a debtor;
(f) the declaration of dividends by subsidiaries and associated companies relating to periods prior to the balance sheet date of the holding company. There is no specific guidance in SSAP 17 as to how a company should treat proposed dividends receivable from an investment other than in a subsidiary or associate;
(g) the announcement of the rates of taxation applicable to the accounting period;
(h) the receipt or agreement of amounts due in respect of insurance claims in the course of negotiation at the balance sheet date; and
(i) the discovery of fraud or errors which had led to the accounts being incorrect.

Non-adjusting events

(a) mergers and acquisitions;
(b) proposals for any form of capital reconstruction scheme;
(c) issues of shares and debentures. SSAP 3 only requires disclosure of a figure for diluted earnings per share when the company has already undertaken to issue the new shares at the balance sheet date. In order to comply with the requirement to disclose an estimate of the financial effect of a material post balance sheet event, it would seem reasonable to show the effect of a post balance sheet dilution on earnings per share;
(d) losses of fixed assets or stocks arising from catastrophes such as fire or flood.
(e) changes in trading activities;
(f) fluctuations in exchange rates;
(g) industrial disputes;
(h) augmentation of pension benefits; and
(i) government action such as nationalisation.

EXAMINATION PRACTICE

24.1 SSAP 17 – definitions

Define and give five examples of:

(a) an *adjusting event;*
(b) a *non-adjusting event.*

24.2 SSAP 17 – treatment

What is a post balance sheet event? Describe the way in which such events should be treated in a set of accounts.

CHAPTER 25

SSAP 19: Accounting for Investment Properties

Background

When ED 15, issued in January 1975, included a requirement to depreciate buildings, the proposal was highly controversial. However, FRS 15 excludes investment properties from this requirement. SSAP 19 offers a definition of investment property and defines the appropriate accounting treatment.

Summary of the statement

Definitions

SSAP 19 defines an *investment property* as 'an interest in land and/or buildings':

(a) 'in respect of which construction work and development have been completed'; and
(b) 'which is held for its investment potential, any rental income being negotiated at arm's length'.

The standard goes on to state that there are two exceptions:

(a) a property owned and occupied by a company for its own purposes is not an investment property; and
(b) a property let to and occupied by another group company is not an investment property either in the company's own accounts or those of the group.

Required practice

SSAP 19 requires that depreciation on investment properties should not be provided as laid down in FRS 15, except where a property is held on a lease, in which case, if the unexpired lease term is less than 20 years, depreciation must be provided.

Investment properties should be included in the balance sheet at their open market value.

Changes in their value should be shown in the statement of total recognised gains and losses, being a movement on the investment revaluation reserve. An exception to this rule is that where a deficit on revaluation of an investment property is expected to be permanent then that deficit, as well as any subsequent reversal, should appear in the profit and loss account.

Compliance with the requirement not to depreciate investment property departs from the requirement of the Companies Acts to depreciate all assets with a finite life. SSAP 19 justifies this departure under the *true and fair view* override provisions, so that the disclosures laid down in UITF abstract 7 should be followed.

Special cases

SSAP 19 applies special rules to certain types of entity:

(a) *charities* are excluded from the scope of SSAP 19;

(b) *investment trust* companies and *property unit trusts* are permitted, in accordance with their articles of association, not to take revaluation deficits in excess of the investment revaluation reserve through the profit and loss account. Instead such deficits must be shown *prominently* in the accounts;

(c) the rules on treatment of property revaluation surpluses and deficits do not apply to pension funds and the long-term business of insurance companies, where changes in value are dealt with in the relevant fund account.

Required disclosure

The accounts should disclose either the name or the qualifications of the valuer, together with the bases of valuation. Where the valuer is an employee or officer of the company or group this fact must be disclosed.

Background

As we have seen, the application of SSAP 19 is to all investment properties, not merely those held by property investment companies, but it was the special problems affecting those companies that caused the special treatment.

Certain special objections to the provision of depreciation have been put forward in relation to investment property, including:

(a) that where there is a clause in the lease requiring the tenant to keep the property in good repair then a depreciation provision becomes unnecessary. This objection fails to take into account the wearing out of the basic structure of the building and the obsolescence factor;

(b) that the total value of an investment property consists of the total of future rents to be received from it discounted to present value, and that a figure of cost less depreciation is meaningless. Now one measure of value of any asset is to take the total of the net future stream of income arising from it and discount this to present value; as each year passes, there is a reduction in the total expected income and a consequent reduction in value. Under our present accounting conventions we recognise that loss in value by making a depreciation charge; and

(c) that the provision of depreciation on investment properties will reduce the distributable profits of property companies to such an extent as to reduce or eliminate their capacity to pay dividends. This, in practice, is the main reason for the opposition of the property companies to property depreciation, and it does seem unacceptable to say that companies should be exempted from following best accounting practice in order to show their results in a better light.

To understand the reasons why the ASC was willing to give special consideration to the problems of investment property it is necessary to consider the special circumstances of property companies. Traditionally such companies fall into two categories, property dealing and property investment. A property dealing company will acquire property with the intention of resale, treating both the rental received and the disposal proceeds as trading income, showing property held at the balance sheet date as a current asset akin to stock, and paying corporation tax in full on its profits; a property investment company will acquire property with the intention of continuing to hold it for the benefit of the rental received which will be shown as the only trading profit from the property, any surplus arising in the event of a disposal being taken direct to reserves and regarded as non-distributable, and corporation tax being payable at the full rate on trading income and at the capital gains tax rate on surpluses on property disposals.

In the early 1970s a rapid increase in property prices combined with a sharp rise in interest rates led to a situation where it was common for property companies to buy property at a price such that rental income was considerably less than the related interest charges, the commercial justification for such a transaction being the prospect of increased rental yields and property values in the future. This is known as deficit financing. Conventional measures of accounting income would result in the company showing substantial losses in the early years of such a venture, even though the transaction had been undertaken in the full knowledge of such losses with the expectation of their being exceeded by related income at a later date. To require the provision of depreciation in the early years of such a transaction would result in further distortion of the company's commercial intention, artificially increasing losses in the early years and increasing profit in later years.

Conclusion

SSAP 19 emerged as a response to vigorous lobbying from the property industry. It resulted in the presentation of useful information, but did so at the cost of a substantial departure from traditional accounting conventions.

EXAMINATION PRACTICE

25.1 Definition

You are required, in relation to Statement of Standard Accounting Practice No 19: Accounting for Investment Properties (SSAP 19), to define the term *investment property*.

CHAPTER 26

SSAP 20: Foreign Currency Translation

Background

When exchange rates are fixed and stable, perhaps with occasional orderly revaluations or devaluations of currency, the difficulties of accounting for exchange rate fluctuations are minimised. However, since the early 1970s most currency exchange rates have been *floating*, being allowed to fluctuate in line with market pressures on a day-to-day basis. In those countries, such as the UK, where companies tend to have substantial foreign trading links, foreign currency loans and foreign investments, the need to find an acceptable solution to the problem of accounting for foreign currency items is particularly important.

There are two main ways in which a company may engage in foreign currency operations:

(a) the company may enter directly into a foreign currency business transaction. It will be necessary to translate these transactions into the currency in which the company reports so that they can be included in the accounting records; or
(b) operations may be conducted through a foreign subsidiary company which maintains accounting records in terms of the local currency; in order to prepare consolidated accounts it will be necessary to translate the accounts of the foreign subsidiary into the currency in which the holding company presents its accounts.

When translating foreign currency items in the accounts the question arises as to what rate of exchange should be used. Generally there are two rates that might be considered.

(a) the *historical rate*, being the exchange rate applicable when the item first entered the accounts; and
(b) the *closing rate*, being the exchange rate applicable at the balance sheet date.

SSAP 20 lays down circumstances in which each rate should be used.

The other main accounting problem in accounting for foreign currency translation is how to account for foreign exchange differences, which a company may be *exposed* to in the two following ways.

Transaction exposure

Transaction exposure arises when there is a difference between the exchange rate at the time when a transaction is entered into and the time when it is completed. These realised gains or losses are quantified by the circumstances of the transaction, and there is general agreement that they should be taken through the profit and loss account.

Translation exposure

Translation exposure arises when there is a difference between the exchange rate at the time when an item is brought into the accounts and the exchange rate used to translate that item at the balance sheet date. Translation differences will only arise in relation to those items translated at the closing rate. There are a number of ways of treating translation differences in the accounts, and SSAP 20 tries to standardise practice in this area.

Summary of the statement

Definitions

SSAP 20 defines a number of terms including:

(a) A *foreign enterprise* is

> a subsidiary, associated company or branch whose operations are based in a country other than that of the investing company or whose assets and liabilities are denominated mainly in a foreign currency.

(b) A company's *local currency* is

> the currency of the primary economic environment in which it operates and generates net cash flows.

Note that this definition, combined with the requirement that individual companies should translate their foreign currency balances into local currency, means that companies are required to report their accounts in the currency of the *primary economic environment* even if this is different from the country of legal incorporation.

(c) The *closing rate* is

> the exchange rate for *spot* transactions ruling at the balance sheet date and is the mean of buying and selling rates at the close of business on the day for which the rate is to be ascertained.

(d) The *average rate* is not covered by the definitions section of SSAP 20. However, the introductory explanatory note to SSAP 20 does consider this issue, pointing out that where there are seasonal trade variations the use of a weighting procedure will be desirable.

(e) *Monetary items* are

> money held and amounts to be received or paid in money and, where a company is not an exempt company, should be categorised as either short-term or long-term. Short-term monetary items are those which fall due within one year of the balance sheet date.

(f) The *net investment* which a company has in a foreign enterprise is

> its effective equity stake and comprises its proportion of such foreign enterprise's net assets; in appropriate circumstances, intra-group loans and other deferred balances may be regarded as part of the effective equity stake.

(g) The *temporal method* is not covered in the definitions section of SSAP 20; the explanatory note states that 'the mechanics of this method are identical with those used in preparing the accounts of an individual company'. SSAP 20 explains that this means translating monetary items at the closing rate and other items at the historical rate. Although SSAP 20 does not specifically mention revalued assets, it may be implied from the use of the term temporal method that revalued assets should be translated by reference to the exchange rate at the date of revaluation, not acquisition.

(h) The *closing rate/net investment* method is again not covered in the definitions section of SSAP 20, but in the introduction to the standard is defined: 'Under this method the amounts in the balance sheet of a foreign enterprise should be translated into the reporting currency of the investing company using the rate of exchange ruling at the balance sheet date' (i.e. the closing rate).

Overview

SSAP 20 requires use of the temporal method in translating foreign currency balances in a company's own accounts. The closing rate method should be used when incorporating the accounts of foreign enterprises into the group accounts, except where the foreign enterprise is heavily dependent on the economic environment of the investing company's home currency when the temporal method should be used. Normally translation differences go through the profit and loss account where they arise from the temporal method and direct to reserves when they arise from the closing rate method, except where a foreign investment is financed by foreign borrowing where a *cover* approach (see below) may be used.

Required practice – individual companies

In the accounts of individual companies all items should be translated at the exchange rate ruling when each transaction occurs (i.e. the historical rate). An average rate for each accounting period may be used as an approximation. At each balance sheet date all monetary items should be retranslated at the closing rate, while non-monetary items will not be altered except where a cover approach (see below) is adopted.

All translation differences will be reported as part of the results for the year arising from ordinary operations, except:

(a) differences arising on extraordinary items should be treated as part of the related extraordinary item;

(b) exchange gains on long-term monetary items normally go through the profit and loss account, but should be taken to reserves where there are doubts as to the convertibility of the currency in question;

(c) where a *cover* approach is adopted.

The possibility of adopting a *cover* approach arises when a company has used foreign currency borrowings to finance or provide a hedge against foreign equity investments. In such a case a company is permitted to adopt a policy of translating the foreign equity investment at the closing rate and taking differences on translation of the investment, net of translation differences on the related loan, direct to reserves. This approach is subject to the following conditions:

(a) in each accounting period translation differences on borrowings may only be offset to the extent of translation differences on the related investments;

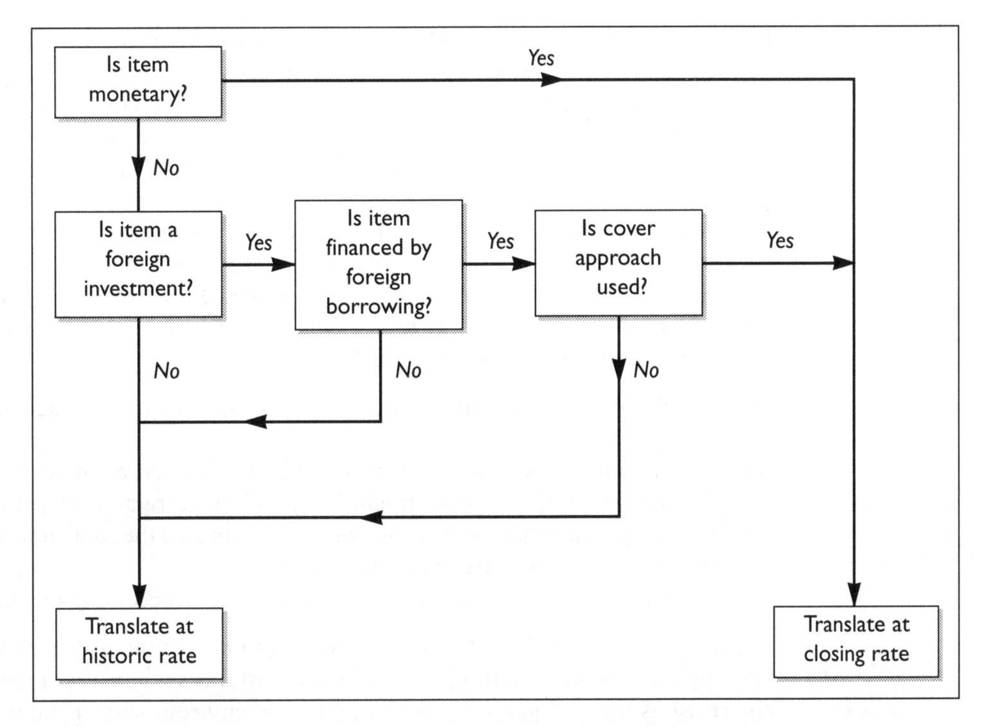

Fig. 26.1 Exchange rate to be used by an individual company

(b) the foreign currency borrowings which are offset must not exceed the total cash expected to be generated from the investments;

(c) where a company chooses to adopt a cover approach, the same accounting policy must be adopted in successive accounting periods.

Figure 26.1 shows the exchange rate to be used at the year end by an individual company.

Required practice – group accounts

When translating the accounts of foreign enterprises (as defined above), the closing rate method should normally be used. The one exception to this rule is that where the trade of the foreign enterprise is more dependent on the economic environment of the investing company's currency than that of its own reporting currency the temporal method should be used. The methods used should be applied consistently unless operational relationships with the investing company change.

When the closing rate method is used, companies are allowed to translate the profit and loss account at either the average or the closing rate. Consequently, translation difference can arise from two causes:

(a) a difference will arise because of retranslation of the opening net investment from the opening to the closing rate; or

(b) where the results for the year are translated at the average rate, a difference will arise when the results are retranslated at the closing rate for inclusion in the balance sheet.

Both types of difference should be recorded as reserve movements.

The conditions under which the *cover* method can be adopted in the group accounts are rather different from those governing the individual company accounts. Where the investing company has adopted a cover approach, the same offset procedure can only be adopted in the consolidated accounts where the foreign equity investment is not a subsidiary or associated company; otherwise the accounting entries related to the cover approach in the individual company's accounts will be reversed on consolidation. SSAP 20 does permit a *cover* approach to be adopted in the group accounts, whereby the exchange differences on foreign currency borrowings in a company's own accounts can be set off against exchange differences on the net equity investments in foreign enterprises, provided that:

(a) the closing rate method is appropriate to translation of the accounts of the foreign enterprise;
(b) the amount of exchange differences offset is limited to the extent of exchange differences on the net investment in the related foreign enterprises;
(c) the foreign currency borrowings should not exceed the total amount of cash that the net investments are expected to generate;
(d) the same accounting policy must be adopted in successive accounting periods.

We have seen that SSAP 20 requires the accounts of foreign enterprises to be translated by the temporal method: 'in those circumstances where the trade of the foreign enterprise is more dependent on the economic environment of the investing company's currency than that of its own reporting currency'.

The explanatory note to SSAP 20 offers some detailed guidance on the factors to take into account in identifying this position:

(a) the extent to which the cash flows of the foreign enterprise have a direct impact upon those of the investing company;
(b) the extent to which the functioning of the foreign enterprise is directly dependent upon the investing company;
(c) the currency in which most trading transactions are denominated;
(d) the major currency to which the operation is exposed in its financing structure.

Examples of situations where the temporal method may be appropriate are where the foreign enterprise:

(a) acts as a selling agency of the investing company;
(b) produces raw materials or other products which are shipped to the investing company for inclusion in its own products;
(c) is located overseas to act as a vehicle for raising finance for other group companies.

SSAP 20 argues that where a foreign enterprise operates in an area of hyperinflation it is desirable that the local currency accounts be adjusted to reflect price level movements before translation takes place.

Required disclosure

SSAP 20 requires disclosure of the methods used in the translation of the accounts of foreign enterprises and the treatment accorded to foreign exchange differences. In practice, this information will normally be given in the accounting policies note.

All companies are required to disclose the net movement on reserves arising from exchange differences.

All companies other than exempt companies (as defined in CA 1985) are required to disclose the net gain or loss on foreign currency monetary items, identifying separately:

(a) amounts offset in reserves under the *cover* method;
(b) the amount taken through the profit and loss account.

Computation in line with SSAP 20

The following example, Hathern Ltd, illustrates the main practical applications of SSAP 20.

Hathern Ltd, a UK company, set up a subsidiary, Hentzau Inc. in Ruritania on 1 January 19X1; the currency of Ruritania is the crown. At the end of the first year of trading Hentzau Inc. presented the following accounts:

Balance sheet as at 31 December 19X1

	Crowns
Share capital	750 000
Retained profit	50 000
	800 000
Plant (purchased 1.1.19X1)	
Cost	600 000
Depreciation	120 000
	480 000
Stock (purchased 20.11.19X1)	390 000
Net monetary current assets	80 000
	950 000
Long-term loan (raised 1.1.19X1)	150 000
	800 000

Profit and loss account year ended 31 December 19X1

	Crowns	Crowns
Sales		470 000
Depreciation	120 000	
Other expenses	280 000	
		400 000
		70 000
Taxation (payable 1.1.19X2)		20 000
		50 000

Exchange rates moved:	*Crowns to the £1*
1 January 19X1	3
Average for 19X1	2.8
30 November 19X1	2.6
31 December 19X1	2.5

In order to finance the investment in Hentzau Inc., Hathern Ltd had raised a long-term loan of 600 000 crowns in Ruritania on 1 January 19X1. The accounts of Hentzau Inc. will be converted to sterling as follows:

(a) By the temporal method:

Balance sheet

	Crowns	*Conversion factor*	*£*
Share capital	750 000	1/3	250 000
Retained profit	50 000	*	32 000
	800 000		282 000
Plant: Cost	600 000	1/3	200 000
Depreciation	120 000	1/3	40 000
	480 000		160 000
Stock	390 000	1/2.6	150 000
Net monetary current assets	80 000	1/2.5	32 000
	950 000		342 000
Loan	150 000	1/2.5	60 000
	800 000		282 000

*Balancing figure

Profit and loss account

	Crowns	*Crowns*	*Conversion factor*	*£*	*£*
Sales		470 000	1/2.8		167 857
Depreciation	120 000		1/3	40 000	
Other expenses	280 000		1/2.8	100 000	
		400 000			140 000
		70 000			27 857
Taxation		20 000	1/2.5		8 000
		50 000			19 857
Exchange difference					12 143
Profit					32 000

Note the principles of translation:

(i) All monetary items in the balance sheet translated at closing rate.
(ii) All non-monetary items in the balance sheet converted at historical rate.
(iii) All revenue and expenditure items are converted at historical rate or, where this is impractical, at average rate.
(iv) The exchange difference is taken through the profit and loss account.

(b) By the closing rate method:

Balance sheet

	Crowns	*Conversion factor*	*£*
Share capital	750 000	1/3	250 000
Reserves	50 000	*	70 000
	800 000		320 000
Plant: Cost	600 000	1/2.5	240 000
Depreciation	120 000	1/2.5	48 000
	480 000		192 000
Stock	390 000	1/2.5	156 000
Net monetary current assets	80 000	1/2.5	32 000
	950 000		380 000
Loan	150 000	1/2.5	60 000
	800 000		320 000

*Balancing figure

Profit and loss account

	Crowns	*Crowns*	*Conversion factor*	*£*	*£*
Sales		470 000	1/2.8		167 857
Depreciation	120 000		1/2.8	42 857	
Cost of sales	280 000		1/2.8	100 000	
		400 000			142 857
		70 000			25 000
Taxation		20 000	1/2.8		7 143
Retained profit		50 000			17 857

Note that it is necessary to translate share capital at the historical rate, and that any pre-acquisition reserves would also be translated at the exchange rate ruling at the date of acquisition. The exchange difference to be taken direct to reserves can be calculated.

	£	£
Opening net investment at closing rate:		
750 000 × 1/2.5	300 000	
at opening rate:		
750 000 × 1/3	250 000	
		50 000
Retained profit at closing rate:		
50 000 × 1/2.5	20 000	
at average rate:		
50 000 × 1/2.8	17 857	
		2 143
		52 143

So the closing balance on the reserves is made up:

	£
Retained profit	17 857
Exchange difference	52 143
	70 000

Note that SSAP 20 would also have allowed the closing rate to be used in translation of the profit and loss account.
In the accounts of Hathern Ltd a loss on foreign currency transactions will arise made up as follows:

	£
Sterling proceeds of 600 000 crown loan @ 1/3	200 000
Year-end liability 600 000 @ 1/2.5	240 000
Loss charged against operating profit	40 000

If the conditions for applying the *cover* approach laid down in SSAP 20 apply, then Hathern Ltd would be allowed to choose an accounting policy for applying the cover approach as follows:

(a) In the company's own accounts the original investment of 750 000 crowns would be translated at the closing rate of 2.5 crowns instead of the historical rate of 3 crowns. A gain would arise of:

$$\left(750\ 000 \times \frac{1}{2.5}\right) - \left(750\ 000 \times \frac{1}{3}\right) = £50\ 000$$

The loss on translating the loan (£40 000) would be offset against this gain, and the net gain (£10 000) is taken direct to reserves.

(b) On consolidation the loss on translating the loan would, if the closing rate method has been used, be offset directly against the translation gain of £52 143, the net gain or loss being taken directly to reserves. If the temporal method of translation has been used then, as we have already seen, use of the cover approach is not permitted.

Controversy over the statement

Economic relationships

Two economic principles are relevant to the controversy over foreign currency translation:

(a) the *Fisher* effect, whereby it is argued that there is a link between interest rates and expectations as to future exchange rate movements, so that the weaker the currency the higher the interest rate. This relationship arises because lenders will expect to receive a high return in the form of interest to compensate for the loss which arises because when the foreign currency loan is repaid it will convert into fewer units of the home currency than when the loan was first made; and
(b) the purchasing power parity effect, whereby it is argued that there is a link between the rate of inflation and the strength of currency, so that the higher the rate of inflation the weaker the currency and vice versa.

It is not claimed that either of these relationships is cast-iron, but research has shown that, over a number of years, both these effects tend to operate in practice.

Choice of translation method

The debate on foreign currency translation has tended to centre on the relative merits of the temporal and closing rate methods.

Benefits of the temporal method have been seen as:

(a) the principles of historical cost accounting are maintained;
(b) the activities of the foreign subsidiary are treated as an extension of those of the parent company, which is in line with the conceptual basis of consolidation;
(c) the method recognises that the risk of translation differences being realised depends on the nature of the item being accounted for.

Benefits of the closing rate method have been seen as:

(a) the accounting ratios in the accounts of the subsidiary are not distorted on consolidation;
(b) the method is simple to operate and understand;
(c) the most up-to-date information on exchange rates is used.

SSAP 20 attempts to justify the closing rate method for foreign subsidiaries with the argument that a company's investment in a quasi-independent foreign subsidiary 'is in the net worth of its foreign enterprise rather than a direct investment in the individual assets and liabilities'. This is why SSAP 20 focuses on the term 'net investment approach'. However, this is inconsistent conceptually with the consolidation of all the assets and liabilities of such a subsidiary into the group accounts on a line-by-line basis.

Translation exposure can be dramatically different for the two methods. For example, if a foreign subsidiary has substantial non-monetary assets but also has net monetary liabilities then under the closing rate method the net investment in the subsidiary, being a net asset, will be *exposed*, while if the temporal method is used then non-monetary assets will give rise to no translation gain or loss, being translated at the historical rates, and only the monetary items, being a net liability, will be exposed. To take a simple example: Nanpantan Ltd invested $100 000 on 1 January 19X6 in a wholly owned foreign subsidiary Bruges SA. Exchange rates moved from $5 to £1 on 1 January 19X6 to $4 to £1 on 31 January 19X6. During the year 19X6 no profit or loss arose, and at both the beginning and end of the year the balance sheet of Bruges SA showed:

	$
Freehold property	1 000 000
Loan	900 000
	100 000
Share capital	100 000

Translation of the balance sheet at 31 December 19X6 will show:

	$	*Translation factor*	*Temporal* £	*Translation factor*	*Closing rate* £
Freehold property	1 000 000	1/5	200 000	1/4	250 000
Loan	900 000	1/4	225 000	1/4	225 000
	100 000		(25 000)		25 000
Share capital	100 000	1/5	20 000		20 000
Gain/(loss) (on translation)	—	*	(45 000)	*	5 000
	100 000		(25 000)		25 000

*Balancing figure.

Translation differences

At different times various proposals on the treatment of translation differences have arisen. These include:

(a) taking translation differences into account when arriving at the figure for operating profit;
(b) showing translation differences on the face of the profit and loss account after the operating profit figure, possibly in conjunction with the extraordinary items;
(c) showing translation differences as a movement on the reserves.

As we have seen, SSAP 20 treats different types of translation difference in different ways. Arguments in favour of different views are taken into account in the SSAP 20 approach as follows:

(a) as we have seen, there is an economic relationship between interest rates and currency fluctuations. SSAP 20 recognises this in that translation differences in a company's own accounts, which relate to monetary items, are shown in the profit and loss account and are therefore matched with interest charges;
(b) where an asset acquisition is financed by a loan it is desirable that translation differences on the two items be matched; SSAP 20 permits this to some extent via the cover method considered in detail above;
(c) translation differences on investments abroad often reflect a form of revaluation adjustment; SSAP 20 normally takes such differences directly to reserve.

Areas of hyperinflation

Paragraph 26 of SSAP 20 argues that where a foreign enterprise operates in an area of hyperinflation it is desirable to adjust the accounts to reflect current price levels before translation of the foreign currency amounts.

We can illustrate the reason for this with a simple example. Supposing a UK company buys a company owning a piece of land in Ruritania for 100 000 crowns, and having no other assets or liabilities, at a time when the Ruritanian crown exchange rate is 2 crowns to the £.

Let us suppose that in the following year rent from the land exactly covers expenses, while Ruritania has inflation of 100 per cent and, in line with the purchasing power parity effect, the exchange rate moves to 4 crowns to the £.

Using the closing rate method of translation the investment in land would be translated for consolidation at:

Opening balance sheet:	
	£
$100 000 × 1/2 =	50 000
Closing balance sheet:	
	£
$100 000 × 1/4 =	25 000

Clearly it is not realistic to regard an unchanged piece of land as having halved in value over the year, since in practice one would expect such a non-monetary asset to maintain its value in real terms. The solution is to revalue the land in crowns before translation.

Conclusion

SSAP 20 tackles a highly complex area in which international harmonisation is particularly important. The provisions of SSAP 20 are very similar to those prescribed in the USA and Canada. Many of the difficult issues of principle involved in currency translation are attributable to differential inflation rates in different countries, and could be resolved more easily within the context of an inflation accounting system.

EXAMINATION PRACTICE

26.1 Foreign currency translation

(a) In terms of the definitions offered in SSAP 20 you are required to distinguish between
(i) the closing rate method;
(ii) the temporal method;
and to explain the circumstances under which each should be used.

(b) The following are the summary accounts of Overseas Ltd, in foreign currency (limas):

Balance sheet as at 31 December 19X9

	Limas
Ordinary share capital	630 000
Retained profits	80 000
	710 000
Plant and machinery, at cost	700 000
Less: Depreciation	70 000
	630 000
Stocks, at cost	210 000
Net monetary current assets	40 000
	880 000
Less: Long-term loan	170 000
	710 000

Profit and loss account, year to 31 December 19X9

		Limas
Sales		900 000
Less: Depreciation	70 000	
Other operating expenses	750 000	
		820 000
Net profit before taxation and appropriations		80 000

During the year, relevant exchange rates were:

	Limas to the £
1 January 19X9	14
Average for the year	12
Average at the acquisition of closing stock	11
31 December 19X9	10

Your UK company, Sterling Ltd, had acquired Overseas Ltd on 1 January 19X9 by subscribing £45 000 of share capital in cash when the exchange rate was 14 limas to the £. The long-term loan had been raised locally on the same date. On that date Overseas Ltd had purchased the plant and equipment for 700 000 limas. It is being depreciated by the straight-line method over 10 years.

You are required to show the balance sheet, profit and loss account and reserve movement of Overseas Ltd in £s, using:
(i) the closing rate method; and
(ii) the temporal method.

(ACCA, adapted)

26.2 Translation

On 1 January 19X5 Chestnut Ltd, a UK company, acquired the entire share capital of Acorn SA, a company registered and trading in Ruritania, for a purchase consideration of 600 000 crowns. To help finance the purchase, a loan of 300 000 crowns was raised in Ruritania by Chestnut Ltd on 1 January 19X5. These were the only foreign currency items recorded in Chestnut's own accounts.

On 1 January 19X5 Acorn SA acquired all the plant currently shown in the balance sheet. During the year to 31 December 19X5 exchange rates moved as follows:

1 January 19X5	20 crowns to £1
Average 19X5	18 crowns to £1
At date stock acquired	16 crowns to £1
31 December 19X5	15 crowns to £1

The accounts of Acorn for the year to 31 December 19X5 showed:

Acorn SA
Balance sheet as at 31 December 19X5

	Crowns	*Crowns*
Plant – Cost		604 800
– Depreciation		86 400
		518 400
Current assets		
Stock	129 600	
Cash	43 200	
		172 800
		691 200
Long-term loan		172 800
		518 400
Ordinary share capital		345 600
Retained profit – At 1 January 19X5	129 600	
– For year	43 200	
		172 800
		518 400

Profit and loss account for the year ended 31 December 19X5

	Crowns	*Crowns*
Sales		864 000
Cost of sales		561 600
Gross profit		302 400
Less:		
Depreciation	86 400	
Other expenses	172 800	
		259 200
Retained profit		43 200

You are required, in compliance with SSAP 20 to:

(a) Translate the accounts of Acorn SA by the closing rate method. Apply the closing rate to profit and loss items.
(b) Translate the accounts of Acorn SA by the temporal method.
(c) Show the exchange differences taken in Chestnut Ltd's own accounts through the profit and loss account and direct to reserves respectively:
    (i) taking a cover approach;
    (ii) not taking a cover approach.

CHAPTER 27

SSAP 21: Accounting for Leases and Hire Purchase Agreements

Background

SSAP 21, issued in August 1984, has been one of the most difficult accounting standards on which to reach agreement. This is caused both by the technical complexity of the subject and by fierce controversy over the basic approach of the standard.

The growth of leasing

A lease is an agreement whereby a *lessor*, who owns an asset, conveys the right to use that asset to a *lessee* for an agreed period of time at an agreed rental. Most lessors in the UK are members of the Equipment Leasing Association, and Table 27.1 shows how the leasing industry had grown over a ten-year period.

Table 27.1 Assets acquired by members of the UK Equipment Leasing Association

	Assets acquired*	*% increase in year*
		£m
1975	340	6
1976	421	24
1977	675	60
1978	1 214	80
1979	1 802	48
1980	2 359	31
1981	2 674	13
1982	2 834	6
1983	2 894	2
1984	4 012	39

*Source: *World Leasing Yearbook 1986*, Hawkins Publishers Ltd.

Leases can be divided into two broad categories;

(a) *Finance leases*, covering most of the life of the asset. Such a lease normally is designed as a mechanism whereby the lessor finances the acquisition of an asset which will in practice be used by the lessee.

(b) *Operating leases* where a lessor acquires an asset to be hired out for successive periods of time to successive users. Such a lease is normally entered into for operational reasons, in circumstances where the lessee does not require the asset for a sufficient length of time to warrant purchase.

The distinction between the two types of lease is obviously blurred, and we consider in detail below how SSAP 21 has tried to draw a distinction between the two.

A major reason for the growth of leasing in the UK has been the combination of the tax system and the economic climate. From 1972 to 1984 companies acquiring plant and machinery enjoyed 100 per cent first-year allowances for tax purposes. Many manufacturing companies found that, with the high levels of inflation of the 1970s, their trading profits were insufficient to cover the full first-year allowance; thus they were unable to enjoy the cash flow benefits on acquisition of new plant which the tax system was designed to give them. By contrast, in times of high inflation financial institutions tend to record high taxable profits. Thus, where a financial institution financed asset acquisition for a client by means of a lease agreement rather than a simple loan, the lessor could enjoy a substantial cash flow benefit from accelerated capital allowances and therefore would be willing to offer finance with lower finance charges than would apply to a simple loan.

The 1984 budget announced the phasing out of first-year allowances and a phased reduction in the corporation tax rate from 50 per cent in 1984 to 35 per cent in 1987. The effect was to boost leasing business substantially in 1984, for two reasons:

(a) fixed assets were being leased early to enjoy the benefit of first-year allowances before they were abolished; and
(b) during the transitional period first-year allowances could be used to defer profit to later years with lower tax rates, giving a combination of cash flow benefits and a saving in actual tax paid.

The basic accounting problem

Accounting for leases presents a wide range of technical problems for both lessees and lessors. These are addressed in detail in SSAP 21, and are considered below. The major accounting problem that arises is that a finance lease is in legal form a rental agreement, while in commercial substance it is a device for borrowing the financial resources to obtain the use of a fixed asset. If we account for a finance lease in line with its legal form then in the accounts of a lessee we would expect the only accounting entry each year to be an item in the profit and loss account, writing off the rental charge. In the accounts of a lessor, following legal form, we would find the asset recorded initially at cost and depreciated systematically, with rental income credited to profit and loss. This approach was common practice in the UK up until the 1980s.

The traditional approach based on *legal form* appears somewhat unsatisfactory if we consider the commercial substance of such a transaction. A lessee has effectively acquired the use of a fixed asset, and has incurred an obligation to pay a series of instalments, normally over a period of several years, to finance the acquisition. Accordingly, it is argued, the lease should be *capitalised* by recording the asset as though it had been purchased, and the related obligation to pay future instalments as a liability. Similarly, lessors are regarded as owning a financial asset, the right to receive future payments under the lease agreement, rather than the fixed asset which is the subject of the lease. During the 1980s this *capitalisation* approach has become more common, and it is the approach taken by SSAP 21.

Hire purchase agreements

So far we have considered matters relating to lease agreements. A hire purchase agreement is a special kind of rental contract under which the hirer has an option to purchase the asset at the end of the rental period.

SSAP 21 requires that hire purchase agreements which are of a financing nature should be treated as finance leases, and other hire purchase agreements should be treated as operating leases. Normally hire purchase agreements involve transfer of the asset at the end of the agreement for a nominal sum, so that the hirer can be expected to exercise the option to purchase; such agreements are clearly similar in character to finance leases.

However, it sometimes happens that a hire purchase agreement may set the option to purchase at a price so high as to raise doubts as to whether the option will be exercised; in such a case, the agreement will have the character of an operating lease.

It should be noted that a hire purchase agreement is treated for tax purposes as the acquisition of an asset by the hirer, while under any form of lease agreement the tax system treats the lessor as acquiring the asset.

Definitions

A major problem in introducing a requirement to capitalise finance leases is that of drawing a distinction between a *finance* lease and an 'operating' lease.

A *finance lease* is

> a lease that transfers substantially all the risks and rewards of ownership of an asset to the lessee.

Having defined a finance lease in principle, SSAP 21 goes on to state that

> it should be presumed that such a transfer of risks and rewards occurs if at the *inception of a lease* the present value of the *minimum lease payments*, including any initial payment, amounts to substantially all (normally 90 per cent or more) of the *fair value* of the leased asset. The present value should be calculated by using the *interest rate implicit in the lease*. If the fair value of the asset is not determinable, an estimate thereof should be used.

Four of the terms used above have been presented in italics, because SSAP 21 offers further definitions of these terms as follows:

(a) The *inception of a lease* is

> the earlier of the time the asset is brought into use and the date from which rentals first accrue.

(b) The *minimum lease payments* are

> the minimum payments over the remaining part of the lease term (excluding charges for services and taxes to be paid by the lessor) and:
>
> (i) in the case of the lessee, any residual amounts guaranteed by him or by a party related to him; or
> (ii) in the case of the lessor, any residual amounts guaranteed by the lessee or by an independent third party.

(c) *Fair value* is

> the price at which an asset could be exchanged in an arm's length transaction less, where applicable, any grants receivable towards the purchase or use of the asset.

(d) The *interest rate implicit in the lease* is

> the discount rate that at the inception of a lease, when applied to the amounts which the lessor expects to receive and retain, produces an amount (the present value) equal to the fair value of the leased asset.

Where this interest rate is not determinable it should be estimated by reference to the rate which a lessee would be expected to pay on a similar lease.

Taking the above definitions together we can see that SSAP 21 both defines what in principle constitutes a finance lease and lays down detailed criteria for identifying such a lease. However, the standard makes it clear that it is the definition with reference to transfer of the 'risks and rewards of ownership' that is crucial, and provides that in exceptional circumstances a lease falling outside the detailed criteria may be shown to be a finance lease, and a lease falling inside the detailed criteria may be shown not to be a finance lease.

An *operating lease* is defined simply as

> a lease other than a finance lease.

Other definitions in SSAP 21 include:

(a) The *lease term* is

> the period for which the lessee has contracted to lease the asset and any further terms for which the lessee has the option to continue to lease the asset, with or without further payment, which option it is reasonably certain at the inception of the lease that the lessee will exercise.

Thus the definition of a *lease term* involves not merely a reading of the minimum term provided in the lease, but also an assessment of how future rights to extend the lease are likely to be used.

(b) The *net cash investment* in a lease is

> the amount of funds invested in a lease by a lessor, and comprises the cost of the asset plus or minus the following related payments or receipts:
>
> (i) government or other grants receivable towards the purchase or use of the asset;
> (ii) rentals received;
> (iii) taxation payments and receipts, including the effect of capital allowances;
> (iv) residual values, if any, at the end of the lease term;
> (v) interest payments (where applicable);
> (vi) interest received on cash surplus;
> (vii) profit taken out of the lease.

This definition is important in the allocation of finance charges by lessors, an issue that will be considered in detail below.

(c) The *gross investment* in a lease is

> the total of the minimum lease payments and any unguaranteed residual value accruing to the lessor.

(d) The *net investment* in a lease is:

> (i) the gross investment in a lease . . . ; less
> (ii) gross earnings allocated to future periods.

Requirements for the lessee

A finance lease must be recorded by the lessee at the inception of the lease as an asset and as an obligation to pay future rentals. The asset and liability at the inception of the lease will both be of the same amount, and in principle the amount should be the present value of the minimum lease payments as discounted by the implicit interest rate. In practice, SSAP 21 points out that *fair value* will normally closely approximate to *present value* and so constitute an acceptable substitute.

The asset should be depreciated over the lesser of the useful life or the lease term; the logic of this is that the asset will only be of use to the lessee for the lesser of these two periods. There is an exception to this rule for hire purchase agreements treated as finance leases, where the asset is simply depreciated over the useful life; the reason for this is that such an agreement carries an option to purchase, so that the asset will be available for use by the company indefinitely.

Rentals payable under the lease agreement should be split between the finance charge, shown as an expense in the profit and loss account, and the reduction of the outstanding lease obligation, being set off against the liability in the balance sheet. The total finance charge should be written off so as to produce a constant periodic rate of charge on the remaining balance of the lease obligation, or a *reasonable approximation* thereto.

It may happen that a lessor offers lease terms whereby the minimum lease payments total less than the fair value of an asset, because of the benefits of government grants and capital allowances. In such a case the amount to be capitalised and depreciated will be restricted to the total of the minimum lease payments.

In the case of an operating lease the rental should be charged to profit and loss on a straight line basis over the lease term, even if the payments are not made on such a basis, unless another systematic and rational basis is more appropriate.

Disclosure by the lessee

For each major class of leased asset held under a finance lease there must be shown the gross amount and the accumulated depreciation. Alternatively, leased assets may be included in the totals disclosed relating to owned fixed assets; in this case the net amount relating to leased assets included in the fixed asset total must be disclosed. The amount of depreciation relating to assets held under finance leases must be disclosed.

The liabilities for finance lease obligations should be separately identified, either on the face of the balance sheet or in the notes to the accounts. These obligations should be analysed into three categories:

(a) amounts due within one year;
(b) amounts due in the second to fifth years; and
(c) amounts due after more than five years.

The analysis can be presented either as a separate analysis of finance lease obligations or, where such obligations are included with other items in the balance sheet, as an analysis of all those items. In the former case the lessee may, instead of showing net obligations, show gross lease payments due with future finance charges deducted from the total.

Total finance charges for the year relating to finance leases must be disclosed. Disclosure should be made of the amount of any commitment in respect of finance leases entered into at the balance sheet date where inception occurs after the year end.

In relation to operating leases the lessee must disclose total lease rentals for the year, split between hire of the plant and machinery and other items. The lessee must also disclose total payments under operating leases committed for the coming year, analysed between:

(a) agreements ending in the coming year;
(b) agreements ending in the second to fifth years; and
(c) agreements lasting more than five years.

This analysis should further be split between commitments relating to land and buildings and other commitments.

Accounting policies relating both to finance leases and operating leases must be disclosed.

Requirements for the lessor

SSAP 21 requires that the amount due from a lessee under a finance lease should be shown as a debtor in the balance sheet, recorded at the net investment (see definitions above) in the lease, less any provision for bad or doubtful debts.

Total gross earnings under a finance lease should normally be allocated to accounting periods to give a constant periodic rate of return on the net cash investment in the lease; alternatively an allocation may be made out of gross earnings equal to the estimated cost of finance, with the balance recognised on a systematic basis. The practical problems of allocating the gross earnings on a finance lease are considered in detail below.

In the case of hire purchase agreements the same principles apply as in the case of a finance lease; in practice, because the lessor's cash flow position is not complicated by capital allowances or grants, SSAP 21 states that allocation of gross earnings to give a constant rate of return on the net investment in the lease will normally be acceptable.

Where a lessor receives tax-free grants against the purchase price of assets acquired for leasing, these grants should be spread over the period of the lease, being dealt with by either:

(a) treating the grant as non-taxable income; or
(b) by grossing up the grant and including the grossed up amount in arriving at profit before tax. In this case the lessor should disclose the extent to which both pre-tax profit and the tax charge have been increased as a result of *grossing up*.

In the case of an operating lease the asset should be recorded as a fixed asset and depreciated in the normal way. Rental income from an operating lease, excluding charges such as insurance and maintenance, should be recognised on a straight line basis over the period of the lease, even if payments are not made on such a basis, unless another more systematic and rational basis can be justified.

The initial direct costs of arranging any lease may be apportioned over the lease period on a *systematic and rational* basis.

Disclosure by the lessor

At each balance sheet date there must be disclosed the net investment in finance leases and in hire purchase contracts. The gross amounts of assets held for operating leases, and related accumulated depreciation, must be shown.

Disclosure must be made of the accounting policies on finance leases, operating leases and finance lease income.

Aggregate lease rentals receivable during the year must be disclosed both for finance and operating leases.

The cost of assets acquired for letting under finance leases during the year must be disclosed.

Special problems

So far we have addressed the basic rules laid down in SSAP 21 for the capitalisation of finance leases, and the techniques used to apply these rules. SSAP 21 also addresses a number of more detailed issues.

Manufacturer/dealer lessor

A manufacturer or dealer in goods may be the lessor of those goods. In such a case, a question may arise as to how the total profit on the transaction should be divided between a *selling profit*, to be taken as income on entering a firm agreement, and finance income, to be spread over the period of the lease. SSAP 21 lays down that a selling profit should be recognised under an operating lease. Under a finance lease a selling profit can be recognised, but is restricted to the excess of the *fair value* of the asset over its cost, less any grants receivable relating to the asset.

Sale and leaseback transactions

Sometimes the owner of an asset will make an arrangement to sell the asset and lease it back from the purchaser. In such a transaction the sale cannot be regarded as being at *arm's length* price, so that it may be inappropriate to take account of any gain or loss in the sale in the normal way. Where the arrangement constitutes a finance lease SSAP 21 requires that the gain or loss be amortised over the shorter of the lease term and the useful life of the asset. In the case of an operating lease:

(a) if the transaction is at fair value the gain or loss should be recorded immediately;
(b) if the transaction is below fair value then again the gain or loss should be recorded immediately, unless the apparent loss is compensated by rentals below market price in which case the apparent loss should be deferred and amortised over the period at the low rentals;
(c) if the sale price is above fair value the excess should be deferred and amortised over the shorter of the lease term and the period to the next rent review.

Application of SSAP 21 by the lessee

Example

Swithland Ltd is the lessee of an asset on a non-cancellable lease contract with a primary term of three years from 1 January 19X7. The rental is £5 404 per quarter payable in advance. The lessee has the right after the end of the primary period to continue to lease the asset as long as the company wishes at a rent of £1 per year. The lessee bears all maintenance and insurance costs. The leased asset could have been bought for cash at the start of the lease for £55 404. The rate of interest implicit in the lease is 3 per cent per quarter. The company expects to continue to employ the asset for one year after the end of the primary term, and use the straight line method of depreciation.

This is a simple example of the terms of a lease agreement. It would clearly constitute a finance lease, since the company will be able to retain the asset indefinitely after the end of the primary period. The cash price of the asset will be taken as fair value, being £55 404, so that total finance charges to be allocated will be:

	£
Total instalments: 12 × £5 404	64 848
Less fair value	55 404
Total finance charge	9 444

Table 27.2 Allocation of finance costs

Quarter	(a) *Initial capital sum before instalment* £	(b) *Instalment* £	(c) *Capital sum after instalment* £	(d) *Finance charge @ 3%* £	(e) *Capital sum at end of period* £
1/X7	55 404	5 404	50 000	1 500	51 500
2/X7	51 500	5 404	46 096	1 383	47 479
3/X7	47 479	5 404	42 075	1 262	43 337
4/X7	43 333	5 404	37 933	1 138	39 071
				5 283	
1/X8	39 071	5 404	33 667	1 010	34 677
2/X8	34 677	5 404	29 273	878	30 151
3/X8	30 151	5 404	24 747	742	25 489
4/X8	25 489	5 404	20 085	603	20 688
				3 233	
1/X9	20 688	5 404	15 284	459	15 743
2/X9	15 743	5 404	10 339	310	10 649
3/X9	10 649	5 404	5 425	157	5 402
4/X9	5 402	5 404	(2)*	2*	—
				928	

*Should be zero – attributable to rounding.

SSAP 21 requires that this charge be allocated in a way that gives a constant periodic rate of finance charge on the outstanding lease obligation. Table 27.2 shows how the finance charge would be apportioned by the *actuarial* method. Column (a) commences on the first line with the opening value of the asset. Column (b) shows on line 1 the first instalment, paid at the beginning of the first quarter, being the amount in column (a) less the amount in column (b). Column (d) shows the finance charge, computed as the quarterly interest rate applied to the outstanding capital sum as shown in column (c). This finance charge is added to the lease obligation shown in column (c) to give the total capital sum outstanding at the end of the period shown in column (e). This then becomes the opening amount of the following quarter, shown in column (a). If the correct interest rate is used then in the final quarter the instalment should exactly clear the final balance. In practice, because of rounding, a small balance will often be outstanding after the final instalment and should be added to or deducted from the finance charge for that year.

The actuarial method is long-winded and complex to apply, particularly if the implicit interest rate in the finance charge is not given and has to be computed. A simpler method of approximating a fair allocation of finance charges is to use a *sum of the digits* method as illustrated in Table 27.3. For each quarter we state the number of rental payments outstanding at the end of the quarter, as shown in column (a). For each year the finance charge is then computed as:

$$\frac{\text{Sum of digits for year}}{\text{Total sum of digits}} \times \text{Total finance charge}$$

Table 27.3 Swithland Ltd – allocation of finance charged by the *sum of the digits*

	(a) *Rentals not yet due*	(b) *Sum of digits for year*	(c) *Total sum of digits*	(d) *Total finance charge*	(e) *Finance charge for year*
1/87	11				
2/87	10	(38	÷ 66)	× 9 444	= 5 437
3/87	9				
4/87	8				
1/88	7				
2/88	6	(22	÷ 66)	× 9 444	= 3 148
3/88	5				
4/88	4				
1/89	3				
2/89	2	(6	÷ 66)	× 9 444	= 859
3/89	1				9 444
4/89	0				
	66				

Finally, the guidance notes to SSAP 21 envisage the possibility of finance charges being apportioned on a simple straight line basis, in circumstances where total finance charges are not a material item in the accounts.

Table 27.4 shows a comparison of finance charges under each method for our example. We can see how the actuarial and sum of digit methods give similar figures, while the straight line method gives a very different picture.

Depreciation on a leased asset is governed by the same principles applied to other fixed assets in SSAP 12. The period over which the asset is depreciated is the lower of:

(a) the lease term, being the primary period of the lease plus any secondary periods which may reasonably be expected to be used by the lessee;
(b) the expected useful life of the asset.

Table 27.4 Swithland Ltd – annual finance charges by each method

	Actuarial	*Sum of digits*	*Straight line*
1987	5 283	5 437	3 148
1988	3 233	3 148	3 148
1989	928	659	3 148

In our example, Swithland Ltd, we are told that the asset is to be leased for a primary period of three years, and that the company expects to lease and use the asset, at a nominal rent, for one further year. Thus the period over which the asset should be depreciated is four years, and using the straight line method annual depreciation will be:

$$\frac{£55\ 404}{4} = £13\ 851$$

Table 27.5 shows balance sheet extracts for our example Swithland Ltd, assuming that the actuarial method has been used to apportion finance charges (*see* Table 25.2). Note that to comply with the Companies Act 1985 we must split obligations within one year and over one year.

Table 27.5 Swithland Ltd – balance sheet extracts

Asset held under finance lease	*19X7*	*19X8*	*19X9*	*19Y0*
	£	£	£	£
Cost	55 404	55 404	55 404	55 404
Less: Depreciation	13 851	27 702	41 553	55 404
Net book value	41 553	27 702	13 851	—

Finance lease obligations:	*19X7*	*19X8*	*19X9*
	£	£	£
Payable within one year	18 383	20 688	—
Payable in more than one year	20 688	—	—

Application of SSAP 21 by the lessor

As we have seen, SSAP 21 requires the lessor to allocate total gross earnings to accounting periods so as to give a constant periodic rate of return on the lessor's net cash investment in the lease. Alternatively an allocation out of gross earnings equal to the lessor's cost of finance may be made, with the balance allocated as above. An example in the guidance notes accompanying SSAP 21 helps both to explain this requirement and to show how figures are computed. The example is summarised below.

Example

A company leases an asset on a non-cancellable lease contract from 1 January 19X7. The rental is £650 per quarter payable in advance. The primary term of the lease is five years, at the end of which it is expected that the asset will be sold for £2 373 and the proceeds will be passed to the lessee as a rebate of rental. The leased asset could have been purchased for cash at the start of the lease for £10 000.

Profit should be taken out of the lease at the following quarterly rate:

Assuming no interest	*Assuming quarterly interest @ 2.5%*
2.06%	0.36%

Tax at the rate of 35 per cent is payable at the beginning of the fourth quarter, nine months after the balance sheet date. A writing down allowance of 25 per cent applies to plant.

In order to compute the net cash investment in the lease we have to identify the cash flows, which will consist of:

(a) the initial outflow of £10 000 to purchase the asset;
(b) the inflow from rentals of £650 at the beginning of each quarter for five years;
(c) corporation tax, based on rental received less capital allowances.

Note that the sale of the asset at the end of the agreement has no cash flow effect, since cash is passed on to the lessee.

Capital allowances are summarised in Table 27.6, as are the annual tax charges payable in the following year. The ASC introduced a rather artificial assumption about the expected sale of the asset at tax written down value into this example to get round the problem that, unless there is such a sale of the asset, writing down allowances on a reducing balance basis would continue indefinitely.

Table 27.6 Capital allowances

19X7	Cost	10 000
	Less: WDA	2 500
19X8	WDV b/fwd	7 500
	Less: WDA	1 875
19X9	WDV b/fwd	5 625
	Less: WDA	1 406
19Y0	WDV b/fwd	4 219
	Less: WDA	1 055
19Y1	WDV b/fwd	3 164
	Less: WDA	791
		2 373
	Less: Balancing allowance	2 373
		0

Table 27.6 *(continued)*

Tax computation

	19X7	*19X8*	*19X9*	*19Y0*	*19Y1*
Rentals	2 600	2 600	2 600	2 600	2 600
Capital allowance	2 500	1 875	1 406	1 055	3 164
Taxable profit @ 35%	100	725	1 194	1 545	(564)
Tax payable	35	254	418	541	(197)

Table 27.7 Actuarial method after tax – no interest payments

Period	*Opening net cash investment* (a) £	*Cash flow in period* (b) £	*Net cash investment after cash flows* (c) £	*Profit @ 2.06%* (d) £	*Closing net cash investment* (e) £
1/X7	10 000	650	9 350	193	9 543
2/X7	9 543	650	8 893	183	9 076
3/X7	9 076	650	8 426	174	8 600
4/X7	8 600	650	7 950	164	8 114
				714	
1/X8	8 114	650	7 464	154	7 618
2/X8	7 618	650	6 968	144	7 112
3/X8	7 112	650	6 462	133	6 595
4/X8	6 595	615 (650 – 35)	5 980	123	6 103
				554	
1/X9	6 103	650	5 453	112	5 565
2/X9	5 565	650	4 915	101	5 016
3/X9	5 016	650	4 366	90	4 456
4/X9	4 456	396 (650 – 253)	4 060	84	4 144
				387	
1/Y0	4 144	650	3 494	72	3 566
2/Y0	3 566	650	2 916	60	2 976
3/Y0	2 976	650	2 326	48	2 374
4/Y0	2 374	232 (650 – 418)	2 142	44	2 186
				224	
1/Y1	2 186	650	1 536	32	1 568
2/Y1	1 568	650	918	19	937
3/Y1	937	650	287	6	293
4/Y1	293	109 (650 – 541)	184	4	188
				61	
1/Y2	188	—	188	4	192
2/Y2	192	—	192	4	196
3/Y2	196	—	196	4	200
4/Y2	200	197	(3)	(3)	—
				9	96 618

Having computed these cash flows we can now consider one method of allocating finance charges, the *actuarial method after tax*, ignoring interest payments. Table 27.7 shows how this would be computed. Column (a) shows the opening net cash investment. Column (b) shows the net cash flow at the beginning of the quarter. Column (c) shows the opening net investment adjusted for this cash flow. Column (d) shows the quarterly profit of 2.06 per cent applied to the figure in column (c); this is then added on to the outstanding net cash investment to give the closing net cash investment in column (e).

The percentage profit to be taken out in each quarter will be the amount to be applied to come to a final nil balance of net cash investment when all cash flows are completed. There is no formula to compute this percentage, and a trial and error process, or some form of iteration, must be used. In practice, computer programs would be used to find this percentage. Note that in our example, as a result of *rounding*, a balance of £3 is left at the end of the agreement; this is not material, and would simply be adjusted against profit allocated to the final year. The total of the closing net investment figures is not needed to apply this method but is shown in the figure because it is relevant to the investment period method considered below.

As we have seen above, SSAP 21 allows finance charges to be allocated either by applying a constant periodic rate of return on the net cash investment to allocate gross earnings, or alternatively by deeming interest to be paid to support the borrowings financing the net cash investment and apportioning the finance charge. Table 25.8 shows how profit to be taken out of the lease would be computed on the basis of the ASCs example for 19X7.

Table 27.8 Actuarial method after tax – including interest

Period	*Opening net cash investment* £	*Cash flow in period* £	*Net cash investment after cash flows* £	*Interest @ 2.5%* £	*Profit @ 0.36%* £	*Closing net cash investment* £
1/X7	10 000	650	9 350	234	34	9 618
2/X7	9 618	650	8 968	224	32	9 224
3/X7	9 224	650	8 574	214	31	8 819
4/X7	8 819	650	8 169	204	29	8 402
				876	126	

The interest for 19X7 would be regarded as an expense reducing the company's tax charge for that year. Thus in the fourth quarter of 19X8 this would be treated as leading to an additional cash inflow of:

$$£876 \times 35\% = £307$$

The effect of taking interest charges into account is to run down the net cash investment regarded as tied up in the lease more quickly, because of tax relief on the interest; consequently finance income will be credited to profit and loss more rapidly by this method.

In our example, Table 27.7 shows how, ignoring interest, the income credited for 19X7 would be £714. By contrast, Table 27.8 shows how, taking interest into account, income taken to profit and loss would be:

	£
Interest	876
Profit	126
	1 002

An alternative to the *actuarial method after tax* is the *investment period method*. This method is based on the figures calculated for the actuarial method after tax, either with or without interest taken into account. The profit taken on the lease for each period is computed as:

$$\frac{\text{Closing net investment at end of period}}{\text{Total of closing net investment at end of all periods}} \times \text{Total profit to be taken}$$

Total profit to be taken on our example is

$$(£650 \times 20) - £10\ 000 = £3\ 000$$

Based on our figures for the actuarial method before tax and ignoring interest, as shown in Table 27.7 above, the profit taken in the first quarter of 19X7 would be:

$$\frac{9\ 543}{96\ 618} \times £3\ 000 = £296$$

Background

From the mid 1970s onwards, the ASC was acutely aware of the need for an accounting standard on leasing, yet SSAP 21 only emerged in August 1984. The main reason for this delay was a protracted debate over the principle of capitalising finance leases, a principle opposed vigorously by the major lessors.

The major conceptual issue has been an argument about the 'substance over form' concept on which capitalisation is based. This concept states that transactions should be accounted for in accordance with their commercial substance rather than their legal form. Opponents of capitalisation questioned the validity of this concept, and also questioned whether a lease could in substance possess the characteristics of a secured loan.

ED 29 on leasing was the first UK exposure draft to refer explicitly to the potential economic consequences of a proposed accounting standard. Three potential consequences were identified:

(a) the ASC referred to the possibility that the capitalisation of finance leases might have an adverse effect on company borrowing powers, because the obligations under finance leases will be regarded as a form of borrowing.

In ED 29 the ASC stated: 'The lawyers we have consulted have advised generally that it is not capitalisation as such which would affect borrowing powers, but the entering into a lease agreement in the first place – if the item is relevant at all. However, borrowing power clauses may vary from document to document and the general advice may not be applicable in every case. Accordingly the ASC particularly request submission from any persons or companies who believe that their position might be affected in their own specific circumstances.' In fact no special problem emerged from this enquiry;

(b) the ASC referred to the argument that a requirement to capitalise finance leases might inhibit companies from entering such agreements, because of the loss of the attractions of 'off balance sheet' finance. In the absence of research on the effect of SSAP 21 in the UK, it is not possible to reach a conclusion on the significance of this issue. In the US a study found a significant number of companies claimed in reply to a questionnaire to have decided to buy assets instead of leasing because of the lease capitalisation requirements of a similar US standard; and

(c) in ED 29 the ASC considered the possibility that in response to any requirement to capitalise finance leases the UK tax authorities might change the tax rules to give capital allowances on leased assets to the lessee instead of the lessor.

The ASC corresponded on this question with the Inland Revenue, and were informed that the publication of an accounting standard on leasing would not in itself lead to any change in the tax treatment of leased assets. However, in ED 29 the ASC recognised that an accounting standard might have an influence on government thinking on any review of tax law on leasing. The ASC made the point that: 'It is fair to assume that the UK Treasury and government would take into account the possible economic consequences of any change in rules before deciding upon such a change.'

In fact prior to the issue of SSAP 21 the UK tax system was changed so that the tax benefits of leasing were substantially removed. This change in tax policy had no apparent connection with the accounting debate over leasing.

In the Republic of Ireland, a special set of conditions applied at the time of ED 29 which included a paragraph: 'By reason of the law at present obtaining in the Republic of Ireland, this exposure draft is not intended to apply to financial statements prepared or audited in the Republic of Ireland.' This exclusion was inserted because tax law in the Republic of Ireland gave capital allowances on leased assets to the party recording depreciation in the accounts. In the Irish Budget in 1984 the tax benefits of leasing were effectively removed, so that accounting practice on leasing would no longer have any effect on the tax position. As a result SSAP 21 now applies in the Irish Republic.

For futher developments see Leases: Implementation of a New Approach in the chapter on Discussion Papers.

Conclusion

The emergence of an accounting standard on leasing has been marked both by the economic issues raised and some knotty technical problems.

EXAMINATION PRACTICE

27.1 SSAP 21 rules

In relation to SSAP 21: Accounting for Leases and Hire Purchase Payments:

(a) What is the difference between a finance lease and an operating lease?

(b) In preparing both the balance sheet and the profit and loss account of a finance company (the lessor) how should you treat:

(i) An asset subject to a financial lease?

(ii) An asset subject to an operating lease?

27.2 Lease calculations

K C Ltd leases a computer from T F Ltd. The terms of the lease are that K C Ltd pays four annual rental payments of £10 000 each, the first payment to be made on 1 January 19X7. Thereafter the computer can be rented indefinitely for a nominal sum of £1 per year. The cost of the computer new would be £34 868, and the finance cost implicit in the lease is 10 per cent per year.

Compute the amount of the lease obligation to be shown at the end of each year in the balance sheet.

CHAPTER 28

SSAP 24: Accounting for Pension Costs

The basic problem

The provision of a pension is part of the benefits provided to many employees. Two types of scheme arise:

(a) a defined contribution scheme involves an employer in making agreed contributions to a pension scheme. The benefits paid to the employee will then depend on these contributions and related investment earnings. This type of scheme is common in smaller businesses. The cost to the employer is easy to identify; and
(b) in a defined benefit scheme the benefits to be paid are defined, often in terms of the employee's final pay. Such schemes are common in larger enterprises. The level of contributions needed to meet benefit requirements is necessarily a matter for estimate. In this case, because of the uncertainty as to the final cost, a number of accounting problems arise.

Actuarial issues

In a defined benefit scheme the choices of assumptions and valuation method made by an actuary can have a major impact on the estimated necessary level of contributions. Major matters to estimate include:

(a) future rates of inflation and pay increases;
(b) increases to pensions in payment;
(c) number of employees joining and leaving the scheme;
(d) deaths of employees before retirement age;
(e) the age profile of employees;
(f) earnings on investments.

Some of these estimates may be related and offsetting. One example is that income from investment yields and costs of pension increases may both be related to inflation.

Funding

Pension schemes are often financed from a special fund managed by independent trustees. Payments into the fund are likely to be linked to actuarial estimates of the required level of funding. From time to time a revised estimate may lead to:

(a) changes in the level of contribution made into the fund;
(b) lump sum payments by the enterprise to the fund or vice versa reflecting changed requirements.

Key definitions

Definitions in SSAP 24 include:

(a) An *ex gratia pension* or a *discretionary* or *ex gratia increase in a pension* is one which the employer has no legal, contractual or implied commitment to provide.
(b) A *defined benefit scheme* is a pension scheme in which the rules specify the benefits to be paid and the scheme is financed accordingly.
(c) A *defined contribution scheme* is a pension scheme in which the benefits are directly determined by the value of contributions paid in respect of each member. Normally the rate of contribution is specified in the rules of the scheme.
(d) An *experience surplus or deficiency* is that part of the excess or deficiency of the actuarial value of assets over the actuarial value of liabilities, on the basis of the valuation method used, which arises because events have not coincided with the actuarial assumptions made for the last valuation.
(e) A *funding plan* is the timing of payments in an orderly fashion to meet the future cost of a given set of benefits.
(f) A *funded scheme* is a pension scheme where the future liabilities for benefits are provided for by the accumulation of assets held externally to the employing company's business.
(g) The *level of funding* is the proportion at a given date of the actuarial value of liabilities for pensioners' and deferred pensioners' benefits and for members' accrued benefits that is covered by the actuarial value of assets. For this purpose the actuarial value of future contributions is excluded from the value of assets.
(h) An *ongoing actuarial valuation* is a valuation in which it is assumed that the pension scheme will continue in existence and (where appropriate) that new members will be admitted. The liabilities allow for expected increases in earnings.
(i) *Past service* is used in the statement to denote service before a given date. It is often used, however, to denote service before entry into the pension scheme.
(j) *Pensionable payroll/earnings* are the earnings on which benefits and/or contributions are calculated. One or more elements of earnings (e.g. overtime) may be excluded, and/or there may be a reduction to take account of all or part of the state scheme benefits which the member is deemed to receive.
(k) A *pension scheme* is an arrangement (other than accident insurance) to provide pension and/or other benefits for members on leaving service or retiring and, after a member's death, for his/her dependents.

Required practice

The principles

SSAP 24 applies to any situation when an employer is committed to a pension scheme. Commitment may arise from legal requirements or contract, it may be implicit in the employer's actions and may arise from discretionary or *ex gratia* payments. The accounting objective is to ensure that the accounts recognise the expected cost of providing pensions on a systematic and rational basis over the period of the employees' services.

Defined contribution schemes

In this case the charge against profits should be the amount of contributions payable to the pension scheme for the accounting period.

Defined benefit schemes

In this case actuarial valuation methods should be used. The actuarial assumptions must be compatible *taken as a whole*, giving the actuary's *best estimate*.

On the basis of these actuarial assumptions pension costs should be allocated over employees' service lives by a *substantially level percentage* of the pensionable payroll.

Where variations from the regular cost arise these should normally be allocated over the expected remaining service lives of current employees in the scheme. Exceptions to this rule are:

(a) changes arise because of a significant reduction in the number of employees in the scheme. Reductions in these circumstances should be recognised as they occur;
(b) prudence may dictate that a material deficit be recognised over a shorter period than the expected remaining service lives of employees in the scheme; and
(c) where a refund to the employer is subject to deduction of tax then the surplus or deficiency may be accounted for in the period in which the refund occurs.

Ex gratia arrangements

The capital costs of granting *ex gratia* pensions or increases, to the extent that these are not covered by a surplus, should be recognised in the period when they are granted.

Balance sheet

The balance sheet should show a *net pension provision* or prepayment for the difference between the cumulative pension cost recognised in the profit and loss account and total of contributions made into the pension fund and pensions paid directly.

Required disclosure

The accounts should state whether the pension scheme is on a *defined benefit* or *defined contribution* basis.

For a defined contribution scheme there should be disclosed:

(a) the accounting policy;
(b) the pension cost charge for the period;
(c) any outstanding or prepaid contributions at the balance sheet date.

For a defined benefit scheme there should be stated:

(a) whether it is funded or unfunded;
(b) the accounting policy and, if different, the funding policy;
(c) whether pension arrangements are assessed on the advice of a professionally qualified actuary, together with the date of the most recent formal actuarial valuation. Where the actuary is an employee of the company or of a group of which the company is part, this fact should be disclosed;
(d) the pension cost charge for the period, with an explanation of significant variations in comparing with the previous accounting period;
(e) any provisions or prepayments in the balance sheet arising from differences between the costs shown in the accounts and payments to the fund;
(f) any commitment to make additional payments over a limited number of years;
(g) the accounting treatment adopted for a refund made subject to deduction of tax.

The following disclosures must also be made, except in the case of a subsidiary company which is a member of a group scheme and has a UK or Irish holding company:

(a) the amount of any deficiency on a current funding level basis, indicating any action being taken on the matter;
(b) an outline of the results of the most recent actuarial valuation or formal review including:
    (i) the actuarial method and main assumptions,
    (ii) the market value of scheme assets,
    (iii) the level of funding expressed in percentage terms,
    (iv) comments on any material actuarial surplus or deficiency.

A subsidiary company which is a member of a group scheme should state this fact and report if contributions are based on the group scheme as a whole. The accounts should state the name of the holding company in whose accounts details of the scheme will be found.

For further developments, see FRED: 20 Retirements Benefits in the chapter on FREDs, and UITF 18 in the chapter on UITFs.

Conclusion

Pension costs are a difficult topic for the accountant because they constitute a major expense subject to fluctuation in the light of events in the long-term future. While the job of making estimates and computing their effects is the responsibility of the actuary, the accountant's role is to report the impact of changes in actuarial valuation in a consistent way.

EXAMINATION PRACTICE

28.1 Pension costs

In conjunction with SSAP 24: Accounting for Pension Costs:

(a) Explain the objective in accounting for pension costs.
(b) How are the following items defined:
  (i) A defined contribution scheme?
  (ii) A defined benefit scheme?
  (iii) An experience deficiency?
(c) What information should be disclosed concerning a formal actuarial valuation of a defined benefit scheme?

CHAPTER 29

SSAP 25: Segmental Reporting

The need for a standard

The Companies Act 1985 requires disclosure of certain segmented information where a company carries on two or more classes of business that differ substantially from each other, or supplies geographical markets that differ substantially from each other. The International Stock Exchange also requires certain segmental information. SSAP 25 provides detailed guidance on the provision of such information, together with some additional requirements.

Definition of terms

SSAP 25 offers the following definitions:

(a) A *class of business* is a distinguishable component of an entity that provides a separate product or service or a separate group of related products or services.
(b) A *geographical segment* is a geographical area comprising an individual country or group of countries in which an entity operates, or to which it supplies products or services.
(c) *Origin* of turnover is the geographical segment from which products or services are supplied to a third party or to another segment.
(d) *Destination* of turnover is the geographical segment to which products or services are supplied.

Basic requirements

If an entity has two or more classes of business, or operates in two or more geographical segments which differ substantially from each other, then it should define these classes in the accounts and report with respect to each class the following:

(a) turnover, distinguishing between turnover from external customers and turnover from other segments of the entity;
(b) profit or loss before tax, minority interests and extraordinary items;
(c) net assets.

The disclosure of geographical segmentation of turnover should be based on origin. Where materially different turnover to third parties by destination should also be disclosed; if this is excluded on grounds of not being materially different that fact should be stated.

The segment profit or loss before tax should normally be before interest earned or incurred; similarly net assets will normally be non-interest-bearing operating assets less non-interest-bearing operating liabilities.

However, where any part of the entity's businesses is to earn or incur interest, or interest income/expense is central to the business, then interest should be taken into account in arriving at the reported segmental profit/loss and related assets/liabilities will form part of reported net assets.

If the total of segmented amounts does not equal the related total in the accounts then a reconciliation between the two shall be provided.

Comparative figures for the previous year should be provided. The directors should redefine segments when appropriate, and the nature and effects of any change should be reported with an appropriate restatement of the previous year's figures.

Associated companies

If associated companies account for at least 20 per cent of either total profit/loss or total net assets then the segmental report should include details of:

(a) the group's share of profit/loss on the same basis as above.
(b) the group's share of net assets, including unamortised goodwill, where possible attributing *fair value* to assets at the acquisition date.

Such information need not be published if it is unobtainable or prejudicial to the associate. In such a case the reason for non-disclosure should be given in a note, with a brief description of the omitted business.

Exemptions

All companies are required to comply with SSAP 25 to the extent that the requirements coincide with company law. The additional requirements only apply where:

(a) the entity is a plc or has a plc subsidiary, or
(b) is a banking or insurance company or group, or
(c) exceeds the criteria, multiplied by ten, for defining a medium-sized company under company law.

Practical problems of compliance

SSAP 25 contains some useful guidance on practical problems of compliance.

In deciding whether a separate class of business is a distinguishable segment, factors to consider include:

(a) the nature of the products;
(b) the nature of the production process;
(c) the markets in which output is sold;
(d) the distribution channels for products;

(e) the manner in which the entity's activities are organised;
(f) any separate legislative framework relating to part of the business.

A geographical segment is an individual country or group of countries where the entity either operates or supplies goods and services. The geographical analysis should enable the user of the accounts to assess the impact of:

(a) expansionist or restrictive economic climates;
(b) stable or unstable political regimes;
(c) exchange control regulations;
(d) exchange rate fluctuations.

Overall, in the case of both business and geographical segments, the user needs to distinguish between areas that:

(a) earn a rate of return out of line with the entity as a whole;
(b) are subject to different degrees of risk;
(c) have experienced different rates of growth;
(d) have different potential for future development.

It is suggested that a segment should be reported on separately if:

(a) third-party turnover is 10 per cent or more of total turnover,
(b) profit or loss is 10 per cent or more of total profits or total losses, whichever is greater, or
(c) net assets are 10 per cent or more of total net assets.

SSAP 25 also considers the situation where common costs or common net assets cannot be apportioned to segments on a basis that is other than misleading, and argues that these should be identified separately.

The example below shows how business segment information might be disclosed.

Fulke plc – Segmental report

	Hotels		*Brewing*		*Group*	
	19X9	*19X8*	*19X9*	*19X8*	*19X9*	*19X8*
	£000	£000	£000	£000	£000	£000
Turnover						
Total sales	33 000	20 000	38 000	36 000	71 000	56 000
Inter-segment sales	—	—	1 000	1 000	1 000	1 000
Sales to third parties	33 000	20 000	37 000	35 000	70 000	55 000
Profit before tax						
Segment profit	5 400	4 000	3 600	3 500	9 400	7 500
Common costs					100	100
Operating profit					9 500	7 600
Net interest					(500)	(500)
					10 000	8 100

	Hotels		*Brewing*		*Group*	
	19X9	*19X8*	*19X9*	*19X8*	*19X9*	*19X8*
	£000	£000	£000	£000	£000	£000
Group share of associated company profits			1 000	900	1 000	900
Group profit before tax					11 000	9 000
Net assets						
Segment net assets	58 000	41 000	37 000	36 000	95 000	77 000
					3 000	3 000
Unallocated net assets					98 000	80 000
Group share of associates' net assets			10 000	9 000	10 000	9 000
Total net assets					108 000	89 000

Geographical segments would be analysed on a similar basis.

EXAMINATION PRACTICE

29.1 SSAP 25

In relation to SSAP 25: Segmental Reporting:

(a) Explain the basis on which disclosure of geographical segmentation of turnover should be made.

(b) Outline the issues to be considered in deciding whether a separate class of business is a distinguished segment.

29.2 Applying the rules

Vorsat plc operates in two business segments, one being a chain of butchers' shops in the UK and the other being a chain of hotels in the UK and Spain. The financial director is applying SSAP 25. He views the two activities as separate business segments but is wondering whether it is also necessary to identify segmental information separately for the hotel operations in each of the two countries.

You are required to explain the factors which the financial director needs to consider.

CHAPTER 30

Financial Reporting Standard for Smaller Entities

Introduction

Successive governments have been concerned about the burden of bureaucracy in small businesses. There is the view that this stifles entrepreneurial initiative and prevents businesses from reaching their full potential. The requirements for financial reporting and auditing were also thought to be part of this burden, particularly as standards were becoming more complex. Therefore, in 1994, the CCAB (the Consultative Committee of Accountancy Bodies) conducted a consultative exercise on the application of accounting standards to smaller entities.

The basic problem

The basic problem is whether all companies, regardless of size, should follow the same accounting standards, or whether there should be one set of accounting standards for large companies and another set for small companies.
This debate was referred to as the Big GAAP/Little GAAP debate. A number of different views were held.

- Some held the view that there should only be one GAAP and this should be applicable to all companies. Whilst they recognised that many of the accounting standards were complex they argued that since only a few of the issues within these standards were relevant to small companies, in practice they did not have to comply. Thus they would argue, for example, that since few small companies had convertible debt they would not have to comply with FRS 4. If they did have convertible debt, then the standard was just as applicable to them as any other company, regardless of size, and they should therefore comply.
- Some argued that the accounting standards are in general aimed at large companies and that an entirely new suite of standards should be prepared for small businesses to meet their specific needs. For example, it may be more relevant to allow small companies to value stock on a variable cost basis rather than the requirement in SSAP 9 to include fixed overheads in stock.
- Another argument was that when each standard was issued, the ASB should determine its relevance to small companies and should limit its scope, if necessary, to a certain size of business. FRS 1, for example, gives exemption to the standard to 'small companies', as defined by company law; SSAP 25 has an exemption criteria based on the company law criteria for a medium-sized

company, multiplied by a factor of ten.
- Others argued that a distinction could be made between measurement issues and disclosure issues. They argued that all companies should use the same measurement techniques but that smaller entities might be allowed exemption from certain of the disclosure requirements.
- Another argument was that the debate was irrelevant because accounting standards were not a burden. They might be a burden to their financial advisers, and this might result in larger fees, but if the information was useful, and it met the cost–benefit criteria, then it should be disclosed.
- Some argued that tailoring accounting standards to smaller businesses was a logical step, given that company law had already allowed recognised different reporting requirements for small- and medium-sized companies.

The result of this debate was that the ASB issued the Financial Reporting Standard for Smaller Entities (FRSSE) in 1997.

Financial Reporting Standard for Smaller Entities – detailed requirements

The FRSSE is an accounting standard; it incorporates all the relevant FRSs and UITF Abstracts in a modified and simplified version relevant for smaller companies. In general, the FRSSE uses the same definitions and accounting treatments as in the 'full' standards but it excludes a number of the disclosure requirements. It is discretionary for those companies who fall within its scope and, if a company adopts the FRSSE, then it need only comply with this single standard. If it chooses not to adopt the FRSSE, then it must comply with all extant standards and UITF Abstracts.

The ASB reviews all standards for their applicability to small businesses and effectively covers them all within this one 'omnibus' standard. The criteria which the ASB uses to assess the applicability of a standard to small businesses are:

General relevance

- Is the standard essential practice for all businesses?
- Is the standard generally relevant to the transactions of small businesses?

User Needs

- Does the standard lead to a transaction being reported in a way that the owner of a small business is likely to understand?
- Does the standard meet the needs of the users of small business accounts?
- Would users who are not shareholders receive the information, given that they may only have access to abbreviated accounts?
- Does the standard give additional information to that required by company law?

Measurement

- Is the standard compatible with that used by the Inland Revenue when computing profit?
- Does the standard provide the least cumbersome way of reporting an item?
- Are the measurement methods practical for small businesses?

If, on balance, the answer to these questions is 'yes', then the full standard should be applied to small businesses; if the answers are generally 'no', then the FRSSE gives exemption or an alternative treatment.

Objective

The objective of the FRSSE is to ensure that companies falling within its scope provide information which meets user needs, but it recognises that there may be an emphasis on providing stewardship information rather than decision-making information in a small company.

Scope

Companies which come within the definition of a small company for purposes of company law may choose to adopt the FRSSE. Where a small business prepares consolidated accounts it may adopt the FRSSE but it must also comply with the accounting standards which apply to group accounts.

The content of the FRSSE

The FRSSE effectively goes through all the SSAPs and FRSs under such headings as fixed assets and goodwill, current assets, taxation, etc. (It is interesting that there is a heading for discounting, which gives a clear indication that the ASB wish to introduce discounting into financial statements and they are preparing the way for smaller companies by introducing this as a separate heading.)
It states under each heading what the standard requires with regard to each item. The FRSSE produces tables which cross-reference the FRSSE paragraphs to the paragraphs in an FRS or SSAP. It categorises for each reference whether it is adopted in full ('complete'), or with minor change or major change. Standards may be dealt with in any of the following ways:

Treatment	**Example**
Adopted in full, i.e. complete	SSAP 17 adopted in full
Disclosure requirements reduced – major change	FRS 3 – no reference to continuing or discontinued operations
Disclosure requirements reduced – minor change	SSAP 4 – no reference to disclosure of accounting policy
No reference, unless consolidated accounts being prepared	FRS 6
No reference – not applicable to small companies	FRS 15 – no mention of renewals accounting
No reference	SSAP 25 – because small company already exempt from its requirements
Additional clarification	FRS 8 – disclosure required re directors' personal guarantees

Financial statements must state if they have been prepared in accordance with the FRSSE.

The FRSSE will need regular revisions to bring it up to date as new standards are issued. The title of a FRSSE will include the date from which it is effective so that it can be distinguished from earlier versions. For example, the FRSSE issued in December 1999 is referred to as FRSSE (March 2000) and includes all FRSs up to FRS 15.

Controversy

Critics of the concept of a FRSSE argue that true and fair is an absolute; there cannot be different concepts of true and fair for different sizes of company. The ASB were clearly concerned about the legality of developing Big GAAP standards for large companies and Small GAAP standards for small companies. They took legal advice which confirmed that this approach was acceptable, providing a rational case could be made for there being different GAAPs. Rational grounds might include:

- the different nature of small and large companies;
- the different user needs in small and large companies.

Furthermore FRSSE states that:

> Where there is doubt whether applying provisions of the FRSSE would be sufficient to give a true and fair view, adequate explanation should be given in the notes to the accounts of the transaction or arrangement concerned and the treatment adopted.

Many of those involved with small businesses would argue that the most relevant primary statement is the cash flow statement. It is therefore strange that small companies are exempt from FRS 1. The ASB acknowledges the force of this argument to the extent that the FRSSE contains a section on 'Voluntary Disclosures' where small companies are 'encouraged' to produce cash flow statements.

A more radical view is that the ASB have tackled this 'back-to-front'. Rather than take existing standards to see if they fit small companies, it would have been preferable to start with small companies and see what standards would be useful to them. However, given the limited resources of the ASB, it seems inevitable that their work will focus on large listed companies because that is where the public interest is at its greatest.

The ASB has failed to acknowledge that shareholders in small companies receive full accounts and other users, for example creditors, only have access to abbreviated accounts. It therefore makes little difference to creditors if Big or Little GAAP is used since abbreviated accounts have few disclosures attached to them anyway. It would be preferable if the whole issue of users of small company accounts were addressed as part of company law reform.

Conclusion

The FRSSE is discretionary. The proof of whether Little GAAP is welcomed by the accountancy profession will be evidenced by the number of accountancy practices which adopt it on behalf of their clients. Some may choose not to adopt it on conceptual grounds, arguing that it does not provide a true and fair view. Some may adopt it believing that it meets their small client needs.

It would be unfortunate if some choose not to adopt it, arguing that it is another burden on small businesses, since this is the very thing that FRSSE was designed to

alleviate. Some consider it a burden because it requires more audit and accountancy preparation time to apply a different GAAP to large and small companies. They argue that since so few of the Big GAAP standards apply to small companies it is more efficient to have one GAAP for all clients.

The original FRSSE was issued in 1997 and this introduced the concept of there being a complete, distinct accounting standard for smaller companies. The ASB intends to undertake a review of how the FRSSE has worked after two years of operation, and this is due to be held in 2000.

EXAMINATION PRACTICE

30.1 What is the role and purpose of the FRSSE?

30.2 What are the arguments for and against the FRSSE?

Statement of Principles for Financial Reporting

Introduction

Many countries have sought to produce a 'conceptual framework', and in the UK this has been titled a 'statement of principles' (SOP). The key issues are:

- the definition of a conceptual framework,
- the development of a conceptual framework.

Definition of a conceptual framework

A conceptual framework is a statement of the theoretical principles which underpin the study of a subject. In the social sciences, such as accounting, a conceptual framework is a basic structure for determining objectives and how these can be achieved. The Financial Accounting Standards Board (FASB) in the US in 1967 defined a conceptual framework as:

> a constitution, a coherent system of interrelated objectives and fundamentals that can lead to consistent standards and that prescribes the nature, function and limits of financial accounting and financial statements

A conceptual framework should be able to provide a 'thread of reason' that extends from abstract objectives to practical applications. In theory it should be possible to take a requirement in an FRS and trace it back to the objectives of accounting; *vice versa,* it should be possible to take an objective of accounting and trace this through to a series of requirements in FRSs.

The development of a conceptual framework

Many countries have embarked on establishing a conceptual framework of accounting, for example the United States, Canada, Australia and New Zealand. In 1989 the International Accounting Standards Committee (IASC) issued 'Framework for the Preparation and Presentation of Financial Statements' which is their conceptual framework. The first attempt at a conceptual framework in the UK was in 1975 when 'The Corporate Report' was issued and the latest is the 'Statement of Principles for Financial Reporting' in 1999.

It is interesting that the attempts to develop a conceptual framework in the countries above all began after they had begun to set accounting standards. This is partly because the need for a conceptual framework was not always agreed upon and partly because of the difficulty in establishing a conceptual framework. The difficulty is partly because of fundamental disagreement on the nature of accounting, for example the use of historic or current values, and partly on the conflict of interest between users and preparers.

This chapter appears after you have read the earlier chapters on SSAPs and FRSs. You will find it useful to refer back to these to see how the SOP provides a theoretical foundation to them, for example FRS 15 and FRS 12 .

Statement of Principles for Financial Reporting – the detail

The SOP is not an accounting standard; it is a statement for guidance. It is applicable to all entities producing financial statements which are intended to give a true and fair view.

The SOP is in eight chapters. The coherence of these chapters is portrayed in Figure 31.1

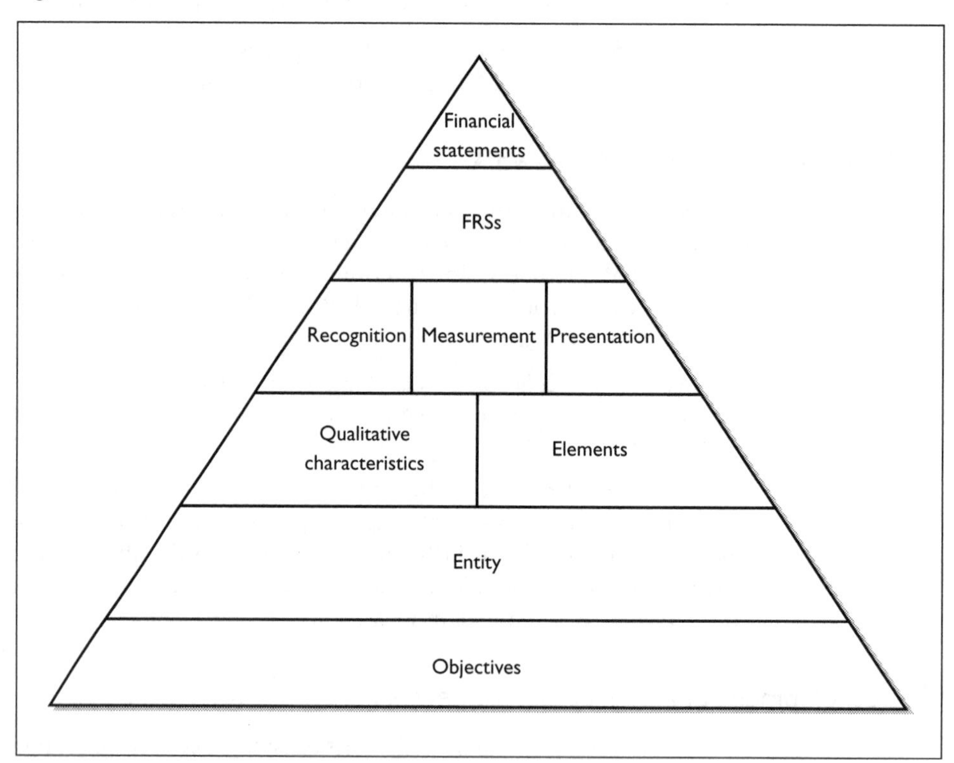

Fig. 31.1 A conceptual framework

At the foundation are the objectives; from this all other issues flow. The reporting entity determines who should report; the characteristics ensure that the information produced is useful and the elements describe the building blocks from which financial statements are constructed. The next level is more practical – what should be recognised, and how to measure and present this information. Finally this results in the release of accounting standards, which are followed when preparing financial statements.

The chapters are:

1. The objectives,
2. The reporting entity,
3. The qualitative characteristics,
4. The elements,
5. Recognition,
6. Measurement,
7. Presentation,
8. Accounting for the interest in other entities.

Chapter 1: The objectives of financial statements

The objective of financial statements is to provide information about the performance, financial position and cash flows which is useful to a wide range of users for assessing the stewardship of management and for decision making. The users and their needs are:

User	Information Needs
Investor	the risk and return on their investment.
Lenders	the payment of interest and the repayment of the principal sum.
Suppliers	the payment of the sum due.
Employees	the 'risk and return' on their labour – the payment of salaries and pensions and whether the company will provide stable employment. This information is needed at a disaggregated level, i.e. subsidiary or branch.
Customers	the continued existence of the company (important for warranty claims) and the supply of goods (important if a monopoly).
Government	the regulation of the economy and the imposition of taxes on a fair basis.
Public	these will vary; an example may be the effect of an entity on a local economy, for example a university.

Although the various user groups have different needs, most of these needs can be met by focusing on investors. Their needs can be met by providing general purpose financial reports; by contrast, special financial reports are usually produced to meet the specific needs of a particular user, as for example when a banker requests financial information as part of a business plan. General purpose financial reports provide information on the financial position (balance sheet), performance (profit and loss account and STRGL) and cash flow / financial adaptability (cash flow statements).

Chapter 2: The reporting entity

Companies should produce financial statements which report on all the activities and resources under their control. In the case of an individual company this will be the resources under its direct control. For groups of companies this will be as for single companies, plus the resources in subsidiary companies.

Chapter 3: The qualitative characteristics of financial information

This chapter is concerned with the qualities of financial information which make it useful. The significant terms and their relationship are expressed in Fig 31.2.

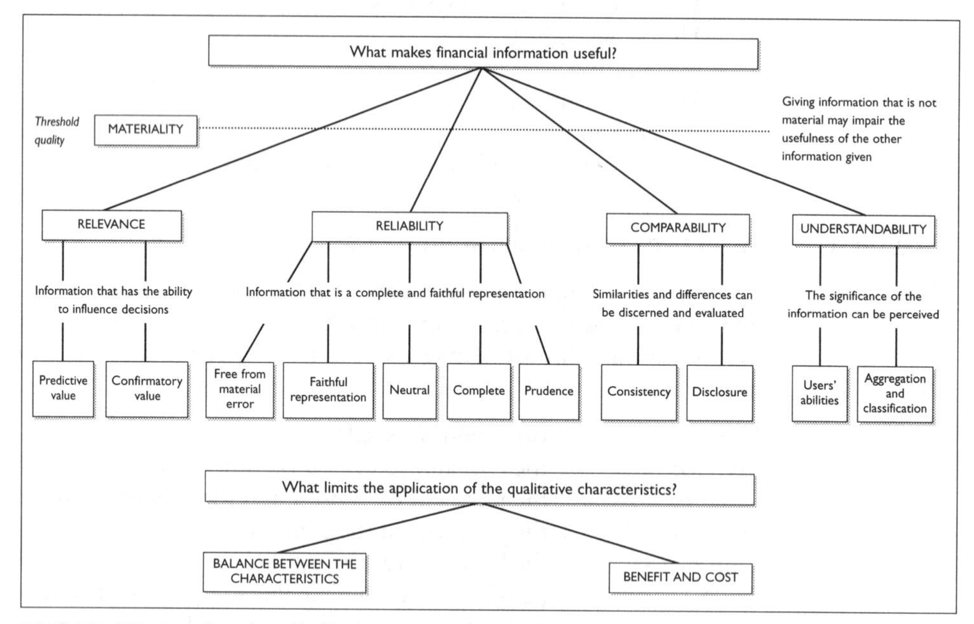

Fig 31.2 The qualitative characteristics of financial information

What makes financial information useful ?

The following is a list of the qualitative characteristics of financial information which make it useful.

Materiality: The threshold for disclosure is materiality. Information is material if its misstatement or omission is likely to influence the decisions of the users. If immaterial information is disclosed this excessive information may cause 'information overload' to the user and the impact of material information may be lessened.

Relevance: Information provided should be relevant, which is defined as information which is likely to influence the decisions of users. Where there is a choice of what information to disclose, this should be resolved by disclosing the information which is most likely to have an impact on users' decisions. Relevant information should enable users to evaluate past events and predict future events, as well as providing information which confirms (or otherwise) their past evaluations and predictions.

Reliability: Reliable information is free from material error. It should faithfully represent what it seeks to represent. FRS 5: Reporting the Substance of Transactions provides an interesting example of whether the portrayal of sale and repurchase agreements as secured loans is a faithful representation. Reliable information should be neutral, that is, it is free from deliberate and systematic bias. Biased information, on the other hand, seeks to influence a user to arrive at a particular point of view. Information should be complete with no material data omitted. Given the uncertainty in financial information, and the importance of making users aware of their risk, it is sensible to exercise a degree of caution in reporting information, and thus financial statements should be prudent.

Comparability: Comparability requires consistency across three dimensions:

- consistency within the entity, for example in branches and subsidiaries;
- consistency from one year to another for the same company;
- consistency between companies.

Disclosure of accounting policies is necessary to determine whether consistency exists; if it does not, then there should be sufficient disclosure to enable meaningful comparisons to be made. An example would be the disclosure of depreciation policies on property in the leisure industry where there has been notable inconsistencies.

Understandability: Whether information is understandable will depend to a large extent on the abilities of the user. What is understandable to the accountant, banker, financial adviser will be very different from what is understood by the average person. The SOP assumes that users :

> have a reasonable knowledge of business and economic activities and accounting and a willingness to study with reasonable diligence the information provided.

The presentation of information will also affect whether it is understood, and this will depend, for example, upon the level of aggregation and classification. The issue of aggregation may be seen in SSAP 25: Segmental Reporting and that of classification in SSAP 19: Accounting for Investment Properties, which defines what is classified as an investment property.

What limits the application of the qualitative characteristics?

Balance between the characteristics: The qualitative characteristics may sometimes be in conflict and this must be resolved in such a way that the objectives of financial statements can still be met.

Examples of conflict are :

Relevance v reliability: An example of this conflict is the measurement of asset values; current value may be more relevant than historic cost, but it is less reliable. Up-to-date information is more relevant than out-of-date information, but it may be less reliable. If preparers of financial statements wait until all information can be checked for reliability it may be too late to be useful. As a simple example, recognising debtors is more relevant than waiting until the cash is paid, but it is less reliable if debtors do not pay.

Neutrality v prudence: It may be argued that the concept of prudence, if applied too rigorously, systematically biases the information to understate assets and overstate liabilities, with a consequent adverse effect on users' decisions.

Relevant, reliable, comparable v understandable: There may be some material information which meets all the qualitative characteristics apart from being understandable, as defined above. There may be few users, however diligent, who will be able to understand, for example, the measurement issues in FRS 4: Capital Instruments.

Chapter 4: The elements of financial statements

The elements are the building blocks from which financial statements are constructed.

There are seven elements:

1. assets,
2. liabilities,
3. ownership interest,
4. gains,
5. losses,
6. contribution from owners,
7. distribution to owners.

Assets

Assets are defined as 'rights or other access to future economic benefits controlled by an entity as a result of past transactions or events'. This definition includes a number of important phrases.

'Rights or other access' makes it clear that it is not the asset itself, or the legal ownership, which is important, but rather the right to receive the benefits. This definition allows leases to be capitalised even though they are not legally owned.

'Future economic benefits' makes it clear that all assets must ultimately yield cash inflow into the business.

'Past transaction or events' is important in emphasising that financial statements are based on past transactions, not on future transactions or intentions.

Liabilities

Liabilities are defined as 'obligations of an entity to transfer economic benefits as a result of past transactions or events'. This is the opposite of an asset in that it is the transfer, not the receipt of economic benefits. The definition also includes the phrase 'past transactions'. This prevents a company making provisions for intended expenditure in the future.

Ownership interest

This is defined as the difference between assets and liabilities. This implies that the owners have a residual interest in the business after all the liabilities have been met.

Gains and losses

Gains are defined as 'increases in ownership interest not resulting from contributions from owners'. Losses are as above, except they are decreases in ownership interest. The definition of gains includes all forms of income and revenue, regardless of whether they are realised or unrealised. Similarly the definition of losses includes expenses and recognised losses, regardless of whether they are realised or unrealised. Gains and losses appear in the statements of financial performance, and, depending on their precise nature, this will be the profit and loss account or the STRGL.

Contributions from owners / distribution to owners

Contributions increase ownership interest, distributions decrease ownership interest, other than from gains and losses. An example of a contribution is a rights issue and dividends are an example of a distribution.

Chapter 5: Recognition in financial statements

An item is said to be recognised if it is included in a financial statement; an item is derecognised when it is eliminated. Recognition concerns the effect of transactions on the elements (see above) in financial statements .

Assets and liabilities

If a transaction creates an asset or liability, it is recognised when there is sufficient evidence that the asset or liability has been created and it can be reliably measured. Assets and liabilities are derecognised when there is sufficient evidence that a transaction has eliminated the asset/liability. Events, as well as transactions, may also give rise to recognition and derecognition. For example, the discovery of a natural resource may create an asset without there being a transaction; a fire may lead to an asset being derecognised without there being a transaction.

There are three stages to recognition:

- initial recognition, when an item is included for the first time in a financial statement;
- subsequent remeasurement, where the carrying value of an existing asset/ liability is changed;
- derecognition, where an existing asset/liability is eliminated.

At its simplest, a debtor is recognised when goods are sold; the debtor may be remeasured if there are doubts about the debt being paid; the debt is eliminated when the cash is received.

When deciding on initial recognition, there are two categories of uncertainty:

- *Element uncertainty* – has an asset or a liability been created. For example, there may be doubt on whether development expenditure is an asset; there may be doubts on where a court case is a liability. These matters are resolved by examining evidence.
- *Measurement uncertainty* – the basis may either be historical cost or current value and there must be sufficient evidence to measure this reliably (see measurement below).

Similarly, there may be uncertainty when deciding on derecognition. Does an asset/liability still exist and can it still be measured reliably?

Revenue recognition

The discussion so far has been on the recognition/derecognition of assets/liabilities, rather than gains and losses. The SOP is quite clear that:

> the starting point for the recognition process is always the effect that the transaction or other event involved has had on the reporting entity's assets and liabilities.

In other words, if assets increase there must be a gain; if liabilities increase there must be a loss (assuming there are no contributions from owners/distribution to owners). The SOP admits that looking at gains and losses is only to help to identify the effect on asset and liabilities. There are two aspects to this process:

- matching,
- critical events in the operating cycle.

Matching

Matching occurs where expenditure is matched to a period of time. Where rent is paid in advance, for example, the part which relates to the current period is expenditure and the part beyond is classed as a pre-payment asset.

Matching also occurs where revenue and expenditure are matched in order to measure profit. Because expenditure typically occurs before revenue is received, it is carried forward as an asset until such time as the revenue is recognised, at which time it is 'expensed'. Taken to its logical conclusion, since nearly all expenditure is incurred in the hope of future benefits, it would be possible to carry forward most expenditure. The SOP prevents this by requiring an asset recognition test; if it does not meet the definition of an asset, for example the receipts of future economic benefits, it must be written off. If the future economic benefits are too uncertain, it must also be written off. Thus matching is not the driving force behind recognition. However, once an asset, for example, has been recognised, then matching is used to allocate that cost to the profit and loss account. This might mean to a single year, (derecognition) or it might mean over a number of years (partial derecognition). In the latter case the asset may need 'subsequent remeasurement'.

Critical events in the operating cycle

A typical operating cycle might be:

1. receipt of raw materials,
2. manufacture,
3. customer places order,
4. goods are sold,
5. customer pays.

Typically the critical point is when the goods are sold and at this time a sale and the asset (debtor) are recognised. In an illegal activity, such as drugs, the dealer might consider that stage 1 was the critical event and recognise an (illegal) profit by valuing the raw materials at market ('street') value. In contrast, a 'barrow boy' selling on credit terms to pedestrians without references or security might consider stage 5 the critical event! The SOP makes it clear that the identification of critical events for the recognition of gains is an aid in ascertaining whether an asset should be recognised, i.e. if there is a gain, there must be an increase in assets.

Prudence

The discussion on recognition can be related back to the qualitative characteristics of financial information. Reliable information should be prudent. This means that more evidence is needed to measure assets than liabilities; greater reliability for the measurement of assets is required than for liabilities. However, prudence should not lead to bias and there is no justification, for example, to deliberately and systematically create hidden reserves by overstating liabilities.

Chapter 6: Measurement in financial statements

Measurement issues involve:

- selecting a measurement basis,

- determining the monetary amount under that basis,
- revising monetary amounts where appropriate.

Selecting a measurement basis

There are a number of alternative models for measuring profit and valuing net assets, and each has an underlying capital maintenance concept. Examples of such models are historical cost, replacement cost and net realisable value. These models may also involve adjustments for inflation, which give rise to models for current purchasing power (CPP) and current cost accounting (CCA). These models may be broadly categorised into historical cost models and current value models. (See Chapter 36, Inflation Accounting in the UK.)

In practice, none of these models exist in its pure form. The historical cost model values assets at the lower of cost and net realisable value. Audit reports frequently refer to 'modified historical cost' where some assets, for example buildings, are at a current value. Even when companies adopt current values, they do not necessarily value all classes of assets at current value. Thus in practice there exists a 'mixed measurement system' where some assets and liabilities are at historical cost and some at current value. The choice for companies within the mixed measurement system is to what extent assets and liabilities should be at historical cost or current value.

Companies, when making their choice, should be guided by the objectives of financial statements and the qualitative characteristics of financial information. The SOP implies (but does not say) that current value is more relevant than historical cost; it also states that it should not be assumed that historical is more reliable than current value. There are many matters of judgement which have to be made in the modified historical cost model, for example the value placed on a self-constructed fixed asset. It also argues that measuring current values is becoming easier and this should not now be seen as a barrier to the adoption of current values.

Determining the monetary amount

When an asset or liability is first recognised it will normally be the same value for both historical cost and current value, assuming that the transaction was at 'arm's length' and was for a fair value.

Revising monetary amounts where appropriate

When using the modified historical cost basis, assets are measured at the lower of depreciated historical cost and recoverable amount and revision to recoverable amount may sometimes be necessary.

When using the current value basis, assets and liabilities are carried at up-to-date current values and will therefore need regular revision.

Three measures of current value are replacement cost, value in use (discounted future cash flows arising from the asset) and net realisable value. These three values can be combined into a single model called 'value to the business' which is a mixed model which allows these three current values to be combined. (This model is sometimes called the 'deprival value model because it answers the question of how much an owner of an asset should be compensated if he / she were deprived of the asset.)

The 'value to the business model' for valuing assets may be presented as shown in Fig 31.3.

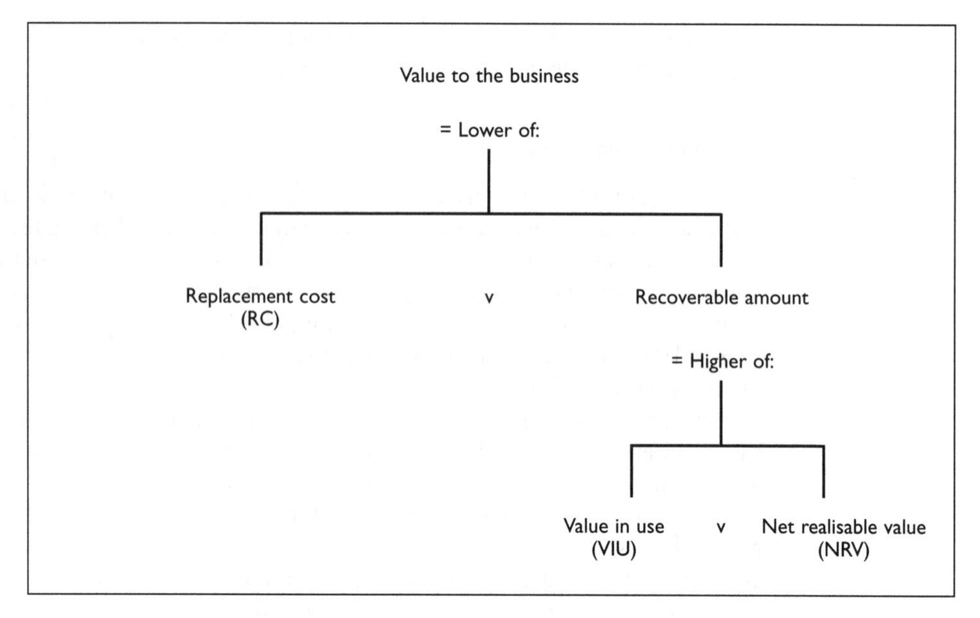

Fig. 31.3 Value to the business model

The following table shows how to apply this model to the valuation of a fixed asset.

Table 31.1

Replacement cost	VIU	NRV	Value to the business
£100	£120	£110	£100
£100	£110	£120	£100
£110	£120	£100	£110
£110	£100	£120	£110
£120	£110	£100	£110
£120	£100	£110	£110

The model is logical as the asset is not carried at a greater value than the recoverable amount; that is the amount it could be sold for or the amount from further use. Since VIU and NRV lie in the future, any gain is not anticipated and the lower RC is used; where either VIU or NRV are lower than RC, then this loss is recognised. The process of identifying if the recoverable amount of a fixed asset is below its carrying amount is known as an impairment review.

Capital maintenance

The valuation of net assets, the measurement of profit, and capital maintenance are all interrelated. Profit may be defined as the 'maximum amount that can be consumed in a period and still be as well off at the end of the period as at the beginning' This may be represented diagrammatically, as shown in Fig. 31.4.

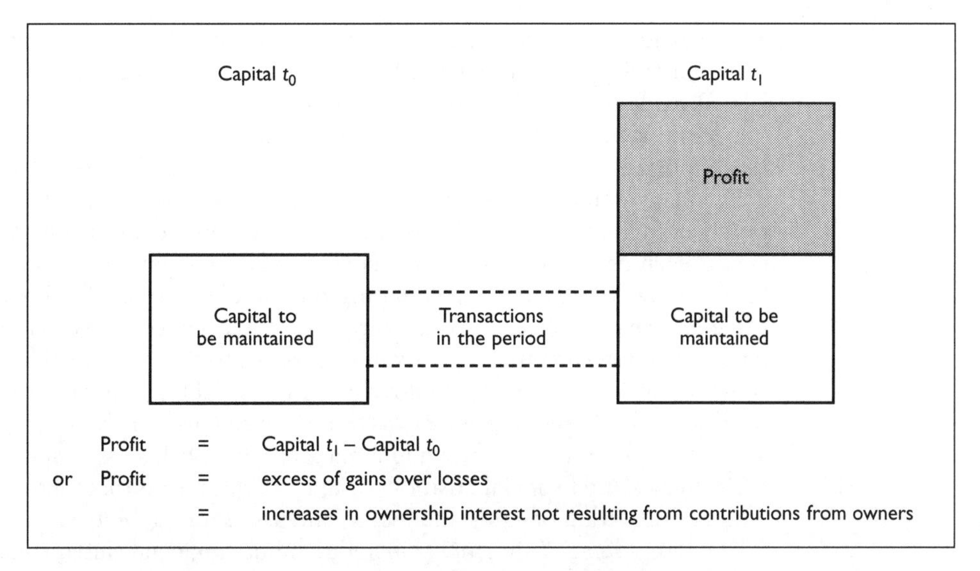

Fig. 31.4 Relationship of net assets, profit and capital maintenance

If the capital at time t_0 is represented by a square then at time t_1 profit must be the excess over this amount, i.e. if profit were consumed (the shaded area), then there would still be the same amount of capital at t_1 as at t_0. The measurement of capital and hence the measurement of profit will depend upon the model used, for example historical cost or current value.

The SOP defines capital as the monetary amount of ownership interest, which is referred to as the financial capital. Profit is the surplus of gains over losses and no further adjustment is required to this profit in order to ensure that capital is maintained.

It may be argued that when there are general price changes there needs to be a transfer from profit to a capital maintenance reserve in order to maintain the purchasing power of the financial capital. Similarly, if there are specific price changes, there needs to be a transfer from profit to a capital maintenance reserve in order to maintain the capital, which in this context is defined as the operating capability (see Chapter 36, Inflation accounting in the UK.)

Chapter 7: Presentation

Chapter 2 in the SOP refers to the qualitative characteristics of financial information. One of these is 'understandability' and to some extent this depends upon how information is aggregated, classified and reported. Information which is understood will help meet the objectives of financial statements, which is to help users assess stewardship and take economic decisions. The primary financial statements should communicate information about the financial performance, financial position and cash flows in a company.

The relationship of the notes to the financial statements is of particular importance. The notes to the accounts may:

- Provide more information about the figures in the accounts. In general, financial statements have main headings and the details may be found in the notes, for example regarding fixed assets.

- Provide an alternative figure to items recognised in the accounts, for example where there is a material difference between carrying value and current value.
- Provide information about events which are not in the accounts, for example contingent liabilities and post-balance sheet events.

It is important that the notes do not confuse users by giving conflicting information.

Financial statements are highly aggregated documents; in a large company the results of millions of transactions are summarised in the four primary financial statements, each of which may be on a single page. Aggregation should help the user to focus on the key issues by eliminating the unnecessary detail. Similarly, the aggregated information is classified into groups so that related items can be compared for purposes of interpretation. For example, users should easily be able to pick out and compare profit and capital employed; sales and debtors; current assets and current liabilities. Good presentation means that the elements, for example gains and losses, assets and liabilities, are shown in a manner which helps users understand financial performance and financial position. In general, this means that there should be a minimum of offsetting of gains and losses, and assets and liabilities.

The term *financial statements* includes annual financial statements, interim financial statements and preliminary announcements (see the chapter on Statements by the Accounting Standards Board). The contents include the financial statements and the notes to the accounts.

Annual reports, as well as including financial statements, may also have an Operating and Financial Review (see the chapter on Statements by the Accounting Standards Board), a Chairman's statement, a Directors' Report and other information required by the Stock Exchange. This information tends to be more discursive than the financial statements and may deal with some matters not in the financial statements, for example a forecast for the next year, and expand upon some matters which are in the financial statements, for example a review of research and development in the Directors' Report. Many users prefer a narrative approach and it is important that this accompanying information is consistent with the information in the financial statements.

Similarly, it is important that, where companies produce 'highlight' tables and calculate key ratios, that this information is comprehensive and not selected in such a way as to show the company in a distorted way.

Chapter 8: Accounting for interest in other entities

Many of the issues raised in Chapters 1–7 in the SOP are relevant to investments in other companies. Rather than deal with these issues within each chapter they are all brought together in a single chapter. Where one company invests in another, the accounting treatment will depend upon whether:

- There is control, in which case consolidated financial statements are prepared.
- There is joint control or significant influence, in which case the equity method of accounting is used which recognises in the investing company's accounts a share of the profits and a share of the net assets.
- There is no influence, in which case the investments are accounted for in the same way as any other asset.

Where consolidated financial statements are prepared, this will either be treated as an acquisition or a merger, depending on the circumstances.

The advantages of the Statement of Principles

The chapter began by defining a conceptual framework and discussing the world-wide development of such frameworks The chapter then focused on the UK's development of a conceptual framework in its SOP. It is worth considering why so much effort has been put into developing a conceptual framework and the benefits which such a conceptual framework should provide.

The advantages of the SOP are:

- it is a source of reference to:
  Standards setters when setting new standards or revising existing standards. The ASB has suggested that when issuing new standards it will include a section on how the standard relates to the SOP.
  Preparers of financial statements who have to apply accounting standards in practice. Where a preparer of financial statements is uncertain about the application of a standard to a particular event then further guidance may be sought from the SOP.
  Users who interpret the information in financial statements. Users will read the notes on disclosure of accounting policies in financial statements and will be aware of the accounting standards, but they may on occasion need to refer back to the SOP in order to understand their applicability to a company's accounts.
  Auditors who have to express an opinion on financial statements. Auditors have to confirm whether financial statements comply with accounting standards and where, for example, a company has apparently departed from a standard, it may be that a reading of the SOP will confirm that the departure was justified.
  Others who are interested in the work of the ASB. The ASB issues discussion papers and exposure drafts for comment and the SOP is a basis on which to form a judgement on a particular standard.
- Where there is an accounting issue but there is no relevant FRS or UITF, then the SOP acts as a guide to preparers, users, auditors and others for judging how the ASB would deal with the issue.
- It avoids the proliferation of accounting standards. It is generally agreed that it is undesirable to have numerous standards, and at various times it has been the aim of standard setters to reduce the number of standards being issued and to concentrate on the revision of exiting standards. Since the SOP provides a framework for setting accounting standards it avoids the need to actually produce a standard for all possible situations. This avoids the situation in the US which has arguably far too many standards on minor issues.
- It assists in reducing the number of alternative accounting policies. The ASB is committed to narrowing choice within standards and the SOP may be used to show how there may be only one permissible policy, for example on the treatment of goodwill.
- It should lead to consistent standards. Standards have been set in the UK since 1970 without an agreed conceptual framework. They have been set on a 'fire-fighting' basis, tackling each small blaze as it breaks out rather than designing a system which would not catch fire in the first place! This is obvious by reading the chapter headings in this book, beginning with the SSAPs. They are not in order of importance but on 'stamping out' an undesirable practice which had emerged. It is therefore not surprising that there are some inconsistencies between

these standards, for example SSAP 2: Disclosure of Accounting Policies states that prudence prevails over matching where there is a conflict, but SSAP 13: Accounting for Research and Development would appear to give precedence over matching to prudence (see the chapter on FREDs and FRED 21). The SOP should act as a single focus for the direction of accounting standards.

- It should save resources and enable accounting standards to be set more efficiently because there is an agreed foundation on which to build.

Controversy over the Statement of Principles

The first draft of the SOP appeared in 1995, twenty years after *The Corporate Report* in 1975. This first draft attracted more comments than any other document by the ASB and the ASB decided to produce a second draft, which was issued in 1999 and finalised in the same year. The ASB's version of events is that the first draft was misunderstood, that its critics had not read the draft and that it only needed to be rewritten to make it clearer, but essentially it did not need changing. The critics' version of events is that the first draft was hastily withdrawn and that the second draft represents a compromise on the issue of current value.

The main controversial areas are :

Current values: A continuing debate in financial reporting is whether the measurement base should be historical cost or current value. Those who argue for historical cost emphasise the importance of the stewardship role in financial reporting; those who argue for current values emphasise the decision-usefulness role. The advocates of historical cost accounting feared that the SOP was an attempt to introduce current value accounting and make it compulsory. A careful reading of the SOP makes it clear that this is not the case although the reader is left in no doubt that the ASB prefer current value accounting.

Recognition: There is a fundamental disagreement on the process of recognition. Some argue that the process begins with the profit and loss account and the matching of revenue and expenditure, and unmatched items are treated as residuals which are recorded in the balance sheet. The SOP argues that the process begins with the balance sheet and the measuring of assets and liabilities; if there are changes in assets and liabilities then these give rise to gains and losses. The ASB is said by its critics to be giving preference to the balance sheet over the profit and loss account. Presumably the reason why it does this is that it regards an asset as more 'solid' than the more nebulous concept of a 'cost'.

SSAP 2: The SOP is inconsistent with SSAP 2 which states that two of the fundamental concepts are accruals and prudence. The SOP states that accruals (matching) is not the main driver of recognition; it is used in a subsidiary role to confirm whether there has been a change in the value of an asset or a liability. Similarly, the concept of prudence is applied when recognising assets and liabilities. The SOP warns against the over-zealous use of prudence and any consequent bias in the information produced (see FRED 21 in the chapter on FREDs).

Performance statements: The SOP's definition of gains and losses includes revenue within gains and expenses in losses. Thus the distinction between the two performance statements, the profit and loss account and the STRGL has become blurred. (This may be deliberate on the part of the ASB as it has a discussion paper on measuring financial performance which does in fact seek to combine these two statements. See 'Reporting financial performance: proposals for change' in the chapter on Discussion Papers.)

Standard Setting: One of the advantages of a conceptual framework is that it supports the standard setters. Principles are, by definition, a 'fundamental truth used as basis for reasoning'. However, the ASB states that the SOP is just one of a number of factors to be considered when setting standards. It would be hoped that the status of the SOP would be more than a mere 'guide' which was departed from if it proved inconvenient.

These other factors to be considered by the ASB include:

- Legal requirements – the SOP was not developed within the constraints imposed by company law. Thus if the SOP supported an approach which was contrary to the law then a new standard would have to depart from the SOP. Whilst this is perhaps a logical approach it is hoped that the ASB would seek to change company law rather than issue inconsistent standards.
- The desirability of evolutionary change. The ASB do not expand on what they mean by this. Whilst one can understand that the ASB would prefer gradual change to radical change, it would be regrettable if this meant that the ASB rushed out standards which were not consistent with the SOP and then embarked on revising them to make them consistent.
- Implementation issues. The ASB do not expand on what they mean by this. It might mean that they would prefer to issue a standard which was inconsistent with the SOP, but which they believe will be accepted, than issue a standard which is consistent with the SOP, but which they believe would not be accepted by the accountancy profession. Whilst this might be a practical response, the ASB need to guard against standard setting becoming a 'political process' whereby standards are unduly influenced by lobbying from pressure groups. In the long term the goal of 'true and fair' is more likely to be met if standards are based on the firm foundation of a conceptual framework. Accounting concepts which underlie financial reporting cannot be proved to be correct. They can only be accepted as principles through consensus. If there is no consensus, then pressure groups will lobby the ASB in order to meet their own self-interest.

Conclusion

The development of a conceptual framework is not a panacea and the process of setting accounting standards will still be fraught with difficulties. To ignore this is to ignore the complexities of accounting.

The influence of the SOP can be seen in many of the standards which have been set since the work on the SOP began. The influence of the SOP can be seen in, for example, FRS 12 and the circumstances in which a provision can be made, and in FRS 15 and the recognition of an asset. There are other cases where the ASB appears to be inconsistent with the SOP, for example the treatment of deferred taxation may be inconsistent with the concept of a liability (see the chapter on FREDs).

The ASB have said that the SOP may need to be revised in response to developments in accounting thought. The ASB also states that it is their intention that each new accounting standard will make clear how the standard relates to the SOP. It will be these revisions and statements that will provide the evidence on which to judge the success of the SOP and whether it is built on a firm foundation or one of shifting sand.

EXAMINATION PRACTICE

31.1 Is the Statement of Principles too theoretical to be applied to accounting standards?

31.2 What are the benefits of developing a conceptual framework, such as the Statement of Principles?

CHAPTER 32

Statements by the Accounting Standards Board

The ASB has issued three Statements which are designed to codify and develop best practice. These Statements are not mandatory, they are not accounting standards, but their adoption is commended.

The three Statements are:

1. The Operating and Financial Review
2. Interim Reports
3. Preliminary Announcements

The Operating and Financial Review

In 1993 the ASB issued a statement on the 'Operating and Financial Review' (OFR). This statement has no mandatory force, but as a recommendation has the support of the Financial Reporting Council, the Hundred Group of Finance Directors, and the Stock Exchange.

It is aimed primarily at listed companies.

The OFR can be included in any part of the annual report. The Review offers a framework for the directors to discuss and analyse the business's performance and the factors underlying its results and financial position, in order to assist users to assess for themselves the future potential of the business.

Key features of the OFR should be:

(a) clear, succinct, readily understood by the general reader, and relevant to investors;
(b) balanced and objective;
(c) an explanation of comments made in previous statements which have not been borne out by events must be offered;
(d) analytical discussion, not just numerical analysis;
(e) individual aspects should be considered in the context of the business as a whole;
(f) any change in accounting policies should be explained;
(g) any ratios or numerical information given must be related to the accounts;
(h) a discussion of:
    (i) trends and factors underlying the business that have affected the results but are not expected to continue in the future,
    (ii) known factors that are expected to have an impact on the business in the future.

The ASB's statement offers detailed guidance on the content needed to meet these objectives.

Statement on interim reports

Introduction

The Stock Exchange requires that listed companies must produce interim reports which cover the first six months of the year; these are sometimes referred to as half yearly reports. These Stock Exchange regulations give no detail on how performance should be measured for the interim period, and the disclosure requirements are inadequate in that they require little more than an abbreviated profit and loss account and forecast by the directors. However the Stock Exchange is reviewing its requirements and there is due to be revised regulations in early 2000.

This deficiency in interim reports might not matter if they were unimportant; however there is evidence that analysts do use them to take decisions. It is fundamental to financial reporting and the working of efficient markets that financial decisions should be based on all relevant and reliable information, given any cost constraints.

This deficiency in interim reports was identified by the Committee on the Financial Aspects of Corporate Governance (the 1992 Cadbury Report) which recommended that the accountancy profession should address this issue.

The objectives of interim reports

The objectives of interim reports are similar to those of annual reports. However, since the reason for the Stock Exchange introducing interim reports was that the interval between annual reports was considered too long, there is an emphasis on 'timeliness', both frequency and speed. Thus half-yearly reports are obviously more frequent than annual reports and a few companies in the UK report quarterly. With regards to speed, the Stock Exchange regulations require interim reports within four months of the period end; this Statement recommends they be produced within 60 days. This is possible because interim reports are unaudited although they are usually 'reviewed'.

The basic problem – integral and discrete methods

There are two methods for measuring interim performance – the integral and the discrete. The integral approach views the interim report as an integral announcement of the annual report, with the interim reports being a progress report on how the year is progressing. Thus the approach of the integral interim report is to predict the annual result and to allocate the revenue and expenditure accordingly to the interim period.

In the discrete approach, the interim report is treated as an accounting period in its own right. The same rules which apply to incomplete transactions, or transactions which have not occurred, are dealt with in interim reports in the same way as annual accounts. (The exception to this is taxation which is considered below.)

The Statement adopts the discrete approach. The reasons for this are that the integral approach can give rise to 'assets' and 'liabilities' in the balance sheet which do not conform with the definitions in the Statement of Principles. Also, it is confusing to have two different treatments for the annual report and the interim report.

Controversy over the integral and discrete method

The Statement gives little detail on measurement issues and some of the examples suggest more of a hybrid approach than the Statement cares to admit. For example, where a company is entitled to a bulk discount and the minimum quantity has not been exceeded at the half year stage, but is expected to be exceeded by the year end, then the interim report should accrue for part of the expected discount. Similarly, where a company pays a bonus based on annual profits above a minimum amount and this has not been exceeded by the half year, this should nevertheless be accrued if it is expected to be paid at the year end.

The two examples above relate to annually determined expenditure where it may be argued that an obligation exists. However there may be discretionary expenditure which the management is committed to spending; for example, should a share of the following expenditure be accrued in the interim reports?

- annual audit fee;
- maintenance where there is a plant shut down in the second half;
- advertising which is all spent in the second half;
- payments to charity and political parties in the second half.

Similarly, should overheads be absorbed into stock where the level of activity is below normal in the first half but is expected to increase in the second half, or be treated as a period cost?

Yes, on an integral basis; no, on a discrete basis.

Another example of the hybrid approach is in relation to discontinued operations. Operations are regarded as discontinued in the interim period if they cease up to three months after the end of the interim period or the date of approving the interim report if earlier.

In other examples in the Statement, it is more clear that a discrete approach should be followed. For example:

- Where the closing rate method of foreign exchange translation is used, then the rate should be that at the end of the period. (In an integral approach, a forward rate might be used.)
- When calculating earnings per share and there is to be a share issue in the second half, the number of shares in the interim period is used, not a projected figure for the year as would be used in the integral approach.

Taxation

The exception to the rule regarding the use of the discrete approach is taxation. The Statement argues that this is an annual charge and it is inappropriate to calculate the tax in the interim report as if it were a discrete period. Thus the Statement requires a prudent estimate to be made of the effective tax rate for the year, taking into consideration (for example) capital allowances on assets expected to be bought in the second half, and to apply this percentage to the half-yearly profit or loss.

This general rule can give rise to some interesting specific situations. The Statement implies that if the effective tax rate is nil per cent then there should be no tax in the interim report. Thus in Table 32.1 although there is an interim report profit of £1 000, the business is expected to break even for the year as a whole and thus there is no tax. An alternative treatment, shown in Table 32.2, is that there should be an equal and opposite tax charge/recovery in each period.

Table 32.1

£	1st half	2nd half	Annual total
Profit/(loss)	1 000	(1 000)	0
Tax rate at annual rate of 0%	0	0	0
Profit/(loss) after tax	1 000	(1 000)	0

Table 32.2

£	1st half	2nd half	Annual total
Profit/(loss)	1 000	(1 000)	0
Tax rate at say 30%	(300)	300	0
Profit/(loss) after tax	700	(700)	0

Where there is a tax loss brought forward and there are profits in the interim period and expected annual profits in excess of these losses, then the loss should be offset in the same proportion as the interim profit bears to the expected annual profit. Thus in Table 32.3 there are losses brought forward of £30 which are allocated to the interim period.

Table 32.3

£	1st half	2nd half	Annual total
Profit	50	100	150
Loss b/f (£30)	(10)	(20)	(30)
	40	80	120
Tax at say 30%	(12)	(24)	36
Profit after tax	38	76	114

An alternative treatment favoured by the International Accounting Standards Committee (IASC) is to utilise tax losses brought forward against the interim report, where this is sufficient. This is shown in Table 32.4. The ASB position fits better with its integral approach for tax since the IASC method is effectively a discrete approach.

Table 32.4

£	1st half	2nd half	Annual total
Profit	50	100	150
Loss b/f (£30)	(30)	0	(30)
	20	100	120
Tax at say 30%	6	30	36
Profit after tax	44	70	114

A final example to illustrate the complexities of the tax charge is shown in Tables 32.5 and 32.6. Where there is a tax loss brought forward, and this is less than the interim profit but more than the forecast profit for the year, there is a choice as shown in these Tables. In Table 32.5 the loss brought forward is allocated; in Table 32.6 it is not allocated. Neither of these approaches seems particularly attractive and thus the ASB stance of showing no tax charge where no annual tax is expected to be paid makes more sense, as shown in Table 32.7.

Table 32.5

£	1st half	2nd half	Annual total
Profit/(loss)	100	(50)	50
Loss b/f (£75) restricted to (£50); allocated IR:AR	(75)	25	(50)
	25	(25)	
Tax at say 30%	(7.5)	7.5	0
Profit/(loss) after tax	92.5	(42.5)	50

Table 32.6

£	1st half	2nd half	Annual total
Profit/(loss)	100	(50)	50
Loss b/f (£75) restricted to (£50)	(50)	0	(50)
	50	(50)	
Tax at say 30%	(15)	15	0
Profit/(loss) after tax	85	(35)	50

Table 32.7

£	*1st half*	*2nd half*	*Annual total*
Profit/(loss)	100	(50)	50
Loss b/f (£75) restricted to (£50); 0% tax charge	0	0	(50)
Tax nil	0	0	0
Profit/(loss) after tax	100	(50)	50

Disclosure requirements

The disclosure requirements of the Statement are:

- a management commentary should be similar, but in less detail, than an Operating and Financial Review (OFR);
- a summarised profit and loss account;
- a statement of total recognised gains and losses;
- a summarised balance sheet;
- a cash flow statement.

Other disclosures required are:

- a statement that the interim report is prepared using the same accounting policies as the annual report (further disclosure is required where this is not the case);
- changes in accounting policy should be made at the interim stage; a note is required where these are not implemented in the interim report but will be in the annual report;
- segmental reports, using the same segments as used in the annual report;
- exceptional items;
- quoted shares should be revalued but not properties; a note stating that the valuations are at the last balance sheet date will suffice. Similarly, for actuarial valuations of pension funds;
- comparative figures for the summarised:
  profit and loss account,
  statement of total recognised gains and losses,
  cash flow statement.
  should be provided for:
  the previous annual report,
  the previous interim report.

With regards to the balance sheet, the only comparative figures required are those of the last annual report. It is interesting that comparative figures for the previous interim report are not required. This is a weakness of the Statement. In a seasonal business, the comparison for example, of a June interim balance sheet with a December annual balance sheet may be misleading, unless there is also the previous June balance sheet. Companies may, however, choose to disclose the balance sheet in the previous interim report.

It is interesting to note that, in line with the discrete approach, materiality in relation to disclosure is in the context of the interim report not the annual report. Thus an item may appear as exceptional in the interim report but not in the annual report where it is immaterial at the year end.

Controversy over interim reports

The Statement recommends the discrete approach to interim reporting. However, it may be argued that an interim report is more than just an 'annual report' prepared for half a year. The desirable characteristics of financial information include relevance and reliability and in this context it may be that the integral is more relevant, albeit less reliable, than the discrete approach. Relevant information should have a predictive and confirmatory role and if the purpose of an interim report is to help predict the year-end results, then the integral approach may be more useful.

Conclusion

Interim reports have been the poor relation of financial reporting for many years. It is an issue which the accountancy profession should have tackled but it was left to the Cadbury Report to take the initiative. Now that it has been tackled in the UK it is to be hoped that this momentum will be maintained so that the interim report will become of equal quality to the annual report, albeit in a slimmer but more timely format.

Statement on preliminary announcements

Introduction

Companies which are listed on the Stock Exchange are required by the Stock Exchange's Listing Rules to make a preliminary announcement of the annual results in advance of the publication of the full annual report.

The accountancy profession had been remarkably silent on preliminary announcements, which was surprising given the strong evidence that preliminary announcements are relied upon and do cause share prices to move. However, in 1998 the ASB issued a Statement on Preliminary Announcements; this is not a standard and is recommended practice for listed companies only.

The Statement codifies best practice. The Listing Rules are minimal and most companies produce preliminary announcements which contain substantially more information than is required. Companies choose to do this to prevent the risk that the limited information in preliminary announcements required by the Stock Exchange may be misunderstood and that share prices would have to be corrected when the annual report is released. For the same reason, companies prefer to disclose this additional information at meetings with analysts and, since the Listing Rules require all investors to have simultaneous access to the same price-sensitive information, then companies must provide this additional information in their preliminary announcement.

Objectives of preliminary announcements

The objective of preliminary announcements is to reduce the period between the end of the accounting year and the release of information to the market. Company annual reports are released on average about 125 days after the year end. However, the company and auditors are aware of the contents of the annual report before this and there is therefore the risk of information being leaked and insider dealing occurring.

Distribution

The only Stock Exchange requirement for the distribution of preliminary announcements is that they must be sent to the Company Announcements Office at the Stock Exchange.

Since an objective of preliminary announcements is to prevent insider dealing, they should be more widely distributed, and this is supported by the Cadbury Report's guidance on openness. The Statement offers a number of possibilities:

- use of the Internet to announce the results;
- press advertisements;
- pre-registration cards used to request receipt of the preliminary announcement when it is published;
- publish an address and telephone number where shareholders may request a copy of the preliminary announcement;
- announce in advance (in the interim report) the date and where the preliminary announcement will be published.

Timeliness

The average time lag between the year end and the release of the annual report is 125 days; the average time between the year end and the preliminary announcement was 86 days, and thus the preliminary announcement improved the timeliness of reporting by 39 days. The Statement encourages companies to issue preliminary announcements within 60 days of the year end and preliminary announcements should therefore be released an average of 65 days before the annual report, although the Statement also wants annual reports to be released as soon as possible after the preliminary announcement. This will be easier, for example, for companies trading mainly in the UK than manufacturing companies with overseas subsidiaries. Currently, only 22 per cent of companies publish their preliminary announcement within 60 days of the year end, according to research by Arthur Andersen (see '*Accountancy*' November 1999).

Reliability

If investors want the same reliability from preliminary announcements as annual reports, then preliminary announcements should not be released until the audit is completed; but if they are prepared to sacrifice reliability for timeliness, then preliminary announcements could be released without any auditor involvement once draft reports have been prepared by the internal accountants and before they have been seen by the directors. The Statement takes a middle position and states that preliminary announcements should be released before the audit is finalised, but after the accounts have been approved by the board of directors and after the auditors have confirmed to the directors that their remaining work is not expected to reveal any material changes to the draft accounts.

Auditors may be reluctant to give this assurance to directors as there is always the risk that audit work, right up to the date of signing the audit report, may reveal errors in the accounts.

Where the auditors know that their report will be qualified, then the details of the qualification must be given in the preliminary announcement. There should therefore be no surprises in the annual report, only more detail.

Content

The content of preliminary announcements are broadly similar to those of interim reports – see above. In summary these are a management commentary, profit and loss account, statement of total recognised gains and losses, balance sheet, cash flow statement and notes to the financial statements. A statement that the audit has yet to be completed, or exceptionally that the preliminary announcement is based on audited accounts, must also be given.

Final interim period

The final interim period may be described as the second half of the financial year, e.g. in a company with a year end of 31 December, it is the period 1 July to 31 December. The first interim period is 1 January to 30 June, which is covered by the 'interim report'. The only new information in an annual report is therefore the final interim period. This, however, is subsumed within the annual report.

The Statement therefore requires companies to comment on the final interim period in the management commentary. Furthermore, the Statement 'encourages' separate presentation of the final interim period, together with corresponding amounts from the final interim period of the previous year where this is necessary to support the commentary. The preliminary announcement thus has a dual function – announcing the full year results and reporting the second half-yearly results.

Controversy over the final interim period

At present, companies produce the annual report (AR) and an interim report for the first half-year (IR1). If an investor wishes to calculate the performance for the final interim period (IR2), then this can simply be calculated as AR – IR1. The proposal to report this final interim period implies that it is something more than AR – IR1. This gives rise to the intriguing question of whether IR1 + IR2 must equal AR. This is illustrated in the simple example below relating to a volume discount, and many other examples could be taken for income and expenditure determined on an annual basis, for example profit sharing bonuses and sales commission.

Example 32.1

Example of IR2 reporting

A company is offered a bulk discount of 10 per cent on all goods if purchases are £100 000 or more. In IR1, purchases were £50 000 and in IR2 were also £50 000.

The total paid for the year was therefore £100 000 – 10% = £90 000.
AR-IR1 is £90 000 – £50 000 = £40 000.
IR2 (on a discrete basis) is £50 000 – 10% = £45 000.
Thus IR1 (£50 000) + IR2 (£45 000) does not equal AR (£90 000)

Possible solutions to this issue are to :

- make a prior period adjustment to IR1 and re-state the figures, such that IR1 + IR2 = AR
- to give a single line adjustment in IR2 so that IR1 + IR2 = AR
- to provide a financial statement of the differences between IR2 and AR – IR1.

The Statement is silent on the issue of linking the two interims with the annual report and the ASB may not perceive this as a problem. The Statement is also silent on the extent of auditor involvement with IR2.

Conclusion

The ASB's Statement of Principles presents the qualitative characteristics of useful financial information. A preliminary announcement meets some of these criteria. Thus, the preliminary announcement gives timely information, although it may not be complete or reliable.

It is therefore unfortunate that, according to recent research by Arthur Andersen (see '*Accountancy*' November 1999), only 22 per cent of companies publish their preliminary announcement within the 60 day period.

The publication of the final interim period should improve the predictive value of the preliminary announcement, although it may be argued that producing these accounts will require considerable effort on behalf of directors and for little gain to investors. In a recent survey by Arthur Andersen less than 40 per cent of companies made any comment on the final interim period, and only one company presented final interim period figures. The ASB should therefore be encouraged to undertake a cost/benefit analysis of producing accounts for the final interim. Recent research shows that more than 60 per cent of companies made no comment on the final interim period, and for those who did, there were usually only a few words. There was only negligible response to producing separate presentation of the second half.

The preliminary announcement has a role and the improvements in this Statement should enhance company reporting in the UK. There is – however – a danger that as the contents of the preliminary announcement expand, and auditors delay approving the release of the preliminary announcement until their audit is completed, the time advantage of the preliminary announcement becomes only the delay due to printing. If this became the situation, then the preliminary announcement ceases to have a role and companies might as well place their full accounts on the Internet and dispense with the preliminary announcement. The ASB has therefore undertaken to review the wider issues connected with year-end financial reporting.

EXAMINATION PRACTICE

32.1 The Operating and Financial Review provides a framework for directors to explain the factors underlying a business's performance and financial position so that users may assess for themselves the potential of the business.

Give two examples of information which directors may disclose for each of the following headings:

- operating results,
- dynamics of the business,
- investments for the future.

32.2 What are the objectives of interim reporting and what are the two methods of measuring interim performance?

32.3 What are the objectives of preliminary profit announcements and to what extent do they meet the qualitative characteristics of timely, complete and reliable information?

CHAPTER 33

Financial Reporting Exposure Drafts

Introduction

This chapter gives a summary of each of the extant financial reporting exposure drafts (FRED). All these FREDs are on topics already covered by an SSAP and so less detail is given as this will already have been given in the chapter dedicated to that SSAP.

Where there is an SSAP and a FRED has been issued on the same topic then the SSAP remains in force until such time as the FRED becomes a new accounting standard.

If a company wishes to anticipate a FRED becoming an FRS, and the FRED does not conflict with any extant accounting standard, then it may be incorporated into the financial statements or provided in a note to the accounts, although companies should be aware that the FRED may be amended before it becomes an FRS.

FRED 19: Deferred Tax

Introduction

The chapter on SSAP 15: Accounting for Deferred Taxation explained the three different approaches to accounting for deferred taxation – flow through, partial deferral and full deferral. The chapter explained how SSAP 15 required the partial deferral method.

The full provision method, however, is favoured internationally and the ASB therefore decided to review SSAP 15. Furthermore, the partial provision basis anticipates future transactions and this is contrary to FRS 12 on provisions. A tax liability should be recognised when there is an obligation to pay tax as a result of past transactions, and this definition supports the full provision method.

It is proposed that FRED 19 will replace SSAP 15.

The detail of FRED 19

- Deferred tax should be provided in full on all timing differences, except:
    - revaluations, unless the company is committed to selling the asset,
    - fair value adjustments on an acquisition (see FRS 7),
    - the unremitted earnings of subsidiaries, associates and joint ventures, unless

dividends have been accrued or there is an obligation from the subsidiary etc. to distribute earnings.

- Deferred tax is not provided on permanent differences.
- Deferred tax provisions should be discounted, where the result would be material. The unwinding of the discount should be recorded in the profit and loss account as a financial charge, next to, but separate from, other financial charges, for example interest paid (see the section on 'Discounting in Financial Reporting' in the Chapter on Discussion Papers).
- When calculating deferred taxation, future originating timing differences are ignored. This is consistent with FRS 12 which requires provisions to be based on past, not future, transactions.
- Deferred tax assets would be recognised only to the extent that they are 'more likely than not' to be recoverable against tax profits.
- Deferred tax would be allocated between the profit and loss account and the statement of total recognised gains and losses in accordance to where the item giving rise to the deferred tax was recorded (this is the same as FRS 16).
- Deferred tax assets and liabilities would be shown separately on the balance sheet, unless they can legally be offset.
- A reconciliation must be given of the current tax charge for the period to the charge that would arise, if the profit were charged at a standard rate of tax. This should provide users of the accounts with an analysis of all the factors which have influenced the tax charge for the period.
- The existing rate of corporation tax should be used. However, if legislation setting a new rate is 'substantively enacted', then that new rate may be used. (This is similar to FRS 16.)
- The notes should disclose an analysis of the tax charge in the profit and loss account and statement of total recognised gains and losses, and an analysis of the deferred tax provision in the balance sheet.

Controversy over FRED 19

Although one of the stated reasons for developing FRED 19 was international harmonisation, the FRED does not in fact follow international practice. It adopts a different methodology with regard to the calculation of a 'full provision'. The international practice is to calculate a full provision which would always include deferred tax on all timing differences, revaluation gains and profits in subsidiaries. These items are not always required under FRED 19; this approach has been referred to as the full provision 'incremental liability' approach.

The US and international standards prohibit discounting of deferred tax provisions, but FRED 19 supports this, although it does acknowledge that the sections relating to discounting may be removed when the actual FRS is published. Some commentators support the view that, since the ASB is committed to the harmonisation of accounting standards, then it should adopt international practice and prohibit discounting. However, it may be argued that if worldwide standard setters simply adopt the US or international standard then this would seriously reduce debate on accounting issues to the detriment of the accounting profession. It is far better for the ASB to produce the standard it believes is best and attempt to persuade the international community to adopt this as best practice.

One reason for issuing FRED 19 is that SSAP 15 is inconsistent with the definition of a liability. However, some argue that FRED 19 does not go far enough in this direction. If a liability is a current obligation for past events, then the true liability is the amount owed to the Inland Revenue and this would therefore be the 'flow through' figure, i.e. the amount on the tax demand and due to be paid.

A survey by PricewaterhouseCoopers on the FTSE 100 companies showed that £24 billion of deferred tax relating to accelerated capital allowances is currently not provided, but which would be provided for under FRED 19, on the assumption that discounting was not permitted. If this sum were provided for, it would reduce distributable profits by 19 per cent; reduce net assets by 10 per cent and increase gearing by 12 per cent. These are significant sums and FRED 19 is therefore likely to make a major impact on financial statements.

FRED 20: Retirement Benefits

Introduction

The subject of pension costs was discussed in the chapter on SSAP 24: Accounting for Pension Costs. The objective of SSAP 24 is to record pension costs on a systematic and rational basis over the period during which the employer benefits from the employees' services. This is achieved by using an actuarial measurement basis and by spreading variations over a number of years.

SSAP 24 was issued by the ASC and the ASB decided to commission research on the operation of SSAP 24. The choices faced by the ASB were:

1. To amend SSAP 24. Two suggested improvements were:

- to continue with the actuarial valuation approach but remove many of the options,
- improve the disclosure requirements.

2. To radically change SSAP 24 and adopt a market value approach based on measuring the pension scheme assets at market value.

The ASB went for the second choice arguing that:

- Since the IASC had produced a standard on retirement benefits which uses market values for pension scheme assets, the ASB wanted to produce a standard on similar lines in the interest of harmonisation.
- The ASB believe that market values reflect the underlying economics of providing defined benefits more closely than the actuarial method.
- The market value basis is more transparent and easier to understand than the actuarial method. (Under SSAP 24, which smoothes out variations, it was possible for the balance sheet to show a liability when the scheme was in surplus, and an asset when the scheme was in deficit.)
- The actuarial profession now uses a more market-based approach to valuing pension schemes.

The detail of FRED 20

FRED 20 covers pensions and other retirement benefits, including medical care, but its main focus is defined benefit pension schemes. It is significantly different from

SSAP 24. The major changes are:

- Pension scheme assets are based on market values. Full actuarial valuations should be obtained every three years, with updates at each balance sheet date.
- Pension scheme liabilities are measured at an approximation of fair value, and are discounted at a rate which reflects the characteristics of the liabilities.
- The surplus /deficit in a defined benefit scheme is the excess/shortfall of the value of the assets in the scheme over/below the value of the liabilities. A surplus should be recognised as an asset and a deficit as a liability in the balance sheet. An asset represents the sum that can be recovered by the employer through reduced contributions and refunds. A liability represents an employer's liability to fund a deficit. The asset or liability will be shown separately on the balance sheet, after other net assets. This is unusual – it may be argued that a pension scheme asset should be included with assets and a pension scheme liability with liabilities.
- Gains and losses arising from changes in assets and liabilities measured at fair values are recognised immediately in the statement of total recognised gains and losses. (Under SSAP 24 these were spread forward in the profit and loss account.)
- The profit and loss account includes:
  - 'Service costs': the current service cost is calculated as the current value of the additional obligation to current members for the year of service. This is included in operating profit.
  - Interest on pension liabilities and return on pension assets: these are disclosed net, next to the financial charges in the profit and loss account. The interest cost on pension scheme liabilities is the unwinding of the interest on the discounted liabilities (see 'Discounting in financial reporting' in the chapter on Discussion Papers).

The profit and loss account should be more stable under FRED 20 than SSAP 25 because:

  - Changes due to the use of market-based values are restricted to the statement of total recognised gains and losses. (However if the statement of total recognised gains and losses and the profit and loss account are combined in one statement this issue becomes irrelevant – see 'Reporting Financial Performance: Proposals For Change' in the chapter on Discussion Papers.) In some other countries smoothing is achieved by allowing actuarial gains and losses to be deferred so long as their cumulative amount is within 10 per cent of the assets or liabilities – the so-called 'corridor' approach.
  - There is no spreading forward of gains and losses within the profit and loss account as there is in SSAP 25.

- The disclosure requirements include a five-year history, of amount and percentage, of key figures. It has been argued, however, that five years may be too short a period; it is important to users to be able to compare valuations at two points in time, and, given that a full actuarial valuation is only required every three years, a five-year period may only cover one full valuation. An alternative is to ensure that the 'history' covers at least two full valuations.

The FRED is consistent with the Statement of Principles in that it adopts a balance sheet rather than a profit and loss account approach. It is more concerned with establishing the most appropriate asset and liability in the balance sheet rather than measuring the expense in the profit and loss account.

FRED 21: Accounting Policies

Introduction

This FRED, once it becomes an FRS, will replace SSAP 2, which has become out of date with the publication of the Statement of Principles (SOP).

Objectives

The objectives are that a company should:

- adopt the most appropriate accounting policies;
- regularly review its accounting policies;
- disclose its accounting polices.

Definitions

Accounting policies

The specific principles, bases, conventions, rules and practices applied by an entity in order to reflect the effects of transactions and other events through recognising, selecting measurement bases for, and presenting assets, liabilities, gains, losses and changes to shareholders' funds. Accounting policies do not include estimation techniques.

Important terms here are 'recognition', 'presentation' and 'measurement base'; a change in any of these is a change in accounting policy (see the section below on Distinguishing Between Accounting Policies and Estimation Techniques).

Estimation techniques

The methods and estimates adopted by an entity to arrive at monetary values, corresponding to the measurement bases selected for assets, liabilities, gains, losses and changes to shareholder funds.

Estimation techniques include:

- depreciation,
- general doubtful debts provision,
- calculation of present values.

Estimation techniques are thus different from accounting policies; a change in an estimation technique is not a change in accounting policy.

Measurement bases

Measurement bases fall into two categories – historical cost and current value. An example of a current value basis is 'value to the business', which is the lower of replacement cost and recoverable amount (where recoverable amount is the higher of value in use and net realisable value).

A change in a measurement base is a change in accounting policy.

It should be noted that FRED 21 has abandoned the notion in SSAP 2 of an accounting base; it does not consider it necessary to distinguish between accounting bases and accounting policies.

Distinguishing between accounting policies and estimation techniques

Examples

A company which previously capitalised interest costs now decides to charge the interest direct to the profit and loss account.

This is a change in recognition, presentation and measurement base and is accordingly a change in accounting policy.

A company changes from reducing balance to straight line depreciation.

This is not a change in recognition, presentation or measurement base. This is a change in an estimation technique and not a change in accounting policy.

A company reclassifies certain overheads from cost of sales to administration expenses.

This is a change in presentation; it is not a change in recognition or measurement. This is a change in accounting policy.

A company which previously valued listed investments at replacement cost now decides to value them at net realisable value.

This is a change in the measurement basis; it is not a change in recognition or presentation. It is a change in accounting policy.

Accounting policies

A company should adopt those accounting policies which are the most appropriate for giving a true and fair view. Where compliance with an accounting standard is inconsistent with giving a true and fair view, then a company may depart from that accounting standard, but it must disclose full details of the circumstances.

Two practices are fundamental to financial statements and therefore affect the selection of accounting policies. These are:

Going concern – the assumption that the company will continue for the foreseeable future.

Accruals – the non-cash effect of transactions and events should be reflected in the financial statements in the accounting period in which they occur and not when any cash is received or paid. However, the non-cash effect of transactions and events should only be included if they can be reliably measured; if they cannot be reliably measured, then recognition should be deferred until reliable measurement is possible.

This explanation of the accruals concept has a different emphasis than that of SSAP 2 and is more in accord with the SOP. SSAP 2 explains the concept in terms of matching revenues and costs and dealing with them in the period to which they relate. FRED 21 is less concerned with the relationship between revenues and costs; it is more concerned with reflecting transactions in the period they occur, not when cash is received or paid. This follows the SOP which views matching as a means of identifying whether an increase in assets (a gain) or increase in liabilities (a loss) has arisen, which is a balance sheet as opposed to a profit and loss account approach.

Objectives and constraints in selecting accounting policies

The criteria which should be used to judge the appropriateness of accounting policies are the same qualitative characteristics of financial information from Chapter 3 of the SOP. These are relevance, reliability, comparability and understandability. The application of these characteristics may be constrained by the need to find a balance between these characteristics where there is tension between them, and to balance the cost of providing the information against the benefit to users.

There may be a tension between neutrality and prudence. FRED 21 states that prudence may lead to bias if this means that gains and assets are understated and losses and liabilities are overstated. FRED 21 states that there is often uncertainty about the existence of, for example, assets and liabilities, and uncertainty about measurement. Prudence requires that, where uncertainty exists, greater confirmatory evidence for the existence and measurement of assets and gains is needed than for liabilities and losses.

The concept of prudence has a different emphasis in FRED 21 than in SSAP 2. The concept of prudence has been used in the past as a means of smoothing profits. In good years, for example, provisions could be overstated, and in bad years these inflated provisions could be written back to the profit and loss account, thus smoothing out profits. This artificial smoothing of profits became a greater problem than the overstatement of profits which was originally at the core of the concept of prudence.

Another distinction between FRED 21 and SSAP 2 with regards to the concept of prudence is its link to the realisation concept. SSAP 2 stated that revenue and profits should only be included in the profit and loss account when realised, which was regarded as prudent. FRED 21 breaks the link between prudence and realisation. Realisation originally, pre-SSAP 2, meant that cash was received; this was considered important if profits were to be distributed by a cash dividend. SSAP 2 extended this to cover cash and cash equivalents, where the ultimate realisation in cash of the cash-equivalent asset was assured. FRED 21 extends this to mean that a gain is recognised when it can be measured reliably, even though no disposal has occurred. Thus FRED 21 breaks the link between realisation and prudence.

Thus the concept of prudence, which was considered fundamental in SSAP 2, is seen to be of lesser importance in FRED 21.

Reviewing and changing accounting policies

A company should review its accounting policies on a regular basis to ensure that they remain the most appropriate for giving a true and fair view. If there is a more suitable accounting policy, then the company should change to that policy. A change in accounting policy may require a prior period adjustment, in accordance with FRS 3.

The requirement to keep accounting policies under review may lead companies to change accounting policies more frequently than previously. It could be argued that this will lead to a lack of consistency, as it will make comparison with previous periods more difficult, not withstanding the use of prior year adjustments. However, FRED 21 argues that the concept of consistency should not impede the introduction of improved accounting policies. Thus the concept of consistency, which was considered fundamental in SSAP 2, is seen to be of lesser importance in FRED 21.

Estimation techniques

Where there are a number of possible estimation techniques which could be used in the application of accounting policies, a company should adopt the most appropriate one. In selecting the most appropriate estimation technique, the same criteria which are used to judge accounting policies should be used, i.e. relevance, reliability, comparability and understandability. The application of these characteristics may be constrained by the need to find a balance where there is a tension between them and to balance the cost of providing the information against the benefit to users.

A company should review its estimation techniques on a regular basis to ensure that they remain the most appropriate. If there is a more suitable estimation technique, then the company should change to that technique. A change in estimation techniques is not a change in accounting policy and will not lead to a prior year adjustment.

A company should adopt those accounting policies and estimation techniques which are the most appropriate for giving a true and fair view. SSAP 2 also requires companies to select the most appropriate accounting policies, but it does not give the criteria by which this should be judged. Now that criteria have been given this may require companies to justify their choice. It has previously been the case that the same auditors have audited the accounts of several companies in the same industry which have used different accounting policies. It may be more difficult in the future to justify this position.

* Disclosures

The following should be disclosed in the financial statements (subject to materiality):

- a description of its accounting policies;
- details of changes in accounting policies, stating why the change and its effect;
- a description of estimation techniques;
- details of changes in estimation techniques and the effect;
- if the financial statements are not prepared on the basis of the going concern and accruals concepts, this should be disclosed with an explanation;
- if a company has departed from an accounting standard or company law, the details of the departure, the reasons and the effect should be given. This statement must be given for each year there is a departure, including where this applies to corresponding figures.

A description of the estimation techniques is required, where material. Materiality is judged by reference to the range of values which other acceptable (i.e. relevant and reliable) estimation techniques would have given. For example, taking the estimation technique of depreciation, if a company uses the straight line method and this gives a charge of £2m per annum, and if the reducing balance method is just as relevant and reliable, and this would give a charge of £3m, and the difference of £1 million is considered material, then the estimation technique, i.e. straight line, should be disclosed.

This means that the directors will have to calculate the effect of all acceptable estimation techniques in order to assess whether they are material. This may be just a short step away from requiring the disclosure of that range so that users can assess the impact on financial statements of different estimation techniques.

Conclusion

SSAP 2 was in existence for 28 years, without change. No other accounting standard has such longevity, but this is not perhaps surprising given that it dealt with concepts rather than matters of practice. However, with the introduction of the SOP it needs to be updated.

EXAMINATION PRACTICE

33.1 What are the most significant differences between SSAP 15 and FRED 19?

33.2 What are the most significant differences between SSAP 24 and FRED 20?

33.3 Compare and contrast SSAP 2 and FRED 21.

CHAPTER 34

Discussion Papers

Accounting issues which appear on the ASB's agenda arise either from its own inquiries or from others bringing issues to its attention. When a suitable issue for an FRS has been identified the ASB will undertake the necessary research. The ASB will normally debate the issue and then it will release a Discussion Paper (DP) for wide consultation which should then be followed by a FRED.

DP: Derivatives and other financial instruments

Introduction

There has been a rapid growth in financial instruments and the ASB recognised that accounting regulation did not give sufficient guidance on how to account for them. This DP was issued in 1996 and is in three parts – scope, measurement and disclosure. FRS 13 was issued in 1998 and covered scope and disclosure. This summary of the DP therefore only covers the issue of measurement. It may be helpful to refer to the chapter on FRS 13 before reading this section on the DP.

Historical cost

At present financial instruments are measured at either historical cost or current value.

The use of historical cost causes the following problems.

- Reported profits do not reflect the events of the year since:
  - Any change in values giving rise to unrealised gains and losses are ignored.
  - When a financial instrument is realised any gains and losses are included in the profit and loss account of a single year even though the gain or loss may have accrued over many years.
  - Companies may manipulate profit by choosing which financial instruments to sell and thus realise gains and losses; in good years, financial instruments showing losses may be sold; in bad years, financial instruments showing profits may be sold.
- Active risk management is not adequately reflected by historical cost. Some companies buy and sell financial instruments in response to current values in an attempt to manage risk. Since the management of the company are using current values it seems appropriate that the external users should have the infor-

mation prepared on the same basis as the internal users, i.e. current value. This should also help in judging how successful the management have been in managing risk.

- The use of historical cost makes it difficult to compare one company with another. Two companies may have identical financial instruments with the same current value, but under the historical cost basis these would appear to be different if they were purchased at different dates when the price was different.
- The use of historical cost makes it necessary to adopt hedge accounting and there are problems with hedge accounting. Hedge accounting is necessary when historical cost is used because risk on a financial instrument measured at historical cost is being mitigated by a financial instrument measured at current value. The problems with hedge accounting are discussed below.

Historical cost and current value

At present, there is a mixed system where some financial instruments are at historical cost and others at current value. For example, financial instruments held for trading purposes are often valued at market value; current asset investments may be at the lower of cost or net realisable value; fixed asset investments may be at historical cost or at a lower value where there has been impairment. It is possible to rationalise this approach and allow some financial instruments to be measured at historical cost and others at current value.

The ASB, however, rejected a 'mixed value' model and concluded that:

- all financial instruments should be valued at current value,
- gains and losses should be recognised as they occur. Some gains and losses would be reported in the profit and loss account, others in the STRGL. In general gains and losses on fixed rate borrowings, interest rate derivatives and currency financial instruments would be in the STRGL, all others in the profit and loss account.

Hedge accounting

The DP considers the question of whether some form of hedge accounting should be allowed and if so what form it should take. Hedge accounting occurs where separate transactions are linked with each other for accounting purposes because one of the transactions is designed to offset the risk arising on the other transaction. In hedge accounting, gains and losses on a financial instrument which is classed as a hedge are deferred until they can be matched with the gains and losses on a hedged position. Hedge accounting assumes that a 'hedge' and a 'hedged position' are matched on a one-to-one basis and that the hedge reduces the risk of the hedged position.

There are numerous problems associated with hedge accounting. For example:

- Hedge accounting works best on a one-to-one matching of a hedge with a hedged position. However, companies often manage risk on a portfolio basis rather than on a one-to-one basis and it is therefore difficult to match individual transactions.

- Many companies engage in active risk management and it is not easy to distinguish between a 'hedge', for which gains and losses are deferred in hedge accounting, and trading in a financial instrument, where gains and losses are recognised as they occur.
- Realised gains and losses on hedges are deferred and included in the balance sheet as liabilities and assets and this makes financial statements less easy to understand.
- The classification of a derivative as a hedge is based on the intention of the management to match it with a hedged position. Management intention is not a sound basis for an accounting technique.

The DP notes that if the proposal to use current values was adopted this would eliminate many of the reasons for hedge accounting.

The DP says there are three views on hedge accounting:

1. Hedge accounting should not be allowed; it is an exception to normal accounting rules and causes more problems than it solves.
2. Hedge accounting should be allowed where it corrects anomalies in the present mixed value accounting model. For example, it can correct the anomaly where a derivative, which is measured at current value, is used to hedge an asset or liability which is measured at historical cost.
3. Hedge accounting may be used to correct anomalies, as above, and also to hedge for uncontracted future transactions. For example, if a company expects to make future sales in a foreign currency, it may seek to protect itself by entering into a forward foreign currency contract. Even if there are gains and losses on this hedge, these will be deferred until such time as the hedged position (the sales) take place, or the company decides not to make the future sales. In this case the company is hedging against future uncontracted sales.

If hedge accounting is allowed, then there are four options:

1. Leave the hedge at cost. The DP does not favour this option since it prefers financial instruments to be at current value.
2. Measure the hedge at current value and enter any gain or loss in a reserve in the balance sheet. The DP does not favour reserve accounting as this is contrary to FRS 3.
3. Measure the hedge at current value and enter any gain or loss in liabilities and assets in the balance sheet.
4. Measure the hedge at current value and enter any gain or loss in the STRGL. The gain or loss would be recycled from the STRGL to the profit and loss account in a future period when the hedged transaction occurred.

The DP is supportive of methods 3 and 4.

Conclusion

The subject of derivatives and other financial instruments is another example where the ASB clearly favour current values but they recognise that there may be opposition to any move away from historical cost. Any FRS is likely to impact upon the disclosures required by FRS 13.

DP: Business Combinations

Introduction

This Discussion Paper was prepared by the US Financial Accounting Standards Board and was based on the work of a working party from the international standard setters group known as G4+1, which includes the UK, USA, Canada, Australia and New Zealand and the IASC. The ASB circulated it for comment without any change, and so the paper uses US terminology, though for purposes of this summary UK terminology is used. The ASB has not debated this paper and so it contains none of their views, as is the case with other DPs.

In the chapter on FRS 6: Acquisitions and Mergers, the difference between the two methods of business combination, the acquisition method and the merger method, were discussed and the criteria for use of the merger method. You may like to refer back to this chapter before reading this summary.

There are numerous differences between UK GAAP and that in other countries, and some examples have been given in this book, for example the difference between the US and UK approach to the full provision method for deferred tax (see FRED 19). However, it may be argued that since business combinations represent the largest transaction that a business may make and the effect may last such a long time that accounting for this issue should be standardised. There is also the economic consequences argument that a more 'generous' accounting treatment in one country may give that country an unfair competitive advantage.

The basic issues

The basic issues are:

- Should there be a single method of accounting for business combination?
- If yes, which should be the preferred method?
- If no, which methods should be allowed and what should be the criteria for their use?

Different methods of business combination

The DP identifies three methods:

- acquisition method,
- merger method,
- fresh-start method.

These three methods are assessed based on the objectives of accounting and the desirable characteristics of useful information (see the SOP).

The acquisition and merger methods are well documented, not least in FRS 6. The 'fresh-start' method is not in use and is less familiar and so this summary of the DP will give a fuller explanation of this method, not because of its importance, but because readers are less likely to be familiar with it.

Fresh-start method

Under the fresh-start method the combined business is treated as a new business on the day of combination and all of its assets and liabilities are measured at fair values.

The method thus combines some of the features of the merger method and some of the features of the acquisition method. This may be summarised as follows:

Table 34.1 Summary of the main differences in accounting outcomes for the three methods of accounting for business combinations

	Merger	*Acquisition*	*Fresh-start*
Fair values or book vales for assets and liabilities	Book values	Fair value: acquiree Book value: acquirer	Fair values
Recognition of goodwill	No	Yes	Yes
Carry forward of predecessor company retained earnings	Yes	Yes: Acquirer No: Acquiree	No
Combination of earnings prior to date of combination	Yes	No	No

In the fresh-start method, it is assumed that none of the predecessor companies continue and that a new company emerges on the day of combination.

Table 34.2 Summary of main differences in the rationales that underlie the three methods of accounting for business combinations

	Merger	*Acquisition*	*Fresh-start*
Is the nature of the consideration relevant?	Yes – equity shares only	No	No
Are the combined *companies* considered parties to the combination?	No – shareholders only	Yes	Yes
Is a new entity created?	No	No – dominant (acquirer) company survives	Yes
Is there a change in control ?	No	Yes – the acquiree loses control	Yes

Recommendations

The DP concludes that the merger method should not be used for business combinations. It rejects the merger method:

- because it uses book values and not fair values, and these are less relevant to users;
- because the use of book values may give rise to subsequent gains and losses on disposal which should properly relate to the period prior to combination;
- because it is not acceptable to combine the profits when a company is purchased during a year and report a profit at the year end as if the companies had been combined for the whole of that year. This is contrary to the facts.

It concluded that:

- there should be a single method;
- although both the acquisition method and the fresh-start method did have merits, the acquisition method was the preferred method.

Conclusion

The ASC struggled with the issue of merger accounting; in 1971 it issued ED 3: Accounting for Acquisitions and Mergers and it issued SSAP 23: Accounting for Acquisitions and Mergers in 1985, some 14 years later! The ASB issued FRS 6, which replaced SSAP 23, in 1994 and in 1998 circulated this DP recommending the abolition of the merger method! It will be interesting to hear the official views of the ASB when it eventually issues its own paper on this topic.

Discounting in financial reporting – working paper

Introduction

It is not the purpose of this book to explain discounting. A description of discounting may be found in most textbooks on finance or management accounting. A simple description of discounting cash flows is that it is a technique for reflecting in the valuation of an asset or liability the time value of money and the risk associated with future cash flows. It is therefore possible to calculate the present value of a future receipt or payment. For example, the receipt of £1 000 in five years time if interest rates are 10 per cent has a present value of £621. Similarly, the obligation to pay a liability of £1 000 in five years time if interest rates are 10 per cent has a present value of £621.

Discounting appears in a number of standards and FREDs.

- In FRED 19 there is a discussion on whether the deferred tax balances should be discounted;
- FRED 20 requires future pension liabilities to be discounted.
- FRS 12 requires provisions to be discounted.
- FRS 11 defines value in use as 'the present value of the future cash flows obtainable as a result of an asset's continued use, including those resulting from ultimate disposal'. FRS 11 requires fixed assets to be valued at 'value in use' where this is greater than net realisable value, but less than carrying value.

ASB Working Paper

The ASB issued a 'Working Paper' in 1997 on discounting. It made the distinction between a Discussion Paper (DP) and a Working Paper (WP) by explaining that whereas a DP should lead to an FRS the Working Paper was not a prelude to an FRS. The merits of whether discounting should be applied to any particular issue would be part of each specific standard. Given that a number of standards now have sections requiring discounting, and no doubt more will do so in the future, the purpose of this WP is to establish principles on discounting so that the technique can be applied on a consistent basis to future standards. It is therefore a reference paper for the ASB itself.

Discounting is implicit in assets and liabilities which directly generate future cash flows and the timing and risk is already encapsulated in the market price; for example, five-year loan investments and five-year loan liabilities do not need to be discounted, as their market price already reflects that the cash flow arises in five years and the interest rate includes an element for risk.

However, where the value of an asset or liability is not valued in a market or by a transaction, then it is necessary to discount. For example, a fixed asset may have a market value but where it is necessary to value it at 'value in use', discounting needs to be applied; similarly, for example, for deferred tax provisions.

It may be argued that if discounting is not used, items which are different will appear similar. For example, if discounting is not used, there is no difference in the balance sheet between £1million due tomorrow, a certain £1 million in five years time and a risky £1 million due in five years time. If these figures were discounted, they would have a different value, which accords with the economic reality.

It might be argued that to reduce a liability from £1 000 to £621 is not prudent. However, discounting is not about reducing the value of a liability but about arriving at its economic value. The concept of prudence is invoked when deciding whether to recognise a liability and at what amount; discounting then arrives at a more precise measurement of that figure.

Discounting is only considered necessary where it is likely to be material; current assets and liabilities are normally due to be received and paid in the near future and discounting these items would rarely be material. Small items due some years in the future would also not need discounting.

The WP discusses the main issues surrounding discounting:

- how to allow for the variability of the cash flow, and discusses the concept of 'expected value', which is the cash flow times the probability of the cash arising;
- how to assess risk and hence what discount rate to use;
- how to incorporate tax into the cash flows;
- how to incorporate inflation into the cash flows.

Over a period of time, the discounted assets and liabilities will change in value and there is a debate as to where to record this movement.

Example 34.1

If a provision is required for £1 000 in five years time, and the discount rate to be used is 5 per cent, then the provision will be measured as follows:

	Year 0	*Year 1*	*Year 2*	*Year 3*	*Year 4*	*Year 5*	*Total*
Present value	784	823	864	907	952	1 000	
1					1 000		
2				1 000			
3			1 000				
4		1 000					
5	1 000						
Interest		39	41	43	45	48	216
		823–784	864–823	907–864	952–907	1 000–952	1 000–784

In year 0, the £1 000 provision is valued at £784; in year 1, the provision is valued at £823. This increase in the provision of £39 is regarded as interest. This repeats itself until in year 5 the provision is measured at £1 000. The total interest is £216, the difference between the provision of £1 000 and its valuation in year 0 of £784.

This is referred to as the 'unwinding' of the interest. It could be argued that this figure is interest or is part of the underlying cost. For example, if the provision relates to abandonment costs, then it could be shown as part of abandonment costs.

The WP argues that the unwinding of a discounted figure is by its very nature interest. However, it argues that it would not be appropriate to include this as part of the normal interest charge, as the latter figure is important for various ratios, for example interest cover. The WP therefore suggests that the unwinding of the discount should be shown adjacent to, and separate from, the normal interest charge. This recommendation appears, for example, in FRS 20 on pensions costs.

DP: Reporting financial performance – proposals for change

Introduction

This paper was developed by the G4 + 1 group of standard setters, which includes the UK, USA, Canada, Australia and New Zealand and the IASC. It is intended that each country will adopt the proposals in its own accounting standards and is therefore an example of international harmonisation. The effect of the DP on any participating member will depend on its existing standards. Thus the ASB has added a Foreword to the DP explaining what impact the DP would have in the UK and particularly with regard to FRS 3.

The DP develops the theme in FRS 3 that the performance in a complex company cannot be measured by a single figure; FRS 3 was designed to highlight a number of key measures of performance and users were encouraged to select the one most relevant to their specific needs, bearing in mind the decisions they need to take.

The detail of the DP

Comprehensive income statement

FRS 3 recognises there are two performance statements; the profit and loss account and the statement of total recognised gains and losses (STRGL). The DP recognises that it is not appropriate to have two statements of performance and therefore suggests that these are combined into a single statement. This single statement would have three parts:

- operating activities,
- financing activities,
- other gains and losses.

The concept of a single statement is referred to as the comprehensive income statement (CIS).

An example is set out below.

Table 34.3

	Statement of financial performance		
			£000
I	*Operating (trading activities)*		
	Revenues		775
	Cost of sales		(620)
	Other expenses		(104)
	Operating income		*51*
II	*Financing and other treasury activities*		
	Interest on debt	(26)	
	Gains and losses on financial instruments	8	
	Financing Income		*(18)*
	Operating and financing income before taxation		*33*
	Taxation on income		(12)
	Operating and financing income after taxation		*21*
III	*Other gains and losses*		
	Profit on disposal of discontinued operations	3	
	Profit on sale of properties in continuing operations	6	
	Revaluation of long-term assets	4	
	Exchange translation differences on foreign currency and net investments	(2)	
	Other gains and losses before taxation	*11*	
	Taxation on other gains and losses	(4)	
	Other gains and losses after taxation		7
			28

The CIS would still include the further analysis of continuing and discontinued activities, but for simplicity these are excluded in the above statement.

The first two parts are broadly the profit and loss account; the third part is the STRGL.

This presentation supports the SOP definition of gains and losses being anything that increases/decreases equity, apart from contributions/distributions to shareholders.

A key issue is how to allocate items between the three headings, and table 34.4 is offered.

Table 34.4

Characteristics more typical of operating items	*Characteristics more typical of other gains and losses*
Operating activities	Non-operating activities
Recurring	Non-recurring
Non-holding items	Holding Items
Internal events (e.g. value adding activities)	External events (e.g. price changes)

An item which predominately has the characteristics of the left column would be in the 'Operating' section; an item which predominately has the characteristics of the right column would be in the 'Other' section.

The DP makes a number of proposals which would impact upon FRS 3; for example, profits and losses on the sale of a business and on the disposal of a fixed asset, would be in the 'Other' section, rather than in the 'Operating' section.

The following table summarises the position on how gains and losses on fixed assets would be reported.

Table 34.5

Component of performance	*Gains and losses*
Operating activities	• depreciation • disposal gains/losses representing adjustments to depreciation • impairment losses and their reversal • disposal losses which are impairments
Other gains and losses	• revaluation gains • disposals gains, which are not depreciation adjustments or reversals of impairments • revaluation and disposal losses, where there is no impairment or adjustments to depreciation

In the UK, dividends paid and proposed are shown on the face of the profit and loss account as a deduction from profit for the year. Dividends are an appropriation of profit and it may be argued that they should not therefore be shown in a performance statement. Accordingly, the DP proposes that dividends should not be shown in the CIS but as a deduction from equity. A related issue is whether a proposed dividend should be regarded as a liability; in the UK proposed dividends are recognised as a current liability; in other countries they are not recognised, on the basis that they are not a liability until approved by the shareholders.

Realisation and recycling.

The DP looks at the issue of recycling, which occurs when the same item is reported in a performance statement in more than one period, but in a different form.

Example 34.2

A fixed asset is bought for £1 000 in year 1; it is revalued at £1 500 in year 2; it is sold for £1 800 in year 3. There is an unrealised gain in year 2 of £500 (£1 500 – £1 000). When the asset is sold, the realised gain is £1 800 – £1 500 = £300.

In the UK, the unrealised gain of £500 is reported in the STRGL in year 2 and the realised gain of £300 in the profit and loss account in year 3. If recycling were permitted, in order to show that the gain had now changed its form (from unrealised to realised) then the £500 unrealised gain could be recycled from the STRGL to the profit and loss account to report a total realised gain of £800. If, however, the distinction between realised and unrealised is not considered important, then recycling is not necessary.

It would be possible to make clear the distinction between realised and unrealised by dividing a performance statement into two parts – realised and unrealised.The performance statement could simply be realised gains in the top half and unrealised gains in the bottom half, and it would be possible to recycle between these sections. It also follows that the balance sheet would distinguish between unrealised and realised reserves. Some argue that it is not the distinction between realised and unrealised which is important but between uncertain and certain and it this change in status which is being reported when an item is recycled. It may be argued that an unrealised gain is uncertain, but that a realised gain is certain.

The division in the CIS is between 'Operating' and 'Other', regardless of whether they are realised or not. In Table 34.3, gains and losses are grouped according to their nature, rather than whether they are realised or not. For example, the revaluation of fixed assets (unrealised gains) are grouped with the profit on sale of fixed assets (realised gains).

Even in the CIS it would be possible to recycle an item within 'Other Gains and Losses' by including it as a revaluation in one period and as a realised profit in a later period. However, the distinction is not important in the CIS and so recycling within a group, and between groups, is not allowed.

The DP concludes that recycling is undesirable; having reported an unrealised gain it is not necessary to report it again if it is realised.

Exceptional items

Where there are several exceptional items relating to different parts of the CIS, these could be:

- combined together into one line,
- be disclosed next to the item they relate to, i.e. 'Operating' or 'Finance' or 'Other'.

The DP proposes that these should be shown on a separate line, next to the line they relate to, arguing that they have more in common with a line item than they do with each other (which would be the implication if they were combined together into one single line).

Tax

The options for the tax charge are to:

- allocate it to each of the three headings in the CIS;
- include it as a line item at the foot of the CIS;
- allocate it to:
    - the total of Operating and Financing,
    - Other Gains and Losses.

As may be seen in Table 34.3 the DP opts for the latter approach.

Changes of accounting policy, correction of errors and changes in estimates

The DP proposes that a change of accounting policy should be applied retrospectively to the previous year to aid comparability. Any cumulative adjustment is made to the opening retained earnings; there is no adjustment to the CIS as it does not affect performance in the current year. A similar treatment is applied to the correction of errors for the same reason.

No changes are made with regard to estimates, as financial statements contain many estimates based on the best judgement at the time and no attempt should be made to amend these estimates retrospectively.

Controversy over the combined income statement

Realised v unrealised gains and losses

The most controversial feature of the CIS is its implicit definition of performance. Performance is taken to be the difference between equity in two balance sheets, disregarding any distribution or contribution to/from shareholders. This is consistent with the SOP where the starting point for measuring gains and losses are changes in net assets; it follows that all such changes in the balance sheet are a measure of performance. This leads the DP to state that, with regard to the measurement of performance, there is no difference between realised and unrealised gains. The DP argues that a realised gain reflects the same economic event as an unrealised gain, although it admits that realised gains are evidenced by a transaction. They are therefore treated in the same way and are both included in the 'Other' section.

However it may be argued that an unrealised holding gain in the 'Other' section is not a measure of performance. In many income models such gains would be taken direct to a non-distributable reserve. This of course depends upon the underlying capital maintenance concept and this is not defined in the DP.

The DP approaches the measurement of performance indirectly, via the change in equity. It may be argued that the concept of performance should first be defined and then a statement constructed around this definition. This would probably lead to certain items in 'Other' being moved to the 'Operating' section, and the remaining 'Other' items being treated as capital maintenance adjustments.

It may be argued in support of the DP that recognising unrealised holding gains smoothes out the measurement of profit, since if they are ignored all the realised gains are recognised in a single year. However, because the DP prohibits re-cycling it is not possible to show these unrealised gains again if they are realised. This problem could be solved by allowing recycling between a realised section and an unrealised in an income statement.

Recurring items

Table 34.4 for judging whether an item should be in the 'Operating' section or the 'Other' section includes the criteria recurring and non-recurring. It may be argued that such items, like exceptional items, have more in common with the section to which they relate rather than being a criteria to distinguish 'Operating' from 'Other' activities. Thus a non-recurring item of an operating nature is better shown in the 'Operating' section.

Conclusion

The ASB are committed to evolutionary rather than revolutionary change. The change brought about by FRS 3 was an important step; a change from FRS 3 to an FRS based on this DP would be yet another step in measuring profit.

DP: Leases – implementation of a new approach

Introduction

The G4+1 international group of accounting standard setters has produced a Position Paper on leases and the ASB has circulated this document as a Discussion Paper in the UK.

The subject of leases was covered in the chapter on SSAP 21 and readers may like to refer back to that chapter before reading this summary of the DP on leases.

An important feature of SSAP 21 is the distinction between finance leases and operating leases. Finance leases are capitalised; i.e. an asset and liability are recognised in the balance sheet of the lessee and the profit and loss account has an interest charge and a depreciation charge. Operating leases are not capitalised; i.e. there is no recognition in the balance sheet and the profit and loss account has only the lease payment.

The definition of a finance lease includes the condition that the present value of the minimum lease payments amount to substantially all (normally 90 per cent or more) of the fair value of the leased asset. The '90 per cent rule' has generally been interpreted such that if the figure is 89 per cent, the transaction is an operating lease, and if it is 90 per cent, then it is a finance lease. This has made it possible for leasing companies, with the support of their customers, to enter into leasing agreements which may be classed as operating leases and thus avoid the onerous conditions of a finance lease. In essence, this means that the operating lease finance is 'off balance sheet'.

It was reported in a recent research project by Goodacre and Beattie (see *Accountancy* June 1999, page 86) that:

- Since the introduction of SSAP 21 in 1984 there has been a significant growth in operating as compared to finance leases and by 1994 operating lease payments were five times larger than finance lease payments.
- Operating lease finance represents 39 per cent of long-term debt.
- Operating lease liabilities were 13 times greater than finance lease liabilities.
- Over 80 per cent of operating leases related to land and buildings rather than to plant and machinery.

The DP makes recommendations to improve the reporting of lease transactions.

Main features of the Discussion Paper

Capitalisation of leases

The DP proposes that the same accounting procedures should be applied to all leases and thus avoid the arbitrary distinction between finance leases and operating leases. All leases would essentially be accounted for as finance leases. Lessees would therefore recognise in their balance sheet the fair value of the rights and obligations from all leases.

Lessors would report as financial assets, i.e. debtors, the amount receivable from the lessee. Where the lessor retained an interest in the residual value of an asset, then this would be reported as a separate financial asset. The reason for this is that the debtor for lease receipts and the debtor for residual value carry different risks; there is a contractual agreement for lease receipts but the residual value will depend upon market conditions.

Land and buildings

Leasing usually refers to the leasing of equipment, but it does also apply to land and buildings. The leasing of buildings is different from that of equipment because:

- equipment leasing often has tax consequences which do not apply to buildings;
- the residual value of buildings is often substantial and belongs to the lessor; for equipment, the amounts are often small and are usually passed from the lessor to the lessee;
- the lease period for buildings may often be 25 years and sometimes 50 years, whereas equipment leases are for much shorter periods.

Leases of buildings have typically been treated as operating leases. Under the proposals in the DP these leases would be capitalised and this would have a significant impact on the balance sheets of lessees and lessors. Furthermore, the lessee would be able to revalue the building, in accordance with FRS 15, and be obliged to undertake impairment reviews, as in FRS 11.

The lessor would normally show two assets – a financial asset for the lease receivables and an interest in the residual value. The profit and loss account would disclose separately:

- finance income,
- lease receivables,
- changes in interest in residual value.

The current position for a lessor is that a building would normally be accounted for as an investment property, under SSAP 19. The main feature of SSAP 19 is that investment properties are carried in the balance sheet at fair value. The DP acknowledges that these proposals would be less useful than those in SSAP 19 and that it would be desirable to keep the advantages of fair value accounting as well as giving information about the lease agreement. The DP therefore recommends that the lessor's interest in the residual value would be reported as the difference between the amount of the lease receivable and the fair value of the property.

A feature of UK property leases is that they often provide for regular rent reviews to reflect market conditions, but these work on a ratchet – the rent may be increased but not reduced. The DP recommends that where leases require that the rentals are to be adjusted to reflect price changes, these price changes should be reflected in the amount of the asset and liability at the inception of the lease. The ASB's view is that it is not practical to estimate such increases and even if it were, this would lead to regular recognition and de-recognition in successive periods as the property market changed. The ASB therefore prefers that only existing rentals would be recognised as assets and liabilities and therefore adjustment would only be required at the time of rent reviews.

Short leases

The DP does not propose any exemption for short leases. Although some have suggested that leases of less than one year should be exempt, the DP does not accept this proposal. The DP argues that even leases of less than one year may give rise to material assets and liabilities. It should therefore be the concept of materiality which determines whether a lease is capitalised, not an arbitrary threshold of a minimum lease period. This should ensure that the leasing industry does not attempt to find a loop-hole so that material leases can remain off balance sheet.

Executory contracts

An executory contract arises where both parties are still to perform to an equal degree the actions promised by and required of them under a contract. For example, a manufacturer may require a monthly delivery from a supplier and agree to pay for these each month. Some commentators have questioned whether such contracts should be accounted for as a lease. The DP is quite clear that they should not; executory contracts are a 'promise for a promise' and as such are unfulfilled. These contracts may be distinguished from leases which are fulfilled when the lessor gives to the lessee right of access to an asset.

Recognition of income by lessors

There are two main methods by which a lessor may recognise income from leases. These are the 'net investment method' and the 'net cash investment' method. (These terms are defined in the chapter on SSAP 21). Both methods allocate income on the basis of a constant periodic rate of return on the lessor's outstanding investment in the lease. The essential difference is that the net investment method is based on the lease payments without taking account of the effect of taxation; on the other hand, the net cash investment does allow for the effect of tax on the lease payments. The DP does not reach any firm conclusion on the preferred method. The ASB, however, prefers the net cash investment method; this is not surprising as this is the required method in SSAP 21.

Fair values

The capitalisation of leases gives rise to financial instruments. (These are defined in the chapter on FRS 13.) These are the financial assets of lessors and the financial liabilities of lessees. Although the DP is written from the perspective of historical cost accounts, the ASB favours a current value model. (See the section in this chapter on the Discussion Paper on Derivatives and Other Financial Instruments.) It therefore seems likely that any move to current value for financial instruments would have an impact on accounting for leases.

Conclusion

The DP recommends that all leases be capitalised, if material. It may be argued that the distinction between operating and finance leases should be maintained, but at a lower threshold for the recognition of a finance lease. However, lessors, with the support of lessees, would probably continue to structure lease agreements in such a way as to artificially enable leases to be construed as operating leases. The removal of thresholds in the DP is therefore a practical solution to preventing such artificial agreements.

The DP is consistent with the SOP's definition of assets and liabilities because it proposes that operating leases should be capitalised and therefore the lessee's balance sheet recognises all its assets and liabilities. The methodology of asset and liability recognition is preferable to the methodology in SSAP 21 which is based on whether substantially all the risks and rewards of the ownership of an asset have been transferred to the lessee.

The DP is also consistent with the importance of the concept of comparability in the SOP. The comparability of financial statements has been adversely affected by the distinction between operating and finance leases, with the consequence that financial statements have been less useful. The classification of leases into operating and finance leases affects the level of debt, gearing, return on capital and interest cover. It is known that analysts have attempted to overcome this problem by estimating the affect if operating leases were capitalised, but the interests of users and preparers would be better served if a common approach to all leases were adopted.

Research by Goodacre and Beattie (see *Accountancy* June 1999, page 86) showed that the capitalisation of operating leases would have a major impact on performance indicators. For example:

- Operating profit would increase from 8.7 per cent to 9.8 per cent (This would occur because depreciation charges would be substituted for rental charges in operating profit, and the interest charge would be included in financial costs.)
- Gearing would rise from 20 per cent to 72 per cent.
- There would be a minimal impact on return on capital employed. (It should be noted that the balance sheet would include both the leased asset and the lease finance obligation.)

The ASB has circulated this G4+1 Position Paper for comment in the UK. It does not agree with all its recommendations but it does support the main thrust of the Paper. The ASB therefore intends to issue a FRED and then an FRS which will replace the current SSAP 21.

Some fear that these changes may have economic consequences which will have an adverse effect on the leasing industry with the result that less finance will be available for British industry. A counter view is that the demand and supply of finance, whether it be lease finance or bank loans, will not be affected.

Others argue that such changes may have an adverse effect on share prices of companies which currently have significant operating leases, for example some travel companies with aircraft on operating leases. However, many believe that analysts and investors are efficient at processing information and that share prices already encapsulate the effect of operating leases.

DP: Year end financial reports – improving communication

Introduction

Company law requires that shareholders should be sent annual financial accounts so that the directors can account to the owners of the company on their stewardship of the resources entrusted to them. The shareholders are only interested in a basic amount of information: are the directors able to account for the capital entrusted to them, has the company made a reasonable return on that capital and other information, such as directors' remuneration. The needs of shareholders may be met largely by providing them with historic cost accounts.

However, accounts which are produced to meet basic stewardship needs are not useful for taking economic decisions, such as whether to buy or sell shares in a company. Analysts and institutional investors need more detailed information and there has therefore developed a regulatory framework which includes the accounting standards, UITFs, company law, stock exchange requirements and European directives. The result is highly complex accounts which are helpful to institutional investors and analysts in making economic decisions.

A consequence of this growth in reporting requirements is that financial statements are no longer understood by the typical private investor. Although the purpose of company law is to meet their stewardship needs these have been denied to them because the needs of analysts have been given preference. As Sir David Tweedie has said 'Financial reporting is useless if it fails to communicate. . . For the informed layman, however, there is a danger that the central features of a company's performance and financial position may get lost in a welter of detail.'

The Statement of Principles (see the chapter on the Statement of Principles) states that 'Those preparing financial statements are entitled to assume that users have a reasonable knowledge of business and economic activities and accounting and a willingness to study with a reasonable diligence the information provided.' It is arguable that accounts fail this qualitative characteristic of 'understandability' since it requires much more than this to understand financial statements.

A contrary argument is that it is not necessary for private investors to understand accounts; their needs are best met by providing detailed information to their advisers, the analysts, from whom they should seek advice before they make any financial decisions.

The basic problem

It has long been recognised that the Annual Report is not understood, or even read, by private shareholders. The Companies Act 1989 therefore allowed listed companies to send summary financial statements to shareholders who did not wish to receive the full accounts. The content was prescribed in the Act and was broadly the financial statements without the notes.

It may be argued that the Act was misguided in that it addressed the wrong issue. Many companies were concerned with the cost of sending out glossy Annual Reports which were immediately discarded; it was believed that sending summary financial statements would save costs if these were substituted for the full Annual Report. Summary financial statements are an extract from a complex document and are therefore themselves no more than a reduced complex document and are not understandable by the typical private investor. Thus the Act addressed the issue of cost rather than the issue of 'understandability'. In the event many listed companies did not produce summary financial statements, as producing both full and summarised financial statements did not save on costs.

The ASB therefore decided to take a broader view of this issue and produced the Discussion Paper 'Year-End Financial Reports: Improving Communication'.

The details of the Discussion Paper 'Year-End Financial Reports: Improving Communication'.

The DP argues that the summary financial report should be used by the vast majority of users and should therefore become the mainstream financial report. This glossy summary financial report should be sent to all shareholders. The full financial report would be a 'plain paper' report which would be used for filing purposes and those who specifically requested the full accounts.

The ASB wanted to meet the twin objectives of saving costs and producing an understandable second report and they have proposed the neat solution that the summarised financial report should be similar to the preliminary announcement (see the chapter on ASB Statements).

There is an important distinction between summarised financial reports and simplified reports. The former are a summary which leaves out much of the detail and uses graphs and ratios where appropriate; the latter use plain language rather than technical jargon, use highlights from the financial statements and use more narratives. Thus full accounts are for analysts; summary accounts for the informed layman; and simplified accounts for the uninformed layman. The DP recognises that only a few companies with large numbers of shareholders would choose to issue simplified accounts.

Internet

The cost of printing different reports is an important consideration for companies. However, if reports were published on the Website of a company then this would reduce these costs. The use of electronic versions of financial statements opens up many exciting possibilities. For example, through the use of hyperlinks, users can relate different areas. It also possible to move from a high-level summary to the underlying data, or to ask for the data to be presented in graphs, pie charts, etc. The ultimate would be for a company to place all its data in a data base which could be accessed by sophisticated users who would use their own models to extract the data and assemble it in a form most suitable to their needs.

If the Internet is used for financial reporting there would of course need to be secure controls over that data.

Conclusion

Accountants have had the goal of effective communication with shareholders for many years. They have also had the fear of misleading shareholders and have erred on the cautious side and disclosed too much information. The approach adopted in this DP is to concentrate on summarising/simplifying the information and giving the user the *caveat* that the accounts may only serve the more limited purpose of stewardship rather than decision taking.

The DP will probably not lead to an accounting standard although it may lead to a statement of good practice. Since any change with regard to disclosing information to shareholders is a matter for company law, it will feed into the current review of company law by the Department of Trade and Industry.

EXAMINATION PRACTICE

34.1 In connection with the DP: Derivatives and Other Financial Instruments:

(a) Why did the DP reject historical cost in favour of current values?

(b) What is hedge accounting?

34.2 What are the implications of the DP: Business Combinations for FRS 6 and why did the DP reach this conclusion?

34.3 A company has a liability of £3 000 in four years time and this is to be measured at its discounted value. Using a discount rate of 8 per cent, show:

(a) how the liability would be measured at the end of each of the four years;

(b) the interest charge in each of the four years.

(You will need to use 'present value' tables or calculate the present value using the formula $1/(1 + r)^t$, where r is the discount rate and t is time in years.)

34.4 What is the most significant difference between FRS 3 and the DP: Reporting Financial Performance.

34.5 What is the most significant difference between SSAP 21 and the DP: Leases.

34.6 What is the difference between full, summarised and simplified financial reports?

CHAPTER 35

Urgent Issue Task Force Abstracts

Introduction

The relationship of the Urgent Issues Task Force (UITF) to the ASB was discussed in Chapter 1. The main role of the UITF is to assist the ASB where a problem has arisen with an accounting standard or a provision of company law. It investigates the problem and then issues an Abstract, which has a similar status to an FRS, on how the issue should be resolved.

UITF Abstract 4: Presentation of long-term debtors in current assets

Under the Companies Act, the current assets figure may include debtors payable after more than one year, with separate disclosure of these in the notes. The abstract requires disclosure of such debtors on the face of the balance sheet where the amount is so material that otherwise 'readers may misinterpret the accounts'.

UITF Abstract 5: Transfer from current assets to fixed assets

This abstract deals with the situation where a decision is taken to use a current asset on a continuing basis in the company's activities. At this stage the fixed asset should be recorded at the lower of cost and net realisable value.

UITF Abstract 6: Accounting for post-retirement benefits other than pensions

This abstract explicitly responds to a new standard in the USA, FAS 106, that requires companies to account for all post-retirement benefits on an accruals basis, in the same way as pensions are treated under SSAP 24. The abstract requires similar treatment in the UK for accounts ending on or after 23 December 1994, while encouraging earlier compliance.

UITF Abstract 7: True and fair view override disclosures

The abstract addresses in detail what disclosure companies should make when invoking the *true and fair view override* provision of the Companies Act 1985. This comprises:

a) a statement of the treatment normally required and that actually adopted;
b) a statement as to why the treatment normally required fails to give a true and fair view;
c) a description of the effect of departing from the normal rules, with a quantification of the effect if this is not shown in the accounts and is practicable.

UITF Abstract 9: Accounting for operations in hyperinflationary economies

As we have seen above, SSAP 20 identifies a need for special treatment of the translation of foreign currency amounts of companies in areas of hyperinflation. UITF 9 defines such an area as one where over three years the cumulative inflation rate approaches or exceeds 100 per cent.

Two adjustment methods are permitted:

(a) adjustment of the local currency accounts to reflect current price levels, with any gain or loss on monetary items taken to the profit and loss account, followed by translation at the closing rate; or
(b) using a relatively stable currency as the *functional* currency, translating the subsidiary's accounts into that currency by the temporal method. The functional currency would then be translated in turn by the closing rate method.

UITF Abstract 10: Disclosure of directors' share options

Directors' share options can form a significant element of their remuneration, and so in principle should be included in the report of aggregate remuneration. Since a meaningful value cannot be provided, UITF 10 opts for an alternative approach to full disclosure. For each director there should be shown:

(a) changes in the number of options held during the year;
(b) the option price;
(c) the market price at the date when any option was exercised: and
(d) the date from which options are exercisable and on which they expire.

UITF Abstract 11: Capital instruments: issuer call options

A capital instrument may include an issue call option, being a right of the issuer to redeem the instrument early, usually on the payment of a premium.

UITF 11 takes the view that if the call option is only exercisable by the issuer then the payment should be accounted for in the year it relates to. An exception to this rule arises where the terms of the instrument are such that the issuer would be commercially obliged to exercise the call option.

UITF Abstract 12: Lessee accounting for reverse premiums and similar incentives

An operating lease may include an up-front cash payment to the lessee, a rent-free period or a contribution to lessee costs.

Normally such benefits should be spread over the lease over the period until an adjustment to a market rent is made. If, exceptionally, it can shown that the incentive is not part of the lessee's market return, another systematic and rational basis may be used.

UITF Abstract 13: Accounting for ESOP trusts

This pronouncement deals, in some detail, with the accounting issues that arise when a company has an Employee Share Ownership Plan (ESOP). It is common for such a scheme to operate through a trust which acquires and holds shares to be sold or transferred to employees in the future; the acquisition is financed by loans either from the company or from a third party loan, often guaranteed by the company. The basic principle of UITF 13 is that the trust should be treated on a 'substance over form' basis, in the spirit of FRS 5, so that until shares are passed unconditionally to the employees, the shares should appear as an asset, and related third-party loans should appear as a liability, in the company's accounts.

UITF Abstract 14: Disclosures of changes in accounting policy

This pronouncement makes a minor addition to the disclosure requirements of FRS 3 when a change in accounting policy is made. This is a requirement to disclose the impact of the change on the current year's results. Where the effect is either immaterial or similar to the reported effect of the prior year, a simple statement to the effect is acceptable. Where it is not practicable to quantify the effect in the present year the reasons for this must be stated.

UITF Abstract 15: Disclosures of substantial acquisitions

FRS 6 specifies additional disclosures required for 'substantial' acquisitions. Substantial is defined by reference to Class 1 or Super Class 1 transactions under the Stock Exchange listing rules. In August 1995 the Stock Exchange revised their rules, removing the Class 1 transactions. UITF 15 specifies that the term 'substantial' should continue to be defined by reference to the criteria that are used to 'identify a Class 1 transaction'.

UITF Abstract 17: Employee share schemes

Share option schemes are a feature of employee remuneration, either as a management incentive or through 'Save As You Earn' schemes that are available to all employees. A more recent development is the increasing use of share awards, either through annual bonuses or longer-term incentive schemes. In such schemes the amount of the award is governed by performance criteria; if these criteria are partially achieved, participants may be entitled to a proportion of the full award. UITF 17 is concerned with the measurement and timing of the charge to be recognised by companies in the profit and loss account.

The UITF concludes that the charge should be recognised over the period in which the employee's performance relates. The amount recognised should be based on the fair value of the shares at the date the employee enters the share scheme (see the chapter on FRS 14 and the section on Employee Share and Incentive Plans).

UITF Abstract 18: Pensions costs following the 1997 tax changes in respect of dividend income

Since 1997 pension schemes are no longer able to reclaim a tax credit on dividend income. This will probably result in a reduction in the actuarial value of the assets in a pension scheme or an increase in the actuarial value of the liabilities. If the scheme is in surplus, the surplus will be reduced. If the scheme has a deficit, the deficit will increase.

This Abstract is concerned with the recognition of this loss in the financial statements of employers sponsoring defined benefit schemes.

The UITF concludes that the loss should be spread over the remaining service lives of current employees, regardless of whether the scheme is in surplus or deficit and regardless of any additional contributions which are made.

UITF Abstract 19: Tax on gains and losses on foreign currency borrowings that hedge an investment in a foreign enterprise

The UITF deals with two issues:

1. Certain gains and losses on foreign currency borrowings that have been used to finance or provide a hedge against equity investments in foreign enterprises are reported in the STRGL. UITF 19 confirms that any related tax should also be reported in the STRGL.
2. Until recently, neither the retranslation of the net investment in a foreign enterprise nor the gain or loss on foreign borrowings had any consequences for tax. Owing to recent changes in UK tax legislation this is no longer always the case. The UITF sets out how these tax consequences should be accounted for when applying the restrictions in SSAP 20 regarding the amount of gains and loses which are dealt with in the STRGL.

UITF Abstract 20: Year 2000 issues – accounting and disclosures

Although the date of 1 January 2000 has now passed, the ASB has stated that the principles of this UITF still remain.

UITF 20 addresses the accounting for external and internal costs of modifying existing equipment, such as software used for internal operational purposes, to achieve year 2000 compliance.

UITF 20 requires all such costs to be charged as expenses unless they are clearly of a capital nature. These costs may be 'exceptional items' and as such should be separately disclosed. In general the costs should be treated no differently from any other expenses and the same disclosure requirements are applicable. It also states that some non-financial disclosures should be made in respect of an entity's general approach to the year 2000 problem.

UITF Abstract 21: Accounting issues arising from the proposed introduction of the euro

UITF 21 considers the accounting treatment of three issues:

1. The treatment of costs incurred in connection with the introduction of the euro and whether these should be charged as an expense or capitalised. Examples of expenditure are administrative, planning, staff training, the provision of information to customers, modification of software and the adaptation of hardware, such as vending machines, retail outlets' cash registers or banks' automatic teller machines.
   UITF 21 requires these costs to be charged as expenses, unless they are clearly of a capital nature.
2. The treatment of cumulative foreign exchange differences which will become permanent now that some national currencies are locked into the euro.
   UITF 21 follows the accepted rules that gains and losses should not be recycled through the profit and loss account and they should therefore remain in reserves.
3. The impact on hedge accounting at the date of the introduction of the euro.
   UITF 21 states that the introduction of the euro should have no impact on hedge accounting; the normal rules governing the deferral of gains and losses on hedged instruments and their matching with the hedged position should still apply.

UITF Abstract 22: The acquisition of a Lloyd's business

Lloyd's syndicates adopt a basis of accounting under which underwriting accounts are not closed for at least three years. Syndicates are managed by managing agents who are usually entitled to commissions equivalent to a share in the syndicates' profits, which will not be known with certainty until the accounts are closed.

UITF 22 is concerned with the recognition of assets and liabilities when a business such as a Lloyd's managing agent is acquired. The issue is whether profit commissions receivable in respect of years that are not yet closed should be included in these assets.

Abstract 22 concludes that on the acquisition of a Lloyd's managing agent all profit commissions receivable in respect of periods before the acquisition, including those periods not yet closed, should be recognised at fair value.

UITF Abstract 23: The application of the transitional rules in FRS 15

FRS 15 requires that where, on adopting FRS 15, companies separate tangible fixed assets into different components with significantly different useful economic lives for depreciation purposes, for example the lifts and heating system in a building, the changes should be dealt with as a prior year adjustment.

Abstract 23 states that such prior period adjustments should be restricted to those components:

- where a provision for repairs and maintenance was eliminated by prior year adjustment on the adoption of FRS 12, or
- there has been a change in policy from writing off repairs and maintenance to a policy of capitalisation because it replaces a separately depreciated component.

Prior period adjustments should not be used for changes to the useful economic lives or residual values of assets.

EXAMINATION PRACTICE

35.1 What is the role of the UITF?

Inflation Accounting in the UK

Introduction

In the English speaking world, inflation rates have generally been low since the mid 1980s, and accordingly inflation accounting has not been a major topic of professional debate. Nevertheless, the subject continues to be a vital part of the training of the professional accountant for four reasons:

1. Internationally a number of countries continue to see inflation rates at a level where unadjusted historical cost accounts are meaningless. A number of Latin American countries have well-established inflation accounting systems. Such systems are likely to be applied in those Eastern European countries with similar problems.
2. Under SSAP 20 on foreign currency translation UK holding companies with foreign subsidiaries operating in countries with hyper inflation must apply inflation accounting to those subsidiaries before translating by the closing rate.
3. During the working life of a professional accountant there is a significant possibility, in most countries, that there will be a period of substantial inflation.
4. Historic cost accounts, even at low levels of inflation, can include material distortions. As an example, one study adjusted accounts of 12 UK companies between 1959 and 1968 when inflation rates varied from 1 per cent to 4.4 per cent. On an inflation adjusted basis it was found that historical cost profit was overstated by some 10 per cent.

In this chapter we:

1. Briefly summarise the problems of historic cost accounting in times of inflation.
2. Summarise the history of official pronouncements on inflation accounting in the UK.
3. Explain the basic principles of the two main approaches to the problem which have been considered in the UK: Current Purchasing Power (CPP) and Current Cost Accounting (CCA).
4. Offer a brief review of the arguments for each of the alternative approaches.

The basic problem

Traditionally historic cost accounting involves the application of two conventions:

1. The 'money measurement' convention, whereby all items are measured in monetary units.
2. The 'historic cost' convention, whereby all items are measured by reference to the amount at which they first enter the accounts.

In times of inflation the monetary unit has a shrinking value while the historic amount at which an item originally entered the accounts loses its significance. The impact depends on whether the item recorded is monetary or non-monetary. Monetary items are assets or liabilities representing an obligation of a fixed monetary amount, such as a bank balance, a trade debtor or a trade creditor. Non-monetary items do not represent any such fixed monetary obligation – examples include land and building, plant and stock.

Four major specific problems that arise for historic cost accounts in times of inflation are:

1. Non-monetary assets are stated at a historic cost amount less than current value, thus giving an unrealistically low picture of net assets.
2. When non-monetary assets are consumed the related expense shown in the profit and loss account will be less than current value, so reporting an unrealistically high profit.
3. The accounts fail to reflect the declining value of monetary items.
4. When considering successive years' accounts, comparison is distorted by the fact that the unit of measurement has a different significance each year.

Official pronouncements in the UK

UK inflation accounting proposals have included:

1973 ED 8 proposed a system of CPP accounting, whereby the effects of general price level movements on shareholders' funds would be shown in statements supplementary to the historical cost accounts.

1974 SSAP 7, issued as a provisional statement and therefore not binding on members of the professional accounting bodies as SSAPs usually are, followed ED 8.

1975 The 'Sandilands Report', being the report of a committee set up by the government to investigate the problem of accounting for inflation, rejected CPP as a solution on the grounds of being 'constrained by the deficiencies of the basic historic cost accounts' and recommended that 'accounts drawn up in accordance with the principles of current cost accounting should as soon as possible become the basic published accounts of companies'.

1976 The Inflation Accounting Steering Group presented ED 18, a proposal for a full system of CCA accounts to replace historical cost accounts.

1977 At a special meeting of the ICAEW members voted to reject ED 18.

1978 Following the vote against ED 18 the ASC published an interim report (The Hyde Guidelines) recommending that quoted companies should show a statement adjusting their historical cost profit to a current cost basis by means of three adjustments, these being one for depreciation, one for cost of sales and one for gearing.

1979 The ASC withdrew ED 18 and issued ED 24; ED 24 evolved from the Hyde guidelines, retaining the proposal for a separate statement giving current cost adjustments to the profit and loss account while separating from the gearing adjustment the working capital items into a separate monetary working capital adjustment, and in addition requiring presentation of a CCA balance sheet and disclosure by listed companies of CCA earnings per share.

1980 The accounting bodies agreed to the issue of SSAP 16, based on ED 24.

1984 ED 35 offered suggestions of amendments to SSAP 16.

1985 ED 35 withdrawn.

1986 ASC issued a handbook, *Accounting for the Effects of Changing Prices*, which considers a range of inflation accounting approaches.
ASC withdrew SSAP 16.

1988 ASC affirmed a continued belief in the validity of CCA, and in the handbook as a basis for future development, while withdrawing SSAP 16.

An interesting analysis of forms of accounting considered in the UK is offered in the Accounting Standards Committee handbook on inflation accounting. This argues that there are three elements to consider in distinguishing between approaches to inflation accounting:

(a) *The valuation base:* Two bases have been used in UK systems, historical cost and current cost (*value to the business*)
(b) *The capital maintenance concept:* All accounting systems arrive at profit after allowing for the maintenance of the opening capital of the business. This *capital* to be maintained can be regarded in three ways:
    (i) as the physical operating capital of the company, referred to in SSAP 16 as 'operating capability';
    (ii) as the measure of opening capital in units of money (money capital);
    (iii) as the measure of opening capital measured in units of general purchasing power, often referred to as *real capital.*
(c) *The unit of measurement:* The principal alternatives here are:
    (i) the monetary unit;
    (ii) a unit of constant purchasing power (CPP), usually defined as the purchasing power of the monetary unit at the closing balance sheet date.

Traditional historical cost accounting measures all items by reference to historical cost, uses money as a unit of measurement and, consistent with the unit of measurement, uses a *money capital* concept of capital maintenance.

The first response of the UK accounting profession to the problem of inflation was to put forward a CPP system in ED 8 (1973) and SSAP 7 (1974). This system also measures all items by reference to historical cost but uses a current purchasing power unit of measurement and, consistent with that unit, uses a *real capital* concept of capital maintenance.

In 1975 the government-appointed Sandilands Committee argued against CPP and in favour of a CCA approach. After a number of proposals from the ASC an agreed CCA standard, SSAP 16, emerged in 1980. This used money as a unit of measurement, current cost as a valuation base and, consistent with the valuation base, had an operating capability capital maintenance concept. Compliance with SSAP 16 was made voluntary in 1985 but the standard was withdrawn in 1986.

In July 1984 the ASC published ED 35, offering some suggested amendments to SSAP 16, and in 1986 published a more wide-ranging review of the inflation accounting issue. The 1986 review continued to support a CCA approach, but suggested that companies be permitted to choose either an *operating capability* (as in SSAP 16) or a *real capital* capital maintenance concept. It is interesting to note that the *real cap-*

ital maintenance concept does not link to either the monetary unit of measurement of the current cost basis of measurement used in CCA. Table 36.1 summarises the key dimensions of SSAP 7 and the two approaches to CCA in the handbook, compared to historic cost.

In 1988 SSAP 16 was formally withdrawn, but the ASC continued to commend the approach in the handbook.

Table 36.1 A comparison of accounting approaches

	HC	*CPP*	*CCA*	
			per SSAP 16	Real terms
Unit of measurement	Money	CPP unit	Money	Money
Basis of valuation	Historic cost	Historic cost	Current cost	Current cost
Capital maintenance concept	Money capital	'Real' capital	Operating capital	'Real' capital

The current purchasing power approach

This approach aims to solve the inflation problem by adopting a different unit of measurement, the current purchasing power unit. This is found by taking an index of general price level movements, such as the retail price index in the UK, and applying to each transaction the factor:

Index at balance sheet date
Index at transaction date

At the year end all monetary items at the balance sheet date are restated at their actual amount, the consequent gain or loss representing the gain or loss from holding fixed monetary commitments in times of inflation.

In practice item-by-item translation of all transactions is not practical.

An approximate result can be found by the 'net change' method:

(a) The opening historical cost balance sheet is restated in CPP units as at the close of the accounting period by applying to all non-monetary items the factor:

$$\frac{\text{Index at closing balance sheet}}{\text{Index at date of acquisition or revaluation}}$$

and applying to all monetary items the factor:

$$\frac{\text{Index at closing balance sheet date}}{\text{Index at opening balance sheet date}}$$

The nominal value of share capital, being a matter of historic record, remains unchanged. Reserves are the balancing figure.

(b) The closing balance sheet is converted to CPP units by applying to all non-monetary items the factor:

$$\frac{\text{Index at closing balance sheet date}}{\text{Index at date of acquisition or revaluation}}$$

Monetary items are not adjusted. Again, the nominal value of share capital remains unchanged. Opening reserves will be as computed in restating the opening balance sheet. Retained profit for the year will be the balancing figure.

(c) The profit and loss accounting is translated into CPP units by applying to each item the factor:

$$\frac{\text{Index at closing balance sheet date}}{\text{Index at transaction date}}$$

The transaction date for depreciation is the date when the related asset was first acquired. For items which spread over the year, such as wages, sales and purchases, an average index for the year is used. In a seasonal business this might be appropriately weighted.

(d) To complete the profit and loss account the gain or loss on monetary items must still be computed. This gain or loss will be made up of:

(i) The difference between historic cost and CPP figures relating to monetary items in the opening balance sheet.
(ii) The difference between historic cost and CPP figures relating to monetary items in the profit and loss account.
(iii) Differences arising from any exchange between monetary items and non-monetary items in the year.

Example 36.1

On 1 December 19X2 Mary bought a bag-making machine for £10 000 and a supply of materials and thread for £5 000. To finance her business she borrowed £8 000 and injected £8 000 of her own savings. The loan was interest free.

During the following 12 months, Mary operated the machine and accumulated a stock of decorated gift bags, using all her original raw material stock, which she sold on 30 November 19X3 for £11 000 cash.

On 30 October 199X3 Mary bought a further £2 000 of raw material, on two months trade credit.

Relevant indices moved:

	Retail Price Index
1 December 19X2	100
30 October 19X3	144
30 November 19X3	148

The machine has a four-year life with no residual value, and is depreciated on a straight line basis.

Mary prepares accounts with a 30 November year end.

The example 'Mary' above offers a simple collection of data for the preparation of CPP accounts. The solution is shown in Table 36.2.

Taking each stage in turn:

(a) Translation of the opening historic cost balance sheet into closing CPP units identifies both the opening equity and the differences on the opening monetary items of the loan and the cash.

(b) The closing balance sheet similarly translates by applying the appropriate CPP factor to non-monetary items, with the profit for the year as the balancing figure.

(c) The profit and loss account involves no adjustment to sales, which took place on the last day of the year. Other items are adjusted by reference to the date of the related transaction with depreciation adjusted by reference to the date of the fixed asset acquisition.

(d) In this simple example, the gain or loss on monetary items consists of the amount relating to the two opening items plus the gain arising from acquiring a monetary asset, the one stock purchase of the year, in exchange for the monetary liabilities of the trade creditor.

Table 36.2 CPP accounts

Mary – Balance sheet at 1 December 19X2

	HC £000	CPP Factor	CPP £000
Equity	8 000	148/100	11 840
Loan	8 000	148/100	11 840
	16 000		23 680
Machine	10 000	148/100	14 800
Stock	5 000	148/100	7 400
Cash	1 000	148/100	1 480
	16 000		23 680

Mary – Profit and loss account for the year ended 30 November 19X3

	HC		CPP	CPP	
	£000	£000	Factor	£000	£000
Sales		11 000	1		11 000
Opening stock	5 000		148/100	7 400	
Purchases	2 000		148/144	2 056	
	7 000			9 456	
Closing stock	2 000		148/144	2 056	
Cost of sales		5 000			7 400
		6 000			3 600
Depreciation		2 500	148/100		3 700
Profit (loss) before		3 500			(100)
Gain on monetary items					3 416
					3 316

Mary – Balance sheet as at 30 November 19X3

	HC £000	CPP Factor	CPP £000
Opening equity	8 000		11 840
Profit for year	3 500	*	3 316
Closing equity	11 500		15 156
Loan	8 000		8 000
	19 500		23 156
Machine	7 500	148/100	11 100
Stock	200	148/144	2 056
Cash	12 000		12 000
Creditor	(2 000)		(2 000)
	19 500		23 156

* Balancing figure

Gain (loss) on monetary items

	£000
Opening cash (1 480 – 1 000)	(480)
Opening loan (11 840 – 8 000)	3 840
Purchases in year (2 056 – 2 000)	56
	3 416

The current cost accounting approach

This approach aims to solve the inflation problem by adopting a different basis of measurement, 'value to the business'. This is discussed in Chapter 31, The Statement of Principles for Financial Reporting, in the section headed, 'Chapter 6: Measurement in financial statements'. A practical example of the application of SSAP 16: Current Cost Accounting follows.

The SSAP 16 approach

Example 36.2

Sanjay bought a car for £20 000 on 1 January 19X3, borrowing £10 000 and using £10 000 of his own cash. The car has a five-year life with no residual value, and is to be depreciated by the straight line method. He rents out the car on a series of one-year letting agreements. At 31 December 19X3 he collects £8 000 being the first year of rental and pays £1 200 interest on the loan. Replacement cost of the car at 31 December 19X3 was £30 000.

Example 36.3

Jenny set up in business on 1 January 19X4. She bought 100 wooden boxes as her initial stock for £1 each. She carves a simple pattern on each box and sells the entire stock to a major store at the end of January for £180. It costs her £120 to replace her stock of 100 wooden boxes.

Example 36.4

Samuel provides a security service. He has ten customers, each of them a shopkeeper. At 1 January 19X3 he charged £100 per month to each shop protected. On 30 June 19X3 he raised his charge to £110. He allows one month's credit to his customers,

SSAP 16 suggested presentation of a statement showing how historic cost operating profit can be adjusted to current cost operating profit with three adjustments.

(a) A depreciation adjustment, reflecting the difference between depreciation on a current cost and a historic cost basis. Taking Example 36.1 above, current cost depreciation would be:

1/5 × £30 000	£6 000
Historic cost depreciation:	
1/5 × £20 000	£4 000
Depreciation adjustment	£2 000

(b) A cost of sales adjustment, being the difference between the value of the business of goods consumed and their historic cost. Taking Example 36.2 above, current cost of sales would be based on replacement cost at the time of consumption £120 per unit:

Current cost	£120
Historic cost	£100
Cost of sales adjustment	£ 20

(c) The two adjustments above are found in all forms of current cost accounting. SSAP 16 introduced a third adjustment, the monetary working capital adjustment.

'Monetary working capital' is the net amount of monetary assets and liabilities that form part of the operating cycle of the business. These are basically trade debtors, trade creditors and any cash or bank balances that fluctuate with the trading activities of the business.

If there is a net asset the adjustment represents the change in net finance needed to support the changing price level of the related stock. If there is a net liability then the adjustment represents an abatement of the cost of sales adjustment to the extent that changes in stock levels caused by price changes are financed by monetary working capital.

Thus, in Example 36.3, if Jenny's supplier of wooden boxes consistently allows her one month's credit then her whole cost of sales adjustment would be reversed by an equal and opposite monetary working capital adjustment. Taking the Example 36.4, at 1 January he will have debtors of 10 × £100 = £1 000, on the basis on one month's credit. At 31 December his debtors will be 10 × £100 = £1 100, but, since this is attributable to a price increase while the underlying activity remains unchanged, the £100 increase will be a monetary working capital adjustment reducing historic cost profit.

Having arrived at a figure of current cost operating profit, SSAP 16 next shows the impact of borrowing. This consists of two elements; one is the interest charge, as in the historic cost accounts. In the current cost accounts another element, the gearing adjustment, appears. This is an abatement of part of the CCA operating adjustments, in proportion to the part of the total operating assets financed by borrowing.

We can illustrate this with our Example 36.2, Sanjay. Throughout the year half the total operating assets have been financed by borrowing. As we have seen above, the depreciation adjustment was £2 000 so that the gearing adjustment will be:

50% × £2 000 =	£1 000

Historical cost operating profit would be:

Rental	£8 000
Depreciation 20% × 20 000	£4 000
Operating profit	£4 000

Thus the current cost profit and loss account in line with SSAP 16 would be as shown in Table 36.4.

Table 36.4

Sanjay – Current cost profit and loss account for the year ended 31 December 19X3 on a SSAP 16 basis

	£	£
Operating profit on a historical cost basis		4 000
Current cost operating adjustments:		
Depreciation		2 000
Current cost operating profit		2 000
Gearing adjustment	1 000	
Interest payable	(1 200)	
		(200)
Current cost profit before tax		1 800

The ASC Handbook

The 1986 ASB Handbook suggested a more flexible approach to CCA. The main area of flexibility is in relation to the capital maintenance concept. Two broad approaches are suggested:

(a) The 'operating capability' approach. This means that profit is arrived at after allowing for maintenance of the value to the business of the operating assets.

On this basis the handbook suggests that companies should be allowed to make three choices:

(i) Whether or not to make a monetary working capital adjustment;
(ii) whether or not to make a gearing adjustment;
(iii) whether the gearing adjustments should be applied just to the CCA operating adjustments, as in SSAP 16, or should apply in addition to revaluation surpluses in the CCA balance sheet.

(b) *The 'real term' approach*. Under the 'real terms' capital maintenance concept an entirely different approach is taken to monetary items. No adjustment is made for monetary working capital or gearing. Instead both realised and unrealised holding gains are added on profit, while an inflation adjustment to shareholders' funds' is deducted. This inflation adjustment is the uplift necessary to maintain opening CCA equity in 'real terms', and is computed as:

$$\text{Opening CCA equity} \times \frac{\text{Closing RPI}}{\text{Opening RPI}}$$

(RPI stands for Retail Price Index)

CPP v CCA

The debate in the UK as to which system of accounting for inflation should be adopted has tended to centre on a discussion of the relative merits of the CPP and CCA approaches. Although the two approaches are not incompatible, in that the CPP approach relates to the unit of measurement while the CCA approach relates to the basis of valuation, so that it would be possible to combine the two by, for example, presenting accounts on a CCA basis expressed in CPP units, in practice the two approaches have generally been seen as alternative and mutually exclusive solutions to the inflation accounting problem.

Advocates of a CPP approach advanced the following arguments:

(a) Inflation is concerned with changes in the general level of prices, so that only CPP can be regarded as a genuine form of inflation accounting.
(b) A CPP approach provides a method of adjusting corresponding amounts, and is of particular value in the five- and ten-year summary of results.
(c) Only CPP provides for a comprehensive recognition of the impact of inflation on holding monetary items.
(d) CPP is evolutionary in its approach, retaining all the characteristics of historical cost accounting, except for the change in the unit of measurement.
(e) CPP accounts will be more objective and verifiable than those prepared on a CCA basis because management is not free to choose which index to apply and there is no use of subjective valuations.
(f) Failure to convert monetary amounts into CPP units means that accounts will aggregate monetary units of widely varying values. A number of supporters of CPP argued that this was similar to failing to translate foreign currency balances!
(g) CPP is based on actual market transactions while CCA is based on hypothetical transactions.

Advocates of a CCA approach argued:

(a) That CCA measures an individual company's experience of inflation by reference to that company's specific pattern of expenditure.
(b) Management will need to be able to plan on the basis of the replacement costs of specific assets, so that a CCA approach will be more relevant to management's information needs.
(c) The historical cost system has already been adapted to allow for fixed asset revaluations, so that CCA can be regarded as evolutionary in its approach.
(d) Some investment analysts have already developed useful methods for making CCA adjustments to historical cost accounts.

A survey in the early 1970s found that most accountants in professional practice preferred a CPP approach, while management accountants tended to prefer a CCA approach. This impression is confirmed by an analysis of comments made to the ASC on ED 8.

During the course of the inflation accounting debate, advocates of the CCA approach as opposed to the CPP approach seem to have persuaded a majority of accountants. Of some 700 comments to the ASC on ED 18 only 10 per cent objected to CCA accounts on the grounds that they would not be useful.

Conclusion

The ASC has formulated both an accounting standard and a detailed discussion document on current cost accounting. In the event that a further attempt at producing such a system be undertaken in the UK, issues to be resolved are likely to include:

(a) the choice of capital maintenance concept;
(b) the treatment of monetary items;
(c) the status of any CCA data to be included in the accounts;
(d) ways in which CCA might be simplified.

EXAMINATION PRACTICE

36.1. On 1 January 1999 Mary bought a machine for £100 000, using £50 000 of her own savings and £50 000 of borrowed money. During the year she rented out the machine to various local factories. On 31 December 1999 all her customers paid their rental, being £40 000 in total, and Mary paid interest on her loan of £3 000. The machine is to be depreciated on the straight-line basis over four years with no residual value. A replacement machine on 31 December 1999 would cost £120 000. The retail price index rose by 8 per cent during 1999.

You are required to:

(a) Prepare a profit and loss account and balance sheet for 1994 under:
  (i) The historic cost basis
  (ii) The current purchasing power basis
  (iii) The current cost accounting basis as described in SSAP 16
(b) Explain the unit of measurement, the basis of measurement and the capital maintenance concept, under each of these three systems.

ADDITIONAL QUESTIONS (BASED ON QUESTIONS SET BY THE ASB)

1. What are accounting standards?
2. Are accounting standards mandatory?
3. It is sometimes suggested that accounting standards are not necessary, because the market can decide what accounting principles to demand. Discuss.
4. How does the ASB decide what subjects to add to its agenda?
5. How does the ASB obtain views before issuing an accounting standard?
6. What has the ASB done about 'creative accounting'?
7. What are the ASB's views on international harmonisation of accounting standards?
8. What is the ASB's Statement of Principles for Financial Reporting? What role does it play in the setting of accounting standards?
9. What are the ASB's views on putting brand names and other intangible assets on the balance sheet?
10. Why does the ASB think that the balance sheet is more important than the profit and loss account? After all, earnings are what is most important to the market.
11. What does the ASB think are the biggest problems in financial reporting today?
12. Will accounting standards ever be complete?

Answers

Answers for the examination practice questions have been carefully written to provide the student with clear answer guides and key facts that would be needed to pass professional accountancy examinations. Additional detail for a fully comprehensive answer is given in the relevant chapter.

1.1 Compliance with accounting standards

The CCAB bodies require their members to observe accounting standards. Members having a responsibility as directors or officers of a company for the publication of accounts and have a duty to ensure that the board are fully aware of the existence and purpose of accounting standards, and should use their best endeavours to ensure that the accounts comply with accounting standards. Members acting as auditors or as reporting accountants are required to ensure that any significant departures from accounting standards are disclosed, and must justify any departure in which they concur. The tradition in the UK that a *clean* audit report is a brief document has made this a powerful factor in persuading companies to comply with accounting standards.

The Stock Exchange expects listed companies to comply with accounting standards.

The Companies Act 1989 has introduced a new provision for large companies, which are now required to state in their accounts whether these have been prepared in accordance with applicable accounting standards. Any material departure from SSAPs must be disclosed and justified.

In the case of a material departure from a SSAP either the Secretary for Trade or the Review Panel may refer this to the court. If the court takes the view that non-compliance results in a failure to give a true and fair view then it may order the company to circulate appropriately revised accounts.

Company directors may be personally concerned at the risk that any costs falling on the company as a result of such an order may be regarded as arising from their failure to perform a legal duty, and so fall on them personally.

2.1 Forecast cash flow statement

Chiron Ltd – cash flow statement for the year ended 31 March 19X7

	£000	£000
Net cash inflow from operating activities		89
Returns on investments and servicing of finance:		
Bank interest paid	(2)	
Net cash outflow from returns on investments and servicing of finance		(2)
Taxation (16 + 26 – 26)		(16)
Capital expenditure:		
Premises	(30)	
Plant purchased	(105)	
Net cash outflow from investing activities		(135)
Equity dividend paid		(16)
Net cash outflow before financing		(80)
Financing:		
Issue of ordinary shares	75	
Net cash inflow from financing		75
Decrease in cash and cash equivalents		5

Notes to the cash flow statement:

1. Reconciliation of operating profit to net cash inflow from operating activities:

	£000
Operating profit	86
Depreciation	28
Stock increase	(30)
Debtor increase	(20)
Creditor increase	24
Accrual increase	1
	89

2. Analysis of net debt:

	Balance at 1 April 19X6 £000	*Cash flow in year* £000	*Balance at 31 March 19X7* £000
Cash	1	1	2
Overdraft	(6)	(6)	(12)
	(5)	(5)	(10)

2.2 Preparation of cash flow statement

Beatem Ltd – cash flow statement for the year ended 31 March 19X8

	£000	£000
Net cash inflow from operating activities		1 295
Returns on investments and servicing of finance:		
Dividend		
Debenture interest	(80)	
Overdraft interest	(140)	
Net cash outflow from returns on investments and servicing of finance		(220)
Taxation		(1 000)
Capital expenditure:		
Plant disposal	565	
Plant acquired	(1 500)	
Land and buildings acquired	(1 700)	
Net cash outflow from investing activities		(2 635)
Equity dividend paid		(180)
Net cash outflow before financing		(2 740)
Financing:		
Share issue	150	
Debenture issue	2 000	
Net cash inflow from financing		2 150
Decrease in cash and cash equivalents		(590)

Notes to the cash flow statement:

1. Reconciliation of operating profit to net cash flow from operating activities:

	£000
Operating profit	1 375
Depreciation	640
Creditors (100 + 80)	(180)
Stock	(285)
Debtors	(300)
Loss on plant disposal	45
Net cash inflow from operating activities	1 295

2. Analysis of net debt

	Balance at 1.4.X7	*Cash flow*	*Balance at 31.3.X8*
	£000	£000	£000
Cash & Bank	500	(340)	160
Overdraft	(1 500)	(150)	(1 750)
	(1 000)	(590)	(1 590)
Debentures	—	(2 000)	(2 000)
	(1 000)		(3 590)

2.3 Treatment of items in the cash flow statement

1. DO	6. I
2. N	7. N
3. R	8. F
4. I	9. AO
5. N	10. N

2.4 Preparing the statement

Vienne Ltd – cash flow statement for the year ended 31 December 19X4

	£000	£000
Cash flow from operations		171
Cash flows from returns on investments and servicing of finance:		
Lease finance	(105)	
Interest paid	(100)	
Interest received	50	
Cash flow from taxation		(155)
Capital expenditure and financial investment		(185)
Sale of plant	50	
Plant purchase	(10)	
		40
Equity dividend paid		(310)
		(439)
Management of liquid resources		(20)
Financing cash flows:		
Lease repayment	(328)	
Debenture issue	500	
		172
Net cash outflow		(287)

Note 1

	£000	£000
Operating profit		
Adjustments		787
Depreciation	108	
Loss on plant sale	105	
Stock increase	(210)	
Debtor increase	(610)	
Prepayment decrease	1	
Creditor decrease	(20)	
Accrual increase	10	
		(616)
Operating cash flow		171

Note 2

Analysis of net debt

	At 1.1.X4 £000	*Cash flow* £000	*Other non-cash exchange* £000	*At 31.12.X4* £000
Bank	120	(95)		25
Cash	31	9		40
Overdraft	—	(201)		(201)
	151	(287)		(136)
Debenture	(1 000)	(500)		(1 500)
Lease	—		(410)	(410)
		(500)	(410)	
Investment	180	20	—	200
Total	669	(767)	(410)	(1 846)

Workings

	£000	£000
(1) Land and buildings		
B/fwd		2 500
Revaluation surplus:		
In reserve	280	
Deferred tax	120	
		400
		2 900

(2) Leased plant

Initial cost	1 108
Depreciation*	108
NBV	1 000

*Balancing figure

(3) Lease

Initial obligation	1 108
Interest	105
Instalments paid*	(435)
Closing obligation	780

*Balancing figure

(4) Interest

	Payable	*Receivable*
B/fwd	50	12
P & L	125	52
Cash	(100)	(50)
C/fwd	75	14

(5) Plant disposal

NBV	155
Sales proceeds	50
Loss on sale	105

(6) Taxation

B/fwd	230
P & L	205
Cash	(185)
C/fwd	250

(7)

Operating profit		787
Interest payable	230	
Interest receivable	(52)	
		809
Profit before tax		
Corporation tax	205	
Deferred tax	4	
		209
		400
Interim dividend	110	
Proposed final dividend	180	
		290
		110
Retained profit b/fwd		1 210
Retained profit c/fwd		1 320

3.1 Exclusion from consolidation

A subsidiary may only be excluded from the consolidated accounts in the following circumstances:

(a) company law permits, and FRS 2 requires, that a subsidiary be excluded from consolidation where severe long-term restrictions substantially hinder the exercise of the rights of the parent undertaking over the assets or management of the subsidiary. If the restrictions were in force at the acquisition date then the subsidiary is carried in the accounts initially at cost; if the restrictions come into force after the accounting date then the investment in the subsidiary at that point in time is shown as though the equity method applied. No further accruals for profit or loss of the subsidiary should then be made unless the restrictions allow *significant influence*, in which case the subsidiary should be treated as an associate;

(b) company law permits, and FRS 2 requires, exclusion from consolidation for a subsidiary held exclusively with a view to resale. Such an investment should be shown at the lower of cost and net realisable value;

(c) company law permits exclusion from consolidation on the grounds that the subsidiary's activities are so different from those of other group undertakings as to make inclusion incompatible with the obligation to give a true and fair view. FRS 2 argues that such cases are 'exceptional' since a true and fair view of different activities can be given by segmental reporting. Where this situation does arise then equity accounting should be used;

(d) company law allows exclusion of subsidiaries where *disproportionate expense or undue delay* would arise from their inclusion. FRS 2 restricts this exemption to situations where the subsidiary is not material to the consolidated accounts.

4.1 FRS 3 – allocation of items

(a) This is part of the gain or loss on termination of an operation, shown on the face of the profit and loss account after operating profit and loss interest as an exceptional item;

(b) this is an exceptional item. To give a true and fair view it should be shown on the face of the profit and loss account under the appropriate format heading;

(c) this is shown as a gain relating to discontinued operations, as an exceptional item shown on the face of the profit and loss account after operating profit and before interest.

4.2 FRS 3 – presentation

(a) The £320 000 is shown as an exceptional item after operating profit and before interest. The related taxation is shown as part of the tax charge;

(b) this is a *fundamental error* giving rise to a prior period adjustment. The comparative figures for the previous period should be adjusted accordingly. The effect of the adjustment will also be shown at the foot of the statement of total recognised gains and losses;

(c) the whole £980 000 is an exceptional item to be included under the appropriate format headings within operating profit;

(d) this is a gain on a fixed asset disposal, and accordingly appears as an exceptional item between the operating profit and the interest charge.

4.3 FRS 3 – conceptual basis

The *all-inclusive* income approach shows on the face of the profit and loss account all extraordinary items and all prior period adjustments, as well as ordinary trading profit. The advantages of this approach are:

(a) analysts can select for themselves the aspect of performance they wish to focus on;

(b) since all income and expenditure is revealed, management does not have the opportunity to manipulate the disclosure in the profit and loss account;

(c) the risk of analysts failing to observe significant non-trading items is reduced.

The *current operating income* approach shows only items relating to the normal recurring activities of the company on the face of the profit and loss account. This has the following advantages:

(a) the profit figure provides a more meaningful guide to future profits, since non-recurring items are excluded;

(b) the profit figure gives a useful indication of management's achievement in running the business.

5.1 Understanding the rules

An exception to the requirement to allocate finance costs evenly over the loan term arises when the required payment is contingent on some future event. Two examples where this might arise are:

(a) In the case of a limited recourse debt where the lender's rights to recover a loan are restricted to the proceeds of sale of a specific security. If the proceeds of that sale fall short of the required repayment then the borrower has enjoyed an abatement of finance costs to the extent of the shortfall but, because the extent cannot be foreseen, this benefit is only recognised when the security is transferred to the lender.

(b) In the case of an index-linked loan, finance costs can only be computed when the index movement has occurred. Accordingly each year finance costs are allocated on the basis of actual index movements.

5.2 Applying the rules

(a) Annual finance costs are:

	£
19X5	8 000
19X6	8 400
19X7	8 832

(b) The journal entry is:

	Dr	Cr
	£	£
Convertible loan stock	116 232	
Ordinary share capital		50 000
Share premium		66 232

Workings

	Balance at beginning of year	*Finance cost for year (8%)*	*Cash paid in year*	*Balance at end of year*
Year				
19X5	100 000	8 000	(3 000)	105 000
19X6	105 000	8 400	(3 000)	110 400
19X7	110 400	8 832	(3 000)	116 232

6.1 FRS 5 defines an asset as a right or other access to future economic benefits controlled by an entity as a result of past transactions or events. The key question here is whether the stock becomes an asset at the date the stock is received or at the date when a legal sale is made.

In the case of dealer A Roadroller does not carry the benefits and risks of ownership until the legal sale, since up to that time:

(a) Rise and fall in price do not affect the company;
(b) Roadroller has no right to retain stock until the point of sale.

In the case of dealer B Roadroller carries the benefits and risks of ownership from the date of consignment in that:

(a) compensation is received if stock is withdrawn;
(b) rise or fall in prices is borne by the company.

6.2 Key issues to justify derecognition of factored debtors are:
(a) there is no recourse to the seller for losses;
(b) transfer is for a single fixed sum;
(c) the seller has no right or obligation for further sums payable by or to the factor.

7.1 Definitions

(a) The *equity method* of accounting involves showing an investment in a company in the consolidated balance sheet at:
(i) the cost of the investment; and
(ii) the group's share of post-acquisition retained profits and reserves of the company; less
(iii) any amounts written off in respect of (i) and (ii) above.

The investing group's share of profits is brought into the consolidated profit and loss account. SSAP 1 prescribed the *equity method* for associated companies, while FRS 2 prescribes the equity method where a subsidiary is excluded from consolidation because of lack of effective control, if all the other requirements for classification as an associate under SSAP 1 are met.

(b) *Acquisition accounting* is a consolidation approach where a business combination is accounted for as an acquisition. The difference between the fair value of the purchase consideration and the aggregate of the fair value of the separable net assets, both tangible and intangible, is identified as *goodwill* and accounted for in accordance with SSAP 22. The results of the acquired company are only brought into the consolidated accounts from the date of acquisition.

(c) *Pooling of interests* is a consolidation approach where a business combination is accounted for as a merger. This means that the cost of a new investment is recorded in the acquirer's books as the nominal value of the shares issued plus the fair value of any additional consideration. On consolidation the book value of assets, liabilities and reserves is added together and any difference between the amount of the investment and the nominal value of the acquired shares is deducted from consolidation reserves if it is a debit balance, and shown as an unrealised reserve if it is a credit balance.

7.2 Merger accounting

Sid Ltd
Consolidated balance sheet 31 December 19X0

	Acquisition £	*Merger* £
Share capital:		
1 280 000 ordinary shares of 25p	320 000	320 000
Share premium	165 000	—
Reserves	300 000	345 000
	785 000	665 000
Fixed assets	270 000	270 000
Goodwill	120 000	—
Current assets	620 000	620 000
	1 010 000	890 000
Current liabilities	225 000	225 000
	785 000	665 000

Workings
Share premium – acquisition method:

	£
Market value 300 000 @ 80p	240 000
Nominal value 300 000 @ 25p	75 000
	165 000

8.1 Fair value

In historic cost accounting a problem arises when consolidated accounts are prepared. On acquisition of a subsidiary on the basis of issuing shares in the acquirer in exchange for shares in the acquiree it is necessary to:

(a) identify the *fair value* of the shares issued so that an appropriate share premium can be computed;

(b) attribute a *fair value* to the identifiable assets and liabilities of the acquired business so that these can be brought into the consolidated accounts.

This is necessary in the context of the historic cost convention because:

(a) the *barter* nature of a share for share exchange means that a *fair value* of the shares issued must be estimated in order to impute a historic cost;

(b) the purchase of a bundle of assets and liabilities as one *batch* within the acquired company makes it necessary to allocate the cost between the individual acquired items.

9.1 Related parties

Since Ghoul only has influence, rather than control, over each of Burnem and Coffin, then the two companies are not deemed to be 'related' unless one of the parties has subordinated its own separate interests. In the absence of such evidence:

(a) Burnem and Coffin are not related.
(b) Thus Mrs Slaughter's relationship to Burnem does not relate her to Coffin.
(c) Therefore, Mr Slaughter's relationship to Wilting does not lead to any related party position with Coffin.

10.1 (a)

Net assets at 1st January 20X1			300 000
Retained profits for the year			10 000
			310 000
Group share	30% × £310 000		93 000
Premium on acquisition			
Net assets 1 January 20X1	£300 000 × 30% =	£90 000	
Price paid		£120 000	
			30 000
			123 000

Alternative calculation:

Fixed assets	
Investment in associates	£
Cost	120 000
Group share of post-acquisition retained profits (30% × £10 000)	3 000
	123 000

(b) Share of profit in associates	30% × £20 000	£6 000

It will exclude the £3 000 dividend received (£10 000 × 30%)

(c) Cash flow statement	30% × £10 000	£3 000

10.2 An associated company is a company in which the investor has a participating interest and over whose operating and financial policies it exercises a significant influence. This means that the investment should be for the long term and that the investor should exercise some control over that investment. The investor should be actively involved with and influence the investee's financial policies with regard to, for example, products, markets, acquisitions and dividends. This will often be achieved by representation on the board of directors. Companies legislation includes a rebuttable presumption that a holding of 20 per cent or more of the shares is a participating interest and that significant influence may be exercised.

A joint venture is a company in which a reporting company has a long-term interest and exercises joint control together with other companies.

A Joint Arrangement that is Not an Entity (JANET) occurs where there is a contractual arrangement under which the participants engage in joint activities, but there is no separate legal entity which engages in its own activities. Examples might be joint marketing and distribution networks, a shared production facility and the construction of a single project.

11.1 (a)
Goodwill calculations

Consolidated balance sheet:

The Cab Group balance sheet as at 31 March 20X0

	£000
Tangible assets	1 800
Goodwill	200
	2 000
Share capital	1 500
Retained profit	500
	2 000

Note that tangible assets are included on the basis of the fair value of the assets of Horse Ltd
(b)
Balance sheets:

		Amortised	
	20X1		*20X2*
	£000		*£000*
Tangible assets	1 830		1 865
Goodwill	180		160
	2 010		2 025
Share capital	1 500		1 500
Reserves	510		525
	2 010		2 025

Profit and loss accounts:

		Amortised	
	20X1		*20X2*
	£000		*£000*
Profit before taxation	300		330
Taxation	160		175
Profit after taxation	140		155
Dividends	130		140
Retained profit	10		15

11.2. (i) Goodwill is defined as the 'difference between the cost of an acquired entity and the aggregate of the fair values of that entity's identifiable assets and liabilities'.

Positive purchased goodwill should be capitalised and included as a fixed asset in the balance sheet. Internally generated goodwill should not be capitalised.

Intangible assets which have been purchased separately from the purchase of a business as a whole should be capitalised at cost. Intangible assets which have been acquired as part of the acquisition of a business should be distinguished from goodwill and capitalised as a separate asset, if their value can be reliably measured.

The intangible assets should be valued at fair value. Where the value of an intangible asset cannot be reliably measured then it should be included within goodwill.

Internally developed intangible assets may be capitalised if there is a readily ascertainable market value.

(ii) Where goodwill and intangible assets have limited useful economic lives, they should be amortised on a systematic basis. There is an expectation that the life of goodwill and an intangible asset will normally be 20 years or less.

Where they have indefinite lives, then they should not be amortised. Indefinite lives or periods longer than 20 years may be used when:

(a) there are grounds for believing that the life exceeds 20 years.
(b) the goodwill or intangible asset is capable of continued measurement.

In calculating the amount of the fair value to be amortised, there can be no residual value for goodwill. There may only be a residual value for other intangible assets where that residual value can be measured reliably. The amortisation method should normally be the straight line method although an alternative method, such as reducing balance, may be used if it can be justified.

The useful economic lives of goodwill and intangible assets should be reviewed at the end of each year.

A review to see whether impairment has occurred must be undertaken at the end of the first full year and at any time that it is believed that impairment may have occurred

Goodwill and intangible assets which are not amortised, or are amortised over a period longer than 20 years, should be reviewed for impairment each year.

12.1 The present value of the future cash flows is £1 200 000.

The impairment loss is therefore £2 415 000 – £1 200 000 = £1 215 000.

Allocation of impairment loss:

Goodwill	£600 000
Property	none
Plant (the balance)	£615 000

	£000
Goodwill	nil
Property	820
Plant	115
Net current assets	265
	1 200
Share capital and reserves	1 200

12.2 (i) An income generating unit is a group of assets, liabilities and associated goodwill that generates income that is largely independent of the reporting entity's other income streams. The assets and liabilities include those directly involved in generating the income and an appropriate proportion of those used to generate more than one income stream.

(ii)

(a) The issue here is whether the feeder routes could be regarded as separate from the main route. However, a feeder route is not an IGU since it is not independent of the main route, and therefore all of the network would be regarded as an IGU.

(b) The issue here is whether each of the sites could be regarded as an IGU. However, each site is dependent on the allocation process and therefore the five sites collectively form an IGU, and each site could not be regarded as a separate IGU.

(c) The issue here is whether each of the stages of production could be regarded as an IGU.
The first stage, the acquisition of raw materials is independent of stages 2 and 3. The external price for the sale of raw materials can be used for the internal transfers. It is therefore an IGU. Similarly, stages 2 and 3 can be regarded as IGUs. The company thus has three IGUs

(d) The issue here is whether each cinema could be regarded as a separate IGU. The income and net assets of each cinema can be determined with some precision and each cinema could therefore be classed as an IGU. However, an individual cinema is unlikely to be material and therefore the cinemas may be grouped into IGUs where the same economic factors affect all the cinemas in a group. For example, the company may have four IGUs for north, south, east and west.

13.1

1. A full provision for £400 000 plus legal costs is needed.
2. A provision will be computed:

2 000 000 × 20%	=	£400 000
8 000 000 × 5%	=	£400 000
		£800 000

3. This is an onerous contract, needing a provision for £200 000.
4. No provision should be made, because there is no obligating event.
5. The proposed approach would mask the impact of two separate issues:
   a) The release of the 150 000 provision for legal action should be disclosed.
   b) A new provision for environment penalties of £150 000 should be made.

13.2 The terms 'provision' and 'contingent liability' both refer to potential liabilities where there is some degree of uncertainty.

A provision is recognised as a liability where it is probable that a transfer of economic benefits will have to be made to settle a present obligation, and a reasonable estimate of the amount can be made.

By contrast, a contingent liability is not recognised as a liability because either:

1. A reasonable estimate of the amount involved cannot be made.

OR

2. The likelihood of the liability arising falls short of 'probable'.
   Contingent liabilities are disclosed unless their probability is remote.

14.1. *Gains and loss on hedges*

	Gains *£m*
Unrecognised gains at 1.1.2001	15
Gains arising in previous years recognised in 2000	5
Gains arising before 1.1.2000 not recognised in 2000	10
Gains arising in 2001 not recognised in 2001	36
Unrecognised gains and losses at 31.12.2001	46
Gains expected to be recognised in 2002	23
Gains expected to be recognised after 2002	23
	46

14.2

(a) The objectives of FRS 13 are that it should ensure that companies disclose sufficient information about their derivatives and other financial instruments to allow users to assess:

- the financial risk of a company,
- the significance of the derivatives and financial instruments to the financial performance, position and cash flows of the company.

(b) The different types of risk identified in FRS 13 are:

- credit risk – for example, non-payment by a debtor,
- liquidity risk – the inability to realise assets to meet financial liabilities when they fall due,
- cash flow risk – the fluctuation in cash flows,
- market price risk – the fluctuation in the value of financial instruments as a result of interest rate changes.

(c) In relation to FRS 13 disclosure:

- Table 14.2 is helpful in forecasting future cash flows and assessing their variability. Variable interest rates will have a positive or negative affect on cash flows if interest rates change, and the disclosure of interest rate and amount of the debt will help users to calculate this affect. Fixed interest rates will identify if the company is paying an excess charge compared to other companies if interest rates fall, and vice versa.
- Table 14.4 is helpful in forecasting future cash flows; the debt will either be paid out of existing cash or out of new finance, and, if the latter, the user will want to be assured that the finance can be raised.
- Table 14.5 is helpful in gauging risk; a company with ample undrawn facilities for future years is less risky than one with no undrawn facilities, or ones which expire in the short term.

(d) FRS 13 requires both narrative and numerical disclosures. It might be thought that just numerical disclosures would be sufficient. However, if users are to understand the numbers they need to be placed in a context. Thus the standard requires the disclosure of objectives, policies and strategies with regard to the management of financial risk.

This narrative disclosure may be included in the Operating and Financial Review. This has the advantage of placing the report on financial instruments in the wider context of the business as a whole. The narrative disclosure should include an analysis of the main reasons for holding or issuing financial instruments .

Where the objectives, policies and strategies have changed from those reported previously, the reasons for the change should be given.

The narrative disclosure should also include commentary on the numerical disclosures. The directors should explain how the numerical data are consistent with their objectives. This will not be possible if the numerical data at the year end are unrepresentative of the position during the year. If this situation occurs, an explanation should be provided.

Where financial instruments are used as hedges, the details of the financial instruments and the risks being hedged should be disclosed.

Thus the narrative disclosures are important in helping users understand the numerical disclosures, which are in turn important for assessing the financial risk of a company.

15.1

Theoretical ex-rights value per share is:

$$\frac{\text{Fair value of current shares} + \text{Amount received from rights issue}}{\text{Number of current shares} + \text{Number of shares issued}}$$

$$\frac{(£3.00 \times 300\ 000 \text{ shares}) + (£2.50 \times 50\ 000)}{300\ 000 \text{ shares} + 50\ 000} = \frac{1\ 025\ 000}{350\ 000}$$

Theoretical ex-rights value		=	£2.93	
Adjustment factor				
Fair value of current shares	=	£3.00	=	1.02
Theoretical ex-rights value		£2.93		

Earnings per share

	20X0	*20X1*	*20X2*
20X0 EPS as originally stated: £35 000 / 300 000 shares	12p		
20X0 EPS restated for rights issue: £35 000 / (300 000 shares × 1.02)	11p		
20X1 EPS allowing for the rights issue: £48 000 / ((300 000 × 1.02 × 3/12) + (350 000 × 9/12))		14p	
20X2 EPS £62 000 / 350 000			18p

15.2

(a) Basic EPS is the earnings divided by the number of issued ordinary shares. Diluted EPS is the earnings divided by the number of ordinary shares, including the issued shares and claims to ordinary shares in the future. Diluted EPS would be calculated, for example, where there are share options.

(b) Dilution will always affect the number of shares, as by definition it occurs when there is a claim to ordinary shares in the future. Dilution will affect earnings when the claim on ordinary shares is from a source of finance which currently receives a return which is included in earnings. For example, if a debenture allows conversion of the loan into ordinary shares then the loan interest will be eliminated and earnings will increase.

(c) Antidilution occurs where the EPS would increase on a claim to ordinary shares being exercised. The implications are that when there are a number of claims to ordinary shares, then the dilutive affect of each should be calculated and then ranked from the most to the least dilutive. EPS is then calculated after each potential claim and if EPS increases then that and any other subsequent claims are ignored for purposes of calculating EPS.

16.1 The accounting treatment would be as follows:

		Year 1 £000
Opening book amount		2 000
Depreciation	1/10	200
Depreciated book amount		1 800
Revaluation gains / (losses)		
STRGL		360
P&L a/c		–
		2 160

Since there has been no previous recognised losses, the whole of the gain of £360 000 is recognised in the STRGL. The property is valued at the valuation figure since this is the lower of the valuation of £2 160 000 and the recoverable amount of £2 200 000.

		Year 2
		£000
Opening book amount		2 160
Depreciation – 9 years remaining	1/9	240
Depreciated book amount		1 920
Valuation		1 500
Loss		420

Initially, the difference between the carrying value and depreciated historical cost would be recognised in the STRGL i.e. £1 920 000 less (2 000 000 × 8/10) = £320 000 and the remaining £100 000 in the profit and loss account. However, since the recoverable amount exceeds the valuation (£1 550 000 less £1 500 000) then a further £50 000 may be recognised in the STRGL, making a total of £320 000 + £50 000 = £370 000. The profit and loss account is charged with the remaining £50 000.

Thus

		Year 2
		£000
Opening book amount		2 160
Depreciation – 9 years remaining	1/9	(240)
Depreciated book amount		1 920
STRGL		(370)
P&L a/c		(50)
Closing book amount		1 500

Extracts from the financial statements would be as follows:

	Year 1	Year 2
Profit and loss account		
depreciation	(200)	(240)
impairment		(50)
Statement of recognised gains and losses		
Surplus / (deficit) on revaluation	360	(370)
Fixed assets		
Cost or valuation at beginning of year	2 000	2 160
Surplus / (deficit) on revaluation	160	(660)
Cost or valuation at end of year	2 160	1 500
Depreciation at beginning of year	nil	nil
Charge for year	200	240
Depreciation written back on revaluation	(200)	(240)
Depreciation at end of year	nil	nil
Net book value	2 160	1 500
Revaluation reserve		
At beginning of year	nil	360
Surplus/ (deficit) on revaluation	360	(370)
At end of year	360	(10)

These figures may be explained as follows. The total loss is £2 000 000 – £1 500 000 = £500 000. Of this, £490 000 is in the profit and loss account, which is the depreciation of £440 000 and the further loss of the difference between depreciated historical cost and recoverable amount (£1 600 000 – £1 550 000 = £50 000). The remaining loss of £10 000 is in the STRGL.

16.2 (a) The company should not start to capitalise interest when it buys the land. It should only start when economic activity commences, that is, when it starts to construct the property. Capitalisation of the interest should cease when the building is finished; it should not wait until the property is let.

(b) The costs incurred in February and March cannot be capitalised. The public house is capable of meeting its target turnover, and therefore these costs cannot be included as start-up costs.

(c) The costs incurred in the period between when the boat is completed and when a licence is received may be capitalised as part of the start-up costs.

(d) The company may depreciate the plant as a single asset, i.e. £700 000 over seven years is £100 000 p.a.

Alternatively, it may capitalise the overhaul as a separate asset. Thus plant would have a cost of £686 000 over seven years = £98 000 p.a., and the 'overhaul' may be capitalised as £14 000 and depreciated over four years = £3 500 p.a.

17.1 (a) £2 111. UK dividend of £1 000, not grossed up, and overseas dividend of £1 111, dividend received plus withholding tax.

(b) The £500 000 should be in the profit and loss account and £100 000 in the STRGL. It is not correct to record all the £600 000 in the profit and loss account.

(c) No adjustment should be made for any notional tax. The profit and loss account should show the actual pre-tax receipts and the actual tax charge.

(d) Since the bill is substantively enacted then the rate in the bill should be used.

18.1 Defining the terms

(a) Fundamental accounting concepts are the broad basic assumptions which underlie the periodic financial accounts of business enterprises.

(b) Accounting bases are the methods developed for applying fundamental accounting concepts to financial transactions and items, for the purpose of financial accounts, and in particular (i) for determining the accounting periods in which revenue and costs should be recognised in the profit and loss accounts and (ii) for determining the amounts at which material items should be stated in the balance sheet.

(c) Accounting policies are the specific accounting bases selected and consistently followed by a business enterprise as being, in the opinion of the management, appropriate to its circumstances and best suited to present fairly its results and financial position.

18.2 Understanding the concepts

(a) The *going concern* concept: that the enterprise will continue in operational existence for the foreseeable future. This means in particular that the profit and loss account and balance sheet assume no intention or necessity to liquidate or curtail significantly the scale of operation.

(b) The *accruals* concept: that revenue and costs are accrued (that is, recognised as they are earned or incurred, not as money is received or paid), matched with one another so far as their relationship can be established or justifiably assumed, and dealt with in the profit and loss account of the period to which they relate.

(c) The *consistency* concept: that there is consistency of accounting treatment of like items within each accounting period and from one period to the next.

(d) The *prudence* concept: that revenue and profits are not anticipated, but are recognised by inclusion in the profit and loss account only when realised in the form either of cash or of other assets the ultimate cash realisation of which can be assessed with reasonable certainty; provision is made for all known liabilities (expenses and losses) whether the amount of these is known with certainty or is a best estimate in the light of the information available.

The relative importance of these concepts will vary according to the circumstances of the particular case. The only provision for putting the four fundamental accounting concepts in any order of priority in SSAP 2 is a requirement that where the accruals concept is inconsistent with the prudence concept the latter should prevail.

18.3 Accounting bases

Examples might include:

Subject matter	*Different bases*
Depreciation	(a) Write off over estimated useful life by the straight line method; (b) write off over estimated useful life by the reducing balance method.
Development expenditure	(a) Write off in the year incurred; (b) write off over the period of commercial exploitation of the related project.
Stock	(a) Value at the lower of cost and net realisable value on a FIFO basis; (b) value at the lower of cost and net realisable value on an average costs basis.
Government grants	(a) Reduce the cost of acquisition of fixed assets by the amount of any related government grant; (b) show government grants relating to fixed assets as a deferred credit, to be transferred to the profit and loss account over the life of the asset.

18.4 Accounting policies

(a) *Turnover*. Turnover represents amounts received and receivable for goods and services supplied exclusive of inter-group sales and VAT.

(b) *Depreciation*. Depreciation is calculated to write off buildings, plant and machinery during their expected normal lives by equal annual instalments. The rates used by the group are:

Buildings	2 %
Plant	15 %
Motor vehicles	25 %

(c) *Stocks*. Stocks are stated at the lower of cost including factory overheads and net realisable value.

(d) *Research and development*. Costs are written off to revenue in the year during which they are incurred.

(e) *Government grants*. Grants relating to fixed assets are treated as deferred credits and are transferred to revenue in equal amounts over the expected life of the asset.

19.1 Accounting for grants

Investment Grant Deferred Credit

		Approach (a) £000	Approach (b) £000			Approach (a) £000	Approach (b) £000
31.12.X4	Profit and loss	—	4	31.1.X4	Cash	—	20
31.12.X4	C/f	—	16				—
			20				20

Plant account

		Approach (a) £000	Approach (b) £000			Approach (a) £000	Approach (b) £000
1.1.X4	Bank	100	100	31.1.X4	Bank	20	—
				31.12.X4	Depreciation	16	20
31.12.X4	C/f depreciation	16	20	31.12.X4	C/f cost	80	100
		116	120			116	120

Balance sheet extracts:

	Approach (a) £000	Approach (b) £000
Fixed assets:		
Plant: Cost	80	100
Depreciation	16	20
	64	80
Deferred liabilities		
Investment grant	—	16

Notes:
Approach (a): reduce the cost of the acquisition of the fixed asset by the amount of the grant.
Approach (b): treat the amount of the grant as a deferred credit, a portion of which is transferred to revenue annually.
For solution see discussion in text.

20.1 VAT and turnover

The turnover figure in a set of published accounts must be shown net of VAT. If a company wishes to show the gross turnover it must also show the related VAT as a deduction to arrive at a net turnover figure.

20.2 VAT and fixed assets

VAT will only be added to the cost of fixed assets where the VAT is irrecoverable, that is where the company is not registered for VAT or is partially exempt.

21.1 SSAP 9

(a) A long-term contract is defined in SSAP 9 as a contract entered into for the design, manufacture or construction of a single substantial asset or the provision of a service (or of a combination of assets or services which together constitute a single project) where the time taken to complete the contract is such that the contract actively falls into different accounting periods. A contract that is required to be accounted for as long-term will usually extend for a period exceeding one year, but this duration is not an essential feature. Some contracts with a shorter duration should be accounted for as long-term if they are so material that exclusion of their turnover and results would result in the accounts failing to give a true and fair view; such a policy must be applied consistently.

(b) The profit and loss account will include:

	£
Sales	1 770
Cost of sales (1 680 + 70)	1 750
	20

The balance sheet will include:

	£
Debtors (classified as amounts recoverable on contracts)	240
Stock (classified as long-term contract balances)	150
Provision for liabilities and charges (classified as long-term contract foreseeable losses)	60

A note to the balance sheet will analyse the stock item:

	£
Net cost less foreseeable losses	190
Applicable payment on account	40
	150

	1	*2*	*3*	*4*	*B/S*	*P&L*
Value of work done	500	350	700	220		1 770 (Sales)
Payments on account	525	200	610	235		
		150	90		240 (Debtors)	
Excess payments on account	25			15		
Offset	(25)			(15)		
	—			—		
Total costs incurred	600	400	720	280		
Transfer to cost of sales	450	400	600	230		1 680 (Cost of sales)
Provision for foreseeable loss		(60)		(10)		70 (Cost of sales)
Classify as provision		(60)		(60)		
Offset	(25)		(15)			
Classify in stock	125		25	150		

21.2 SSAP 9 terminology

(a) *Net realisable value* is the estimated selling price less all costs to completion and all cost relating to the sales of the product.

(b) *Replacement cost* is not in itself an acceptable basis of valuation, in that to value stock at replacement cost when net realisable value is greater will result in increasing the loss in the current period in order to create a future artificial profit; however, SSAP 9 acknowledges that there are occasions when replacement cost will form the best guide to net realisable value.

(c) *Cost* as defined in SSAP 9 consists of both the *cost of purchase* and the *cost of conversion*. Cost of conversion consists of all the expenses, both direct and indirect, attributable to bringing the product to its present location and condition. Thus production overheads will be included in cost, absorption being based on normal production levels and excluding abnormal costs. Normally other overheads will not be included, with certain exceptions including:

(i) costs of service departments, e.g. the accounting department, will be apportioned between the main functions of the business, so that a portion of these costs will be included in production overheads and consequently in stock;

(ii) interest charges on borrowings specifically relating to long-term contracts may be included in the cost of related work in progress;

(iii) expenses of obtaining firm sales contracts, including marketing and design costs, may be included in the cost of related work in progress.

(d) (i) Adjusted selling price, a technique used mainly by retail stores, is calculated by deducting from stock valued at selling price the estimated gross profit percentage. This method is acceptable under SSAP 9 only where no other method is practical and where it can be demonstrated that the result gives a reasonable approximation of the actual cost;

(ii) first in, first out is a method whereby the cost of stock and work in progress is calculated on the basis that the quantities in hand represent the latest purchases or production;

(iii) last in, first out is a method whereby the cost of stock and work in progress is calculated on the basis that the quantities in hand represent the earliest purchases or production;

(iv) base stock is a method whereby the cost of stock and work in progress is calculated on the basis that a fixed unit value is ascribed to a predetermined number of units of stock, any excess over this number being valued on the basis of some other method. If the number of units in stock is less than the predetermined minimum, the fixed unit value is applied to the number in stock.

22.1 Allocation of R&D items

Simple Ltd

SSAP 13 divides research and development expenditure into the following categories:

(a) pure research, being original investigation undertaken to gain new scientific or technical knowledge, not aimed at a specific objective;

(b) applied research, being original investigation undertaken to gain new scientific or technical knowledge directed at a specific objective;

(c) development, being the use of scientific or technical knowledge in order to produce new or substantially improved materials, devices, products, processes, systems or services prior to the commencement of commercial production.

The statement requires that pure and applied research expenditure be written off in the year that it is incurred. Development expenditure must also be written off in the year that it is incurred unless the following conditions are met:

(a) there must be a clearly defined project;

(b) expenditure relating to the project must be separately identified;

(c) there must be a *reasonable certainty* as to the technical feasibility and commercial viability of the project;

(d) there must be a reasonable expectation that the total of further development costs and related production, selling and administration costs will be covered by revenues arising from the project; and

(e) adequate resources must be available to cover completion of the project, including working capital requirements.

If these conditions are met then the company is allowed to defer development expenditure to the extent that its recovery can 'reasonably be regarded as assured', being amortised over the period of commercial production. Even where the conditions are met in full, the company may choose to write off development expenditure. The policy chosen must be applied consistently.

In choosing between a write-off and a deferral policy for development expenditure meeting these conditions, a company will consider:

(a) whether its planning and forecasting systems are adequate to comply with the conditions for deferral;
(b) the policy followed by other companies in the same industry, since it is desirable that accounts be comparable;
(c) since deferment of development expenditure involves disclosure of movements in the balance on the deferred asset account, companies anxious to preserve commercial secrecy may prefer a write-off policy;
(d) where development expenditure fluctuates substantially from year to year, it may be particularly desirable to follow a deferral policy;
(e) a deferral policy is only worth pursuing where the amounts involved are material.

Considering the problem posed by the Research and Development suspense account of Simple Ltd:

1. The term *applied research* has been used in the question to describe expenditure of £500 000 relating to a specific project. If the description used is correct, then this expenditure must be written off as it is incurred. Even if the description *development expenditure* would be more accurate, *cautious* optimism does not sound a strong enough expression of expectation to justify deferral.
2. Expenditure of £50 000 in pure research must clearly be written off when it is incurred.
3. Project Y clearly falls within the definition of *development expenditure* given in SSAP 13. If the project meets the conditions laid down in SSAP 13, therefore, the expenditure may be deferred.
4. Similarly, expenditure on Project Z may, if it meets the conditions laid down in SSAP 13, be deferred. The company must be consistent in its choice of policy. In amortising the expenditure it should be borne in mind that patents have a maximum life of 16 years.
5. Purchased *know-how* is similar in character to development expenditure, although not, strictly speaking, falling within the scope of SSAP 13. It would, therefore, be reasonable to defer this expenditure upon the same conditions as development expenditure.

22.2 Treatment of R&D

Venture Ltd

(a) *Definitions:*
   (i) *Pure research expenditure* is on original investigation undertaken in order to gain new scientific or technical knowledge or understanding, not directed towards any specific practical objective.
   (ii) *Applied research expenditure* is on original investigation undertaken in order to gain new scientific or technical knowledge directed towards a specific practical objective.
   (iii) *Development expenditure* relates to the use of scientific or technical knowledge in order to produce new or substantially improved materials, devices, products, processes, systems or services prior to the commencement of commercial use or production.

(b) *Deferral:* Expenditure on fixed assets for the purpose of research and development should be capitalised and depreciated over their estimated useful life. Expenditure fully recoverable under a firm contract from a customer should, in so far as it has not been reimbursed at the balance sheet date, be carried forward as work in progress.

All other expenditure on pure and applied research must be written off in the year it is incurred. Development expenditure should normally be written off in the year it is incurred but *may* be written off under the following conditions:

(i) there must be a clearly defined project, expenditure on which should be separately identifiable;
(ii) the project must be technically feasible and commercially viable, bearing in mind market conditions and legal requirements;
(iii) total revenues from the project must be reasonably expected to cover total costs; and
(iv) there must be good reason to believe that adequate resources exist, or will become available, to carry through the project.

The policy chosen in respect of development expenditure must be applied consistently.

(c) *Treatment:* Projects 3 and 4 both fall within the scope of development expenditure, while Project 5 will be included in work in progress. Treatment of Projects 3 and 4 will depend on:
(i) whether the projects meet the criteria for deferral laid down by SSAP 13;
(ii) whether the company has chosen to adopt a deferral or a write-off policy in respect of such expenditure.

Expenditure on Projects 3, 4 and 5 will therefore be reflected in the accounts as follows:
(i) the balance sheet will include £35 000 additions to plant;
(ii) the balance sheet will, if the deferral method is used, include a note as follows:

	£	£
Deferred development expenditure at the beginning of the year		x
Development expenditure incurred (including £36 000 relating to Projects 3 and 4)	x	
Development expenditure amortised	x	x
Deferred development expenditure at the end of the year		x

(iii) the amount for work in progress in the balance sheet will include £44 500 in respect of Project 5, less any payments on account received;
(iv) the figure for depreciation shown in the published profit and loss account will include £3 500 relating to fixed assets used on Projects 3, 4 and 5;
(v) the notes on the company's accounting policies will include a note on the policy adopted in respect of research and development expenditure and on stock and work in progress.

Workings

1. *Projects 3 and 4 – deferred expenditure*

	3	*4*	*Total*
Salaries	5 000	10 000	15 000
Overheads	6 000	12 000	18 000
Depreciation	1 000	2 000	3 000
	12 000	24 000	36 000

2. *Project 5 – work in progress*

Salaries	20 000
Overheads	24 000
Depreciation	500
	44 500

23.1 The rules in SSAP 15

(a) SSAP 15 requires that deferred tax should be provided if it is *probable* that a liability or asset will crystallise.

(b) (i) deferred taxation will be shown as a prior year item only when it arises from a change in accounting policy or correction of a fundamental error;

(ii) deferred taxation arising from a reserve movement, e.g. a fixed asset revaluation, will be taken direct to reserves.

(c) Under the liability method the taxation effects of timing differences are regarded as liabilities for taxes payable in the future; thus the deferred tax balance each year will be calculated on the basis of the most recent rate of tax. Under the deferral method the taxation effects of timing differences are regarded as deferrals of taxation payable or recoverable to be allocated to future periods when the differences reverse; thus the deferred tax balance will not change in line with changes in the rate of taxation.

23.2 Deferred taxation

(a) (i) *Permanent differences* arise because certain types of income or expenditure shown in the accounts are tax free or disallowable, while there may also be certain types of tax charge or allowance which are not reflected in the accounts.

(ii) *Timing differences* arise because there are items which are included in the financial statements of a period different from that in which they are dealt with for tax purposes.

(b) (i) *Short-term timing differences* arise from the use of the receipts and payments basis for tax purposes and the accruals basis in the accounts. Examples include interest receivable, interest or royalties payable, and bad debt provisions.

(ii) Accelerated capital allowances arise when capital allowances in the tax computation differ from the related depreciation charges in the accounts.

(iii) Revaluation of fixed assets leads to a timing difference in that the realisation of the asset might lead to a tax liability on the surplus.

(iv) Rollover relief leads to a timing difference in that the relief is subject to potential clawback in the event of a replacement asset being disposed of without further replacement.

(v) Losses lead to a timing difference in that tax relief may only be obtained by offset against profits of a future accounting period.

(c) Deferred tax should be provided for to the extent that it is probable that a liability or asset will crystallise, and should not be provided for to the extent that it is probable that crystallisation will not occur. A prudent view should be taken in the assessment of the probability of crystallisation.

24.1 SSAP 17 – definitions

(a) An *adjusting event* may be defined as a post balance sheet event which provides new or additional evidence of conditions existing at the balance sheet date. Examples include:

(i) a valuation of property showing a permanent diminution in value;
(ii) the receipt of information regarding rates of taxation;
(iii) the discovery of errors or frauds which show that the accounts were incorrect;
(iv) the receipt of the accounts from a company in which an investment is held giving evidence of a permanent diminution in the value of the investment;
(v) the receipt of evidence after the year end showing the net realisable value of stock held at the year end.

(b) A *non-adjusting event* may be defined as a post balance sheet event concerning conditions which did not exist at the balance sheet date. Examples include:

(i) issues of shares or debentures;
(ii) a decline in the value of property which occurs after the year end;
(iii) strikes or other labour disputes;
(iv) losses of assets as a result of some type of catastrophe;
(v) nationalisation.

Note: Chapter 21 lists further examples of *adjusting* and *non-adjusting* events.

24.2 SSAP 17 – treatment

Post balance sheet events may be defined as 'those events, both favourable and unfavourable, which occur between the balance sheet date and the date on which the financial statements are approved by the board of directors'. Such events fall into two categories:

(a) *Adjusting events* are those which provide new or additional evidence of conditions existing at the balance sheet date. Where the effect is material the amounts stated in the accounts should be adjusted for these items.

(b) *Non-adjusting events* are those which concern conditions which did not exist at the balance sheet date. Disclosure of these items should be made in the accounts in either of two cases:
   (i) where the event is so material that non-disclosure would affect the ability of those using the accounts to have a proper understanding of the financial position of the company;
   (ii) where the nature of the event is to reverse or complete a transaction entered into before the year end, the substance of which was primarily to alter the appearance of the company's balance sheet.

   In these cases disclosure will consist of:
   (i) a description of the nature of the estimate;
   (ii) an estimate of the financial effect before tax and of the taxation implications.

25.1 Definition

An *investment property* is defined in SSAP 19 as 'an interest in land and/or buildings':

(a) 'in respect of which construction work and development have been completed', and
(b) 'which is held for its investment potential, any rental income being negotiated at arm's length'.

This definition excludes any property occupied by a company for its own purposes or rented out to any other member of the same group of companies.

26.1 Foreign currency translation

(a) (i) The *closing rate* method is a method whereby assets and liabilities denominated in foreign currencies are translated using the closing rate. Revenue items are translated using an average rate of exchange for the period.
   (ii) The *temporal* method is a method whereby 'assets, liabilities, revenues and expenses are translated at the rate of exchange ruling at the date on which the amount recorded in the financial statements was established at the balance sheet date. Any assets or liabilities which are carried at current values are retranslated at the closing rate'. The *temporal* method must be used where the trade of a foreign subsidiary is a direct extension of the trade of the holding company; in all other circumstances the *closing rate* method must be used.

(b) (i) *Closing rate method:*

Balance sheet 31 December 19X9

	Limas	*Conversion factor*	£
Ordinary share capital	630 000	1/14	45 000
Retained profits	80 000	*	26 000
	710 000		71 000

*Balancing figure

	Limas	*Conversion factor*	£
Plant and machinery:			
Cost	700 000	1/10	70 000
Depreciation	70 000	1/10	7 000
	630 000		63 000
Stock	210 000	1/10	21 000
Net monetary current assets	40 000	1/10	4 000
	880 000		88 000
Less: Long-term loan	170 000	1/10	17 000
	710 000		71 000

Profit and loss account for the year ended 31 December 19X9

	Limas	*Limas*	*Conversion factor*	£	£
Sales		900 000	1/12		75 000
Depreciation	70 000		1/12	5 833	
Other operating expenses	750 000			62 500	
		820 000			68 333
		80 000			6 667

Retained profit movements	£
B/fwd	0
Exchange differences*	19 333
Profit for the year	6 667
C/fwd	26 000

*Balancing figure

	£	£
Opening share capital and reserves at closing rate: 630 000 × 1/10	63 000	
Less: Opening share capital and reserves at opening rate: 630 000 × 1/14	45 000	
		18 000
Profit for year at closing rate 80 000 × 1/10	8 000	
Profit for year at average rate 80 000 × 1/12	6 667	1 333
		19 333

(ii) *Temporal method:*

Balance sheet 31 December 19X9

	Limas	*Conversion factor*	£
Ordinary share capital	630 000	1/14	45 000
Retained profits	80 000	*	6 091
	710 000		51 091

*Balancing figure

	Limas	Conversion factor	£
Plant and machinery:			
Cost	700 000	1/14	50 000
Depreciation	70 000	1/14	5 000
	630 000		45 000
Stock	210 000	1/11	19 091
Net monetary current assets	40 000	1/10	4 000
	880 000		68 091
Less: Long-term loan	170 000	1/10	17 000
	710 000		51 091

Profit and loss account for the year ended 31 December 19X9

	Limas	Limas	Conversion factor	£	£
Sales		900 000	1/12		75 000
Depreciation	70 000		1/14	5 000	
Other operating expenses	750 000	820 000	1/12	62 500	67 500
					7 500
Exchange differences					1 419
					6 091

26.2 Translation

(a) *and* (b): *Translation of the accounts of Acorn*

Balance sheet:

	Crowns	Crowns	Conversion factor	Closing rate £	Closing rate £	Conversion factor	Temporal £	Temporal £
Plant: Cost		604 800	1/15		40 320	1/20		30 240
Depreciation		86 400	1/15		5 760	1/20		4 320
		518 400			34 560		25 920	
Current assets								
Stock	129 600		1/15	8 640		1/16	8 100	
Cash	43 200		1/15	2 880		1/15	2 880	
		172 800			11 520			19 980
		691 200			46 080			36 900
Loan		(172 800)	1/15		(11 520)	1/15		(11 520)
		518 400			34 560			25 380
Ordinary share capital		345 600	1/20		17 280	1/20		17 280
Retained profit: 1.1.X5	129 600		1/20	6 480		1/20	6 480	
For year	43 200		*	10 800		*	1 620	
		172 800			17 280			8 100
		518 400			34 560			25 380

*Balancing figure

Profit and loss:

	Crowns £	Crowns £	Conversion factor	Closing rate £	Closing rate £	Conversion factor	Temporal	Temporal
Sales		864 000	1/15		57 600	1/18		48 000
Cost of sales		561 600	1/15		37 440	1/18		31 200
		302 400			20 160			16 800
Less:								
Depreciation	86 400		1/15	5 760		1/20	4 320	
Expenses	172 800		1/15	11 520		1/18	9 600	
		259 200			17 280			13 920
Net profit		43 200			2 880			2 880
Exchange gain/(loss)		—	*		7 920	*		(1 260)
		43 200			10 800			1 620

*Balancing figure to balance sheet retained profit

(c) (i) *Taking a cover approach:*

	Crowns	£	£
Investment:			
As originally translated	600 000 × 1/20 =	30 000	
As retranslated	600 000 × 1/15 =	40 000	
Gain			10 000
Loan:			
Originally	300 000 × 1/20 =	15 000	
At 31.12.X5	300 000 × 1/15 =	20 000	
Loss			(5 000)
Net gain taken direct to translation reserve			5 000

(ii) *Not taking a cover approach:*
Investment not retranslated – loss of £5 000 taken through profit and loss account.

27.1 SSAP 21 rules

(a) A finance lease is defined in SSAP 21 as a lease that transfers substantially all the risks and rewards of ownership of an asset to the lessee.

Such a transfer is normally assumed to have taken place when at the inception of the lease the present value of the minimum lease payments amounts to substantially all (90 per cent or more) of the fair value of the leased asset. Present value is computed using the interest rate implicit in the lease. This assumption may be refuted by other evidence.

An operating lease is any lease other than a finance lease, i.e. one that fails to meet the above conditions.

(b) (i) An asset subject to a finance lease will be regarded as a debtor, recorded in the balance sheet at the net investment in the lease. Total gross earnings under the lease should be allocated to accounting periods to give a constant periodic rate of return on the net cash investment;

(ii) an asset subject to an operating lease should be recorded as a fixed asset, with depreciation provided over the estimated useful life. Rental income from the asset should be recognised on a straight line basis over the period of the lease, even if payments are not made on such a basis, unless another more systematic and rational basis can be justified.

27.2 Lease calculations

Balance sheet extracts:

Lease obligations

	£
Opening obligation	34 868
Less: First payment	10 000
	24 868
Interest at 10%	2 487
Outstanding loan – end year 1	27 355
Second payment	10 000
	17 355
Interest at 10%	1 736
Outstanding loan – end year 2	19 091
Third payment	10 000
	9 091
Interest at 10%	909
Outstanding loan – end year 3	10 000
Final payment	10 000
Outstanding loan – end year 4	—

28.1 Pension costs

(a) The objective is that the employer should recognise the expected cost of providing pensions on a systematic and rational basis over the period during which benefit is derived from the employees' services.

(b) (i) A defined contribution scheme is a pension scheme where the benefits are directly determined by the value of the contributions paid in respect of each member. Normally the rate of contribution is specified in the rules of the scheme;

(ii) a defined benefit scheme is one where the rules specify the benefits to be paid and the scheme is financed accordingly;

(iii) an experience deficiency is that part of the deficiency of the actuarial value of assets compared to actuarial value of liabilities which arises because events have not coincided with the actuarial assumptions made for the last valuation.

(c) Information given in the accounts should include:

(i) the actuarial method used and a brief description of the main actuarial assumptions;
(ii) the market value of scheme assets at the date of the valuation;
(iii) the level of funding expressed in percentage terms;
(iv) comments on any material actuarial surplus or deficiency.

29.1 SSAP 25

(a) Disclosure of geographical segmentation of turnover should be made on the basis of origin. Where materially different turnover to third parties by destination should also be shown.

(b) In deciding whether a separate class of business is a distinguishable segment, factors to consider include:

(i) the nature of the products;
(ii) the nature of the production process;
(iii) the markets in which output is sold;
(iv) the distribution channels for products;
(v) the manner in which the entity's activities are organised;
(vi) any separate legislative framework relating to part of the business.

29.2 Applying the rules

SSAP 25 requires that where two or more geographical segments differ from each other then they should be shown separately. Issues to consider are:

(a) Does either segment earn a rate of return out of line with the company as a whole?
(b) Are there different degrees of risk in the two countries?
(c) Have the two segments experienced different rates of growth?
(d) Do the two segments have different potential for development?
(e) Does either country have a particularly expansionist or restrictive political regime?
(f) Do the political regimes in the two countries differ in stability?
(g) Is the geographical segment subject to exchange control regulations?
(h) Is either country subject to major exchange rate fluctuations?

30.1 The objective of the FRSSE is to ensure that companies falling within its scope provide information which meets user needs, but it recognises that there may be an emphasis on providing stewardship information rather than decision-making information in a small company.

The FRSSE is an accounting standard; it incorporates all the relevant FRSs and UITF Abstracts in a modified and simplified version relevant for smaller companies. In general, the FRSSE uses the same definitions and accounting treatments as in the 'full' standards but it excludes a number of the disclosure requirements. It is discretionary for those companies who fall within its scope and if a company adopts the FRSSE, then it need only comply with this single standard. If it chooses not to adopt the FRSSE, then it must comply with all extant standards and UITF Abstracts.

It was generally recognised that accounting standards were aimed at large companies and this made them particularly onerous for small companies. The purpose of the FRRSE is therefore to reduce the burden on small companies by providing them with a more straightforward standard which nevertheless ensures a true and fair view. Thus within the 'Scope' section of the FRS's there is usually a reference which states that those companies applying the FRSSE are exempt from the standard.

30.2 The arguments regarding the FRSSE may be divided into three groups:

(a) those who argue in favour of the FRSSE;
(b) those who argue that small companies need different accounting standards, but that the FRSSE is the wrong approach;
(c) those who argue that no distinction should be made between small and large companies.

(a) Compliance with complex accounting standards which are mainly designed for large businesses is an unnecessary burden on small businesses and they should therefore be allowed to comply with a simplified version of those standards, i.e. the FRSSE.

(b) (i) Accounting standards are onerous for small companies and new accounting standards specifically designed for small businesses should be issued, rather than just 'cut-down' versions of the full standard.

(ii) When accounting standards are issued, the ASB should determine their relevance to small companies and should limit their scope, if necessary, to a certain size of business.

(iii) A distinction should be made between measurement issues and disclosure issues. All companies should use the same measurement techniques, but smaller entities might be allowed exemption from certain of the disclosure requirements.

(c) (i) There should only be one GAAP since all companies are required to prepare financial statements which give a true and fair view. Small companies should follow the same accounting standards as large companies but since their structures and transactions are normally less complex than for a large company then many of the standards would not be relevant to them and therefore they would not have to comply.

(ii) The debate is irrelevant because accounting standards are not a burden. They might be a burden to their financial advisers, and this might result in larger fees, but if the information was useful, and it met the cost–benefit criteria, then it should be disclosed.

31.1 It may be argued that it is necessary for standard setters to issue both conceptual as well as practical standards. SSAP 2 may be regarded as a theoretical standard since it deals with the nature of accounting concepts and the reasons for disclosure of accounting policies. SSAP 2 has had an affect on other standards because of the influence of the fundamental concepts, for example on SSAP 13 and accounting for development expenditure and the conflict between the accruals and prudence concepts.

Similarly it may be argued that FRS 5 on substance over form deals with a theoretical issue which has had an affect on other, more practical, standards.

The SOP is therefore a logical development of these more theoretical standards. Good accounting standards need a theoretical base and the affect of the SOP can be seen on many of the standards which have been issued during its development. Examples are:

FRS 15 depends upon the definition of an asset in the SOP.
FRS 12 depends upon the definition of a liability in the SOP.
FRED 21 is a natural development of the SOP

It may therefore be argued that the SOP is not too theoretical to be applied to accounting standards.

However, there are some anomalies between existing accounting standards and the SOP which the ASB will need to tackle. Perhaps the most important issue is whether the ASB, when faced with tough decisions, will have the courage to use the SOP as the basis for their arguments. The ASB have stated that the SOP is one of a number of factors to be taken into consideration when setting standards and it is to be hoped that it would be more than a guide which was abandoned if it proved inconvenient.

31.2 The benefits of developing a conceptual framework, such as the Statement of Principles are:

- It is a source of reference to:
  standards setters when setting new standards or revising existing standards.
  preparers of financial statements who have to apply accounting standards in practice.
  users who interpret the information in financial statements.
  auditors who have to express an opinion on financial statements.
  others who are interested in the work of the ASB.
- Where there is an accounting issue but there is no relevant FRS or UITF, then the SOP acts as a guide to preparers, users, auditors and others for judging how the ASB would deal with the issue.
- It avoids the proliferation of accounting standards. Since the SOP provides a framework for setting accounting standards it avoids the need to actually produce a standard for all possible situations.
- It assists in reducing the number of alternative accounting policies. The SOP may be used to show how there may be only one permissible policy.
- It should lead to consistent standards as the SOP should act as a single focus for the direction of accounting standards.
- It should save resources and enable accounting standards to be set more efficiently because there is an agreed foundation on which to build.

32.1

- operating results:
  changes in market conditions,
  new products introduced;

- dynamics of the business:
  scarcity of raw materials,
  product liability;
- investments for the future:
  advertising campaigns,
  training programmes.

32.2. The reason for the Stock Exchange introducing interim reports was that the market required more timely information, defined as both frequency and speed. Thus half yearly reports are obviously more frequent than annual reports and a few companies in the UK even report quarterly. With regards to speed, the ASB Statement recommends that interim reports should be produced within 60 days of the period end.

There are two methods for measuring interim performance – the integral and the discrete. The integral approach views the interim report as an integral announcement of the annual report, with the interim report being a progress report on how the year is progressing. Thus the approach of the integral interim report is to predict the annual result and to allocate the revenue and expenditure accordingly to the interim period.

In the discrete approach, the interim report is treated as an accounting period in its own right. The same rules which apply to incomplete transactions, or transactions which have not occurred, are dealt with in interim reports in the same way as annual accounts.

32.3 The objective of preliminary announcements (PA) is to release to the market price-sensitive information about the performance, financial position and cash flows of a company as soon as practical.

PAs are clearly timely as they are released ahead of the full annual report. However, they are not complete as they provide only a summary of the full financial statements, which are in the annual report. There is the risk that the information may not be reliable as PAs are released without an audit report. Although the auditors confirm to the directors before they release a PA that the remaining audit work is not expected to reveal any material changes there is always the risk that it might.

33.1 The most significant differences between SSAP 15 and FRED 19 are:

- FRED 19 adopts the full provision approach whereas SSAP 15 adopts the partial provision approach. The full provision approach is different from the one described, but rejected, in SSAP 15 and has been described as the 'full provision incremental liability' method. The incremental liability approach normally ignores revaluations on assets, fair value adjustments on acquisition and unremitted earnings from subsidiaries, etc.
- FRED 19 supports the discounting of deferred tax provisions whereas SSAP 15 makes no mention of this.

33.2 The most significant differences between SSAP 24 and FRED 20 are:

- FRED 20 adopts a market value approach; pension scheme assets are based on market values and pension scheme liabilities are measured at an approximation of fair value.
- Pension scheme liabilities are discounted.
- The surplus / deficit in a defined benefit scheme should be recognised as an asset and a deficit as a liability in the balance sheet.
- Gains and losses arising from changes in assets and liabilities measured at fair values are recognised immediately in the statement of total recognised gains and losses.

33.3 Both SSAP 2 and FRED 21 are concerned with accounting policies and concepts of accounting. They each require the disclosure of accounting policies as a note to the accounts.

There are however a number of differences between FRED 21 and SSAP 2. The most significant are:

- FRED 21 introduces the term 'estimation technique' which is defined as the methods and estimates adopted by an entity to arrive at monetary values, corresponding to the measurement bases selected, for assets, liabilities, gains, losses and changes to shareholder funds. The term 'accounting bases' in SSAP 2 is no longer required.
- The four fundamental concepts of SSAP 2 are no longer termed fundamental. Going concerns and accruals are said to be 'pervasive', but there is a reduced role for consistency and prudence.
- Both SSAP 2 and FRED 21 require companies to select the most appropriate accounting policies; FRED 21, however, gives the criteria by which the most suitable policies should be judged.

34.1 (a) The DP rejected historical cost in favour of current values because:

- Reported profits under the historical cost convention do not reflect the events of the year since:
  - any change in values giving rise to unrealised gains and losses are ignored.
  - when a financial instrument is realised any gains and losses are included in the profit and loss account of a single year even though the gain or loss may have accrued over many years.
  - companies may manipulate profit by choosing which financial instruments to sell and thus realise gains and losses.
- Active risk management is not adequately reflected by historical cost. Some companies buy and sell financial instruments in response to current values in an attempt to manage risk. Since the management of the company are using current values it seems appropriate that the external users should have the information prepared on the same basis as the internal users, i.e. current value. This should also help in judging how successful the management has been in managing risk.
- The use of historical cost makes it difficult to compare one company with another. Two companies may have identical financial instruments with the same current value, but under the historical cost basis these would appear to be different if they were purchased at different dates when the price was different.
- The use of historical cost makes it necessary to adopt hedge accounting and there are problems with hedge accounting.

(b) Hedge accounting occurs where separate transactions are linked with each other for accounting purposes because one of the transactions is designed to offset the risk arising on the other transaction. In hedge accounting, gains and losses on a financial instrument which is classed as a hedge are deferred until they can be matched with the gains and losses on a hedged position. Hedge accounting assumes that a 'hedge' and a 'hedged 'position' are matched on a one-to-one basis and that the hedge reduces the risk of the hedged position.

34.2 FRS 6: Acquisitions and Mergers lists the criteria when the merger method should be used. The DP rejects the use of the merger method and if it became an accounting standard FRS 6 would be withdrawn.

The DP rejects the merger method:

- because it uses book values and not fair values, and these are less relevant to users.
- the use of book values may give rise to subsequent gains and losses on disposal which should properly relate to the period prior to combination.
- it is not acceptable to combine the profits when a company is purchased during a year and report a profit at the year end as if the companies had been combined for the whole of that year.

34.3

	Year 0	Year 1	Year 2	Year 3	Year 4	Total
Balance sheet	2 205	2 382	2 571	2 778	3 000	
1				3 000		
2			3 000			
3		3 000				
4	3 000					
Interest P&L a/c		177	189	207	222	795
		2 382–2 205	2 571–2 382	2 778–2 571	3 000–2 778	3 000–2 205

In year 0, the £3 000 provision is valued at £2 205; in year 1, the provision is valued at £2 382. This increase in the provision of £177 is regarded as interest. This repeats itself until in year 4 the provision is measured at £3 000. The total interest is £795, the difference between the provision of £3 000 and its valuation in year 0 of £2 205.

34.4 The most significant difference between FRS 3 and the DP: Reporting Financial Performance is that the profit and loss account and the STRGL would be combined into a single statement. This single statement would be divided into three parts:

- operating (trading) activities
- financing and other treasury activities
- other gains and losses.

Transactions and other events would be divided between operating activities and 'other gains and losses' using the following criteria:

Operating items
- operating activities,
- recurring,
- non-holding items,
- internal events (e.g. value added activities).

Other gains and losses
- non-operating activities,
- non-recurring,
- holding items,
- external events (e.g. price changes).

Depreciation, for example, would be in 'operating items' and revaluation gains and disposal gains would be in 'other gains and losses'. Thus the new statement would make no clear distinction between realised and unrealised gains and losses.

34.5 The most significant difference between SSAP 21 and the DP: Leases is that the DP proposes that all leases should be accounted for as finance leases, whereas SSAP 21 makes a distinction between operating leases and finance leases.

Finance leases are capitalised, i.e. an asset and liability are recognised in the balance sheet of the lessee, and the profit and loss account has an interest charge and a depreciation charge. Operating leases are not capitalised, i.e. there is no recognition in the balance sheet and the profit and loss account has only the lease payment.

Thus the adoption of the DP would mean that all material leases would be recognised in the balance sheet; there would no longer be a category of leases (operating leases) which were 'off balance sheet'. Perhaps the most significant impact of this would be for the lease of land and buildings which are currently treated as operating leases. The buildings would now appear in the financial statements of the lessee rather than the lessor.

34.6 Full accounts are those which comply with all the regulatory framework, including company law, accounting standards and stock exchange regulations. They would be produced on 'plain paper' and would be used for filing purposes and for those sophisticated users who requested them.

Summarised accounts are a summary of the full accounts. They should be brief and yet should give an overall impression consistent with that conveyed to knowledgeable users by the full financial statements. The Discussion Paper proposes that these should be similar to Preliminary Announcements, i.e. the accounts without all the notes, and supplemented by graphs and ratios where appropriate. These would be the normal accounts sent to shareholders.

Simplified accounts are for those shareholders who would not understand the summarised accounts. They would use plain language rather than technical jargon, highlights from the financial statements rather than the financial statements themselves and would be supported by a narrative description of the performance and financial position of the company. Only those companies with a large number of uninformed shareholders would probably choose to issue simplified accounts.

35.1 The role of the UITF is to assist the ASB where unsatisfactory or conflicting interpretations have developed (or seem likely to develop) about the requirements of an accounting standard. The UITF seeks to arrive at a consensus on the accounting treatment that should be adopted in the context of the ASB's declared aim of relying on principles rather than detailed prescription. UITF consensuses are published in the form of UITF Abstracts. Compliance with UITF Abstracts is necessary in accounts that claim to give a true and fair view.

36.1 (a) *Mary – Profit and loss account for the year to 31 December 1999*

	HC		*CPP*	
	£	£	£	£
Sales		40 000		40 000
Interest	3 000		3 000	
Depreciation	25 000		27 000	
		28 000		30 000
		12 000		10 000
Gain on monetary items				4 000
Profit		12 000		14 000
CCA basis				
HC operating profit				15 000
Depreciation adjustment				5 000
CC operating profit				10 000
Gearing adjustment			(2 500)	
Interest			3 000	
				500
Profit for the year				9 500

Mary – Balance sheet as at 31 December 1999

	HC	*CPP*	*CCA*
Machine	75 000	81 000	90 000
Cash	37 000	37 000	37 000
	112 000	118 000	127 000
Opening equity	50 000	54 000	50 000
Profit	12 000	14 000	9 500
Capital maintenance			17 500
	62 000	68 000	77 000
Loan	50 000	50 000	50 000
	112 000	118 000	127 000

(b)	*Unit of measurement*	*Basis of measurement*	*Capital maintenance concept*
Historic cost	Monetary unit	Historic cost	Monetary amount of equity
CCP	CPP unit	Historic cost	Purchasing power of equity
CCA	Monetary unit	Value to the business	Operating capability of equity

ADDITIONAL QUESTIONS (BASED ON QUESTIONS SET BY THE ASB)

1. Accounting standards are authoritative statements of how particular types of transaction and other events should be reflected in financial statements. Accordingly, compliance with accounting standards will normally be necessary for financial statements to give a true and fair view.

Accounting standards issued by the Accounting Standards Board are designated 'Financial Reporting Standards' (or FRSs). Those issued by its predecessor bodies, and adopted by the Board when it was created in 1990, are designated 'Statements of Standard Accounting Practice' (or SSAPs). Adoption by the Board gave the SSAPs the status of 'accounting standards' within the terms of Part VII of the Companies Act 1985. The Board reviews these SSAPs individually as appropriate opportunities arise during the course of its work.

The consensus pronouncements of the Board's Urgent Issues Task Force, which are contained in UITF Abstracts, do not have the same legal status as accounting standards, but the courts are likely to hold that compliance with Abstracts is also necessary for financial statements to give a true and fair view.

2. Companies legislation does not directly require compliance with accounting standards. However, the Companies Act 1985 requires accounts (other than those prepared by small or medium-sized companies) to state whether they have been prepared in accordance with applicable accounting standards and to give particulars of any material departure from those standards and the reasons for it.

Directors of companies are required by the Act to prepare accounts that give a true and fair view of the state of affairs of the company and of its financial position at the end of the financial year. The accountancy profession (as represented in the Consultative Committee of Accountancy Bodies – CCAB) is committed to promoting and supporting compliance with accounting standards by its members, whether as preparers or auditors of financial information. Under the Companies Act, both the Financial Reporting Review Panel (FRRP) and the Department of Trade and Industry have procedures for receiving and investigating complaints regarding the annual accounts of companies in respect of apparent departures from the accounting requirements of the Act, including the requirement to give a true and fair view.

The Accounting Standards Board has received and published legal advice that the courts would be likely to hold that compliance with accounting standards is necessary to achieve a true and fair view, as required by the Act.

In short, accounting standards should be regarded as mandatory (except in very rare and special circumstances where the requirement to give a true and fair view makes it necessary to depart from accounting standards).

3. Most of the accounting scams of the 1980s, such as off balance sheet finance, window dressing, the presentation of debt as equity and the abuse of reorganisation provisions, were practised in areas of accounting that were not the subject of accounting standards. Experience shows therefore that, in the absence of regulation, financial reporting may not give the information that users need to make informed assessments of companies. Accounting standards aim to promote comparability, consistency and transparency, in the interests of users of financial statements. Good financial reporting not only promotes healthy markets, it also helps to reduce the cost of capital because investors can have faith in companies' reports.

4. In the ASB's early years its agenda for new standards was influenced by the legacy of unfinished projects it inherited from its predecessor body and the need to take resolute action to clean up the inadequacies revealed by the accounting scams of the 1980s. In other words, some of the early standards were of the nature of anti-abuse regulation. In recent years, however, the ASB's work has been driven largely by the need to get ahead of the agenda of the International Accounting Standards Committee, to enable the views of the business community in the UK to be properly represented and taken into account in the international debates in which the ASB participates.

However, the ASB remains sensitive to the need to deal with important domestic issues that are of no international interest: an example is the development, and issue in 1998, of a mandatory Application Note to FRS 5, giving guidance on the treatment of Private Finance Initiative and similar contracts.

5. In accordance with the ASB's 'due process' new standards normally go through a lengthy, formal two-stage process of public consultation before they are issued. The first stage is the publication of a Discussion Paper, which describes and analyses the problem in question and sets out possible ways of dealing with it. At that stage the ASB may not necessarily have decided on a preferred option. The Paper will typically set out a list of questions that respondents are invited to address, and a comment period of, usually, three months is given.

The ASB analyses and considers the responses it receives. It will give far greater weight to the quality of the arguments advanced than to the volume of responses. It will then develop firm proposals, which are eventually published as a draft standard in 'exposure draft' form as a Financial Reporting Exposure Draft (or FRED). Again, at this second stage of public consultation, respondents are usually invited to comment within a three-month period, but on the basis of the specific proposal.

Again, the ASB analyses and considers the responses. Having modified its proposal as appropriate, the ASB will then issue its accounting standard as an FRS.

In addition, throughout this two-stage formal process the ASB typically meets and discusses its proposals with a wide variety of interested parties, including representative organisations, companies and others.

6. 'Creative accounting' is primarily a journalistic term; it has no official standing and no agreed definition.

The ASB's task is to improve the quality of financial statements, a task that obviously took as its starting point the standards of financial reporting that existed when the Board was established in 1990. In its Statement of Aims (1991), the ASB adopted certain guidelines for conducting its affairs. The first was

> To be objective and to ensure that the information resulting from the application of accounting standards faithfully represents the underlying commercial activity. Such information should be neutral in the sense that it is free from any form of bias intended to influence users in a particular direction and should not be designed to favour any group of users or preparers.

If, for convenience, it is assumed that 'creative' accounting is the opposite of what the ASB favours – i.e. accounting that does not faithfully represent the underlying commercial activity and is not neutral – then it would be correct to say that the ASB aims to eliminate 'creative' accounting.

In developing accounting standards, the ASB set itself five principal objectives:

1. Exclude from the balance sheet items that are neither assets nor liabilities.
2. Make 'off balance sheet' assets and liabilities more visible by putting them on the balance sheet whenever practicable.
3. Ensure that all gains and losses are reported prominently so that nothing can be overlooked.
4. Reverse the 'bottom line' mentality by focusing performance reporting on the components of income.
5. Use up-to-date measures, when appropriate, if other measures such as historical costs are ineffective.

These objectives have underpinned the ASB's work, and it could perhaps be argued that the more successfully the ASB attains them, the more honest and faithful financial reporting will become. Much of the ASB's earlier work focused initially on eradicating the worst problems it perceived in financial reporting practices in the 1980s. For example, FRS 3: Reporting Financial Performance dealt with the abuse of 'extraordinary items'; FRS 4: Capital Instruments tackled the problem of debt being portrayed as equity; off balance sheet finance was addressed by FRS 5: Reporting the Substance of Transactions; the abuse of acquisition provisions was dealt with by FRS 6: Mergers and Acquisitions and FRS 7: Fair Values in Acquisition Accounting; and the problem of hidden related party transactions was tackled in FRS 8: Related Party Disclosures.

To the extent that these standards have been reflected by improved financial reporting, users may now feel able to place greater reliance on financial statements. On the other hand, given the ingenuity of the human mind in circumventing the purpose of any regulations, it would perhaps be a delusion to think that it was possible to prevent the future development of accounting practices whose purpose was to mislead the user. All the ASB can hope to do is to remain alert to the possible abuse of the existing rules and to act promptly. Indeed, it was exactly this thought that lay behind the ASB's establishment of its Urgent Issues Task Force.

Many of the practices the ASB has sought to eradicate – for example those mentioned above – have been described in the media as 'creative accounting'.

7. The ASB's Statement of Aims (1991) sets out the fundamental guidelines that the ASB follows in conducting its affairs. One of the guidelines is:

> To ensure that through a process of regular communication, accounting standards are produced with due regard to international developments.

The ASB accepts that, in principle, there should be only one way of accounting for similar transactions throughout the world. The ASB therefore tries to ensure that its standards are consistent with International Accounting Standards (IASs), and every FRS includes a section explaining how it relates to the relevant IAS. Ideally, adherence to the provisions of the ASB's standards should result in compliance with IASs.

However, on certain topics the ASB believes that the international solution is not appropriate for conditions in the UK, or that the international approach is simply out of date. The ASB will therefore support harmonisation with IASs but reserves the right to disagree with the international consensus where a better solution to UK problems exists. In cases where the ASB has adopted an accounting standard that differs from the predominant practice internationally, the ASB believes the position should be reviewed after some experience has been gained to see if, in the light of that experience, there is scope for further harmonisation. Ideally, the ASB will persuade others that its view should prevail and become the international standard (FRS 12 was an example of this) but if the ASB's view is not accepted the ASB would debate the issue after a few years to decide whether to come into line with international practice.

8. The Statement of Principles for Financial Reporting was published in December 1999. The Statement of Principles is a description of the fundamental approach that the ASB believes should, in principle, underpin the financial statements of profit-oriented entities. The Statement is intended to be a comprehensive and reasonably detailed description of that approach, and the approach itself is intended to be internally consistent, up-to-date and in line with the approaches adopted elsewhere in the world. Although the Statement describes fundamental principles, it does not contain requirements on how financial statements should be prepared or presented. (Company accounts will therefore continue to be prepared under the requirements of company law and accounting standards.) Instead, the Statement's primary purpose is to provide a frame of reference to help the ASB as a standard-setter in developing and reviewing accounting standards. As such the Statement will be one of the factors that the ASB takes into account in developing and reviewing standards. Other factors taken into account will include legal requirements, implementation issues, industry-specific issues, cost–benefit considerations and the desirability of evolutionary change. Indeed, experience shows that the influence of these other factors may result in an accounting standard adopting an approach that is different from the approach suggested by the Statement.

9. The ASB's views on this question are set out in FRS 10: Goodwill and Intangible Assets, which was issued in December 1997. The ASB thinks that brands, mastheads and many other intangible assets are actually similar in nature to goodwill and so should be accounted for in the same way as goodwill. FRS 10 allows goodwill to be capitalised only if it has been purchased (rather than generated internally). So it also allows most intangible assets to be capitalised only if they have been purchased.

The ASB is aware that internally generated intangibles can be just as important to a business. But it does not believe that this in itself justifies putting such intangibles on the balance sheet, especially given the difficulties in arriving at a reliable value for them. Instead, the ASB has encouraged companies to discuss significant intangibles in the operating and financial review (OFR) that accompanies their financial statements. Many companies now do this, disclosing, for example, the amount that they have spent on building up their brands in the year and/or statistics demonstrating the strength of these brands.

10. The Statement of Principles places great emphasis on assets and liabilities and even defines the items that are to be included in the profit and loss account in terms of assets and liabilities. It is, incidentally, the approach that has been adopted in the framework documents of all the major financial reporting standard-setters around the world.

Adopting such an approach does not, however, mean that the ASB thinks the balance sheet is more important than the profit and loss account. Users focus primarily on financial performance and, therefore, on the profit and loss account and other performance statements. The

ASB can see no reason to try to change that focus and has not sought to do so. Similarly, it recognises that the balance sheet is, and is likely to remain for the foreseeable future, an accounting statement that has some limitations.

The ASB believes that the approach adopted in the Statement will lead to improvements in the quality of financial statements in general and, through the discipline that the definitions will impose on the recognition of gains and losses, improvements in the quality of the profit and loss account in particular. Quite simply, every expenditure is either a charge to the profit and loss account or an asset. Similarly, every source of funds is either income or has to be repaid (a liability). By defining assets and liabilities the ASB makes it clear that all other items are either income or a charge to the profit and loss account. In this way all income and all expenses will appear in the profit and loss account and will not be deferred on the balance sheet as pseudo-assets or pseudo-liabilities. This clear-cut approach should protect the profit and loss account from manipulation.

11. It would be foolish to single out one issue, or even several issues, as being 'the biggest problems in financial reporting today', but there are several topics that must be mentioned in any consideration on this point. Financial instruments – including derivatives, such as forward contracts and swaps – are clearly one of these. The number and complexity of these instruments has grown hugely in recent years and has outpaced innovations in accounting practice. One of the problems in this area is that instruments can be acquired for small cost, and yet their value can quickly change leading to large profits reporting and losses. Under present accounting practice these profits and losses can go unreported until the instrument is settled. There is also no clear answer in present practice to the many questions that arise in connection with hedge accounting – i.e. departures from normal accounting that are made because it seems to be necessary to reflect the intent underlying the transactions. There is no consistent approach in practice to defining precisely what the circumstances are in which hedge accounting should be used (if any) and how hedge accounting itself should work. The ASB has on its agenda a project that has already resulted in a standard that requires detailed disclosures in this area and work is in hand towards a standard that would prescribe how financial instruments should be treated in the main financial statements.

Another problem area is that of leases. Existing lease accounting standards require a radically different treatment depending on whether a lease is an 'operating lease' or a 'finance lease'. Operating leases are treated simply as short-term rental agreements, whilst finance leases are treated as equivalent to the purchase of an asset on credit. Hence a lessee shows a large asset and liability in the case of a finance lease, and no asset or liability at all for an operating lease. As the difference between an operating lease and a finance lease may in some cases be very small, this approach does not result in similar transactions being accounted for similarly. The ASB has a project in hand that seeks to identify the assets and liabilities arising under all lease contracts and to ensure that all are accounted for similarly.

12. Accounting standards need to keep abreast of changes in the law, business practice and users' expectations. Since these are constantly changing, it is difficult to envisage a time when accounting standards will not need to change

Index